Dialogue and cooperation are motives well-known in public relations theory, often with a normative bent. With this publication Chuck Marsh rallies evolutionary biology for the cause, acting as matchmaker between natural science and humanities. Through a well-written, well-read, sophisticated, yet accessible discussion, professor Marsh introduces nine tenets for public relations emphasizing cooperation and justice as leitmotifs, even from a self-interested perspective. A highly enjoyable read.

Øyvind Ihlen, Professor,
University of Oslo, Norway

How lucky we are to have Charles Marsh weave us such a seamless tapestry of theory—from a variety of fields—that demonstrates how social harmony, not competition, is the superior basis for a successful approach to public relations. From ancient philosopher Isocrates to evolutionary biologist E.O. Wilson, the voices that speak through this text provide solid evidence in support of cooperation and pave the way toward an understanding of public relations practice that privileges justice in the creation of successful relationships.

Jessalynn Strauss, Assistant Professor,
Elon University, USA

A great read and provocative multidisciplinary-based empirical argument outlining how social harmony and cooperative communication approaches to public relations may outlast other frameworks in guiding the field of public relations into the future—a classic yet contemporary academic revelation.

Michael Palenchar, Associate Professor,
The University of Tennessee, USA

Public Relations, Cooperation, and Justice

Modern approaches to public relations cluster into three camps along a continuum:

- conflict-oriented egoism, e.g. forms of contingency theory that focus almost exclusively on the wellbeing of an entity;
- redressed egoism, e.g. subsidies to redress PR's egoistic nature; and
- forms of self-interested cooperation, e.g. fully functioning society theory.

Public Relations, Cooperation, and Justice draws upon interdisciplinary research from evolutionary biology, philosophy, and rhetoric to establish that relationships built on cooperation and justice are more productive than those built on conflict and egoistic competition. Just as important, this innovative book shuns normative, utopian appeals, offering instead only empirical, materialistic evidence for its conclusions.

This is a powerful, multidisciplinary, and well-documented analysis, including specific strategies for the enactment of PR as a quest for cooperation and justice, which aligns the discipline of public relations with basic human nature. It will be of interest to scholars and advanced students of public relations and communication ethics.

Charles Marsh is the Oscar Stauffer Professor of Journalism and Mass Communications at the University of Kansas. He is author of *Classical Rhetoric and Modern Public Relations: An Isocratean Model* (Routledge) and co-author of *Public Relations: A Values-Driven Approach* (Pearson) and *Strategic Writing* (Routledge).

Routledge New Directions in Public Relations and Communication Research

Edited by Kevin Moloney

Routledge New Directions in Public Relations and Communication Research is a new forum for the publication of books of original research in PR and related types of communication. Its remit is to publish critical and challenging responses to continuities and fractures in contemporary PR thinking and practice, and its essential yet contested role in market-orientated, capitalist, liberal democracies around the world. The series reflects the multiple and inter-disciplinary forms PR takes in a post-Grunigian world; the expanding roles which it performs, and the increasing number of countries in which it is practised.

The series will examine current trends and explore new thinking on the key questions which impact upon PR and communications, including:

- Is the evolution of persuasive communications in Central and Eastern Europe, China, Latin America, Japan, the Middle East and Southeast Asia developing new forms or following Western models?
- What has been the impact of postmodern sociologies, cultural studies and methodologies which are often critical of the traditional, conservative role of PR in capitalist political economies, and in patriarchy, gender and ethnic roles?
- What is the impact of digital social media on politics, individual privacy and PR practice? Is new technology changing the nature of content communicated, or simply reaching bigger audiences faster? Is digital PR a cause or consequence of political and cultural change?

Books in this series will be of interest to academics and researchers involved in these expanding fields of study, as well as students undertaking advanced studies in this area.

Communicating Statehood
Public relations strategies in promoting palestine
Ibtisam Abu-Duhou, Jeannie Fletcher, Chris Galloway

Public Relations, Cooperation, and Justice

From Evolutionary Biology to Ethics

Charles Marsh

Routledge
Taylor & Francis Group

LONDON AND NEW YORK

First published 2017
by Routledge

2 Park Square, Milton Park, Abingdon, Oxfordshire OX14 4RN
52 Vanderbilt Avenue, New York, NY 10017

Routledge is an imprint of the Taylor & Francis Group, an informa business

First issued in paperback 2019

British Library Cataloguing in Publication Data
A catalogue record for this book is available from the British Library

Library of Congress Cataloging in Publication Data
Names: Marsh, Charles, 1955– author.
Title: Public relations, cooperation, and justice / Charles Marsh.
Description: 1 Edition. | New York : Routledge, [2017] | Includes
bibliographical references and index.
Identifiers: LCCN 2016046506 (print) | LCCN 2017010937 (ebook) |
ISBN 9781138944206 (hardback : alk. paper) | ISBN 9781315672038
(ebk)
Subjects: LCSH: Public relations—Philosophy.
Classification: LCC HM1221 .M36 2017 (print) | LCC HM1221 (ebook) |
DDC 659.201—dc23
LC record available at https://lccn.loc.gov/2016046506

ISBN: 978-1-138-94420-6 (hbk)
ISBN: 978-0-367-87418-6 (pbk)

Typeset in Times New Roman
by Florence Production Ltd, Stoodleigh, Devon, UK

Contents

Figures

Acknowledgments

I'm very grateful to the editors at Routledge, particularly Jacqueline Curthoys and Kevin Moloney, for encouraging this book and to the University of Kansas for providing a research sabbatical that allowed me to complete the final chapters. I certainly am grateful to John Stauffer and the Stauffer family for funding the Oscar Stauffer Professorship and its research stipend.

As always, I'm grateful to my family, especially Kris, for enduring the messes I make, literally and figuratively, during my research projects. I'm particularly grateful to my brother, Clay, for listening to my thoughts about this project as we hiked toward Lake Helene in the Rocky Mountain National Park and suggesting that I read Kropotkin.

Portions and, in some cases, earlier versions of my prior research publications appear in this book. Chapter 1 is derived in part from *Journal of Public Relations Research*, *22*: 359–377, 2010, available online: www.tandfonline. com/DOI: 10.1080/10627261003801396; *Public Relations Inquiry*, *1*: 313–335, 2012, available online: http://pri.sagepub.com/ DOI: 10.1177/2046147 X12448583; *Journal of Public Relations Research*, *25*: 426–441, 2013, available online:www.tandfonline.com/DOI: 10.1080/1062726X.2013.795861; and *Journal of Mass Media Ethics*, *29*: 210–224, 2014, available online: www. tandfonline.com/ DOI: 10.1080/08900523.2014.949565. Chapters 4 and 5 are derived in part from *Public Relations Inquiry*, *1*: 313–335, 2012, available online: http://pri.sagepub.com/ DOI: 10.1177/2046147X12448583; and *Journal of Public Relations Research*, *25*: 426–441, 2013, available online: www. tandfonline.com/DOI: 10.1080/1062726X.2013.795861. Chapter 8 is derived in part from *Journal of Mass Media Ethics*, *29*: 210–224, 2014, available online: www.tandfonline.com/ DOI: 10.1080/08900523.2014.949565. Chapter 9 is derived in part from *Journal of Mass Media Ethics*, *29*: 210–224, 2014, available online: www.tandfonline.com/ DOI: 10.1080/08900523.2014.949 565. Chapter 11 is derived in part from *Classical Rhetoric and Modern Public Relations: An Isocratean Model* (Routledge, 2013); *Journal of Mass Media Ethics*, *16*: 78–98, 2001, available online: www.tandfonline.com/ DOI: 10.12 07/S15327728JMME1602&3_2; *Public Relations Review*, *29*: 351–367, 2003, available online: www.journals.elsevier.com/public-relations-review/ DOI:

10.1016/S0363–8111(03)00039–0; and *Journal of Public Relations Research*, *27*: 229–243, 2015, available online: www.tandfonline.com/ DOI: 10.1080/ 1062726X.2015.1024249. Chapter 12 is derived in part from *Classical Rhetoric and Modern Public Relations: An Isocratean Model* (Routledge, 2013); *Journal of Mass Media Ethics*, *16*: 78–98, 2001, available online: www. tandfonline.com/ DOI: 10.1207/S15327728JMME1602&3_2; and *Public Relations Review*, *29*: 351–367, 2003, available online: www.journals. elsevier.com/public-relations-review/ DOI: 10.1016/S0363–8111(03)00039–0. I'm grateful to the editors of these publications for their earlier guidance and for permission to use some of that research here.

Finally, I'm grateful that distinguished modern scientists such as Edward O. Wilson, Martin Nowak, Stephen Jay Gould, and Richard Dawkins—as well as their predecessors Charles Darwin, Peter Kropotkin, and Thomas Henry Huxley—are such skilled and entertaining writers. Reading their work has been one of the greatest pleasures of this project.

Part I

Introduction

Chapter 1

Introduction

A consilience of cooperation

A question and a consilience: The study that became this book began with a question, and the answer (or, at least, *an* answer) has become a consilience, a point of multidisciplinary consensus.

The question addresses one of my deepest professional interests: Why, of all the rhetorics of classical Athens and the later Hellenic and Roman worlds, was the community-building rhetoric of Isocrates (436–338 BCE) the most successful? Why, in the high-stakes arenas of early Greek politics, did his version of strategic communication clearly outperform the elitist rhetoric of Plato and the competitive, conflict-oriented rhetoric of Aristotle? Why did the greatest of the Roman rhetoricians, Cicero and Quintilian, strongly prefer Isocratean rhetoric to its rivals? Why Isocrates' victory has receded into the shadows of history is a separate issue—but, in Chapters 11 and 12, I'll strive to provide concise evidence, both ancient and modern, for his significant success vis-à-vis better-known rivals.

The answer to this question—the theme of this book—matters: The answer, I believe, can tell us much about which frameworks of public relations are most effective. The answer can describe those most-effective frameworks and tell us how to achieve them. The answer will lead us into three very different disciplines—evolutionary biology, philosophy, and rhetoric—that have much to contribute to modern public relations.

Here is the main point, the focus of this book, the thread that runs through all chapters: Evidence from evolutionary biology, philosophy, and rhetoric— overwhelming multidisciplinary evidence, in my opinion—shows that social harmony approaches to public relations, such as fully functioning society theory, outperform more egoistic, conflict-oriented approaches, such as some forms of contingency theory. Outperform in what manner? In resource acquisition, perhaps the most widely accepted function of public relations, as I'll document below. And just as this book has a main point, it has a crucial main method: Only empirical, materialistic, even egoistic evidence will be presented. There will be no appeals to idealism, to altruism, or to what *ought* to be rather than what *is*. There will be no attempts to cast normative ideals as practical realities. Instead, humans will be presented as self-interested creatures in steadfast pursuit of the resources they need to survive and flourish. And that approach will lead us not to conflict and competition but, rather, to cooperation and justice. The goal of this book is to establish a multidisciplinary foundation for the comparative effectiveness of public relations' social harmony frameworks.

Pulitzer Prize-winning evolutionary biologist Edward O. Wilson (1998), an important voice in Chapter 6 of this book, holds that a consilience is a "unity of knowledge . . . the linking of facts and fact-based theory across disciplines to create a common groundwork of explanation" (p. 8). The value of such multidisciplinary consensus, he writes, "is in the prospect of intellectual adventure and, given even modest success, the value of understanding the human condition with a higher degree of certainty" (1998, p. 9). The main point of this book, again, is that empirical, materialistic evidence from evolutionary biology, philosophy, and rhetoric coalesces into one such area of heightened certainty: A consilience of cooperation. Further, that consilience can be stated fairly simply. According to evolutionary biologist Richard Dawkins (Chapter 6), author of *The Selfish Gene*, relationships characterized by cooperation and forgiveness generally out-produce relationships built on egoism and conflict. Or, according to skeptical Scottish philosopher David Hume (Chapter 9), a well-known respect for the integrity of others' resources is the best way to secure and build our own resources. Or, according to Isocrates himself (Chapter 12), justice toward others and moderation in our own wants are the surest paths to political and economic security. And at the center of each assertion is the materialistic concept of resource dependency.

Finally, by way of introduction, each of the three disciplines clearly suggests one best strategy for material success: Indirect reciprocity, assisting others without the expectation that they can or will return our cooperative actions. Indirect reciprocity builds reputation and wins willing relationship partners who have observed or learned of our behavior and, consequently, have come to trust and respect us. I did not anticipate this particular multidisciplinary finding when I began my research. I knew that Isocrates insisted upon this strategy: I did not know that the disciplines of evolutionary biology and materialistic philosophy would powerfully support his contention. As I complete this manuscript, I wish that I had more time and more pages—because tentative research shows that related disciplines such as economics and psychology are coming to the same conclusion, a particularly wide-ranging consilience: We ultimately fare best, in a material, economic sense, when we assist others.

Resource dependency theory

Given the exciting "paradigmatic variety" (Edwards, 2012, p. 7) and growth of "pluralistic approaches" (Coombs & Holladay, 2012, p. 880) that now characterize the envisioning and enactment of public relations, many scholars have recommended seeking common ground among the different frameworks (Bardhan & Weaver, 2011; Edwards, 2012; Ihlen & Verhoeven, 2012). Resource dependency theory surely has become a significant part of that common ground, a subset that could hardly be characterized as idealistic or normative. Drawing upon the work of Pfeffer and Salancik (1978) and L.A. Grunig, J.E. Grunig, and Ehling (1992), Guth and Marsh (2017) summarize resource dependency theory as consisting of three basic points:

1. To fulfill their values-driven goals, organizations, and other entities need resources such as raw materials, fair media coverage, and employee dedication and commitment.
2. Some of those key resources are not controlled by the organization or entity.
3. To acquire those resources, organizations, and other entities build productive relationships with the publics that control the resources. (p. 19)

In brief, resource dependency leads to relationships.

Over the past 25 years, resource dependency theory has been shown to be fundamental to an understanding of excellence theory (L.A. Grunig, J.E. Grunig, & Ehling, 1992); encroachment by marketing (Lauzen, 1993); organization-public relationships (Broom, Casey, & Ritchey, 2000); crisis communication (Christen, 2005); fully functioning society theory (Heath, 2006); strategic issues management (Dougall & Straughan, 2006; Heath, 2009); corporate social responsibility (Golob & Bartlett, 2007); power and power disparities (Waymer & Ni, 2009); reputation (Xifra & Ordeix, 2009); publicity (Hallahan, 2010); tactics (Yang & Taylor, 2010); stakeholder management (Smudde & Courtright, 2011); activist public relations (Sommerfeldt, 2011); and jobs in public relations (Guth & Marsh, 2017). Finally, as we shall see below, resource dependency theory has a strong connection to the reflective paradigm of public relations, which includes the core belief that social legitimacy is the primary uncontrolled resource to be acquired (Waeraas & Ihlen, 2009).

Frameworks of public relations

By using the word *framework*, I hope to avoid the blurry distinctions between paradigms, theories, models, and approaches to public relations—each of which has been used to describe a general theory that has been or can be applied to the actual practice of public relations (Curtin, 2011). By *framework*, I mean an applied or applicable theory (and, for those who prefer another term, I certainly don't insist upon this usage). In keeping with this book's materialistic view that humans are self-interested creatures driven to secure the resources we need to survive and flourish, we can distinguish between two general frameworks of public relations, separated primarily by the nature of their egoism, or self-interest. As we shall see in Part II of this book, which addresses evolutionary biology, there are essentially two forms of egoism:

- an independent egoism in which an entity tends, within relationships, to be self-centered in its self-interested quest to secure needed resources. Thus, independent egoism, as a default setting, tends to view relationships as venues of conflict and competition. For example, the definition of public relations as the "strategic management of competition and conflict for the benefit of one's own organization—and when possible—also for the mutual benefit of the organization and its various stakeholders or publics" (Wilcox & Cameron, 2009, p. 7) indicates how an independently egoistic view can characterize relationships as arenas of conflict and competition.
- a dependent egoism in which an entity tends, within relationships, to be relationship-centered and concerned about the wellbeing of relationship partners in its self-interested quest to secure needed resources. Thus, dependent egoism, as a default setting, tends to see relationships as areas for cooperation and justice. And here is a key point: There is nothing inherently more noble about dependent egoism. It is every bit as self-interested as independent egoism. It simply seeks to acquire needed resources in a different manner. Philosophers and neuroscientists do tend to agree that the long-term practice of such things as cooperation and justice can indeed transform those survival strategies into natural human values (Chapter 8)— but, for our purposes in this book, viewed empirically and materialistically there is nothing noble in their initial practice beyond the nobility of survival.

To avoid the cumbersome terminology of independent and dependent egoism, this book, once past this section, generally will follow traditional usage in simply using the term *egoism* to denote independent egoism.

A variety of public relations frameworks tend to skew toward independent egoism:

Contingency theory. Contingency theory places highly independent-egoistic tendencies at a "pure advocacy," self-centered extreme on a continuum of relationship-building stances and highly social, collectivist tendencies at a "pure accommodation" extreme of that continuum (Cancel, Cameron, Sallot, & Mitrook, 1997, p. 31). In "the middle of the continuum" are "mixed-motive" stances that attempt to balance the competing extremes; achieving a midpoint balance, however, is precarious and rare (Cancel, Cameron, Sallot, & Mitrook, 1997, pp. 33, 34, 49). Contingency theory identifies 80-plus variables that affect an organization's continuum-related stance vis-à-vis a particular public (Cancel, Cameron, Sallot, & Mitrook, 1997, p. 33). Influenced, perhaps, by Cameron's definition of public relations, cited above, as the "strategic management of competition and conflict for the benefit of one's own organiza-tion—and when possible—also for the mutual benefit of the organization and its various stakeholders or publics" (Wilcox & Cameron, 2009, p. 7), contingency theory seemingly has evolved from its origins as the "contingency theory of accommodation" (Cancel, Cameron, Sallot, & Mitrook, 1997, p. 31) to the "contingency theory of conflict management" (Pang, Cropp, & Cameron, 2006, p. 374). This shift lends some support to the idea that independent egoism ("for the benefit of one's own organization") does tend to envision relationships as venues of competition and conflict. Contingency theory has become "a theory to understand how the inevitable competition and conflicts that occur in a complex world can be managed" (Cameron, Pang, & Jin, 2008, p. 136). "Such a view," Kent, Sommerfeldt, and Saffer maintain (2016), "is clearly demonstrative of a functional, rather than cocreational view of public relations" (p. 95).

Two-way asymmetry. The two-way asymmetrical model is one of the four basic models of public relations posited by excellence theory. A two-way asymmetrical approach to relationships uses research to create strategies and tactics that will engineer consent, winning essential publics over to the independent-egoistic organization's viewpoint. Two-way asymmetry strives "to change the behavior of publics without changing the behavior of the organization" (J.E. Grunig & White, 1992, p. 39). Two-way asymmetrical public relations is "the use of communication to manipulate publics for the benefit of organizations" (J.E. Grunig, 1989, p. 18).

Adversarial society theory. Adversarial society theory holds that persuasive communication operates in an adversarial society that, although it cannot condone untruths, must accept the delivery of self-interested, selective truths by public relations practitioners. In an influential article in *Journal of Mass Media Ethics*, then-editors Ralph Barney and Jay Black (1994) offered this definition of the framework:

> An adversarial society assumes that spokespersons with alternative views will emerge to balance the advocate. If that doesn't work, some will argue the journalist or some other consumer advocate, motivated by an objectivity and stewardship ethic, will assure some balance in the public messages.
>
> The reality is that there is no guarantee in the court of public opinion that adversaries will square off. Yet, just as a lawyer has no obligation to be considerate of the weaknesses of his opponents in court, so the public relations person can clearly claim it is another's obligation to provide countering messages . . .
>
> In an adversary society, truth is not so important as the obligation of opposing counsel to create scenarios that conflict with those of their opponents.
>
> (pp. 241, 244)

Five years later, Barney and Black (1999) still classified public relations practitioners as "an adversary group" (p. 67).

Friedman economics. Though technically not a framework of public relations, the social-responsibility philosophy of Nobel Prize-winning economist

Milton Friedman informs basic notions of corporate independent egoism. In *Capitalism and Freedom* (2002), Friedman declares, "There is one and only one social responsibility of business—to use its resources and engage in activities designed to increase its profits" (p. 133).

The independent-egoistic frameworks of public relations, which, again, tend to view relationships in an adversarial manner, can be summarized by a comment in an anonymous review of an article I wrote on social harmony frameworks for *Public Relations Inquiry* (Marsh, 2012). Though the reviewer generously accepted my article, he or she wrote:

> [Public relations] is not for instance actually a "striving for harmony." Only the most naïve or propagandists would make this claim. This is my problem with communitarian approaches . . . Public relations is only the pursuit of "harmony" if you believe the spin. What it in fact is, is advocacy which tries to stay on the correct side of the ethical contingency of the particular contemporary social milieu which it operates within.

This was, for me, a particularly useful review because it pushed me even deeper into evolutionary biology to see why such key figures as Charles Darwin (Chapter 4) and Richard Dawkins (Chapter 6) do indeed argue for the superiority of cooperative approaches toward relationships and resource acquisition. Surely *they* are not naive. My additional research now constitutes Part II of this book.

A number of public relations frameworks do skew to the social harmony, dependent-egoist view of resource acquisition. The general concept of social harmony can seem so clear that public relations scholars often use that phrase without definition (J.E. Grunig & White, 1992, p. 39; Kruckeberg, 1993, p. 30; Leeper & Leeper, 2001, p. 464; Molleda & Ferguson, 2004, p. 332; Toth, 2002, p. 248). Citing the works of British sociologist L.T. Hobhouse, historian J.T. Stuart (2008) has defined social harmony as "mutual support between two or more elements of a whole" (p. 62). Such mutual support on a societal scale is an expressed goal of several frameworks within public relations, including two-way symmetry, communitarianism, fully functioning society theory, and Isocratean rhetoric. Social harmony may also be an outcome, if not a primary goal, of the reflective paradigm.

Two-way symmetry. Of the two-way symmetrical model of public relations championed by excellence theory, J.E. Grunig (2000) has written, "With the two-way symmetrical model, practitioners use research and dialogue to bring about symbiotic changes in the ideas, attitudes, and behaviors of both the organization and its publics" (p. 32). Of his hopes for the evolution of symmetry, J.E. Grunig (2006) adds, "I now believe that the concept of relationship cultivation strategies is the heir to the models of public relations and the two-way symmetrical model, in particular." He envisions such development as being part of a "theoretical edifice that I call the strategic management role of public relations" (J.E. Grunig, 2006, pp. 153, 168). In *Excellence in Public Relations and Communication Management*, J.E. Grunig and White (1992) establish the role of social harmony within excellence theory, citing "interdependence" and "social harmony" as characteristics of the worldview inherent in "excellent public relations practice" (pp. 43, 56, 61).

Communitarianism. Starck and Kruckeberg (2001) observe:

> Public relations is best defined and practiced as the active attempt to restore and maintain a sense of community . . . lost because of the development of modern means of communication/transportation . . . Community building can be proactively encouraged and nurtured by corporations with the guidance and primary leadership of these organizations' public relations practitioners.
>
> (pp. 58, 59)

The "harmony" inherent in communitarianism need not exist "at the level of specific issues, where genuine disagreements can and do exist, but at the level of community cohesion and values that, hopefully, will lead to harmony, or at least understanding, on basic underlying values and issues" (Leeper & Leeper, 2001, p. 462).

Fully functioning society theory. Robert Heath (2006) explains:

> The fully functioning society theory (FST) of public relations rests on systems, rhetoric, and norm compliance to build relationships . . . At its center, it embraces Quintilian's principle of the good person communicating well as a foundation for fostering enlightened choices through dialogue in the public sphere. FST draws on the norms of exchange whereby community members seek to maximize outcomes and minimize costs of personal and collective association and decision making . . . An essential requirement for public relations according to this theory is to be a steward (K.S. Kelly, 2001) of multiple (the public interest?) interests in harmony and collaboration.
>
> (pp. 96, 97)

Maureen Taylor (2010) notes that fully functioning society theory is a "cocreational approach to public relations" (p. 6)—as opposed to the aforementioned independent-egoistic/functional approach (Kent, Sommerfeldt, & Saffer, 2016)—and that it correlates with "civil society theory," which champions a "process grounded in information, communication, and relationships" that is particularly tolerant of "different ideas" (Taylor, 2010, p. 7).

Isocratean rhetoric. Takis Poulakos (1997) asserts:

> Isocrates . . . changed the art of rhetoric from the way it was when he inherited it. The version of rhetoric he left behind is, unequivocally, a

> rhetoric for the polis [community] . . . He mobilized his version of rhe-
> toric in order to advocate courses of action that safeguarded the interests
> of the citizens and promoted the general welfare of the city-state . . . The
> values associated with hegemony (power and safety) take second seat
> to values associated with unity (cooperation, trust, and friendship).
>
> (pp. 3, 4, 85)

"If kings are to rule well," Isocrates (trans. 1928/1991) declares in his essay *Nicocles*, "they must try to preserve harmony, not only in the states over which they hold dominion, but also in their own households and in their places of abode. . ." (41). Haskins (2004) holds that in *Panathenaicus*, his final essay, Isocrates compares himself to Agamemnon, leader of the Greek forces in the Trojan War, because of his own "lifelong literary labors of promoting *homonoia*, or unity, among the Greek states" (p. 95). Poulakos (1997) adds that Isocrates sought "to address and resolve problems of division and coopera-tion—in other words, problems extremely pertinent to our own times" (p. 1).

The reflective paradigm. Holmström (2009) has defined reflection as "the production of self-understanding in relation to the environment" (p. 191); it is, she maintains, "the core demand on organisations" (2004, p. 126). Reflective organizations understand that they exist within a complex and dynamic frame-work of social needs in which "societal legitimation" (Van Ruler and Verčič, 2005, pp. 239, 263) is indispensable. To earn and sustain such legitimacy, reflective organizations develop the "capability of foreseeing potential conflicts between social systems, of evaluating their consequences, and of transforming the reflective observations into organisational learning processes" (Holmström, 2004, p. 125). Holmström (2009) attributes the origins of the reflective para-digm to the communication theories of German sociologist Niklas Luhmann.

In the reflective paradigm, however, harmony is more an incidental bypro-duct than a goal. In fact, Holmström (2004) declares, "The reflective paradigm . . .opposes ideas of harmony and consensus, and analytically uncovers how society learns to cope with its constitutive conflicts" (p. 131). Within the paradigm, "dialogic interaction with publics" designed to co-create meaning is openly "based more on a battle of interests than on harmony of interests" (van Ruler and Verčič, 2005, p. 250). Despite the reflective paradigm's rele-gation of social harmony to a possible outcome rather than a goal, Heath and Frandsen (2008) maintain that working toward an expansive enactment of social harmony might well, for an organization, help create the social legitimacy that is the aim of the reflective paradigm:

> Is the role of ethical public relations to strive for collaboration and enligh-
> tened choices inside and about organizations that seek and perhaps achieve
> the level of being truly in the "public interest" or the larger interest of
> many? This position assumes that rather than merely creating harmony

between an organization and one or more market, audience, or public that the more important challenge is to foster a functional dialogue so that collectively the best decisions can be made, problems solved, challenges met, harmony achieved, and legitimacy earned.

(p. 354)

Thus, the reflective processes of uncovering and coping with the constitutive conflicts of society, to use the terms employed by Holmström (2004), can foster harmonious relationships that bolster an entity's legitimacy within society.

In *Rethinking Public Relations*, Kevin Moloney stakes out an interesting midground between these egoistic and social harmony frameworks of public relations. In that work, Moloney (2006) holds that "PR reflects and generates social competition, not harmony" (p. 14)—but he also asserts that the discipline should work toward a reduction of unfair competition generated by disparities in communication resources:

A principal aim of [*Rethinking Public Relations*] is to argue for a PR system based on this idea of communicative equality, and for a funded, practical system of subsidy to ensure it . . . Communicative equality sets a minimum threshold for PR "voice," not a maximum. It does not limit free speech; it is a device to offer it to those not heard.

(p. 169)

Moloney's concept of redress and balance is an idea to which we will return in Chapter 5.

Cooperation and justice

A core contention of this book is that the social harmony frameworks of public relations are built upon the related concepts of cooperation and justice—and so, before proceeding, we should define those concepts. Since at least the time of Darwin, evolutionary biologists have been fascinated by "the problem of cooperation" (Axelrod, 2006, p. 3)—the mystery, that is, of why social organisms assist others at, possibly, an initial cost to themselves. For those biologists, cooperation is "a form of working together in which one individual pays a cost . . . and another gains a benefit as a result" (Coakley & Nowak, 2013, p. 4). In sustained relationships, evolutionary biologists note, the roles of cost-payer and benefit-receiver can alternate, ensuring that both partners ultimately benefit from the act of working together (Axelrod, 2006; Nowak & Highfield, 2011). As we shall see, one of the most significant findings of the book—strongly supported by evolutionary biology, philosophy, and rhetoric—is that the concept of indirect reciprocity, of helping someone without the prospect of return (positive or negative), is arguably the most successful strategy in a sustained program of resource acquisition. Again, the logic of this seeming anomaly is that, particularly in a society with strong and varied channels of communication, this form of cooperation wins the notice, respect, and trust of other potential partners, who then seek resource-sharing relationships with the initial cooperator.

As students of law and philosophy know, justice is more difficult to define. Because we are focusing on the sustained acquisition of resources, this book will focus primarily on the division of justice termed "transactional justice" by legal scholar Peter Koller (2009, p. 188). For Koller (2009), transactional justice applies to "exchange relationships" and "demands that . . . transactions occur in a way which makes sure that, in general, they are to the benefit of all parties involved, so that none of them has a legitimate reason to complain about the outcome" (pp. 188, 188–189). Such transactions, Koller (2009) asserts, "are between independent parties who agree on a mutual transfer of certain goods or services" (p. 188). For Hume, Rawls, and the philosophers analyzed in Part III of this book, justice is symbiotic with cooperation: A self-interested desire for secure resources and reliable resource exchange leads to forms of transactional justice, which, of necessity, involve cooperation. Resource dependency, in short, prompts justice, which both sustains and is sustained by social cooperation. Cooperation and justice, again, are the twin pillars of public relations' social harmony frameworks.

Chapter summaries and the Nine Tenets of public relations' social harmony frameworks

The consilience of cooperation established by the forthcoming sections on evolutionary biology, philosophy, and rhetoric supports Nine Tenets of public relations' social harmony frameworks. These Nine Tenets, in other words, arise from the findings in those chapters. In logical order, I hope, the Nine Tenets are these:

I   A core function of public relations is resource acquisition. Resources range from small to large, from tangible to abstract, from raw materials to employee commitment to social legitimacy.
II   Cooperation is the relationship strategy best suited to resource acquisition. Evidence from evolutionary biology, philosophy, and rhetoric shows that, in general, cooperative relationships are more successful in sustained resource acquisition than relationships based on egoism, conflict, and competition.
III Cooperative relationships are not merely normative, idealistic, or utopian. Rather, evidence from evolutionary biology, philosophy, and rhetoric shows that cooperation is a stronger instinct within human nature than the competing instincts of egoism, conflict, and competition.

IV   Justice begins in the social defense of resources, both our own and the resources of others. Based in self-interest, a quest for justice is not normative or contrary to human nature. Justice is inseparable from the processes of sustainable resource acquisition and thus is inherent within the processes of cooperation and public relations.

V   Biological and social tensions between individualism and collectivism are most sustainably resolved in favor of collectivism that defends individualism.

VI   Ethical behavior that accommodates the needs of others has enduring foundations in the biological and social origins of cooperation. Such behavior is not normative, idealistic, or contrary to human nature.

VII   Building relationships on the principles of cooperation and justice does not exclude the option of refusing to cooperate with hostile or destructive publics.

VIII   Acts of cooperation and justice are the most effective builders of a positive reputation. A positive reputation is a powerful, productive force within the processes of public relations and resource acquisition.

IX   Public relations practitioners can take specific actions, drawn from evolutionary biology, philosophy, and rhetoric, to build and enhance relationships built upon cooperation and justice.

These tenets emerged only after I had completed this book's first draft. Rather than guiding the direction of the chapters, they arose from the consilience established by the chapters' findings. As evolutionary biologist Thomas Henry Huxley, a major presence in the chapters to come, wrote in 1860, "My business is to teach my aspirations to conform themselves to fact, not to try and make facts harmonise with my aspirations" (L. Huxley, 1901a, p. 235). Each chapter of each disciplinary section concludes with two things: A summary of specific findings relevant to modern public relations and the linkage of those summary points to the Nine Tenets.

Chapter 2 is quid pro quo: One goal of this book is to show that evolutionary biology has much to offer public relations theory. If that relationship could somehow be characterized as intentional, it also could be characterized as reciprocal—because evolutionary biology owes its beginnings, in part, to one of the most successful public relations campaigns in history. The purpose of Chapter 2 is to review that campaign and, not so incidentally, to introduce individuals and ideas important to the forthcoming chapters.

Chapter 3, the introductory chapter to Part II on evolutionary biology and public relations, reviews scientific analyses of the command center of our species' cooperative instincts, the human brain. If, indeed, evolutionary processes have shaped us—and continue to shape us—to seek cooperation over egoistic conflict, then biological evidence of this reality must exist. Studies of the human brain within modern neuroscience provide that evidence.

Chapter 4 focuses on Charles Darwin's analysis of human evolution. In *The Descent of Man* (1871), unlike his earlier *On the Origin of Species* (1859), Darwin focuses on humans—and in Chapters 4 and 5 of that work, he addresses "the problem of cooperation" (Axelrod, 2006, p. 3) within our species. In Darwin's (1871/1998) own words from *Descent*, "Communities, which included the greatest number of the most sympathetic members, would flourish best, and rear the greatest number of offspring . . . Selfish and contentious people will not cohere, and without coherence nothing can be effected" (pp. 110, 134). For Darwin, a quest for social harmony is an acceptance, not a denial, of human instincts developed via natural selection.

Chapter 5 reviews Russian scientist Peter Kropotkin's theory of mutual aid. At the same time Darwin was writing *The Descent of Man*, Kropotkin was exploring Siberia as an officer in the Russian army. Of the competition for survival among animal species in that unforgiving environment, Kropotkin (1902/1989) later wrote:

> I failed to find—although I was eagerly looking for it—that bitter struggle for the means of existence, among animals belonging to the same species. . . . I saw Mutual Aid and Mutual Support carried on to an extent which made me suspect in it a feature of the greatest importance for the maintenance of life, the preservation of each species, and its further evolution.
>
> (pp. xxxv, xxxvii)

With his consequent book *Mutual Aid: A Factor of Evolution*, Kropotkin, even more than Darwin, became a keen advocate of the superior power of cooperation, vis-à-vis conflict, in natural selection.

Chapter 6 is my favorite chapter in the book. Three of the most honored and, in terms of publications, best-selling evolutionary biologists of the twentieth and twenty-first centuries—Stephen Jay Gould, Richard Dawkins, and Edward O. Wilson—profoundly, publicly, caustically, and wittily disagree on the mechanics of evolution. There is, however, one powerful point of consensus: Each champions the power of cooperation within evolutionary processes. Most telling, perhaps, is Dawkins' (2006a) acknowledgment in the third edition of *The Selfish Gene* that a good alternative title for that work "would have been *The Cooperative Gene*" (p. ix).

Chapter 7 reviews the findings of evolutionary biologists and social scientists who specialize in applied game theory—that is, in sophisticated, often computerized, resource acquisition games. Their findings show that cooperation, far from being overly idealistic and utopian, outperforms egoistic strategies in such experiments. Game theory experiments, particularly multigenerational models, help prove that cooperation is not merely aspirational: It is a basic human instinct, increasingly developed through natural selection operating in both the biological and cultural spheres.

Chapter 8, the introductory chapter to Part III on philosophy and public relations, addresses the inherency of justice within cooperation. Theories of justice, of course, have been the province of philosophy since at least Plato's *Republic*. However, the chapter also reviews the concept of philosophical materialism and its relationship to cooperation, justice, ethics, and the power of habit. Philosophical materialism positions itself against idealism; it holds that matter, divorced from any idealistic or supernatural influences, is the basis of all reality. Throughout Part III, justice, cooperation, and ethics will be presented as material, not normative, idealistic, or aspirational, concepts. (Again, the methodological approach of this book's advocacy of public relations' social harmony frameworks is, I believe, important: Only empirical, materialistic, even egoistic evidence will be presented. There will be no appeals to idealism, to altruism, or to what *ought* to be rather than to what *is*.)

Chapter 9 examines Scottish philosopher David Hume's compelling assertion that justice not only is essential to social cooperation; justice also engenders the society sustained by cooperation. For Hume, justice predates and creates society—and, fortunately for our materialistic, utopia-shunning viewpoint in this book, Hume's vision of justice begins not with altruism but with pure human self-interest. Ideally, this chapter will demonstrate that, far from being a normative ideal, justice—as defined by Hume—is inextricably embedded within resource dependency theory. In Hume's estimation, to work for the sustainable transfer of resources is inevitably to work for justice. Some measure of a quest for justice, then, seems both unavoidable and advisable within the practice of public relations. Hume further asserts that respect for the integrity of another's resources is the greatest driver of a positive reputation.

Chapter 10 focuses on American philosopher John Rawls' justice-as-fairness theory. In fact, the key points of Rawls' vision are the touchstones of this book: Self-interest, property/resources, cooperation, justice, reciprocity, reputation, relationships, reflection, rhetoric, legitimacy, power disparities, and society. Like Hume, Rawls—particularly in his later work—begins with practical, materialistic self-interest, which inevitably creates justice; justice, in turn, catalyzes cooperation, which helps to build an enduring society—or, regrettably, an inadequate form of justice may fail to do so. In his later work, Rawls does *not* consider what kind of justice is moral. Rather, he focuses on what kind of self-interested justice succeeds in catalyzing the cooperation necessary to sustain a "property-owning democracy" (Rawls, 2001, p. 140).

Chapter 11, the introductory chapter to Part IV on rhetoric and public relations, reviews the multidisciplinary debate within ancient Athens—history's first democracy—regarding the nature of the new art of public persuasion. DePaul University Professor of Philosophy Michael Naas (1995) acknowledges, "From tragic drama to philosophical dialogue to lyric poetry, discourses and arguments about the nature of persuasion can be found just about everywhere" in classical Athens (p. 8). Led by the dramatist Aeschylus, the philosopher Plato, and the rhetorician Isocrates, the Athenians did build their own consilience regarding persuasion. At its best, they concluded, persuasion is honest, respectful of others, and mindful of community wellbeing.

Chapter 12 analyzes the most successful rhetoric of Western civilization, the rhetoric of Isocrates. The chapter will document the achievements of Isocrates' school and its graduates, particularly compared with the rival institutions and students of Plato and Aristotle, and will highlight Isocrates' steadfast focus on the core values of justice, moderation, and the solicitation of dissent.

Chapter 13 details Isocrates' legacy, particularly in the ancient rhetorics of Cicero and Quintilian—which had to function in the tumultuous courtrooms and assemblies of ancient Rome—and in the modern rhetorics of I.A. Richards and Kenneth Burke. Of particular importance, I believe, is the linkage of Burke's concepts of identification and consubstantiality to new discoveries in neuroscience, including the functioning of mirror neurons and the human prefrontal cortex. Neuroscientists have discovered biological foundations for the core elements of Burkean rhetoric.

Chapter 14 concludes the book. It links all the chapter summary points to the Nine Tenets (collecting the evidence for the consilience of cooperation), offers suggestions from modern scientists for the furtherance of cooperation, and closes with 20 specific, evidence-based strategies for enacting public relations' social harmony frameworks.

The findings within these chapters create an empirical, materialistic consilience of cooperation, one driven in particular by indirect reciprocity. Of importance to our utopia-shunning approach is that none of the scientists, philosophers, or rhetoricians in this book believes that generations of humans have been walking a straight, unvarying path toward ever-increasing cooperation and justice. Though increasing cooperation indeed is the eons-long trend, in the words of Peter Kropotkin (trans. 1924/1992), "We certainly must abandon the idea of representing human history as an uninterrupted chain of development from the pre-historic Stone Age to the present time" (p. 17). Of the related decline in violence over the history of our species, Harvard Professor of Psychology Steven Pinker (2011) adds, "The decline, to be sure, has not been smooth; it has not brought violence down to zero. . ." (p. xxi).

One closing note: It surely will escape no one's notice that the primary sources in this book—the featured voices from evolutionary biology, philosophy, and rhetoric—are Western white males. That is a severe shortcoming, created in part, certainly, by the grossly unlevel playing field of history—but redressed somewhat within these pages, I hope, by the diversity of modern public relations scholars and of other sources, such as Arabella Buckley (Chapter 5), who anticipates Kropotkin's philosophy of mutual aid, and feminist philosopher Nel Noddings (Chapter 3), who challenges the idea that we can understand moral imperatives simply by examining self-interested, biological origins. Given this biased focus, however, one key finding of this book perhaps gains strength: Research amassed by psychologist Steven Pinker and neuroscientist Donald Pfaff, among others, indicates that one of the clearest paths to indirect reciprocity and enhanced social harmony is the empowerment of women. This book, again, concludes with 20 specific strategies for the enactment and furtherance of public relations' social harmony frameworks—and one of the 20 is this: "Empower women, particularly through equal rights that include equal access to education and equal paths to all levels of employment and leadership." That such a finding could emerge from such an uncongenial environment is both encouraging and a strong endorsement.

Summary

This chapter's review of resource dependency theory leads us to at least one important point for the understanding and practice of public relations:

1. Whether we envision public relations as a quest for social legitimacy, as the management of relationships with key stakeholders, as a function of marketing, or as something else altogether, the securing of resources controlled by others is, in all likelihood, central to our vision of the discipline.

   This point addresses one of the Nine Tenets of public relations' social harmony frameworks outlined in Chapter 1:

I   A core function of public relations is resource acquisition. Resources range from small to large, from tangible to abstract, from raw materials to employee commitment to social legitimacy.

Chapter 2

The public relations
of evolution

On Wednesday, April 26, 1882, Thomas Henry Huxley, Joseph Dalton Hooker, and Alfred Russel Wallace cooperated one last time for Charles Darwin. With six other men, including two dukes, an earl, an ambassador, and the president of the Royal Society, they served as pallbearers for Darwin's coffin on the day of his interment in Westminster Abbey (Browne, 2002). Historian Iain McCalman (2009) christened the three men "Darwin's armada" (p. 13): Like Darwin, they had spent much of their youth aboard ship en route to their investigations of organisms and terrain that few other Britons had seen. "There was no place for formality or affectation between fellow sailors," McCalman (2009) explains. Within months of meeting one another, Darwin and the members of his armada were "addressing each other with the familiarity of old friends" (McCalman, 2009, p. 299). In an 1893 speech to the Royal Society, in fact, Huxley (1894/1983) compares Darwin's *On the Origin of Species* to "a ship laden with a cargo of rich value" (p. 111).

Huxley, Hooker, and Wallace had cooperated before on Darwin's behalf, and that collaboration had changed the world. In part because of Darwin's reticence and poor health, the three were the public faces and voices of what historians have variously called a "great PR campaign" (Wolfe, 2016, p. 48), "a triumph by publicity" (Caudill, 1994, p. 441), "a systematic publicity operation," a "propaganda campaign," and "the marketing of evolutionary theory—a heady publicity campaign" (Browne, 2002, pp. 84, 155, 135). Huxley, Hooker, and Wallace were chief strategists and agents in the campaign for public acceptance of *On the Origin of Species*, with its natural selection, survival of the fittest, and evolution—a fusion termed "Darwin's dangerous idea" by philosopher Daniel Dennett (1995, p. 5). Born into poverty, Huxley (1825–1895) had shouldered his way into the elitist top echelons of British science, becoming secretary of the Royal Society and, by the end of his life, standing second only to Darwin, probably, as the United Kingdom's best-known and most-respected modern scientist. Hooker (1817–1911) was the son of a famous botanist and became director of the Royal Botanical Gardens. Like Huxley, Wallace (1823–1913) came from humble origins. Through his own research and travels, he had worked out a similar theory of natural selection, but had graciously ceded precedence to Darwin. Before their deaths, all three were recognized as among the greatest scientists of the nineteenth century.

Within evolutionary biology, one enduring explanation of "the problem of cooperation" (Axelrod, 2006, p. 3)—of why members of social species assist each other at occasional cost to themselves—has been termed *reciprocal altruism*, more familiarly summarized by the aphorism "You scratch my back, and I'll scratch yours" (Dawkins, 2006a, p. 166). Much of this book, certainly the next five chapters, will strive to show that evolutionary biology has much to offer public relations theory: Primarily, powerful validation of cooperative, social harmony frameworks such as fully functioning society theory, communitarianism, two-way symmetry, and Isocratean rhetoric. If this interdisciplinary contribution could somehow be characterized as intentional, it also could be characterized as reciprocal—because evolutionary biology owes its beginnings, in part, to one of the most successful public relations campaigns in history. The purpose of this chapter is to review that campaign and, not so incidentally, to further introduce individuals and ideas important to the forthcoming chapters.

Odds were against the success of *On the Origin of Species*, first published in 1859. Darwin presented his book to a Western world ruled by natural theology, which posited a deity as the intentional creator of everything. Natural theology is typified by British theologian William Paley's analogy of a watch and a watchmaker: Just as the intricacies of a pocket watch indicate the inevitable presence of an intentional watchmaker, so the intricacies of the universe indicate the inevitable presence of an intentional creator. Just as the watch was designed toward a specific end, so life on Earth has divine purpose (Paley, 1837). Richard Owen, director of the British Museum, and Louis Agassiz, Harvard professor of zoology and geology, spoke and published in defense of natural theology. The belief in a theological form of what, in the twenty-first century, is termed intelligent design "was virtually a constitutive element of science in mid-century Britain" (Campbell, 2003, p. 234). In publishing *On the Origin of Species*, Darwin was asking millions "to believe in what was then thought to be unbelievable" (Browne, 2002, p. 139). Few public relations campaigns have been launched into less promising environments.

On the Origin of Species, however, was not without rough precedent. The French biologist Jean-Baptiste Lamarck earlier had written that acquired characteristics were inherited. Geologist Charles Lyell, Darwin's mentor and author of the influential *Principles of Geology*, had shown that Earth was more ancient than many had believed and was continuously shaped by natural processes. Darwin's own grandfather, Erasmus Darwin, had suggested that warm-blooded animals might have a common ancestor. Fifteen years before the publication of *On the Origin of Species*, Scottish polymath Robert Chambers anonymously published *Vestiges of the Natural History of Creation*, in which he suggested that all forms of matter had naturally evolved from earlier versions. In condemning *Vestiges*, Adam Sedgwick, Darwin's professor of geology at Cambridge, found the book to be full of "deformity and foulness" yet so gracefully written that "I cannot but think the work is from a woman's pen" (Clark & Hughes, 1890, p. 85). For Sedgwick, however, female author-ship would have been a further detriment: He explained that science advances in successive steps, and "petticoats are not fitted for the steps of a ladder" (Clark & Hughes, 1890, p. 85). In 2010, 165 years after Sedgwick's comments, the Royal Society acknowledged that generations of previous members had "actively" denied membership to women (Ferry, 2010, p. S163).

Such was the environment into which Darwin prepared to introduce *On the Origin of Species* with its key explanations of species change: Variation and natural selection. His efforts, combined with those of his armada and other supporters, certainly can be characterized as public relations. Their coordinated strategies and tactics enacted resource dependency theory in seeking the resources of acceptance and approval from a variety of readers (Pfeffer & Salancik, 1978; L.A. Grunig, J.E. Grunig, & Ehling, 1992). In a quest—led by Darwin's gracious and sincere consideration of dissent—to win the ultimate resource of social legitimacy for the radical idea that species evolve through the processes of variation and natural selection, the campaign also enacted the reflective paradigm of public relations (Holmström, 2004). Finally, many of the rhetorical tactics deployed by Darwin and his armada, including speeches, personal letters, and articles of support, are time-honored practices of public relations. Like the evolutionary processes (and consequent public relations frameworks) described in this book, Darwin and his armada sought cooperation but did not shun unavoidable conflict. This chapter divides the campaign for "Darwin's dangerous idea" into three phases: Prepublication, the text of *On the Origin of Species*, and postpublication.

Prepublication

It would be guesswork to label any single measure as Darwin's first step in the campaign for *On the Origin of Species*. Certainly an early tactic, however, was a January 11, 1844, letter to Hooker. In a chatty note that combined requests for information with gossip about other naturalists, Darwin closed with a self-effacing first, albeit veiled, announcement of natural selection and the origin of species:

> I have been now ever since my return engaged in a very presumptuous work & which I know no one individual who w^d not say a very foolish one . . . I am almost convinced (quite contrary to opinion I started with) that species are not (it is like confessing a murder) immutable. . .I think I have found out (here's presumption!) the simple way by which species become exquisitely adapted to various ends.—You will now groan, &

think to yourself 'on what a man have I been wasting my time in writing to.'—I shd, five years ago, have thought so.

(Burkhardt & Smith, 1987, p. 2)

But Hooker did not reject Darwin's presumption. He wrote of his "great interest" and hope that their correspondence might "ascend to grand causes," and soon their frequent letters between Darwin's home in Kent and Hooker's in London carried the salutations "My dear Hooker" and "My dear Darwin" (Burkhardt & Smith, 1987, pp. 15, 16, 17, 18)

His "presumptuous work" having survived such a diffident overture, Darwin progressed in September 1844 to suggesting to Hooker that isolation played a role in his developing theory:

I cannot give my reasons in detail: but the most general conclusion, which the geographical distribution of all organic beings, appears to me to indicate, is that isolation is the chief concomitant or cause of the appearance of *new* forms (I well know there are some staring exceptions).

(Burkhardt & Smith, 1987, p. 61)

Once again, Hooker entertained the oblique new idea: "Your communication was indeed most interesting & much food for me," he declared in October, but added that his own research was too "narrow a base" to support Darwin's vaguely expressed ideas about "the cause of the appearance of new forms" (Burkhardt & Smith, 1987, pp. 69, 71). Darwin responded that he (Darwin) "must have been cracked to have written it"—but he added:

In my most sanguine moments, all I expect, is that I shall be able to show even to sound Naturalists, that there are two sides to the question of the immutability of species;–that facts can be viewed & grouped under the notion of allied species having descended from common stocks.

(Burkhardt & Smith, 1987, p. 79)

Far from rebuking his new friend, Hooker agreed to visit in December 1844. Darwin had recruited his first great ally.

A major tactic in what Campbell (1989) has termed Darwin's "third-party strategy" for the promotion of *On the Origin of Species* was an April 1856 meeting at Darwin's home, Down House in Kent, three years before publication (p. 55). Present were Darwin, Hooker, and Huxley—christened "the Darwinian triad" by Caudill (1994, p. 459)—as well as two other naturalists. McCalman (2009) describes the gathering very much in the language of public relations—as "a strategic weekend meeting" with "key targets" (p. 297). A primary objective of the meeting was to solidify Hooker's support and to enlist a third sailor, Thomas Henry Huxley:

It was no less urgent to win over Thomas Huxley, who had long called himself an "active doubter" about evolution . . . Darwin's sailorly warmth and lack of social pretension had gone a long way towards disarming this *enfant terrible* . . . [Huxley] recognized that he shared [a bond] with Hooker and Darwin . . . The genial host led his guests on a tour of the gardens, greenhouses, and dovecotes—a ploy aimed at instilling doubts about the fixity of species . . . Why was [Huxley] so resistant, Darwin asked, to the idea that the modern horse might be descended from the small, three-toed Eocene fossil?

(McCalman, 2009, pp. 304, 313)

In the face of gentle but relentless logic from a fellow sailor, Huxley's resistance ebbed—but even after the publication of *Origin*, he still declared, "Mr. Darwin does not so much prove that natural selection does occur, as that it must occur" (1860, p. 568). It was only after his 1876 meeting with a Yale paleontology professor named Charles Marsh (who, I immodestly must point out, was a distant cousin via our common ancestors Zachary and Mary Marsh of Salem, Massachusetts) that Huxley wholly embraced the principle of natural selection (L. Huxley, 1901a, pp. 495, 497).

Knowing of the April 1856 meeting, geologist Charles Lyell wrote to Darwin the following month, urging him to publish, though he remained troubled by Darwin's heretical ideas:

I hear that when you & Hooker & Huxley . . . got together you made light of all species & grew more & more unorthodox . . . I wish you would publish some small fragment of your data . . . if you please & so out with the theory & let it take date—& be cited—& understood.

(Burkhardt & Smith, 1990, p. 89)

Six months later, Darwin wrote to Lyell, "I am working very steadily at my big Book" (Burkhardt & Smith, 1900, p. 265).

Over the next several months, Darwin shared excerpts from the first draft of *Origin* with Hooker and Huxley (Browne, 2006; McCalman, 2009)—but Lyell's concern that Darwin needed to quickly take public ownership of his theory was validated when, on June 18, 1858, Darwin received a letter from naturalist Alfred Wallace, whom he had not yet met, with an attached article titled "On the Tendency of Varieties to Depart Indefinitely from the Original Type." On the same day, Darwin wrote this to Lyell:

Your words have come true with a vengeance that I shd be forestalled. You said this when I explained to you here very briefly my views of "Natural Selection" depending on the Struggle for existence.— I never saw a more striking coincidence. if Wallace had my M.S. . . . he could not have made a better short abstract! Even his terms now stand as Heads of my Chapters.

(Burkhardt & Smith, 1991, p. 107)

Darwin then dispiritedly told Lyell that, with Wallace's permission, he would send the article to any journal that Wallace preferred.

Lyell and Hooker, however, had other ideas. They arranged to read Wallace's article *and* key passages from Darwin's writings, which predated the Wallace manuscript, at the July 1858 meeting of the Linnean Society of London. Darwin's papers and the Wallace manuscript were then published in the society's journal (Browne, 2002, pp. 40, 43). McCalman (2007) speculates that Huxley may have helped fashion these tactics but moved in the background because he could not yet afford the society's membership dues (p. 327). In his *Autobiography*, Darwin (1887/1983) recalled that "our joint productions excited very little attention"—and that the little attention gained was negative (p. 72). Though the devout Lyell never fully supported Darwin's theory of natural selection, Darwin biographer Janet Browne included him as one of the "Four Musketeers" (Hooker, Huxley, Lyell, and American botanist Asa Gray) who served as early promoters and defenders of *On the Origin of Species* (Browne, 2002, p. 126). Throughout his life, Wallace generously acknowledged Darwin's precedence in formulating the idea of evolution through the processes of variation and natural selection.

Now rushing to finish his lengthy manuscript (in part condensing the even larger version he had planned), Darwin continued to share passages with Hooker and Huxley. Though Huxley held fast to his concerns about proof of natural selection, Hooker, in Darwin's opinion, came to believe in the concept even more fervently than Darwin himself (Irvine, 1955, p. 79). An additional, unavoidable element of Darwin's third-party strategy was his voluminous correspondence with other naturalists and explorers who possessed the corroborating information and examples that Darwin ultimately would pack into *On the Origin of Species*. Tirelessly developing what Browne (2002) termed "knowledge-producing relationships," Darwin even "attached a mirror to the inside of his study window, angled so that he could catch the first glimpse of the postman turning up the drive" (p. 13). In the text of *Origin* itself, Darwin frequently named these contributors, thus building partnerships in the venture and, surely, increasing the odds of acceptance. In 1859, Darwin finished the manuscript and began preparing it for print. *On the Origin of Species* was published in England on November 24, 1859. The first edition of 1,250 copies sold out in 24 hours (Irvine, 1955).

The text of *On the Origin of Species*

Professor of rhetoric John Angus Campbell (1989) has termed Darwin "the invisible rhetorician" (p. 55) and, indeed, Darwin's *On the Origin of Species* is in many ways a masterpiece of rhetoric. Absent the conclusive proof of natural selection that Huxley and others desired, Darwin had to craft a case for the probability of that process—and probability, as Aristotle (trans. 1954) notes, is the realm of rhetoric (1357a). In the words of his biographer Janet Browne (2002), Darwin "had no equations to establish his case. Everything in his book was to be words—persuasion, revisualisation, the balance of probabilities. . ." (p. 55). Darwin (1859) himself conceded that his book was "one long argument" (p. 459)—an argument that he ceaselessly refined, both before publication and in subsequent editions. (The six key editions of *Origin* exist at Darwin Online, http://darwin-online.org.uk.) "Darwin reveals unexpected talents as a debater," historian William Irvine (1955) concludes. "Confused, stammering, and unsyntactical in the presence of triumphantly articulate people like Huxley, he is deadly in the careful and premeditated quiet of the study" (p. 92). The rhetorical nature of *On the Origin of Species* can clearly be discerned if we examine the work through the lenses of the traditional divisions of rhetoric (Cicero, trans. 1949/1976, I.vii.9), particularly content (invention), organization, and expression (voice and diction).

The content of *Origin*

Two familiar, related rhetorical tactics saturate the early chapters of *On the Origin of Species*—one described by Aristotle as *paradeigma (example)* and the other, by Kenneth Burke (Chapter 13), as *identification*. Specific *paradeigmata*/examples are inherent, of course, in an inductive, empirical pro- cess. Identification—a hallmark of "new" rhetoric for Burke (1951, p. 203)— involves the establishing of common ground, or "consubstantiality," between speaker and audience (Burke, 1950/1969, p. 46). With the opening words of Chapter 1 of *On the Origin of Species*, Darwin (1859) forecasts the prevalence of both tactics: "When we look to the individuals of the same variety or sub- variety of our older cultivated plants and animals . . ." (p. 7). In other words, *we* (not *I*) will examine specific, persuasive examples of species familiar to us all. Before launching into thousands of words on the well-known science of pigeon breeding, which "fascinated the Victorians by keeping nature close at hand yet under control" (Secord, 1981, p. 171), Darwin (1859)—still in his first chapter—trotted out, so to speak, the following familiar examples:

> wheat . . . cart and race-horses, long and short-horned cattle . . . [the] terrier . . . foxes . . . sheep and goats . . . European cattle . . . horses . . . ducks and rabbits . . . the Italian greyhound, the bloodhound, the bull-dog, or Blenheim spaniel . . .
>
> (pp. 8, 15, 17, 18, 19)

Using these familiar species (a list he increased in later editions), Darwin began to connect "what took place in farmyards and what might be presumed to happen in the wild" (Browne, 2002, p. 56). He may ultimately have used his exhaustive study of barnacles to persuade himself of natural selection (Irvine, 1955), but those comparatively obscure creatures do not appear until Chapter 5. Instead, Darwin analyzes species familiar to his readers. In establishing Burkean identification, Darwin (1859) analyzes "*our* knowledge . . . *our* domestic animals and fruits . . . *our* dogs . . . *our* flower and kitchen gardens" (pp. 4, 15, 17, 37, emphasis added). In Chapter 1 alone, he uses the word *our* 44 times.

Such examples in *On the Origin of Species* not only were familiar; they also were almost overwhelming in number, surely a tactic designed to prove natural selection by the sheer mass of supporting information. In his *Autobiography*, Darwin (1887/1983) more than once expressed his distrust of deduction, of moving to an important conclusion by beginning with general principles (pp. 64, 85). *On the Origin of Species* is, conversely, dramatic confirmation of his preference for building up to the general principle via a "heap of facts," in the admiring words of British cleric and novelist Charles Kingsley (Burkhardt & Smith, 1991, p. 379). As Campbell (2003) notes, Darwin's determination to patiently build an irrefutable inductive, empirical case for natural selection also did much for his personal credibility: "From the standpoint of ethos, the variety of Darwin's resources shows him to be a man of common sense as well as theory" (p. 213). In amassing his own voluminous examples in support of the superior power of cooperation—or mutual aid, as he put it—in evolution, the great Russian naturalist Peter Kropotkin surely must have been influenced by the power of Darwin's extensive examples in *On the Origin of Species*.

One species, however, was conspicuously absent from *Origin*—and that absence surely was a rhetorical tactic: Darwin avoided using humans as examples of variation and natural selection. Lyell "used always to caution me to slip over man" Darwin wrote to Hooker in 1860 (Burkhardt et al., 1993, p. 34)—and perhaps Lyell's prescience in foreseeing the coming of Wallace persuaded Darwin to listen to his cautious mentor. "Whatever the reasons," Browne (2006) concludes, "[Darwin] systematically drained the manuscript of human beings" (p. 49). Huxley's insistence on controversially linking humans to earlier primates, however, ensured that the idea of apes as grandparents entered public debates on natural selection soon after the publication of *Origin* (Hellman, 1998). Though he "could not avoid the belief that man must come under the same law" (Darwin, 1887/1983, p. 78), Darwin did not openly discuss humans as products of natural selection until 1871 with *The Descent of Man*.

Mindful of the prevalence of natural theology, Darwin perhaps disingenuously included two quotations on the flyleaf of the first edition of *Origin* that suggested a divine presence behind the workings of natural selection— an idea of great appeal to his American champion Asa Gray. In the second edition of *Origin*, published in January 1860, he also revised the final paragraph to include the idea of a creator setting natural laws into motion:

"There is grandeur in this view of life . . . having been originally breathed by the Creator into a few forms or into one . . ." (1860, p. 490). Darwin (1859), however, did refer to a "Creator" throughout his first edition, particularly, in Chapter 6, in the passage detailing natural selection's refinement of the eye (p. 188). In all probability these tactics were attempts at identification—and religious reassurance—that Darwin himself did not actually share (Browne, 2002, p. 67). In Campbell's (2003) opinion, "Darwin clearly lied about his theological views to advance the cultural penetration of his theory" (p. 217).

Finally, Darwin devoted Chapter 6 of the first edition to objections to his theories and, with the eventual sixth edition, added a second chapter of objections. In his *Autobiography*, Darwin (1887/1983) recalls spending years collecting every objection he could envision, always writing them down to ensure their inclusion and, ideally, their rebuttal in his finished work (p. 73). Chapter 6, titled "Difficulties on Theory" (revised to "Difficulties of the Theory" in the 1869 fifth edition) begins with the seemingly genuine humility and self-effacement that did so much to build Darwin's (1859) ethos as the messenger of a revolutionary new idea:

> Long before having arrived at this part of my work, a crowd of difficulties will have occurred to the reader. Some of them are so grave that to this day I can never reflect on them without being staggered; but, to the best of my judgment, the greater number are only apparent, and those that are real are not, I think, fatal to my theory.
>
> (p. 171)

"There was certainly no man" Huxley later wrote, "whose personal character should have afforded a better safeguard against attacks . . . malignity and . . . shameless impertinences" (F. Darwin, 1888, p. 182).

By the time of the sixth edition in 1872, however, having seen *On the Origin of Species* succeed beyond his hopes (or at least beyond his fears), Darwin (1872) allowed a trace of testiness to enter his tone as he added a new chapter of objections for consideration and refutation:

> I will devote this chapter to the consideration of various miscellaneous objections which have been advanced against my views, as some of the previous discussions may thus be made clearer; but it would be useless to discuss all of them, as many have been made by writers who have not taken the trouble to understand the subject.
>
> (p. 168)

Near the end of Chapter 7, titled "Miscellaneous Objections to the Theory of Natural Selection," Darwin (1872) was able to calmly state, "That many species have been evolved in an extremely gradual manner, there can hardly be a doubt" (p. 202).

The organization of *Origin*

In 1854, Darwin (1887/1983) began to arrange "my huge pile of notes" as a prelude to a volume that, originally, was to be much larger than the eventual *Origin* (p. 70). With the advent of Wallace's 1858 article on natural selection, however, Darwin (1887/1983) whittled that larger work into *On the Origin of Species* in "13 months and ten days [of] hard labour" (p. 73). Despite that relative haste, he was very much aware of the importance of the organization of his book, particularly of the order of the chapters: "With my larger books I spend a good deal of time over the general arrangement of the matter" (Darwin, 1887/1983, p. 82).

The rhetorical organization of *On the Origin of Species* will be familiar to strategic communicators who deliver bad news or sensitive information: Rather than beginning with the theory of natural selection, with its inherent removal of a deity who continuously and personally shapes species, a theory he termed "the key-stone of my arch" (Burkhardt & Smith, 1991, p. 278), Darwin began with the aforementioned presentation of familiar examples. The first six chapters of *Origin* show Darwin painstakingly building to his keystone, then delivering and detailing it, and finally defending it. Chapter 1 is titled "Variation under Domestication." Chapter 2 is "Variation under Nature." Chapter 3 is "The Struggle for Existence." Chapter 4 is the keystone of *Origin*: "Natural Selection." Chapter 5 is "Laws of Variation," and Chapter 6 is "Difficulties on Theory." Irvine (1995) asserts that the book "begins with the humdrum and the prosaic, and moves almost imperceptibly into the vast and mysterious" (p. 89). Browne (2006) adds that *Origin* has been compared to the bulky Victorian masterpieces *Great Expectations* and *Middlemarch* "in the complexity of its interlacing themes and . . . ability to handle so many continuous threads at the same time" (p. 66). In his *Autobiography*, Darwin (1887/1983) confessed a great love for such novels (p. 83).

Voice and diction within *Origin*

Historian Iain McCalman (2009) believes that the plainspoken "sailorly warmth" (p. 304) that Darwin had used to recruit Hooker and Huxley also appealed to the mass audience of *On the Origin of Species*. Similarly, in a comment that evokes Burke's notion of identification, Campbell (2003) writes that Darwin skillfully "beckons the discerning reader to become his coconspirator" (p. 220). Darwin (1887/1983) himself suggested that he agonized over achieving the clear, deferential prose style that stands as one of the most powerful appeals of his controversial work:

> I have as much difficulty as ever in expressing myself clearly and con-
> cisely; and this difficulty has caused me a very great loss of time; but it
> has had the compensating advantage of forcing me to think long and

intently about every sentence . . . There seems to be a sort of fatality in my mind leading me to put at first my statement or proposition in a wrong or awkward form. Formerly I used to think about my sentences before writing them down; but for several years I have found that it saves time to scribble in a vile hand whole pages as quickly as I possibly can, contracting half the words; and then correct deliberately. Sentences thus scribbled down are often better ones than I could have written deliberately.

(p. 82)

Even one of Darwin's severest critics, Bishop Samuel Wilberforce (1860), declared of *Origin*, "It is a most readable book; full of facts in natural history, old and new, of his collecting and of his observing; and all of these are told in his own perspicuous language, and all thrown into picturesque combinations . . ." (p. 118). Browne (2006) finds Darwin's voice to be "sympathetic and genial, creating a distinctive magic between author and reader" (p. 68)—again, Burke's identification—but her extensive studies of Darwin also show that to achieve such rhetorical power, he "relentlessly" tightened and refined the larger prior work that, in 1859, would become *On the Origin of Species* (Browne, 2002, p. 54).

In the years from 1859 to 1872, Darwin constantly revised *Origin* to address new findings and objections, ultimately generating six editions. "Though considerably added to and corrected in the later editions," he wrote in his *Autobiography*, "it has remained substantially the same book" (1887/1983, p. 73).

Postpublication

As Huxley had warned (L. Huxley, 1901a, p. 189), reaction against *On the Origin of Species* was swift and harsh, calling upon prodigious efforts from the overlapping circles of Darwin's armada, the Darwinian triad, and the Four Musketeers to counter the derision and disbelief. Decades later, Huxley singled out a July 1860 *Quarterly Review* article by Wilberforce as the nadir of dishonorable attacks upon Darwin and natural selection (F. Darwin, 1888, p. 182); such reviews generally were unsigned, but Wilberforce was known to be the author of the *Quarterly Review* attack (Browne, 2002, pp. 103, 114). In his review, Wilberforce (1860)—primed, seemingly by British Museum Director Richard Owen (Browne, 2002)—praised Darwin's prose style but alternately mocked and savaged his conclusions and character: "If Mr. Darwin can with the same correctness of reasoning demonstrate to us our fungular descent, we shall dismiss our pride, and avow, with the characteristic humility of philosophy, our unsuspected cousinship with the mushrooms" (p. 121). In Wilberforce's (1860) eyes, however, Darwin could not provide such demonstration: "When subjected to the stern Baconian law of the observation of facts, the theory breaks down utterly; for no natural variations from the specific type favourable to the individual from which nature is to select can anywhere be found" (p. 125). This supposed failing led to Wilberforce's (1860) disingenuous assessment of Darwin's character:

> Mr. Darwin writes as a Christian, and we doubt not that he is one. We do not for a moment believe him to be one of those who retain in some corner of their hearts a secret unbelief which they dare not vent; and we therefore pray him to consider well the grounds on which we brand his speculations with the charge of such a tendency . . . However unconsciously to him who holds them, such views really tend inevitably to banish from the mind most of the peculiar attributes of the Almighty . . . That Mr. Darwin should have wandered from this broad highway of nature's works into the jungle of fanciful assumption is no small evil.
>
> (pp. 134–135, 135, 137)

Darwin's willingness to forgive the bishop failed to move Huxley: "The kindliness with which Mr. Darwin speaks of his assailant, Bishop Wilberforce . . . is so striking an exemplification of his singular gentleness and modesty, that it rather increases one's indignation against the presumption of his critic" (F. Darwin, 1888, p. 182).

On the eve of the Wilberforce review, however, Huxley exacted a powerful counterstroke. Having eagerly cast himself as "Darwin's bulldog" (Browne, 2002, p. 105), he had pledged to Darwin to sharpen "my claws and beak in readiness"—and later acknowledged the pleasure of "jamming common-sense down the throats of fools" (L. Huxley, 1901a, p. 189; 1901b, p. 23). Darwin (1887/1983) himself wrote that Huxley's "mind was as quick as a flash of lightning and as sharp as a razor" (p. 62)—and Huxley applied those qualities at a meeting of the British Association for the Advancement of Science in June 1860. Though accounts of the clash vary (Campbell, 1989; Browne, 2006), Wilberforce apparently concluded his remarks by facing Huxley and asking, before the "700 persons or more" (L. Huxley, 1901b, p. 195) present, "whether it was through his grandfather or his grandmother that he claimed his descent from a monkey" (Hellman, 1998, p. 86). At those words, Huxley muttered to an acquaintance, "The Lord hath delivered him into mine hands" (L. Huxley, 1901b, p. 197). *Macmillan's Magazine* offers the following account of Huxley's famous retort:

> Mr. Huxley slowly and deliberately arose. A slight tall figure stern and pale, very quiet and very grave, he stood before us and spoke those tremendous words . . . He was not ashamed to have a monkey for his ancestor; but he would be ashamed to be connected with a man who used great gifts to obscure the truth. No one doubted his meaning and the effect was tremendous. One lady fainted and had to be carried out: I, for one, jumped out of my seat.
>
> ("A Grandmother's Tales," 1898, pp. 433–434)

When the tumult had subsided, Joseph Hooker spoke of his own movement from disbelief to acceptance of natural selection and asserted that Wilberforce "obviously had not read" *On the Origin of Species* (Hellman, 1998, p. 87).

Before the notorious clash with Wilberforce, Huxley also had written two highly favorable reviews, one in the *Times*—"no living naturalist and anatomist has published a better monograph" (T.H. Huxley, 1908, p. 106)— and one in *The Westminster Review:* "The chapters on Variation, on the Struggle for Existence, on Instinct, on Hybridism, on the Imperfection of the Geological Record, on Geographical Distribution, have not only no equals, but, so far as our knowledge goes, no competitors" (T.H. Huxley, 1860, pp. 569–570). "By harnessing such powerful organs of Victorian opinion," McCalman (2009) concludes, "[Huxley] showed that the Darwinists were a force to be reckoned with" (p. 343). Huxley assisted with several other reviews and maintained constant correspondence with Darwin and his other allies (Caudill, 1994). So powerful were his efforts that Irvine (1955) suggests that "Darwin caused history and Huxley made it" (p. 8).

Hooker, meanwhile, also wrote and encouraged favorable reviews and, via letters, drew upon his reputation as a leading botanist to encourage his colleagues to support Darwin (Browne, 2002; McCalman, 2009). In the intro-duction to his 1860 *Flora Tasmaniae (The Botany of Tasmania)*, he frequently cited Darwin and, early in that work, declared, "Of these speculations [regarding species mutation] by far the most important and philosophical is that of the delimitation of species by natural selection, for which we are indebted to two wholly independent and original thinkers, Mr. Darwin and Mr. Wallace" (1860, p. xi). It was Hooker, again, who had worked with Lyell to link the research of Darwin and Wallace at the July 1858 meeting of the Linnean Society of London. "I shd have liked to have heard you triumphing over the Bishop," Darwin wrote to Hooker in July 1860. "I am astounded at your success and audacity" (Burkhardt et al., 1993, p. 272).

Though he generally remained at Down House, Darwin himself continued to write letters, some 500 annually in the years immediately after publication of *Origin* (Browne, 2006). He sent dozens of copies of *Origin*, with cover letters, to journals and to colleagues, including almost certain critics such as Louis Agassiz of Harvard (Irvine, 1955, p. 114). One of his least successful tactics, however, was a December 1859 meeting with Richard Owen in London, a significant venture given Darwin's shyness and poor health. "Polite as this meeting was," Browne (2002) summarizes, "it signalled the beginning of the end for the two naturalists" (p. 99). Four months later, the influential Owen, the United Kingdom's most prestigious scientific advocate of natural theology, savaged Darwin in an *Edinburgh Review* assessment of *Origin*. Darwin's work, Owen (1860) wrote, "betrays not only the confusion of ideas as to the fact and the nature of the law, but an ignorance or indifference to the matured thoughts and expressions of some of those eminent authorities on this supreme question in Biology" (p. 501). Appalled by the venom and inaccuracy of Owen's attacks on himself and his supporters, Darwin responded with rare, for him, harsh words. To Asa Gray, he wrote, "[Owen] misquotes & misrepresents me badly, & how he lauds himself.—But the manner in which he sneers at Hooker is scandalous" (Burkhardt et al., 1993, p. 166). To Hooker he wrote, "What a base dog [Owen] is" (Burkhardt et al., 1993, p. 162). Years later in his *Autobiography*, Darwin (1887/1983) said of Owen, "His power of hatred was certainly unsurpassed" (p. 61).

Once again, however, Huxley rose as Darwin's champion. Just as Bishop Samuel Wilberforce had provided Huxley an opening with his ape-as-ancestor gibe, Owen also presented a vulnerability: He had, in part, based his rejection of natural selection upon an anatomical error, repeatedly asserting that, alone among primates, humans had a brain segment then called the hippocampus minor. That singularity, he maintained, argued against Darwin's concept of descent with modification and for the primacy of a unique, favored species fashioned by a divine creator. Huxley attacked Owen on this mistaken singularity at the same meeting at which he had attacked Wilberforce (Browne, 2002): The hippocampus minor, Huxley noted, was not unique to humans. He then escalated both his evidence and rancor in an 1861 *Natural History Review* article in which he concluded that Owen was "guilty of wilful and deliberate false-hood" (Gross, 1993, p. 495). Finally, in his *Evidence as to Man's Place in Nature*, Huxley (1863/2001) marshaled overwhelming evidence and agree-ment from colleagues that Owen's "erroneous assertions" were "remarkable"— and that "far from retracting the grave errors into which he had fallen, Professor Owen has persisted in and reiterated them" (pp. 116, 117, 118). Huxley, in short, had "bluntly called Owen a liar" (McCalman, 2009, p. 351). Huxley's attacks were "superb Darwinian propaganda" (Irvine, 1955, p. 135) and "played a major role in finally defeating Owen" (Gross, 1993, p. 496).

Alfred Russel Wallace and Asa Gray also defended Darwin in print (Campbell, 1989; Browne, 2002; McCalman, 2009). Still engaged in research, Wallace did not return to England until 1862, but he published responses to two critics of Darwin and natural selection: Geologist Samuel Haughton and Royal Society member George Campbell, the Duke of Argyll (Browne, 2002; McCalman, 2009). In the United States, Gray successfully debated Agassiz on natural selection (Irvine, 1955). Though Darwin could not accept Gray's theory that natural selection had divine origins, he paid for the packaging of Gray's essays on that topic into a supportive pamphlet, and he further financed the advertising and distribution of the pamphlet (Caudill, 1994). With Gray, at least, Darwin was honest about his reservations:

> I grieve to say that I honestly cannot go as far as you do about Design. I am conscious that I am in an utterly hopeless muddle. I cannot think that the world, as we see it, is the result of chance; & yet I cannot look at each separate thing as the result of Design.
>
> (Burkhardt et al., 1993, p. 496)

Of the contributions of his core supporters, particularly Huxley, Hooker, Lyell, and Gray, Darwin wrote to Huxley, "As I am never weary of saying I shd have been utterly smashed had it not been for you & three others" (Burkhardt et al., 1993, p. 277).

Aftermath

Biographer Janet Browne (2002) believes that carefully managed cooperation among Darwin's allies helped generate the eventual success of *On the Origin of Species*: "As a group that worked as a group, they were impressive . . . Darwin's opponents failed to achieve anything like the same command of the media or penetration of significant institutions" (p. 129). Irvine (1995) says that the Darwinians had won the day by 1863. McCalman (2009) puts the date at 1866, and Caudill (1994) holds out for "the end of the 1860s" (p. 454). Given his contributions to the campaign, however, Darwin's bulldog deserves the final word. By 1894, one year before his death, Huxley declared that Darwin's revolutionary idea was "disputed by no reasonable" individual (L. Huxley, 1901b, p. 397).

Part II

Evolutionary biology, public relations, and cooperation

Chapter 3

Introduction to Part II

Evolutionary biology, neuroscience, and cooperation

Anthropologists tell us that every broad culture has creation stories, tales of how we, as humans, came to be (Sproul, 2013). The intertwined urges to tell such stories seem obvious: We want to know where we came from because we want to understand who we are and where we're going. Such stories help us make sense of the world and our place in it; they contribute meaning, importance, and, perhaps, purpose to our lives. Evolutionary biology tells one such story of creation, albeit a tale with many disputatious narrators. In the words of E.O. Wilson (1975), evolutionary biology is "the collective disciplines of biology that treat the evolutionary process and the characteristics of populations of organisms, as well as ecology, behavior, and systematics" (p. 584). The purpose of Part II of this book is to establish the primary, compelling role of evolutionary biology within the consilience of cooperation: Evolutionary biology shows that far from being combatants in a genetically prompted, Hobbesian war of all against all, humans are cooperators. The four chapters that follow this introduction describe the creation stories of leading evolutionary biologists past and present, particularly Charles Darwin, Peter Kropotkin, Richard Dawkins, Stephen Jay Gould, Edward O. Wilson, and Martin Nowak. Though much divides these brilliant and, in some cases, contentious individuals, they do alight on common ground: The empirical, materialistic conclusion that humans are a communal species, that our biological creation story steers us, not to conflict, competition, and adversarial societies, but, rather, to cooperation. In the words of Harvard psychologist Jerome Kagan, "Although humans inherit a biological bias that permits them to feel anger, jealousy, selfishness, and envy, they inherit an even stronger biological bias for kindness, compassion, cooperation, love, and nurture—especially toward those in need" (Goleman, 2006, p. 62). The purpose of this introductory chapter to Part II is to review scientific assessments of the command center of cooperation, the human brain. If, indeed, evolutionary processes have shaped us—and continue to shape us—to seek cooperation over conflict, there must be biological evidence of this reality. Studies of the human brain within modern neuroscience and neuropsychology provide that evidence.

However, just as we can call upon evolutionary biology to provide a foundation for modern cooperative frameworks of public relations, we can call upon cooperative relationships, driven by communication, to play a foundational role in evolutionary biology. Don Ross (2011) is a University of Cape Town professor of economics whose study of neuroeconomics has drawn him into both cellular and evolutionary biology. In "Naturalism: The Place of Society in Nature," he offers this summary of what French embryologist Rosine Chandebois (1976) has termed "cell sociology" (p. 71):

> Development of multicellularity [compared with original, single-celled life forms] required the evolution of mechanisms to mediate conflict among units . . . Another crucial dimension to the evolution of multicellularity was the refinement of new mechanisms of intercellular signaling necessary for coordination . . . The various phenomena just reviewed as associated with the evolution and maintenance of multicellularity—coalition formation, intergroup conflict, regulation and policing of outlaws, and signaling for coordination—are the daily preoccupation of all social sciences . . . This justifies the idea that sociality is a basic kind of natural process, at least on Earth, and that it vastly pre-dates human culture.
>
> (pp. 127, 128)

Ross' description of the processes of sustainable multicellularity sounds strikingly similar to those of public relations: Even at the cellular level, effective communication aims at building cooperative structures—and one of those cooperative structures, the human brain, now promotes cooperation over conflict in human relationships. The consilience of cooperation extends more deeply into our history and our nature than many of us (certainly myself) suspected.

In *The Better Angels of Our Nature*, his mammoth study of the documentable decline of violence over human history, Harvard psychology professor Steven Pinker (2011) concludes:

> The way to explain the decline of violence is to identify the changes in our cultural and material milieu that have given our peaceable motives the upper hand . . . Humans are not innately good (just as they are not innately evil), but they come equipped with motives that can orient them away from violence and toward cooperation and altruism . . .
>
> (pp. xxiii, xxv)

The human brain, of course, is part of the "material milieu" that has nurtured the increasing tendency toward cooperation rather than conflict within the history of our species. "In the brain," writes neuroscientist Donald Pfaff (Pfaff & Sherman, 2015), "such selection pressures [from social environments] caused the development of powerful neural mechanisms for empathy and goodwill that were uncovered over the last couple of decades" (p. 45). Pfaff, a professor of neuroscience at the Rockefeller University in New York, holds the Daniel S. Lehrman Lifetime Achievement Award from the Society for Behavioral Neuroendocrinology. Of the brain's evolving role in what Charles Darwin (1871/1998) termed the "social instincts" (p. 113), Pfaff (Pfaff & Sherman, 2015) writes, "Cooperation (i.e. altruistic behaviors benefiting both recipient and actor) is the greatest tool in the human Swiss Army knife of survival . . . The foundation of cooperation, kindness, and even altruism are intrinsic parts of the nerve cell biology of the human cerebral cortex" (pp. 139–140). Altruistic brain theory (ABT) is Pfaff's explanation for how, within the human brain, sensory input from our social environment leads to cooperative output. For this chapter, ABT provides an effective template for the consolidation of modern research from neuroscience and neuropsychology.

In *The Altruistic Brain* (2015), Pfaff charts the progress—the path within human brains—of initial sensory input to some form of output, generally a decision to take, or not take, a particular action. Though the path also works with the sense of hearing (Pfaff & Sherman, 2015, pp. 78, 93), it is perhaps easiest to visualize (no pun intended) by beginning with our eyes. Light reflects from an object of perception to our eyes and travels as electrical signals through our optic nerve, turning either toward a rapid response area or, for our purposes in this chapter, toward the thalamus, which sits near the center of the brain, near the top of the brain stem, which itself sits atop the spinal cord. The thalamus routes the signal to the visual cortex at the far back of the brain, where images form. Those data then are transferred both to the amygdala, an ancient source and regulator of emotions between the thalamus and the brain stem, and to the more recent prefrontal cortex, just behind our foreheads. Those two regions, ancient and modern, assess, communicate with each other, and relay a proposed action to the insula, near our brain stem and spinal cord, which also can pass judgment on a proposed action. The insula then communicates with our motor control areas—and an action is taken or not taken (Pfaff & Sherman, 2015). Modern neuroscience suggests that an answer to "the problem of cooperation" (Axelrod, 2006, p. 3) —or, in the words of evolutionary biologists Martin Nowak, Corina E. Tarnita, and Edward O. Wilson (2010), "genetically prescribed selfless behaviour"—begins with the processing of data in the visual cortex (Pfaff & Sherman, 2015).

Aligning with this complex path, Pfaff's (Pfaff & Sherman, 2015) altruistic brain theory consists of five stages:

1. Acknowledgment of an action we are considering
2. Development of an image of the person our action will affect
3. Fusion of that individual's image with our own
4. Evaluation of the consequences of the considered action
5. Decision and action

In Pfaff's (Pfaff & Sherman, 2015) view, "The human brain is actually programmed to make us care for others . . . We are 'hardwired' for producing altruistic behaviors" (pp. 5, 39). Psychologist and science journalist Daniel Goleman (2006) uses the same language for the same conclusion in his work *Social Intelligence*: "We are wired to connect . . . Our sociability has been the primary survival strategy of primate species, including our own" (pp. 4, 56). This chapter will use Pfaff's five stages of altruistic brain theory to consolidate findings regarding the biological origins of human cooperation.

Stage 1: Acknowledgment of an action we are considering

As we consider an action toward someone else, particularly a probable one, a neurological process termed "corollary discharge" occurs: "Corollary discharge signals inform the sensory areas [of the brain] of the upcoming movements and allow them to prepare for the . . . consequences of the movement" (Goldstein, 2010, p. 325). As we contemplate our proposed action, neurological signals rush both to the motor-control areas and to the judgment areas of our brains. "We always represent an impending action to ourselves," Pfaff (Pfaff & Sherman, 2015) writes (p. 79)—and this corollary discharge allows a period for assessment of consequences and, ultimately, judgment before we take an action. Shakespeare's (1969) Brutus knew as much when he contemplated the murder of Julius Caesar:

> Between the acting of a dreadful thing
> And the first motion, all the interim is
> Like a phantasma or a hideous dream.
> The genius and the mortal instruments
> Are then in council, and the state of man,
> Like to a little kingdom, suffers then
> The nature of an insurrection.
>
> (II.i.63–69)

What Shakespeare and Brutus viscerally knew to be true is now accepted as biological reality—generally moving faster than conscious thought—by neuroscientists.

Stage 2: Development of an image of the person our action will affect

As we see an individual and contemplate an action—or even imagine a representative individual and contemplate an action (Pfaff & Sherman, 2015, p. 91)—neurons in our visual cortex begin to construct an image of the potential recipient. As lightning-fast as this process is, however, it can be bypassed for a speedier option in the face (literally) of a perceived threat:

Images of the brain showed an intense response of the amygdala to a threatening picture [of a hostile face] ... The information about the threat probably traveled via a superfast neural channel that feeds directly into a part of the brain that processes emotions, bypassing the visual cortex that supports the conscious experience of "seeing." The same circuit also causes ... angry faces (a potential threat) to be processed faster and more efficiently than ... happy faces.

(Kahneman, 2011, p. 301)

Our altruistic brain, in other words, doesn't weaken our defenses. Should the visual signals reach the visual cortex, however, they engage "large ensembles of neurons for recognizing faces"—even if the face is a generic portrayal of a larger group (Pfaff & Sherman, 2015, pp. 82, 91).

In *Thinking, Fast and Slow*, Nobel Prize-winning economist and psychologist Daniel Kahneman (2011) notes that the bypass reaction to a perceived threat can be wrong, often operating more on "biases" and "cognitive illusions" than on facts and considered judgments (pp. 25, 27). Learning to recognize our bypass moments and, when not endangering ourselves, subjecting those moments to the judgment of a slower thinking process can improve self-control and decision-making, Kahneman (2011) contends—and, important for much of public relations, he adds, "Organizations are better than individuals when it comes to avoiding [such] errors because they naturally think more slowly and have the power to impose orderly procedures" (p. 418).

Stage 3: Fusion of that individual's image with our own

Had this next stage of altruistic brain theory not been brilliantly anticipated (as we shall see) by philosopher David Hume (Chapter 9) and rhetorician Kenneth Burke (Chapter 13)—and, within evolutionary biology, by Charles Darwin's great colleague Thomas Henry Huxley (Chapter 3)—it would seem magical (and I should confess that, to me, it still seems so). Here is how Pfaff (Pfaff & Sherman, 2015) describes stage three of altruistic brain theory:

In everyone's brain a set of firing nerve cells constitutes a unified image of the person toward whom one will act, as well as a neural image of oneself. (We always have an image of ourselves in our brain.) ... An increase in the excitability of cortical neurons [is] such that when the nerve cells representing the other are firing signals, the nerve cells representing self are also firing ... In the brain of the person who will initiate the act toward another person, the difference between the target person's image and his own will unconsciously be brought to zero ... The brain now produces a merged image where images of the two persons coalesce.

(pp. 58, 59)

In describing the same neurological process, Goleman (2006) writes, "We slip into the other's shoes to share what they experience" (p. 58)—even if we are simply anticipating what the other might experience. The process is not a conscious choice; rather, it is an automatic function within the human brain (Pfaff & Sherman, 2015, p. 11; Goleman, 2006, pp. 51–52). Again, however, if we believe that "the other" wishes us harm, a faster process—termed "the low road" by Goleman (2006, pp. 15) and "System 1" by Kahneman (2011, p. 13)—occurs, bypassing evaluation in the cortex and urging immediate action.

Just as Pinker (2011) resists the idea of a brain-based "empathy center with empathy neurons" in favor of "complex patterns of activation and modulation" (p. 578) that steer us toward cooperation and away from conflict, Pfaff rejects a single, clean explanation of the fused images. Rather, he cites four neurological instigators of the merger that are "independent" of one another but "are not exclusive of each other—they could work in various combinations" (Pfaff & Sherman, 2015, p. 65): The development of tunnel-like connections between nerves cells that speed "electrical excitation"; increased release of acetylcholine, a "neurotransmitter" chemical that, again, increases the excitability of neurons; the inhibition of image-separating functions within the cortex; and, finally, the presence of mirror neurons, which "unite the actions of another person with our own" (Pfaff & Sherman, 2015, pp. 58, 89). Tunnels and chemical stimulants are, comparatively, easy to understand—but cortical inhibitions and mirror neurons? The inhibition of traditional neurological processes that might reduce the possibility of the merger can be achieved by reducing the production of chemicals such as gamma-aminobutyric acid that traditionally slow the speed of communications among nerve cells; increased speed would accelerate excitement and merger (Pfaff & Sherman, 2015, p. 87). Whatever the combination of these processes may be, they demonstrate a materialistic basis for cooperation, compassion, and altruism. "As our understanding of the neural basis of altruistic decision making grows, we will need to revisit the common notion of altruism as pure, unadulterated, other-directed concern, without any admixture of self-directed motives," acknowledges Maurice Lee (2013), a professor of religious studies at Westmont College (p. 193).

Pfaff (Pfaff & Sherman, 2015) observes that neuroscientists have called the discovery of mirror neurons "the most important discovery in biology since DNA" (p. 91). Goleman (2006) offers this summary of mirror neurons:

> Mirror neurons . . . sense both the move another person is about to make and their feelings, and instantaneously prepare us to imitate that movement and feel with them . . . They reflect back an action we observe in someone else, making us mimic that action or have the impulse to do so . . . Neuroscientists call that mutually reverberating state "empathic resonance," a brain-to-brain linkage that forms a two-person circuitry.
>
> (pp. 9, 41, 43)

A University of Hawaii research team led by psychologist Elaine Hatfield concludes that mirror neurons offer "insight into why people may so readily 'catch' the emotions of others and why it is so easy for people to be in sync with other people's thoughts, emotions, and behaviors" (Hatfield, Bensman, Thornton, & Rapson, 2014, p. 170). Theologian Sarah Coakley and Martin Nowak, director of Harvard University's Program for Evolutionary Dynamics, go even further: "Our human brains already are hard-wired for cooperation through 'mirror neurons'" (2013, p. 12). Mirror neurons, declares Pfaff (Pfaff & Sherman, 2015), "allow one person to put himself in another person's place" (p. 87). As rhetorician Kenneth Burke (Chapter 13) would say, mirror neurons can make us "consubstantial" with the other (1950/1969, p. 21)—or, in Pfaff's terminology, they help merge the image of the other with the image of the self.

Pfaff (Pfaff & Sherman, 2015) considers the fusion of images and the resultant empathy to be a "new insight," though a profoundly well-documented one within neuroscience (p. 58). However, as we shall see in a moment, other disciplines within our consilience of cooperation have anticipated this finding (Hume's philosophy and Burke's rhetoric)—and within evolutionary biology, Huxley's nineteenth-century speculations provide a compelling antecedent. In Pfaff's (Pfaff & Sherman, 2015) defense, however, I should add that early in *The Altruistic Brain*, he writes, "Several years ago, I read philosophy and religion extensively, and realized with a growing excitement that religious and philosophical demands for reciprocally benevolent behavior appeared to be remarkably consistent across all of those writings" (p. 11). Pfaff certainly predates me in studying a consilience of cooperation.

In his *Treatise of Human Nature*, Scottish philosopher David Hume (Chapter 9) notes the empathic effects of considering the other and calls upon science to discover the source of such fellow feeling:

> No quality of human nature is more remarkable, both in itself and in its consequences, than that propensity we have to sympathize with others, and to receive by communication their inclinations and sentiments, however different from, or even contrary to our own . . . A chearful coun-tenance infuses a sensible complacency and serenity into my mind; as an angry or sorrowful one throws a sudden damp upon me. Hatred, resent-ment, esteem, love, courage, mirth, and melancholy; all these passions I feel more from communication than from my own natural temper and disposition. So remarkable a phænomenon merits our attention, and must be trac'd up to its first principles.
>
> (1739/1968, pp. 316–317)

Hume even anticipates the image of oneself fusing with the image of the other:

> 'Tis evident, that the idea, or rather impression of ourselves is always intimately present with us, and that our consciousness gives us so lively

a conception of our own person, that 'tis not possible to imagine, that any thing can in this particular go beyond it. Whatever object, therefore, is related to ourselves must be conceived with a like vivacity of conception ... And tho' this relation shou'd not be so strong as that of causation, it must still have a considerable influence. Resemblance and contiguity are relations not to be neglected ... 'Tis obvious, that nature has preserv'd a great resemblance among all human creatures, and that we never remark any passion or principle in others, of which, in some degree or other, we may not find a parallel in ourselves ... This resemblance must very much contribute to make us enter into the sentiments of others, and embrace them with facility and pleasure.

(1739/1968, pp. 317–318)

Hume earns the right to tell modern neuroscientists, "I told you so."

As noted above (and again in Chapter 13), twentieth-century rhetorician Kenneth Burke (1950/1969) also anticipates the merger of images with his concepts of identification and consubstantiality:

A is not identical with his colleague, B. But insofar as their interests are joined, A is *identified* with B. Or he may *identify himself* with B even when their interests are not joined if he assumes they are, or is persuaded to believe so ... In being identified with B, A is "substantially one" with a person other than himself ... To identify A with B is to make A "consubstantial" with B.

(pp. 20, 21)

Sounding like a modern neuroscientist describing the function of mirror neurons and neurochemistry, Burke (1950/1969) holds that an individual experiencing identification and consubstantiality is "both joined and separate, at once a distinct substance and consubstantial with another" (p. 21).

Finally, in *Evolution and Ethics*, Thomas Henry Huxley (1897) describes an important "check upon [the] free play of self-assertion, or natural liberty, which is the necessary condition for the origin of human society":

The most important [check] is the tendency, so strongly developed in man, to reproduce in himself actions and feelings similar to, or correlated with, those of other men ... By a purely reflex operation of the mind, we take the hue of passion of those who are about us, or, it may be, the complementary colour. It is not by any conscious "putting one's self in the place" of a joyful or a suffering person that the state of mind we call sympathy usually arises; indeed, it is often contrary to one's sense of right, and in spite of one's will ...

(pp. 27, 28–29)

Pfaff, Goleman, and others would later confirm that the merger of images is involuntary, operating at lightning speed at subconscious levels (Pfaff & Sherman, 2015, p. 11; Goleman, 2006, pp. 51–52).

Stage 4: Evaluation of the consequences of the considered action

In Stage 4 of Pfaff's altruistic brain theory, the analytical prefrontal cortex of the human brain, in collaboration with the older, more emotional amygdala, ponders the proposed action in regard to the merged image of the self and the other (Pfaff & Sherman, 2015, pp. 59, 94; Wilson, 2012, p. 17). "We automatically envision the consequences as pertaining to our own self. . .," Pfaff (Pfaff & Sherman, 2015) writes. "Brain neurons are unable to register the difference between the effects on the target and on [our own self]" (pp. 60, 63). The prefrontal cortex and amygdala then render a " 'good' or 'bad,' 'do' or 'don't do' " decision (Pfaff & Sherman, 2015, p. 60). "It is for these reasons that [the prefrontal cortex] is often called the central executive, or CEO of the brain," concludes neuroscientist Daniel Levitin (2014, p. 165).

By design, our cortical CEO generally renders a cooperative, empathetic "prosocial decision" (Pfaff & Sherman, 2015, p. 60)—but, of course, not always: Motivations for selfish or antisocial behavior "permitted by mechanisms that we still don't fully understand [can] overwhelm the neural circuitries that make up the Benevolent Brain" (Pfaff & Sherman, 2015, p. 211). At the extreme end of antisocial behavior, psychopaths tend to have undersized amygdalas and orbitofrontal cortexes, the portion of the prefrontal cortex behind and slightly above our eyes (Pinker, 2011, pp. 506, 510).

Produced in the hypothalamus (Greek for "under the thalamus"), the chemical oxytocin encourages the prefrontal cortex, in consultation with the amygdala, to render a prosocial, cooperative decision regarding the contemplated action. Pinker (2011) calls oxytocin "the cuddle hormone" because "its original evolutionary function was to turn on the components of motherhood" (p. 579). Both Pinker and Pfaff note oxytocin's evolved role in reducing social anxiety and distrust of the other; Pinker, in fact, cites an experiment in which participants who inhaled oxytocin were more generous in charitable giving to strangers than participants not exposed to the chemical (Pinker, 2011, p. 579; Pfaff & Sherman, 2015, pp. 121, 123). Pfaff (Pfaff & Sherman, 2015) asserts that the prefrontal cortex and the amygdala are particularly suited to respond to oxytocin:

> The genes coding for the peptide oxytocin (OT) and its specialized receptor (OTR) have received a great deal of scientific attention. I theorize that high OT activity working through OTR in the amygdala and the prefrontal cortex would enforce a switch position that yields prosocial behaviors.
>
> (pp. 121, 123)

Throughout *The Altruistic Brain*, Pfaff (Pfaff & Sherman, 2015) refers to the prefrontal cortex-amygdala tandem as an "ethical switch" that places positive/ prosocial or negative/antisocial assessments on proposed actions (p. 93). He hastens to add, however, that the altruistic brain is not moral or ethical in origin; rather, it is a survival mechanism and part of a neurological design "that spans many species" (Pfaff & Sherman, 2015, pp. 81).

Stage 5: Decision and action

In Stage 5, we act on the advice from the prefrontal cortex-amygdala tandem. In particular, output from the prefrontal cortex seems to flow to the insula, near the low center of the brain, which communicates with motor-control functions (Pfaff & Sherman, 2015, pp. 61, 97). And the insula provides yet another assessment of behavior: Though it registers emotions, as does the amygdala (Goleman, 2006), and is a locale for "literal and metaphorical gut feelings" (Pinker, 2011, p. 578), the insula also provides another evaluation and, generally, prosocial judgment:

> Evidence for nervous system equivalence between terrible tastes [of foods, for example] and terrible behavior comes from a part of our cerebral cortex hidden from view, the insula . . . The same brain region that responds to disgusting tastes can also be related to disgusting psychological situations, including morally disgusting acts . . . Even as we avoid eating garbage, we avoid distasteful social behavior.
>
> (Pfaff & Sherman, 2015, pp. 219–220)

Through the insula, we reject both distasteful food and distasteful/antisocial behavior, avoiding the mental anguish triggered, according to Darwin (1871/1998), by uncooperative behavior (pp. 101, 107). From the insula, a decision moves to our brain's motor-control areas—and we act (or not).

Sigmund Freud and the rechanneled libido

The neuroscientists cited in this chapter offer voluminous evidence for our brain's preference for cooperation over conflict—and Pfaff, Pinker, and Goleman in particular are optimistic about what this might mean for the future of human relationships. Again, Pfaff (Pfaff & Sherman, 2015) insists that the altruistic brain is not moral or ethical in origin; rather, it is a survival mechanism and part of a neurological design "that spans many species" (p. 81). Psychoanalyst Sigmund Freud (1856–1939), however, offers an interesting counterpoint to the empirically based optimism of these scientists, a viewpoint that both laments and confirms our species' bias toward cooperation. In *Civilization and Its Discontents*, Freud (trans. 1961) clearly holds that his new science of psychoanalysis is based in genetics (p. 12), but, unlike Pfaff, Pinker, and others, he uses a scientific negative (from his perspective) to acknowledge the dominance within society of "altruistic" instincts (p. 87) and cooperation: That negative is the suppression and repression of the human libido.

Why introduce Freud at this juncture? One important theme of this book is that we need not turn to idealism or wishful thinking to show the superior power, within human history and human nature, of cooperation vis-à-vis conflict and competition: The empirical, materialistic findings of science, philosophy, and rhetoric all champion the amoral legitimacy of the social harmony frameworks of public relations. I introduce Freud at this point because he arrives at the conclusion of Pfaff, Pinker, Goleman, and other scientists by a very different route. Like them, he acknowledges an increasing impetus toward social cooperation within the human species. Unlike them, however, he shuns optimism: He finds social cooperation to be a negative because, for him, the cost is too high. He meets the optimism of the previous pages of this chapter with the view that human cooperation may well be inevitable—but it comes at the cost of neuroses and unhappiness. In short, via Freud, even detractors of cooperation affirm its power. In Chapter 8, Friedrich Nietzsche and his scathing analysis of social cooperation and justice will perform much the same function.

In *Civilization and Its Discontents*, Freud (trans. 1961) asserts that humans' greatest desire is for happiness—and that our greatest happiness comes from "sexual (genital) love" (pp. 23, 48). To decrease the unhappiness created by predatory neighbors, modern humans form civilizations built upon justice and restraint—but those same social arrangements undermine sexual freedom and unchecked libidos, particularly in men (again, according to Freud [trans. 1961, pp. 36, 50, 56]). To gain the benefits of society, we suppress the sexual/genital orientation of our libidos, rechanneling that energy to essential—and nonsexual—social relationships such as friendship; societies encourage this rechanneling by repressing the free play of the original libido in favor of monogamy (Freud, trans. 1961, pp. 44, 51, 52). "Civilization . . . summons up aim-inhibited libido on the largest scale so as to strengthen the communal bond by relations of friendship," Freud (trans. 1961), writes. "In order for these aims to be fulfilled, a restriction upon sexual life is unavoidable" (pp. 55–56).

Without mentioning Freud, Pfaff (Pfaff & Sherman, 2015) disputes the presence of a pain-inducing repressed libido, holding that "acting altruistically produces a profound pleasure on the continuum with that derived from sexuality" (p. 104). Like Pinker (2011), he believes that oxytocins associated with sexual behavior and motherhood have broadened their scope to bolster wider social relationships (p. 105).

But in Freud's (trans. 1961) view, the consequences of individual suppression and social repression of the libido are unhappiness and neuroses:

> When we start considering [the causes of our increasing unhappiness], we come upon a contention which is so astonishing that we must dwell

upon it. This contention holds that what we call our civilization is largely responsible for our misery, and that we should be much happier if we gave it up and returned to primitive conditions . . . A person becomes neurotic because he cannot tolerate the amount of frustration which society imposes on him in the service of its cultural ideals.

(pp. 34, 35)

Our neuroses, Freud maintains, result from the struggle between self-pre-servation (enhanced by sociality) and our rebellious, repressed libidos. Self-preservation has prevailed, he concludes, but "at the price of severe sufferings and renunciations" (Freud, trans. 1961, p. 65). In Chapter 9, philosopher David Hume offers a more positive view of the origins and effects of justice and civilization—but, again, Freud is a valuable voice in our consilience of co-operation. He affirms its victory—but he believes that the cost has been too high.

Caveats

Even Isocrates, the most ancient of the key sources in our consilience of cooperation, understood that mutual aid, to use Kropotkin's term, is not always socially beneficial. Of social harmony [*homonoia*], Isocrates (trans. 1929/1992) concedes, "We shall find that it is in some instances the cause of very many blessings, but in others of the greatest evils and misfortunes" (*Panathenaicus*, 225). He adds that "pirates or brigands or men given to other forms of injustice" may well "enjoy concord among themselves and thereby seek to destroy all others" (*Panathenaicus*, 226). Within small groups, Pfaff (Pfaff & Sherman, 2015) notes, cooperation sometimes "clashes with social norms" that unite a broader society (p. 212). Citing the loyalty within some organized-crime groups, Pfaff (Pfaff & Sherman, 2015) acknowledges that "the brain's neurochemistry does not make distinctions between legal and illegal; rather, it sees opportunities for reciprocity" (p. 215). Likewise, Pinker (2011) asserts that, driven by cooperation and reciprocity, "groups can breed a number of pathologies of thought. One of them is polarization. . ."—but he adds that "open societies with freedom of speech and movement and well-developed channels of communication are less likely to fall under the sway of delusional ideologies (pp. 557, 564). Nowak's game-theory experiments (Chapter 7) con-firm that cooperation increases as personal networks of interaction increase. Pfaff (Pfaff & Sherman, 2015) offers a similar optimism: "We cannot allow ourselves to become stymied by the outcrop of bad, even egregious behavior. In the aggregate, we are *going* to display socially useful traits" (p. 53).

Conclusion

In "Altruism, Normalcy, and God," philosophy professor Alexander Pruss (2013) complains that "modern science specializes in explaining nonnormative facts in terms of further nonnormative facts" (p. 329)—an echo of feminist philosopher Nel Noddings' (2010) belief that "we would make a mistake to assume that, once we have uncovered the roots of morality in evolutionary events, we now have the whole story on morality" (p. 17). However, a non-normative explanation for nonnormative social behavior (social cooperation) is exactly what I seek in this book: Evolutionary biology, philosophy, and rhetoric all tell us that we are mistaken if we believe that conflict and competition are human default settings; those disciplines, instead, dispassionately show the opposite to be true. Championing the social harmony frameworks of public relations is not a normative or idealistic task. Rather, those frameworks are grounded in a multidisciplinary, nonidealistic consilience of cooperation. "What is remarkable," Nowak (Nowak & Highfield, 2011) writes, "is that these familiar religious ideas come from cold hard science" (p. 273). Pfaff (Pfaff & Sherman, 2015) Pinker (2011), and Goleman (2006) all express the belief that an increased understanding of our neural processes—particularly the realization that those processes urge us toward cooperation—might strengthen and expand humans' ability to work peacefully together toward common goals. "If we could more easily accept each other's inherent decency. . .," Pfaff (Pfaff & Sherman, 2015) concludes, "we might be better equipped to cooperate and, ultimately, develop a kind of practical trust" (p. 14).

In this chapter, Pfaff, Pinker, Goleman, and others have explained the automatic neural processes that promote cooperation over conflict and competition. In the other chapters of Part II, Charles Darwin and Peter Kropotkin will make evolutionary biology's first claims that humans' social instincts outweigh our competing egoistic urges (Chapters 4 and 5); the modern evolutionary biologists Richard Dawkins, Stephen Jay Gould, and Edward O. Wilson will deeply disagree on the workings of evolution but will find common ground in asserting that humans are a cooperative, not a combative, species (Chapter 6); and mathematical biologist Martin Nowak (Chapter 7) will use computer-assisted game theory to show that, rather than self-centered competitors, humans are generous "SuperCooperators" (Nowak & Highfield, 2011, p. 283).

Summary

The findings of modern neuroscience lead us to at least three important points for the understanding and practice of public relations:

1. Rather than being "wired" for conflict and competition, humans are neurologically wired for cooperation. Cooperation, not conflict, is our default setting.
2. The way we begin relationships and individual encounters matters: Studies of mirror neurons and similar neurological phenomena show that the self we initially present to others influences their immediate reaction to us as well as their consequent behavior within the relationship.

3. An early impulse toward violence or distrust, particularly in the face of a perceived threat, can literally short-circuit the evaluative functions of the human brain. Recognizing our snap judgments and, when advisable, subjecting them to slower, more considered assessments—including organizational decision-making processes—offers the possibility of better decisions and improved relationships.

These three points address two of the Nine Tenets of public relations' social harmony frameworks outlined in Chapter 1:

III. Cooperative relationships are not merely normative, idealistic, or utopian. Rather, evidence from evolutionary biology, philosophy, and rhetoric shows that cooperation is a stronger instinct within human nature than the competing instincts of egoism, conflict, and competition.

IX. Public relations practitioners can take specific actions, drawn from evolutionary biology, philosophy, and rhetoric, to build and enhance relationships built upon cooperation and justice.

Chapter 4

Re-envisioning Charles Darwin

Critics from Robert Downs (2004), former president of the American Library Association, to the Editorial Advisory Board of Easton Press (2006) have deemed Charles Darwin's *On the Origin of Species* the most consequential book ever published. A 2015 poll sponsored by academic book publishers declared *Origin* to be "the most influential academic book ever written" (Flood, 2015, para. 1), topping works by Plato, William Shakespeare, Immanuel Kant, Albert Einstein, and Simone de Beauvoir. The very success of *Origin*, however, may overshadow Darwin's later elaboration, in *The Descent of Man*, of the role of cooperation in natural selection and evolution, particularly as it relates to humans. In *Books That Changed the World*, Downs (2004) devoted a full chapter to *On the Origin of Species* and one sentence to *Descent of Man*. That latter work did not make the "Top 20" list in the 2015 academic books poll (Flood, 2015, para. 2). In "Evolutionary Theory: The Missing Link for Conceptualizing Public Relations," scholar Cary Greenwood (2010), who introduced "the concept of using Charles Darwin's . . . evolutionary theory as the metatheory for conceptualizing public relations thought" (p. 456), richly explores *Origin* but affords *Descent* only one sentence.

In *The Descent of Man*, unlike *On the Origin of Species*, Darwin focuses on humans—and in Chapters 4 and 5 of that work, he addresses "the problem of cooperation" (Axelrod, 2006, p. 3) within our species. In those seminal chapters of *Descent*, Darwin (1871/1998) writes:

> The social instincts, which must have been acquired by man in a very rude state, and probably even by his early ape-like progenitors, still give the impulse to some of his best actions . . . A tribe including many members who, from possessing in a high degree the spirit of patriotism, fidelity, obedience, courage, and sympathy, were always ready to aid one another, and to sacrifice themselves for the common good, would be victorious over most other tribes; and this would be natural selection.
>
> (pp. 113, 137)

In Darwin's (1871/1998) own words, thus, "natural selection" favors societies in which individuals are "always ready to aid one another" (p. 137). With that assertion—seemingly running counter to portions of *Origin*—Darwin launched a debate that continues to this day. Though modern evolutionary biologists generally concur on the prominence of cooperation within the processes of natural selection—and their concurrence is important for public relations theories and frameworks—they disagree bitterly on which unit or units among genes, individuals, groups, and species are selected for survival (see Chapter 6 of this book).

In the earlier *On the Origin of Species*, Darwin indeed touches upon the power of intra-species cooperation compared with competition and conflict, but he does not dwell upon the topic or extend his theory to humans. In that earlier work, Darwin (1859) writes:

> In social animals [natural selection] will adapt the structure of each individual for the benefit of the community; if each in consequence profits by the selected change . . . The subject well deserves to be discussed at great length, but I will here take only a single case, that of working or sterile ants . . . If such insects had been social, and it had been profitable to the community that a number should have been annually born capable of work, but incapable of procreation, I can see no very great difficulty in this being effected by natural selection.
>
> (pp. 87, 236)

In discussing the sociability of ant colonies, he concludes in *Origin* (to the delight of modern proponents of group selection, such as Edward O. Wilson), "Selection may be applied to the family, as well as to the individual, and may thus gain the desired end" (Darwin, 1859, p. 237). He makes a similar point in regard to bees that sting and die to defend the hive: "If on the whole the power of stinging be useful to the community, it will fulfil all the requirements of natural selection, though it may cause the death of some few members" (Darwin, 1859, p. 202).

Twelve tumultuous years after the publication of *On the Origin of Species*, Darwin, in *The Descent of Man*, again presents his conclusion that natural selection, in tandem with variation, is the driving force in evolution—but he now courageously extends his theory to the human race:

> Although Darwin's major work remains *On the Origin of Species* . . . it is *The Descent of Man* . . . that focuses on the origin and history of our own species. Having deliberately left out any treatment of the human animal in his *Origin* volume, Darwin then became confident enough to extend his theory of evolution to account for the emergence and nature of our species in his *Descent* volume published twelve years later.
>
> (Birx, 1998, pp. ix–x)

In a letter to Alfred Russel Wallace in December 1857, two years before the publication of *Origin*, Darwin concedes, "You ask whether I shall discuss 'man';—I think I shall avoid [the] whole subject, as so surrounded with prejudices, though I fully admit that it is the highest & most interesting problem for the naturalist" (Burkhardt & Smith, 1990, p. 515). The success of *Origin* and Thomas Henry Huxley's *Man's Place in Nature* in 1863, however, helped prepare readers for the eventual appearance of *Descent*, with its strong focus on the evolutionary importance of cooperation within the human species. This chapter will review Darwin's (1871/1998) important assessment of the "social instincts" (p. 113) within humans and will address the related topics of so-called social Darwinism; Darwin's focus on the connection of cooperation and ethics; the nonidealistic materialism with which he supported his theories; and his assessment of two additional topics of importance to public relations: Reputation and reciprocity.

Natural selection and social instinct

In *The Descent of Man*, after more than a decade of reflection since the publication of *On the Origin of Species*, Darwin (1871/1998) insists that human cooperation is every bit as much an artifact of natural selection as our fight or flight instincts: "Social qualities, the paramount importance of which to the lower animals is disputed by no one, were no doubt acquired by the progenitors of man in a similar manner, namely, through natural selection, aided by inherited habit" (p. 134). Of the human species' impetus toward social harmony via "social instincts," Darwin (1871/1998) adds:

> These sensations were first developed in order that animals would profit by association, in the same way that the sense of hunger impels us to eat . . . Sympathy . . . will have been increased through natural selection; communities with the most sympathetic members would flourish best, rearing the greatest number of offspring.
>
> (pp. 113, 108, 110)

Modern experiments in neuroscience, in fact, show that the human brain's "reward signals" for satisfying hunger and for contemplating acts of charity are "indistinguishable" (Pfaff & Sherman, 2015, p. 126); conversely, Harvard psychology professor Steven Pinker (2011) writes that "whatever causes violence, it is not a perennial urge like hunger" (p. 482). Darwin's use of the word *sympathy* as an inherent motivation for cooperation runs throughout *Descent*. In *The Psychology of Sympathy*, Lauren Wispé (1991) notes that "Darwin did not make clear exactly what he meant by the concept of sympathy, but he was clear that it played an important role in his evolutionary theory— especially in the development of the social and moral capacities" (p. 31). In comparison, the word *sympathy* scarcely appears in *Origin*—and, even then, not in the sense of a catalyst for cooperation. In *Descent*, however, Darwin used the term dozens of times. The fellow feeling, leading to cooperation, denoted by *sympathy* is a persistent theme in that work.

Thomas Henry Huxley, who, as we know, was willing to challenge Darwin even on natural selection, echoes his great colleague on this key point about the history and power of cooperation. In *Evolution and Ethics*, Huxley (1897) declares:

> As in the hive, the progressive limitation of the struggle for existence between the members of the family would involve increasing efficiency as regards outside competition . . . In the struggle for existence with the state of nature and with other societies, as part of it, those in which men were thus led to close co-operation had a great advantage.
>
> (pp. 26, 36)

For Huxley, historian William Irvine (1955) finds, "the competition between individuals is drastically modified and in large part replaced by a competition between societies, in which the ethically superior tend to survive" (p. 351).

Developed and reinforced through the processes of natural selection, the social instinct, in the estimations of Darwin and Huxley—and Russian naturalist Peter Kropotkin (Chapter 5) and modern evolutionary biologists (Chapters 6 and 7)—has become an integral part of human nature and a powerful prompter of human actions. As a basic instinct, its gratification generally produces pleasure, and its suppression generally, if eventually, produces pain (again, as Darwin suggested, much like hunger). Honoring the impetus to help one another thus produces satisfaction; disavowing it causes pain:

> As soon as the mental faculties had become highly developed, images of all past actions and motives would be incessantly passing through the brain of each individual: and that feeling of dissatisfaction, or even misery, which invariably results, as we shall hereafter see, from any unsatisfied instinct, would arise, as often as it was perceived that the enduring and always present social instinct had yielded to some other instinct, at the time stronger, but neither enduring in its nature, nor leaving behind it a very vivid impression . . . With respect to the impulse which leads certain animals to associate together, and to aid one another in many ways, we may infer that in most cases they are impelled by the same sense of satisfaction or pleasure which they experience in performing other instinctive actions; or by the same sense of dissatisfaction as when other instinctive actions are checked.
>
> (Darwin, 1871/1998, pp. 101, 107)

Similarly, modern game-theorist Robert Axelrod (2006) describes the "moral regret" that stems from "having violated a situation of trust" (p. 85). As the

Greek rhetorician Isocrates (trans. 1928/1991) succinctly put it, in this conflict of instincts we have the choice between "pain following upon pleasure" and "pleasure after pain" (*To Demonicus*, 47).

Psychoanalyst Sigmund Freud and neuroscientist Donald Pfaff both echo Darwin's important assertion that honoring the social instinct produces pleasure—and, from vastly different perspectives (Chapter 3), each believes that the social instinct has origins in sexual behavior: Freud (trans. 1961) derides that instinct as the repression and rechanneling of a no-longer socially acceptable indiscriminate libido, and Pfaff (Pfaff & Sherman, 2015), less provocatively, sees it as the extension feelings that began with sexual attraction and parenthood. Both, however, ground Darwin's social instinct in a powerful foundation.

So strongly did Darwin (1871/1998) believe that the human impetus toward cooperation is a powerful instinct that he repeats the point later in *The Descent of Man*:

> At the moment of action, man will no doubt be apt to follow the stronger impulse; and though this may occasionally prompt him to the noblest deeds, it will more commonly lead him to gratify his own desires at the expense of other men. But after their gratification when past and weaker impressions are judged by the ever-enduring social instinct, and by his deep regard for the good opinion of his fellows, retribution will surely come. He will then feel remorse, repentance, regret, or shame . . . He will consequently resolve more or less firmly to act differently for the future; and this is conscience; for conscience looks backwards, and serves as a guide for the future.
>
> (p. 117)

Darwin, writes Pulitzer Prize-winning biologist Edward O. Wilson (2012), "was the first to advance the idea that instinct evolves by natural selection" (p. 158). In describing the current direction of related research in psychology, Pinker (2011) echoes Darwin's fusion of instincts and emotions, and he alights, seemingly unintentionally, on Darwin's chosen word—*sympathy*:

> Much of our guilt is anticipatory—we refrain from actions that would make us feel bad if we carried them out . . . Guilt [goes] hand in hand with empathy . . . The sense of empathy we value the most, though, is a distinct reaction that may be called sympathetic concern, or sympathy for short. Sympathy consists in aligning another entity's well-being with one's own, based on a cognizance of their pleasures and pains.
>
> (pp. 552, 581, 576)

The Roman rhetorician Cicero (trans. 1939/1971), in fact, attributed much of his eloquence in judicial speeches to an empathy for his clients that grew to powerful sympathy: In *Orator*, he declares, "I owe my reputation for excellence on such occasions, not to any natural gift, but to a genuine sympathy" (XXXVII.130). Pinker and others might argue that such "genuine sympathy" actually *is* a "natural gift."

Darwin's comprehensive definition of *sympathy* nearly gained status as a term of art in public relations scholarship. At the beginning of excellence project, sponsored by the International Association of Business Communicators Research Foundation, Fred C. Repper, a member of the team that produced *Excellence in Public Relations and Communication Management*, speculated that "sympathetic communication" might be a preferable term to "two-way symmetry":

> I have never been entirely pleased with the title *two-way symmetrical communication*. It sounds too academic and sterile to me. Perhaps a kinder, gentler, and more descriptive title might be *sympathetic communication*. Sympathetic, according to Webster, means having "the ability to understand the needs and feelings of others and to alter or adjust your actions to meet those needs and feelings.". . .If you expect the members of a public to change the way they act toward your organization—then the organization must also change the way it thinks and acts toward the public.
>
> (Guth & Marsh, 2000, p. 250)

In more recent public relations research, *sympathy* has acquired a narrower scope, appearing primarily as a crisis response strategy (Coombs & Holladay, 2008; DiStaso, Vafeiadis, & Amaral, 2015).

Darwinian sympathy exists within the tension between broad social interests and individual/organizational interests that is a mainstay of public relations theory; that tension is denoted in the concepts of symmetry, asymmetry, and mixed-motive models (J.E. Grunig & White, 1992) as well as in the reflective paradigm (Holmström, 2004) and the advocacy/accommodation extremes of contingency theory (Cameron, Pang, & Jin, 2008). Darwin and Kropotkin both described the evolution of such tension and the consequent need to discover and justify an ideal equilibrium. Noting that the presence of cooperation did not, of course, mean the end of conflict and competition, Darwin (1871/1998) viewed the tension as a struggle between basic human instincts—and he believed the struggle would increasingly be resolved in favor of social interests:

> It is not surprising that there should be a struggle in man between his social instincts, with their derived virtues, and his lower, though momentarily stronger impulses or desires . . . If with the temptation still before us we do not yield, it is because either the social instinct or some custom is at the moment predominant, or because we have learnt that it will appear to us hereafter the stronger, when compared with the weakened impression

of the temptation, and we realise that its violation would cause us suffering. Looking to future generations, there is no cause to fear that the social instincts will grow weaker, and we may expect that virtuous habits will grow stronger, becoming perhaps fixed by inheritance. In this case the struggle between our higher and lower impulses will be less severe, and virtue will be triumphant ... Selfish and contentious people will not cohere, and without coherence nothing can be effected.

(pp. 129, 134)

Kropotkin developed a similar resolution of this tension in his analysis of a "double tendency" within human nature (Chapter 5).

As following chapters in this book will indicate, modern evolutionary biologists, including Richard Dawkins, Stephen Jay Gould, Edward O. Wilson, and Martin Nowak, do agree with Darwin on the origin and power of cooperation. That said, the related debates that divide them occasionally deviate into questionable representations of the ideas of the individual who began their profession. In 2012, Richard Dawkins wrote:

With the exception of one anomalous passage in *The Descent of Man*, Darwin consistently saw natural selection as choosing between individual organisms. When he adopted Herbert Spencer's phrase "survival of the fittest" at the urging of A.R. Wallace, "fittest" meant something close to its everyday meaning, and Darwin applied it strictly to organisms: the strongest, swiftest, sharpest of tooth and claw, keenest of ear and eye.

(para. 12)

Given the repeated references, cited above, from both *Origin* and *Descent*, to the operation of natural selection on families and communities, this seems unfair to Darwin. Dawkins' unusual characterization of Darwin's conclusions may, in this instance, be influenced by context: He was in the midst of a provocative attack on Wilson's defense of group selection; Wilson had challenged Dawkins' advocacy of gene selection. Of the more common misperception that Darwin's vision of natural selection echoes philosopher Thomas Hobbes' (1651/1985) famous characterization of life as "nasty, brutish, and short" (p. 186)—a war of all against all, Pinker (2011) laments, "Thomas Hobbes and Charles Darwin were nice men whose names became nasty adjectives. No one wants to live in a world that is Hobbesian or Darwinian. . ." (p. 31).

However, in the view of Darwin and later evolutionary biologists, natural selection has shaped humans to sympathize and cooperate—hardly a bleak worldview. Egoism and its related conflicts, in the estimation of these scientists, work against powerful social instincts. However, Darwin refused to cast this encouraging process as anything other than biology. "The so-called moral sense," he declares in *Descent*, "is aboriginally derived from the social instincts"—and not vice versa (Darwin, 1871/1998, p. 123). "Darwin initially resisted the word [*evolution*] because his theory embodied no notion of general advance as a predictable consequence of any mechanism of change," Stephen Jay Gould (1990) explains (p. 36). And on this key point, Kropotkin (trans. 1924/1992) firmly agrees:

> Darwin pointed out that the social instinct . . . has been developed by natural selection for its own sake, as it was useful for the well-being and the preservation of the species . . . Unhappily, the religious teachers of men prefer to ascribe to such feelings a supernatural origin.
>
> (pp. 37, 283)

In public relations theory, Brown (2006) has counseled scholars—particularly those who advocate symmetry—not to confuse evolution with "evolutionism," which holds that natural selection works as a quasi-religious force of moral improvement (p. 207). Both Darwin and Kropotkin avoided evolutionism: Instead, their notion of the social instinct, affirmed by modern evolutionary biologists, provides a scientific foundation for social harmony frameworks within public relations, such as fully functioning society theory, as well as for public relations functions, such as corporate social responsibility. Rather than looking askance at such frameworks and functions as being overly idealistic or wishful thinking, we can view them as gratifications of a powerful social instinct derived through natural selection.

Darwin and social Darwinism

Social Darwinism is an even more enduring misinterpretation of Darwin's thought. Halliday's (1971) 7,000-word exploration of the broadly defined concept details a range of meanings but settles on positioning social Darwinism as a highly uncooperative doctrine. Acknowledging that an exact description is "uncertain and negotiable," Halliday (1971) holds that "Social Darwinism is defined as that discourse arguing for eugenic population control" (p. 401). He further notes an economic tangent: "Social Darwinism is a synonym for laissez-faire and an antonym of state-socialism or collectivism" (1971, p. 390). In nineteenth-century England, the philosophy that later came to be known as social Darwinism discouraged sympathy, via governmental and private-sector assistance programs, for socioeconomic and genetic "others":

> The adherents of eugenics were opposed to socialism on the particular grounds of demography . . . The practice of socialism in providing welfare, medical, and insurance services was thought to upset a population's biological stability by aiding the survival of the unfit . . . Pauperism, for instance, whether of the native or alien variety, was the sign for genetic inferiority and unemployment the token of hereditary incapacity.
>
> (Halliday, 1971, pp. 398, 399)

Historian Theodore Roszak (2009) offers a famous example of social Darwinism—a fictional character created by a contemporary of Darwin's:

> Social Darwinism . . . was the view of life that Charles Dickens would attribute to Ebenezer Scrooge . . . Asked what he would do about the starving paupers who would not endure the discipline of the workhouse, Scrooge answers, "If they would rather die, they had better do it, and decrease the surplus population."
>
> (p. 229)

Taking aim at Nietzsche (trans. 1913/2003) and his defense of the "magnificent blond brute" archetype against the lesser "slaves" who, in their weakness, unite and rebel (pp. 22, 19), Peter Kropotkin (trans. 1924/1992) viewed nineteenth-century European societies as being torn between social Darwinism and a retreat to religious fervor:

> We certainly see public opinion floating between the two extremes— between a desperate effort, on the one side, to force oneself to return to the obscure creeds of the Middle Ages, with their full accompaniment of superstition, idolatry, and even magic; and, on the opposite extreme, a glorification of "a-moralism" and a revival of that worship of "superior natures," now invested with the names of "supermen" or "superior individualizations," which Europe had lived through in the times of Byronism and early Romanticism.
>
> (p. 11)

The supposed contrast between individualism and collectivism, Kropotkin (trans. 1924/1992) believes, "brought Nietzsche to conclude that all morality must be thrown overboard if it can find no better foundation than the sacrifice of the individual in the interests of the human race" (p. 28). Darwin's own son Leonard, however, showed himself perfectly willing to sacrifice the individual interests of "aments" (those with intellectual disabilities) for the betterment of society. As president of England's Eugenics Education Society from 1911 to 1928, he wrote in *The Need for Eugenic Reform* (a work dedicated to his father):

> No doubt we all dislike any interference with liberty; but liberty implies a certain degree of equality, and as equality between aments and the normal population does not and cannot exist, mental defectives can under no circumstances enjoy true liberty . . . The popular belief in the innate equality of all men is . . . slowly but surely disappearing in the face of irrefutable facts, and it will not be long before it is generally recognized that there does exist a large class of human beings whose *fertility should as far as possible be diminished* for the sake of posterity.
>
> (1926, pp. 198–199, 206–207)

British historian Jonathan Conlin (2014) has written that it is "impossible" to read Leonard Darwin's advocacy of eugenics "and not be aware that within five years the German Parliament would pass a Sterilisation Law, heralding the horrors of the eugenic 'final solution'" (p. 163). Given these associations, the actual term *social Darwinism* rarely appears in modern public relations research save in a historical sense. It generally is cited as a laissez-faire economic policy that, historically, practitioners either accepted, sometimes conditionally (Lamme, 2015), or rejected (Hallahan, 2003).

Ideally, it is unnecessary here to say that Darwin (1871/1998) himself rejected social Darwinism: We have seen already his belief that the social instinct, sympathy, and an individual's "deep regard for the good opinion of his fellows" (p. 117) all lead to cooperation. "Darwin was not a social Darwinist," declares science historian James Moore (1979, p. 161). Similarly, Wispé (1991) concludes, "Although the idea of conflict and competition is closely associated with Darwin's name, it is important to remember that he himself strongly defended the social and moral aspects of human life" (pp. 41–42). Pinker (2011) holds it "unjust" to associate Darwin with social Darwinism: "Darwin himself was a thoroughgoing liberal humanist" (p. 187). Here, then, is the importance for public relations: Charles Darwin's defense of natural selection does not, via social Darwinism, offer perverse (and surely unwanted) support for egoistic, conflict-oriented approaches to relationships. Rather, Darwin's views of natural selection argue for the social harmony frameworks within the discipline.

Like Darwin, Huxley (1897) thoroughly rejected social Darwinism, speculating that "one must be very 'fit,' indeed, not to know of an occasion, or perhaps two, in one's life, when it would have been only too easy to qualify for a place among the 'unfit'" (p. 39). Social Darwinism, he believed, skewed too far toward competitive individualism:

> The fanatical individualism of our time attempts to apply the analogy of cosmic nature to society . . . The duties of the individual to the state are forgotten, and his tendencies to self-assertion are dignified by the name of rights.
>
> (1897, p. 82)

Huxley (1897) concludes, "I suspect that this fallacy has arisen out of the unfortunate ambiguity of the phrase 'survival of the fittest'" (p. 80). More than a century later, Martin Nowak (Nowak & Highfield, 2011) agreed that the phrase "signaled the introduction of Darwinian thinking into the political arena" (p. 14). Although Darwin did use the phrase *survival of the fittest*, borrowed from biologist and philosopher Herbert Spencer, in *On the Origin of Species* (not adding it until the fifth edition, however, when he used it more than a dozen times), he used it only four times in the even lengthier second edition of the *Descent of Man* (1871/1998). "Huxley would grow increasingly troubled by the social ideas being disseminated under the name of Darwinism," asserts historian Iain McCalman (2009, p. 371).

Natural selection and ethics

Far from extending "survival of the fittest" to eugenics or laissez-faire economics, Darwin believes that natural selection helped create a social instinct that is the source—the materialistic source—of relationship-oriented ethics, the ethics that characterize public relations' social harmony frameworks. Within public relations theory, J.E. Grunig (2006) has described the importance of ethics within symmetrical models of public relations, just as Heath (2006) has noted the indispensability of "deontological ethics" within "corporate responsibility" (p. 103). In detailing the ethical nature of the Isocratean framework, Marsh (2003) has quoted the assessment of historian Henri Marrou that, with Isocrates, "rhetoric is gradually transformed into ethics" (p. 366). Leeper (2001) has outlined the challenge, within communitarianism, of establishing a body of ethics "that is comparative rather than objective" (p. 98). Van Ruler and Verčič (2005) hold that a reflective approach to public relations is not automatically "based on morality or ethics as a deontological principle, but on the empirical question of what is good and justifiable to (the members of) society" (p. 266). Clearly, the quest to define ethical behavior is inherent in cooperative, social harmony frameworks of public relations.

Darwin's attribution of relationship-oriented ethics to natural selection and the social instinct helps remove such values and principles from the realm of the normative and utopian. Almost a century before *The Descent of Man*, Immanuel Kant (trans. 1836) issued his frustrated query regarding the origins of social duty: "Whence thy original? And where find we the root of thy august descent?" (p. 136). In other words, if an impetus toward social harmony, an impetus toward duty to one another, does indeed exist, why? And is it a casual, intermittent impulse, unworthy of shaping public relations frameworks—or is it something more? Of Kant's question regarding the provenance of duty, Darwin (1871/1998), in *The Descent of Man*, asserts, "This great question has been discussed by many writers of consummate ability . . . As far as I know, no one has approached it exclusively from the side of natural history" (p. 100). As would Peter Kropotkin a generation later, Darwin (1871/1998) holds that the sense of social duty that engenders ethics is an artifact of the social instinct created by natural selection:

> Ultimately our moral sense or conscience becomes a highly complex sentiment—originating in the social instincts, largely guided by the approbation of our fellow-men, ruled by reason, self-interest, and in later times by deep religious feelings, and confirmed by instruction and habit.
>
> (p. 137)

Kropotkin (trans. 1924/1992) is even more explicit in detailing Kant's consternation and Darwin's success in explaining the origins of duty:

> The most important point in the ethical theory of Darwin is, of course, his explanation of the moral conscience of man and his sense of duty and remorse . . . Kant, as is known, utterly failed, in his otherwise excellent work on morality, to explain why his "categorical imperative" should be obeyed at all, unless such be the will of a supreme power . . . After having thought intensely upon this subject, and written about it for four years, he acknowledged . . . that he was unable to find the explanation of the origin of the moral law. In fact, he gave up the whole problem by recognizing "the incomprehensibility of this capacity, a capacity which points to a divine origin . . ." Such a decision, after four years of meditation, is equivalent to a complete abandoning of this problem by philosophy, and the delivering of it into the hands of religion . . . We have thus, in Darwin for the first time, an explanation of the sense of duty on a naturalistic basis.
>
> (pp. 38–39, 40, 41)

Kropotkin's (trans. 1924/1992) *Ethics: Origin and Development* develops Darwin's theory that "the social instinct is the common source out of which all morality originates" (p. 37). In that work, Kropotkin (trans. 1924/1992) writes:

> Darwin pointed out that the social instinct . . . has been developed by natural selection for its own sake, as it was useful for the well-being and the preservation of the species . . . Nature has thus to be recognized as the first ethical teacher of man. The social instinct, innate in men as well as in all the social animals,—this is the origin of all ethical conceptions and all the subsequent development of morality.
>
> (pp. 37, 45)

Even earlier, in *Mutual Aid*, Kropotkin (1902/1989) concludes, "It is especially in the domain of ethics that the dominating importance of the mutual-aid principle appears in full. That mutual aid is the real foundation of our ethical conceptions seems evident enough" (p. 298). If Darwin and Kropotkin—and, as we shall see in forthcoming chapters, modern evolutionary biologists—are correct, then the relationship-oriented ethics that infuses the social harmony frameworks and cooperative practices of public relations is not an idealistic pipedream. Rather, it is genetic reality, reinforced by "reason, self-interest . . . deep religious feelings, and confirmed by instruction and habit" (Darwin, 1871/1998, p. 137). It is an inseparable part of humanity.

Darwin's materialism

In philosophical materialism, "the sole reality is matter and everything is a manifestation of its activity"; in materialism, "there are no nonmaterial entities such as spirits, ghosts, demons, angels. Immaterial agencies do not exist" (Angeles, 1981, p. 161). For our purposes, idealism can be seen as the contrary of materialism; idealism, in general, is the belief that sheer matter cannot explain everything. In idealism's extreme forms, "matter, the physical, does not exist" (Angeles, 1981, p. 120). To explain humans, René Descartes (1596–1650), in what has come to be known as Cartesian Dualism, tried to synthesize these disparate philosophies: "Descartes characterized an individual person as a composite thing, a combination of body (a corporeal substance) and a rational soul (an incorporeal substance)" (Baker & Morris, 2005, p. 60)— somewhat similar to Alfred Russel Wallace's belief (abhorrent to Darwin) that natural selection could explain all organic development except the human mind, which must have a higher origin (McCalman, 2009, p. 361). This brief section will review Darwin's own acknowledgement of the materialism inherent in his view of natural selection and the origin of the social instinct. Again, Darwin's lack of traditional idealism helps ground the origins and power of cooperation in materialism and empiricism, not in wishful thinking.

Darwin was well aware of the nonidealistic, materialistic direction of his decades of research. In private, the growing heresy sometimes delighted him: In his notebooks that preceded the publication of *Origin*, he writes, in 1838, "Oh you Materialist! Why is thought, being a secretion of the brain, more wonderful than gravity a property of matter? It is our arrogance, it [sic] our admiration of ourselves" (Barrett et al., 1987, p. 291). In his own notebooks, Huxley (1983) recalls, "I maintained that it cannot be proved that matter is *essentially*—as to its base—different from the soul" (p. 92). Only months after labeling himself a materialist in his notebooks, however, Darwin—assessing, no doubt, the probable public reaction to his theory of the origin of species— adds that he must "avoid stating how far, I believe, in Materialism" (Barrett et al., 1987, p. 532). "He knew," Stephen Jay Gould (1977) concludes of Darwin, "that the primary feature distinguishing his theory from all other evolutionary doctrines was its uncompromising philosophical materialism" (p. 24). "God knows what the public will think," Darwin wrote to Wallace on the eve of *Origin's* publication (Burkhardt & Smith, 1991, p. 375).

Gould, in fact, doesn't accept the explanation that the delay between Darwin's notebooks of the 1830s and the eventual publication of *Origin* in 1859 was, primarily, Darwin's diligence in amassing evidence. Instead, he maintains that Darwin could envision all too well the impact of his materialistic explanation of the origin of species—and, thus, the origin of humans:

> [Darwin's notebooks] include many statements showing that he espoused
> but feared to expose something he perceived as far more heretical than

evolution itself: philosophical materialism—the postulate that matter is the stuff of all existence and that all mental and spiritual phenomena are its by-products ... This belief ... was so heretical that Darwin even sidestepped it in *The Origin of Species* (1859) ... Only in 1871 did he gather the courage to publish *The Descent of Man*.

(Gould, 1977, pp. 24, 25, 50)

Darwin's concern, of course, was well founded. After a first reading of *Origin*, Darwin's Cambridge geology professor, Adam Sedgwick, for example, wrote the following to his former student:

There is a moral or metaphysical part of nature as well as a physical. A man who denies this is deep in the mire of folly. Tis the crown & glory of organic science that it *does* ... link material to moral ... You have ignored this link; &, if I do not mistake your meaning, you have done your best in one or two pregnant cases to break it.

(Burkhardt & Smith, 1991, p. 397)

In a later review, Sedgwick denounces the book's "unflinching materialism" (Browne, 2002, p. 108). Darwin's scientific explanation for the social instinct and cooperation, thus, consciously and deliberately shuns any form of idealism. For Darwin, cooperation is a product of natural selection, not a normative ideal for his own species.

Darwin, social instinct, and reputation

We need not look far within public relations research for evidence of the importance of reputation. As noted earlier, a chief aspect of the reflective paradigm is the process of "societal legitimation" (van Ruler & Verčič, 2005, pp. 239, 263) that organizations undergo to ensure their continued operation. Additionally, the surge of scholarship that addresses crisis communication and image repair discourse testifies to the importance of an entity's image and reputation. Lyon and Cameron (2004), among others, posited a difference between image—"how the company wants to be viewed"— and reputation, which "is owned by the publics" (p. 215). Within corporations, "'reputation management' is gaining ground as a driving philosophy" (Hutton, Goodman, Alexander, & Genest, 2001, p. 247). And, as the reflective paradigm demonstrates, reputation surely is tied to resource dependency theory. Game theory research (Chapter 7), for example, shows a direct relationship between a reputation for cooperation and the acquisition of desired resources.

Both Darwin and Kropotkin hold that the human need for public approval and a favorable reputation stems from the processes of natural selection that, over eons, have established the desire to cooperate as a powerful instinct.

In *The Descent of Man*, as we have seen, Darwin (1871/1998) grounds a human's "deep regard for the good opinion of his fellows" and desire for "the approbation of our fellow-men" (pp. 117, 137)—in other words, staples of public relations—in our species' social, cooperative instinct. In *The Descent of Man*, he further declares:

> However great weight we may attribute to public opinion, our regard for the approbation and disapprobation of our fellows depends on sympathy, which, as we shall see, forms an essential part of the social instinct, and is indeed its foundation-stone . . . It should, however, be borne in mind, that the enforcement of public opinion depends on our appreciation of the approbation and disapprobation of others; and this appreciation is founded on our sympathy, which it can hardly be doubted was originally developed through natural selection as one of the most important elements of the social instincts.
>
> (Darwin, 1871/1998, pp. 102, 148)

Darwin already was developing this idea in his private notebooks, which he asserts in the terse style of those volumes:

> If [a human's] passions strong & his instincts weak, he will have many struggles, & experience only will teach him, that the instinctive feeling in its nature being always present. & his passion shortlived, it is to his interest to follow the former; & likewise . . . then receive the moral approbation of his fellow men.
>
> (Barrett et al., 1987, p. 621)

In Chapter 9, we shall see Scottish philosopher David Hume's similar belief that an individual's personal enactments of justice toward others do more than anything else to enhance his or her reputation. And, again, the computerized game theory experiments of Axelrod, Nowak, and others—detailed in Chapter 7—have established that a reputation for cooperation helps an individual secure the resources that lead to evolutionary success, thus increasing the scope of cooperation within a society. Much earlier, Isocrates (Chapter 12) held that attention to the needs of others helps build a reputation that leads to economic success. In other words, reputation, that great desideratum of public relations, is inextricably tied to our cooperation with and consideration for others. To sum up: Our desire for a good reputation arises from feelings of sympathy and from our desire, nurtured through natural selection, to secure resources— and acts of cooperation help build a good reputation.

Referring to the above passages in Darwin's *Descent of Man*, Kropotkin (trans. 1924/1992) adds, "The effect of public approbation and disapprobation depends entirely upon the development of mutual sympathy. It is because we feel in sympathy with others that we appreciate their opinions"

(p. 34). In modern public relations theory, Benoit (1995) makes much the same point in *Accounts, Excuses, and Apologies: A Theory of Image Restoration Strategies*:

> Attacks on our reputation are serious matters, for our image or reputation is extremely vital to us. Face, image, or reputation not only contributes to a healthy self-image, but it also can create important favorable impressions on others. Conversely, a bad reputation may interfere with our interactions with others . . . When our image is threatened, we feel compelled to offer explanations, defenses, justifications, rationalizations, apologies, or excuses for our behavior.
>
> (p. 2)

Were Benoit, in fact, to tie this compulsion to a social instinct derived from natural selection, such a passage might easily appear within the works of Darwin or Kropotkin.

Finally, in his *Autobiography*, written as he was organizing his notes for *Origin*, Darwin (1887/1983) crafts one of his longest explorations of how the social instinct and reputation nurture each other:

> A man . . . looks forward and backwards, and compares his various feelings, desires, and recollections. He then finds, in accordance with the verdict of all the wisest men that the highest satisfaction is derived from following certain impulses, namely the social instincts. If he acts for the good of others, he will receive the approbation of his fellow men and gain the love of those with whom he lives; and this latter gain undoubtedly is the highest pleasure on this earth. By degrees it will become intolerable to him to obey his sensuous passions rather than his higher impulses, which when rendered habitual may be almost called instincts. His reason may occasionally tell him to act in opposition to the opinion of others, whose approbation he will then not receive; but he will still have the solid satisfaction of knowing that he has followed his innermost guide or conscience.
>
> (p. 55)

Huxley (1897), interjecting his wry sense of humor into his sentiments, as he so often does, echoes Darwin:

> However complete may be the indifference to public opinion, in a cool, intellectual view, of the traditional sage, it has not yet been my fortune to meet with any actual sage who took its hostile manifestations with entire equanimity. Indeed, I doubt if the philosopher lives, or ever has lived, who could know himself to be heartily despised by a street boy without some irritation . . . It is needful only to look around us, to see that

the greatest restrainer of the anti-social tendencies of men is fear, not of the law, but of the opinion of their fellows . . . While people endure the extremity of physical pain rather than part with life, shame drives the weakest to suicide.

(p. 29)

If Darwin—and Isocrates, Hume, Huxley, Kropotkin, Nowak, and others—are correct, then egoistic frameworks of public relation that de-emphasize acts of cooperation can work against the acquisition and maintenance of reputation and, thus, against the acquisition of other resources.

Darwin, reciprocity, and reputation

Evolutionary biologists maintain that reputation is primarily built upon a particular kind of cooperation, one well known in public relations research: Reciprocity. In *The Social Conquest of Earth*, Edward O. Wilson links reputation to the concept of indirect reciprocity. Direct reciprocity (I help you in hopes of you, in turn, helping me) ideally secures immediate resources. However, indirect reciprocity (I help you without expectation of a direct return) ideally secures eventual resources by means of earned "reputation and trust," which are won by seemingly selfless acts (Wilson, 2012, p. 54). Humans, writes Wilson (2012), "enhance reputation by what researchers have called indirect reciprocity, by which a reputation for altruism and cooperativeness accrues to an individual" (p. 249). Martin Nowak (Nowak & Highfield, 2011) calls indirect reciprocity "the power of reputation" and has declared it to be one of the key mechanisms that explain cooperation, and consequent resource acquisition, within humans (p. 52). "To understand the indirect form [of reciprocity]," he concludes, "we need to recognize the power of reputation . . . Making a reputation has been shown to engage much of the same reward circuitry in the brain as making money"(Nowak & Highfield, 2011, pp. 52, 55). Thus, cooperation in the form of reciprocity—primarily indirect reciprocity—helps create reputation. Rather than being improbably idealistic behavior, cooperation in the form of helping others without expectation of immediate or direct repayment is a scientifically established reputation-building strategy.

In *Excellence in Public Relations and Communication Management*, J.E. Grunig and White (1992) analyze "the norm of reciprocity" (p. 46), from the works of sociologist Alvin Gouldner, and they link the norm to corporate social responsibility and symmetry:

Excellent organizations realize that they can get more of what they want by giving publics some of what they want. Reciprocity means that publics, too, will be willing to give up some of what they want to the organiza-tion . . . The norm of reciprocity is the essence of what generally is called social responsibility ... The norm of reciprocity ... is an integral part of the symmetrical worldview that is an essential part of excellent public relations.

(pp. 46, 47, 48)

J.E. Grunig and White (1992) further note that reciprocal relationships can have the "mixed motives" of selfishness/enlightened self-interest and disinterested concern for others (pp. 46–48). In her application of political scientist Robert Putnam's theory of social capital to public relations, Luoma-aho (2009) links reciprocity to economically successful relationships: "For Putnam, social trust, norms of reciprocity, and networks of civil engagement are mutually reinforcing ... Moreover, norms and networks of trusting behavior contribute to economic prosperity and are in turn reinforced by that prosperity" (p. 234).

A century before Gouldner or Putnam, Darwin presented the concept of reciprocity, forged by the processes of natural selection, as a founding principle of social harmony. In discussing the sympathy derived from the social instinct, Darwin (1871/1998) declares:

[In sympathy], we are led by the hope of receiving good in return ... In the first place, as the reasoning powers and foresight of the members became improved, each man would soon learn that if he aided his fellow-men, he would commonly receive aid in return. From this low motive he might acquire the habit of aiding his fellows; and the habit of performing benevolent actions certainly strengthens the feeling of sympathy which gives the first impulse to benevolent actions.

(pp. 110, 135)

This is hardly a normative explanation for the presence and power of coopera-tion in the guise of reciprocity. This staple of human behavior, one that infuses the social harmony frameworks of public relations, stems from, in Darwin's own words, the "low motive" of self-interest. Within public relations research, indirect reciprocity—explored more thoroughly in Chapter 7—helps explain the logic and productivity of such frameworks as fully functioning society theory and the reflective paradigm. In the former, we advance socioeconomic wellbeing not only because indirect reciprocity is in our very nature, but also because such behavior advances reputation and the attached social capital. In the latter, indirect reciprocity would seem to strengthen our quest for the most desired resource: Social legitimacy.

In his essay *Plataicus*, Isocrates draws upon his decades-long observations of Greek politics to make much the same point about the linkage of indirect reciprocity and reputation. Writing in support of the city-state Plataea, recently conquered by Thebes, he reminds his fellow Athenians that in a recent conflict with Sparta they had acted not in their own immediate interests but, rather, "in behalf of those who were being deprived of their autonomy in violation of the oaths and covenants" (Isocrates, trans. 1945/1986, *Plataicus*, 17). Such selfless actions, he concludes, "will cause many to desire your friendship. For . . . who will be so insane as to prefer to join those who try to enslave than to be in company with you who are fighting for their freedom?" (Isocrates, trans. 1945/1986, *Plataicus*, 43). Rhetoricians understood the origin and power of reputation/ethos long before the biologists.

Public relations surely is not exclusively a striving for social harmony; in developing his theory of natural selection, Charles Darwin repeatedly acknowledged the power of individualism. Given his assessment of the social instinct, however—an assessment echoed by top evolutionary biologists past and present—it is not naive or disingenuous to posit social harmony a goal of public relations. Again, Darwin (1871/1998) himself has written, "Communities, which included the greatest number of the most sympathetic members, would flourish best, and rear the greatest number of offspring . . . Selfish and contentious people will not cohere, and without coherence nothing can be effected" (pp. 110, 134). If he is correct, then a quest for social harmony is an acceptance, not a denial, of basic human nature.

Summary

Darwin's theory of natural selection, particularly as developed in *The Descent of Man*, leads us to at least five important points for the understanding and practice of public relations:

1. The social instinct in humans, which gives rise to empathy and coopera-tion, is not an aberration. It is a powerful product of natural selection. Denying the social instinct is painful for humans. Acting against that instinct is increasingly contrary to our nature.
2. The biological basis for cooperation is not idealistic. Rather, that basis is grounded in materialism and empiricism.
3. Cooperation is an evolutionary advantage. Cultures in which individuals cooperate outcompete less cohesive cultures.
4. Modern relationship-oriented ethics originates in the same social instinct, derived through natural selection, that gives rise to cooperation.
5. Reputation, with its inherent social capital, is built primarily by acts of cooperation and indirect reciprocity.

These five points address four of the Nine Tenets of public relations' social harmony frameworks outlined in Chapter 1:

II. Cooperation is the relationship strategy best suited to resource acqui-sition. Evidence from evolutionary biology, philosophy, and rhetoric shows that, in general, cooperative relationships are more successful in sustained resource acquisition than relationships based on egoism, conflict, and competition.

III.   Cooperative relationships are not merely normative, idealistic, or utopian. Rather, evidence from evolutionary biology, philosophy, and rhetoric shows that cooperation is a stronger instinct within human nature than the competing instincts of egoism, conflict, and competition.

VI.   Ethical behavior that accommodates the needs of others has enduring foundations in the biological and social origins of cooperation. Such behavior is not normative, idealistic, or contrary to human nature.

VIII.   Acts of cooperation and justice are the most effective builders of a positive reputation. A positive reputation is a powerful, productive force within the processes of public relations and resource acquisition

Chapter 5

Peter Kropotkin and mutual aid

At the same time Charles Darwin was writing *The Descent of Man*, Russian scientist and anarchist Peter Kropotkin (1842–1921) was exploring Siberia as an officer in the Russian army (Woodcock, 1989). Of the competition for survival among animal species in that unforgiving environment, Kropotkin (1902/1989) later wrote:

> I failed to find—although I was eagerly looking for it—that bitter struggle for the means of existence, among animals belonging to the same species, which was considered by most Darwinists (though not always by Darwin himself) as the dominant characteristic of struggle for life, and the main factor of evolution . . . I saw Mutual Aid and Mutual Support carried on to an extent which made me suspect in it a feature of the greatest importance for the maintenance of life, the preservation of each species, and its further evolution.
>
> (pp. xxxv, xxxvii)

With his consequent book *Mutual Aid: A Factor of Evolution*, Kropotkin, even more than Darwin, became a keen advocate for the power of cooperation within natural selection.

Fleeing political persecution in Russia, Kropotkin traveled to Switzerland and then to England, where he remained for 40 years before returning to Russia, where, shortly before his death, he wrote *Ethics: Origin and Development*. As the philosopher who "without a doubt contributed more than anyone to the development of anarchist theory" (Morris, 2004, p. 13), Kropotkin spent time in prisons in Russia and France and was deported from Switzerland. While in England, he was a regular contributor "on scientific subjects for *Nature*, the leading scientific journal [of which Thomas Henry Huxley was a founder], and for the *Times*" (Woodcock, 1989, p. xvii). He was the author of more than a dozen books and dozens of essays.

Kropotkin merits a chapter in this book for many reasons: Again, more so than even Darwin, he championed the presence and power of cooperation within natural selection. Like Darwin, he was a materialist, building a meticulous empirical case for the power and presence of social harmony; is theory of mutual aid is, today, endorsed by top modern evolutionary biologists. As an atheist, he saw no divine direction in the blind forces of nature. As a scientist and anarchist, he strove to understand the origins and relationships of the competing instincts of individualism and collectivism within human nature and behavior. Within this book's central goal of establishing a non-utopian, non-idealistic, scientific basis for the social harmony frameworks of public relations, Kropotkin is, thus, a key figure. This chapter will review Kropotkin's unique contributions to that goal and compare them with those of Charles Darwin as well as those of Darwin's bulldog, Thomas Henry Huxley.

After approximately five years in Siberia and Manchuria, Kropotkin resigned from the army and returned, in 1868, to St. Petersburg, where he had attended military school. Kropotkin (1902/1989) attributed the revival of his interest in mutual aid to a presentation by Karl Kessler, dean of the University of St. Petersburg, in the 1880s:

> Kessler's idea was, that besides the law of Mutual Struggle there is in Nature the law of Mutual Aid, which, for the success of the struggle for life, and especially for the progressive evolution of the species, is far more important than the law of mutual contest. This suggestion—which was, in reality, nothing but a further development of the ideas expressed by Darwin himself in *The Descent of Man*—seemed to me so correct and of so great an importance, that since I became acquainted with it (in 1883) I began to collect materials for further developing the idea, which Kessler had only cursorily sketched in his lecture, but had not lived to develop.
>
> (p. xxxviii)

Inspired by Kessler, Kropotkin began work on *Mutual Aid*, published in 1902, in which he seconds Darwin's assertion, in *The Descent of Man*, that the quest for cooperation and social harmony is driven by a powerful instinct for survival that has been developed and reinforced through natural selection. Kropotkin biographer Brian Morris (2004) characterizes *Mutual Aid* as "presenting a wealth of empirical data to substantiate his thesis, namely, the importance of mutual aid in both the life of animals and in human societies throughout history" (p. 138). In the later *Ethics: Origin and Development*, published posthumously, Kropotkin develops his belief that the foundation of modern ethics is the biological instinct, derived through natural selection, to harmonize individualistic and collectivist tendencies within a framework of mutual aid. Of Kropotkin's *Ethics*, English critic Herbert Read declared, "No better history of ethics has ever been written" (Woodcock, 1992, p. xix).

In *Descent of Man*, "the problem of cooperation" (Axelrod, 2006, p. 3) is one strand among many in Darwin's exploration of how our species came to be. In Kropotkin's hefty *Mutual Aid*, however, cooperation as a main driver of evolution is the core idea. Perhaps inspired by the relentless empiricism of *On the Origin of Species*, Kropotkin fills *Mutual Aid* with examples of cooperation among ants, beetles, bees, crabs, parrots, wolves, monkeys, and dozens of other life forms. For example, pelicans, he notes, "always go fishing in numerous bands, and after having chosen an appropriate bay, they form a wide half-circle in face of the shore, and narrow it by paddling towards the shore, catching all fish that happen to be enclosed in the circle" (1989, p. 23). Kropotkin's *Mutual Aid* is not as well known as Darwin's *Descent of Man*, but modern evolutionary biologists, including those studied in forthcoming chapters of this book, have concurred with the book's basic premise. "The central logic of Kropotkin's argument is simple, straightforward, and largely cogent . . . In fact, I would hold that Kropotkin's basic argument is correct," writes Stephen Jay Gould (1991b, pp. 334, 338), and Martin Nowak (Nowak & Highfield, 2011) concurs: "I believe that our ability to cooperate goes hand in hand with succeeding in the struggle to survive, as surmised more than a century ago by Peter Kropotkin" (p. xvi). Without mentioning Kropotkin, evolutionary biologist Marc Hauser (2013) declares, "Cooperation is not only a stable evolutionary strategy . . . but, critically, forms the basis for what we perceive as universal moral responses in humans and other social animals" (pp. 254–255).

Historian Thomas Dixon (2013) notes that Arabella Buckley, secretary to Darwin's mentor Charles Lyell, anticipated Kropotkin by asserting, in 1882, that "one of the laws of life which is as strong, if not stronger, than the law of force and selfishness, *is that of mutual help and dependence*" (p. 68). Buckley, however, persisted in drawing moral lessons and intent from this finding (Dixon, 2013). Conversely, Kropotkin, as we shall see, finds the origins of morals in biological behavior.

Like modern advocates of social harmony frameworks in public relations, Kropotkin (1902/1989) understood that the theory of mutual aid was, in the eyes of some critics, "Utopian" (p. 228). To establish mutual aid as a part of nature more powerful even than the competitive individualistic tendencies suggested by the phrase "survival of the fittest," Kropotkin painstakingly clarifies three facets of mutual aid: It has a scientific basis in evolutionary biology and the processes of natural selection; it increasingly works with, not against, individualistic tendencies; and it is not equivalent to continuous accommodation—there are some entities, in Kropotkin's estimation, that undermine mutual aid and with which, thus, we should not seek harmonious relationships.

Mutual aid as an artifact of natural selection

For public relations practitioners, Kropotkin offers another respected, scientific assessment that cooperation, far from being hopelessly idealistic, is inherently more powerful than conflict and competition within human nature. Though he transformed Darwin's term *sympathy* into his preferred *mutual aid*, Kropotkin

(1902/1989) joins Darwin in attributing the human race's impetus toward cooperation to the processes of natural selection:

> [The] instinct . . . is a feeling infinitely wider than love or personal sympathy—an instinct that has been slowly developed among animals and men in the course of an extremely long evolution, and which has taught animals and men alike the force they can borrow from the practice of mutual aid and support, and the joys they can find in social life.
>
> (p. xli)

Two decades later, in *Ethics*, Kropotkin (trans. 1924/1992) reasserts the role of natural selection in establishing mutual aid:

> [Mutual aid] represents the best weapon in the great struggle for life which continually has to be carried on in Nature against climate, inundations, storms, frost, and the like, and continually requires new adaptations to the ever-changing conditions of existence . . . The instinct of mutual aid pervades the animal world, because natural selection works for maintaining and further developing it, and pitilessly destroys those species in which it becomes for some reason weakened . . . And the same principle is confirmed by the history of mankind.
>
> (pp. 14, 43)

Darwin (1871/1998) himself does use the phrase *mutual aid* in the earlier *Descent of Man*:

> [Primeval men] would have felt uneasy when separated from their comrades, for whom they would have felt some degree of love; they would have warned each other of danger, and have given mutual aid in attack or defence. All this implies some degree of sympathy, fidelity, and courage. Such social qualities, the paramount importance of which to the lower animals is disputed by no one, were no doubt acquired by the progenitors of man in a similar manner, namely, through natural selection, aided by inherited habit.
>
> (p. 134)

Gould (1996) notes that Darwin distinguishes between "biotic" (organism versus organism) and "abiotic" (organism versus physical environment) struggles for survival, but Gould credits Kropotkin for showing how the rigors of abiotic competition actually encourage cooperation within a species, thus reducing intra-species biotic conflict (pp. 142, 144). Alfred Russel Wallace, Darwin's colleague and early rival, held that the development of "the human mind" transferred human initiative away from intra-species biotic conflict and toward abiotic challenges to survival (McCalman, 2009, p. 353).

For those of us who might cite the latest war or human atrocity as depressing but compelling counter evidence, Kropotkin (trans. 1924/1992), like Darwin, holds that the gradual evolution of mutual aid within humanity has not been a path of continuous progress: "We certainly must abandon the idea of representing human history as an uninterrupted chain of development from the pre-historic Stone Age to the present time. The development of human societies was not continuous" (p. 17). Nonetheless, for Kropotkin (trans. 1924/1992), "the importance of sociality, of mutual aid, in the evolution of the animal world and human history may be taken, I believe, as a positively established scientific truth, free of any hypothetical assumptions" (p. 30). In his richly detailed, 800-plus page *The Better Angels of Our Nature: Why Violence Has Declined*, Harvard Psychology Professor Steven Pinker (2011) comes to a similar conclusion:

> This book is about what may be the most important thing that has ever happened in human history . . . Violence has declined over long stretches of time . . . The problem I have set out to understand is the reduction in violence at many scales—in the family, in the neighborhood, between tribes and other armed factions, and among major nations and states . . . To my repeated astonishment, the global trends in almost all of them, viewed from the vantage point of the present, point downward . . . Declines of violence are a product of social, cultural, and material conditions.
>
> (pp. xxi, 671)

Given the political tumult and conflict within his own life, Kropotkin's enduring belief in the growing power, over time, of mutual aid is a compelling endorsement.

Reconciling mutual aid and individualistic tendencies

A second barrier to accepting social harmony frameworks and their inherent cooperation within public relations is the issue of coordinating individualistic and collectivist tendencies, which has long been a central challenge within the discipline's scholarship and practice. In positing "collaboration" as "the core value of public relations," J.E. Grunig (2000) declares, "Public relations brings an essential element of collectivism into the commonly individualistic worldview of most Western organizations" (p. 25). Similarly, in presenting communitarianism as a framework for public relations, Leeper (2001) writes, "A major part of the programmatic communitarian agenda is . . . to shift the balance from extreme individualism to more of a community orientation. . ." (p. 99). An individualist focus is clear within the contingency theory-oriented definition of public relations as the "strategic management of competition and conflict for the benefit of one's own organization—and when possible—also for the mutual benefit of the organization and its various stakeholders or publics" (Wilcox & Cameron, 2009, p. 7).

Kropotkin was well aware of such tensions. In *Ethics: Origin and Development*, first published in English in 1924, he writes:

> The chief demand which is now addressed to ethics is to do its best to find . . . the common element in the two sets of diametrically opposed feelings which exist in man, and thus to help mankind find a synthesis, and not a compromise, between the two. In one set are the feelings which induce man to subdue other men in order to utilize them for his individual ends, while those in the other set induce human beings to unite for attaining common ends by common effort . . . These two sets of feelings must, of course, struggle between themselves, but it is absolutely essential to discover their synthesis whatever form it takes. Such a synthesis is so much more necessary because the civilized man of to-day, having no settled conviction on this point, is paralyzed in his powers of action. He cannot admit that a struggle to the knife for supremacy, carried on between individuals and nations, should be the last word of science; he does not believe, at the same time, in solving the problem through the gospel of brotherhood and self-abnegation . . .
>
> (trans. 1924/1992, p. 22)

Kropotkin (trans. 1924/1992) refers to the contrasting motivations of egoism and collectivism as a "double tendency" within humans:

> We are enabled to conclude that the lesson which man derives both from the study of Nature and his own history is the permanent presence of a *double tendency*—towards a greater development, on the one side, of *sociality*, and, on the other side, of a consequent increase of the intensity of life, which results in an increase of happiness for the *individuals* . . . Thus the principal problem of ethics at present is to help mankind to find the solution for this fundamental contradiction.
>
> (pp. 19–20, 22)

Though he disagrees, as we shall see, on a solution, Huxley (1897) shares Kropotkin's belief both in the existence of the double tendency and the need to resolve it:

> We cannot do without our inheritance [intra-species conflict and competition] from the forefathers who were the puppets of the cosmic process; the society which renounces it must be destroyed from without. Still less can we do with too much of it; the society in which it dominates must be destroyed from within . . . The check upon this free play of self-assertion,

or natural liberty . . . is the necessary condition for the origin of human society.

(pp. viii, 27–28)

Modern evolutionary biologist Edward O. Wilson (2012) attributes this enduring double tendency to multiple levels of selection within natural selection: Wilson believes that the processes of evolution can select both individuals and groups, a situation that, to oversimplify, would promote both selfish and altruistic qualities—and he links "the conflicted nature of [our] motivations" to this situation (pp. 273–274, 290). Pinker (2011), citing the research of anthropologist Richard Shweder, casts the double tendency as a clash between two universal moral norms: Autonomy and community (p. 625). In contingency theory, Cancel et al. (1997) describe this double tendency as "conflicting organization and public interests" (p. 38), and they cite Pearson's (1989) conclusion that "serving client and public interests simultaneously is the seeming impossible mission of the public relations practitioner" (p. 67). J.E. Grunig and White (1992), however, hold that reciprocal relationships within public relations can have the "mixed motives" of selfishness/enlightened self-interest and disinterested concern for others (p. 46).

Like Darwin, Kropotkin believes that the findings of evolutionary biology point toward the growing strength of the social instinct. In *Mutual Aid*, however, Kropotkin (1902/1989) further asserts that the synthesis of sociality and individualism exists in an increasingly mature social instinct that recognizes and supports a need for individual latitude and interests:

We may safely say that mutual aid is as much a law of animal life as mutual struggle, but that, as a factor of evolution, it most probably has a far greater importance, inasmuch as it favours the development of such habits and characters as insure the maintenance and further development of the species, together with the greatest amount of welfare and enjoyment of life for the individual, with the least waste of energy . . . The Europeans came to work out in medieval times a new form of organization [cities interlaced with guilds and associations] which had the advantage of allowing great latitude for individual initiative, while it largely responded at the same time to man's need of mutual support.

(pp. 6, 224)

Simply put, Kropotkin's resolution of the enduring dichotomy holds that a maturing social instinct draws strength from its support of individual rights; individual rights, conversely, are sustained by the enabling power of social harmony.

In *Ethics*, Kropotkin further explains that the synthesis of individualism and collectivism is, essentially, a chain of three phenomena: (1) Mutual aid is (as we have seen) a powerful human instinct, derived from natural selection;

(2) mutual aid engenders justice; and (3) the justice derived from mutual aid ultimately leads to increasing and increasingly secure individual liberties. This chain of ideas, if accurate, provides one version of the sought after synthesis of individualism and collectivism—a synthesis, as we shall see, that directly addresses the worldwide collectivism/individualism dichotomy identified by Hofstede and cited frequently in public relations scholarship (Choi & Cameron, 2005; Grunig, 2000; Vasquez & Taylor, 1999). In essence, the justice inherent in mutual aid increasingly identifies and defends individual rights:

> In the same instinct [mutual aid] we have the origin of those feelings of benevolence and of that partial identification of the individual with the group which are the starting-point of all the higher ethical feelings. It is upon this foundation that the higher sense of justice, or equity, is developed . . . In proportion as mutual aid becomes an established custom in a human community, and so to say instinctive, it leads to a parallel development of the sense of justice, with its necessary accompaniment of the sense of equity and equalitarian self-restraint.
>
> (Kropotkin, trans. 1924/1992, pp. 16, 30)

In other words, as natural selection increasingly cultivates mutual aid as a powerful instinct—no more noble an instinct, as Darwin suggests, than hunger —justice, with an inherent and individually beneficial balance of individualistic and collectivist tendencies, takes root. In Chapter 9 of this book, philosopher David Hume comes to a similarly non-idealistic finding: Justice is originally self-serving, stemming from and supporting self-interest.

Kropotkin's (trans. 1924/1992) synthesis of individualistic and collectivist tendencies culminates in his belief that justice provides the milieu in which individualism can flourish:

> [Ethics] tells man that if he desires to have a life in which all his forces, physical, intellectual, and emotional, may find a full exercise, he must once and forever abandon the idea that such a life is attainable on the path of disregard for others. It is only through establishing a certain harmony between the individual and all others that an approach to such complete life will be possible, says Ethics, and then adds: "Look at Nature itself! Study the past of mankind! They will prove to you that so it is in reality."
>
> (p. 25)

Within the synthesis that he envisions, however, Kropotkin (trans. 1924/1992) remains adamant that individualism and individual rights are not sacrificed to a utilitarian philosophy of the greatest good for the greatest number:

> The aim of ethics [is] to create such an atmosphere in society as would produce in the great number, entirely by impulse, those actions which best

lead to the welfare of all *and the fullest happiness of every separate being* . . . A most important condition which a modern ethical system is bound to satisfy is that it must not fetter individual initiative, be it for so high a purpose as the welfare of the commonwealth or the species.

(pp. 26, 27, emphasis added)

Rather, Kropotkin believes that the continuing emergence of justice, which unites members of society, fosters the continuing emergence of individual rights.

Kropotkin's synthesis of individualistic and collectivist tendencies thus forecasts and supports Holtzhausen's (2000) vision of a postmodern framework for public relations and society in which "a vibrant, participative democracy . . . reconciles freedom and justice" (p. 96). Throughout *Ethics: Origin and Development*, Kropotkin strives to explain this justice-driven synthesis of individualism and collectivism by placing it within a variety of clarifying contexts. He addresses, for example, the troublesome notion of enlightened self-interest and self-serving altruism that public relations and evolutionary biology scholars alike have condemned as an unworthy foundation for collectivism (Martinson, 1994; Baker, 1999):

There are actions which may be considered as absolutely necessary, once we choose to live in society, and to which, therefore, the name of "altru-istic" ought never to be applied: they bear the character of reciprocity, and they are as much in the interest of the individual as any act of self-preservation.

And there are, on the other hand, those actions which bear no character of reciprocity. One who performs such acts gives his powers, his energy, his enthusiasm, expecting no compensation in return, and although such acts are the real mainsprings of moral progress, they certainly can have no character of obligation attached to them. And yet, these two classes of acts are continually confused by writers on morality, and as a result many contradictions arise in dealing with ethical questions.

(Kropotkin, trans. 1924/1992, pp. 24–25)

Kropotkin's synthesis of individualism and collectivism thus moves beyond the simple compromise of reciprocity (e.g. "I'll be a good collectivist so that I may reap the benefits of enhanced individualism"). Rather, Kropotkin— again, like Darwin—holds that, primarily, humans assist one another because to deny that instinct is to deny who we are; to reject that instinct is to reject the impetus to mutual aid that natural selection has instilled within us. Darwin (1871/1998) writes that humans assist one another "in the same manner as the sense of hunger . . . induce[s] animals to eat" (p. 108), and Kropotkin (trans. 1924/1992) echoes that humans act as social beings "entirely by im-pulse" (p. 26).

Finally, Kropotkin (trans. 1924/1992) grounds his synthesis of individualism and collectivism in Darwin's assessment of the double tendency: "Darwin, who knew nature, had the courage boldly to assert that of the two instincts— the social and the individual—it is the social instinct which is the stronger, the more persistent, and the more permanently present. And he was unquestionably right" (p. 43). Derived from the processes of natural selection and innate instincts, Kropotkin's synthesis may reduce our ability to congratulate ourselves when we act selflessly, but it does have the virtue of defending the synthesis against charges of disingenuousness and naive optimism.

Beyond helping to resolve the individualism versus collectivism dichotomy within society, Kropotkin's (trans. 1924/1992) focus on justice and "self-restraint" (p. 30) echoes the two governing values of justice and self-control that characterize an Isocratean framework for public relations, detailed in Chapter 12 of this book. And as Chapter 8 will review, justice also has been identified as a core value for public relations by a variety of scholars, including L.A. Grunig, Toth, and Hon (2000), Holtzhausen (2000), Curtin and Boynton (2001), Marsh (2001), Leichty (2003), McKie and Munshi (2007), Bowen (2010), and Simmons and Walsh (2012). Kropotkin thus shows how a core value of public relations—justice—might serve to resolve an enduring individualistic/collectivist tension within the discipline.

Mixed-motive mutual aid

Kropotkin's status as a political philosopher—again, the individual who "without a doubt contributed more than anyone to the development of anarchist theory" (Morris, 2004, p. 13)—helps him address a third barrier to accepting social harmony, with its inherent cooperation, as a goal of public relations: The notion that cooperation and social harmony entail an unflaggingly accommodative stance toward all publics. Kropotkin's anarchistic rejection of centralized governments, indicates that, in defense of mutual aid, he preferred a mixed-motive approach to relationships:

> With all anarchists, Kropotkin believed that man is good and that external authority is evil. He differed from the main body of anarchists in his emphasis on the natural solidarity, as contrasted with the natural individualism, of men. This instinct is the subject of his best-known work, *Mutual Aid.* It was Kropotkin's deepest hope that a way could be found to bring city and country, factory and farm, into a harmonious working relationship. He was open-minded as to the means, insisting only that the state had to be abolished before any other measures could be undertaken.
>
> (Fried & Sanders, 1992, p. 345)

Fried and Sanders (1992) add, "[Kropotkin] was a first-rate geologist and naturalist, which may be the reason he later made it one of his chief tasks to reconcile Darwinism and anarchocommunism" (p. 344).

As we shall see, Kropotkin does not oppose all governments; he can, for example, accept a loose federalism that embraced the independence of smaller constituent communities (Berneri, 1942). Rather, he resists only "the crushing powers of the centralized State" (1902/1989, p. 292), a government form that he believes forcibly usurps the innumerable small enactments of mutual aid that characterized free and harmonious communities, thus fulfilling a powerful human instinct. To use the language of contingency theory, Kropotkin's concept of mutual aid clearly skews closer to cooperative accommodation than egoistic advocacy—but his rejection of harmonious relationships with centralized governments, coupled with his strong defense of individual rights, shows mutual aid to champion a mixed-motive philosophy. Mutual aid includes the right, again in the language of contingency theory, to "prohibit compromise with . . . a reprehensible public engaging in untruths founded on 'wrong' thinking" (Cancel et al., 1997, p. 34). As a theoretical foundation, thus, mutual aid does not anchor public relations' social harmony frameworks at an inflexible extreme of accommodative behavior.

For Kropotkin (1902/1989), the "all-absorbing authority of the State" undermined mutual aid through its aggressive aggregation of resources within two broad domains: "centralization of functions" and "territorial centralization" (pp. 224, 179). A persistent theme in his writings, for example, is the state's usurpation of the functions of workers guilds, forerunners of today's labor unions and professional associations (Mattelart, 1996): "The guilds were spoliated of their possessions and liberties, and placed under the control, the fancy, and the bribery of the State's official" (Kropotkin, 1902/1989, p. 226). In Kropotkin's (trans. 1924/1992) view, centralized governments—increasingly expanding in territory but contracting in the locus of power—operate in the interests of the rich and powerful: "Every State constitutes an alliance of the rich against the poor, and of the ruling classes, i.e., the military, the lawyers, the rulers, and the clergy, against those governed" (pp. 259–260). Kropotkin believes that the acquisitive, divisive nature of centralized governments is antithetical to the processes of mutual aid.

Kropotkin traces the historical origins of centralized states to three sources: Egoistic rulers who desired increased power, wealth, and territory (Kropotkin, 1902/1989, p. 205); "merchant aristocracy, which held the cities in the hollow of their hands, supporting alternately the Pope and the Emperor when they were striving for possession of a certain city" (Kropotkin, trans. 1924/1992, pp. 80–81); and, in particular, the Christian church, which—in Kropotkin's (1902/1989) view—having failed in its own attempts to establish a centralized state, gained power by endorsing the similar efforts of others:

The Christian Church, once a rebel against Roman law and now its ally, worked in the same direction. The attempt at constituting the theocratic Empire of Europe having proved a failure, the more intelligent and ambitious bishops now yielded support to those whom they reckoned upon for reconstituting the power of the Kings of Israel or of the Emperors of Constantinople. The Church bestowed upon the rising rulers her sanctity, she crowned them as God's representatives on earth . . .

(p. 217)

This combination of church and state, Kropotkin (1902/1989) maintains, views nongovernmental acts of mutual aid—such as the work of the guilds—as intolerable threats to their authority: "The Christian Church has aided the State in wrecking all standing institutions of mutual aid and support which were anterior to it, or developed outside of it" (p. 283). His unrestrained condemnation of centralized governments underscores again that, even for Kropotkin, the instinct for social harmony does not extend to accommodation with publics holding irrevocably opposed worldviews. His views on cooperation and harmony in the face of, in his opinion, an oppressive fusion of centralism and capitalism may fit well with the civil disobedience tactics of modern activist public relations.

Kropotkin does not condemn all forms of government—only those that, in quests to consolidate land and power, consciously undermine nongovernmental sources of mutual aid. He favors guilds and independent communities, confederated or not, as the historical models most conducive to mutual aid. Of early Venice, for example, he writes, "Each island was an independent political community. It had its own organized trades, its own commerce in salt, its own jurisdiction and administration, its own forum" (1902/1989, p. 180). Such governmental configurations, he believes, created

> a close union for mutual aid and support, for consumption and production, and for social life altogether, without imposing upon men the fetters of the State, but giving full liberty of expression to the creative genius of each separate group of individuals in art, crafts, science, commerce, and political organization.
>
> (1902/1989, p. 186)

Inherent in these communities were trade and professional guilds, organizations that established business standards and rules of commerce but also grew to foster other social norms such as the arts and methods of justice. Of this model, which he links to modern labor unions (Mattelart, 1996), Kropotkin (1902/1989) writes:

> It answered to a deeply inrooted want of human nature; and it embodied all the attributes which the State appropriated later on for its bureaucracy and police, and much more than that. It was an association for mutual support in all circumstances and in all accidents of life . . . and it was an organization for maintaining justice—with this difference from the State, that on all these occasions a humane, a brotherly element was introduced

instead of the formal element which is the essential characteristic of State interference.

(p. 176)

Kropotkin, however, is not dogmatic in his advocacy of the city-state and guild models. In *Mutual Aid* (1902/1989), he concludes that evolving forms of such models will "proceed from all of them, and yet be superior to them in [their] wider and more deeply humane conceptions" (p. 222). Such models, in fact, might include enlightened organization-public relationships, defined by Ledingham and Bruning (1998) as "the state that exists between an organization and its key publics that provides economic, social, political, and/or cultural benefits to all parties involved. . ." (p. 62).

Though modern evolutionary biologist Richard Dawkins (Chapter 6) echoes Kropotkin's belief in the natural-selection origins of cooperative behavior, he offers a directly antithetical view of central governments. According to Dawkins (2006a), such governments began, in part, as altruistic enterprises to further the aims of mutual aid:

Since we humans do not want to return to the old selfish ways where we let the children of too-large families starve to death, we have abolished the family as a unit of economic self-sufficiency, and substituted the state. But the privilege of guaranteed support for children should not be abused . . .

The welfare state is perhaps the greatest altruistic system the animal kingdom has ever known.

(pp. 117, 117–118)

Philosopher David Hume (Chapter 9) believes governments began, in part, as enforcers of justice, which had its origins in self-interested defense of personal property.

Resistance through cooperation and harmony

Though he does not discount the effectiveness or the likelihood of violence in addressing irreconcilable differences, Kropotkin (1995) favors resistance through harmony—that is, though a process of establishing, via "voluntary popular organization" (p. 99), an irresistible coalition of resistance united by mutual aid. In terms of resistance to centralized governments, for example, he declares:

We believe that if a revolution begins, it must take the form of a widely spread popular movement, during which movement, in every town and village invaded by the insurrectionary spirit, the masses set themselves to the work of restructuring society on new lines . . . without waiting for schemes and orders from above . . . The collective spirit of the masses is necessary for this purpose.

(1995, pp. 100, 101)

Kropotkin believes that a refusal to seek accommodation with forces of excessive competition is, like mutual aid itself, evolutionary. Resistance begins with "isolated individuals" who "little by little" grow into "small groups"; eventually, it becomes "impossible to remain indifferent: people [arc] compelled to declare themselves for or against the aims pursued by these individuals" (Kropotkin, 1995, p. 103). Such an approach would seem to follow the same lines as "coalition building" efforts within public relations (J.E. Grunig, 2000; Hallahan, 2001). Evolutionary biologist Martin Nowak has come to a similar conclusion in his computer-generated cooperation/ conflict games (Chapter 7): Determined pockets of cooperators can—as they assist one another—survive, thrive, and expand in hostile environments.

Similarly, Kropotkin (1902/1989) believes that the artificial imposition of the centralized state—guided by individualistic tendencies of its leaders— cannot forever resist the stronger force of the social instinct:

Neither the crushing powers of the centralized State nor the teachings of mutual hatred and pitiless struggle which came, adorned with the attributes of science, from obliging philosophers and sociologists, could weed out the feeling of human solidarity, deeply lodged in men's understanding and heart, because it has been nurtured by all our preceding evolution.

(p. 292)

Ethics and the social instinct

As we saw in Chapter 4, relationship-oriented ethics systems are inherent in public relations' social harmony frameworks. Darwin and Kropotkin, again, maintain that such ethics are an artifact of the social instinct, which itself, they agree, is born of self-interest and created by natural selection—hardly a normative, idealistic phenomenon. Kropotkin's *Ethics: Origin and Development* (trans. 1924/1992) amplifies their idea that "the social instinct is the common source out of which all morality originates" (p. 37). In that work, Kropotkin (trans. 1924/1992) writes, "Nature has thus to be recognized as the first ethical teacher of man. The social instinct, innate in men as well as in all the social animals,—this is the origin of all ethical conceptions and all the subsequent development of morality" (p. 45). Even earlier, in *Mutual Aid*, Kropotkin (1902/1989) concludes, "It is especially in the domain of ethics that the dominating importance of the mutual-aid principle appears in full. That mutual aid is the real foundation of our ethical conceptions seems evident enough" (p. 298).

Kropotkin's rich development of Darwin's much briefer gloss on ethics is particularly important given the direction of Thomas Henry Huxley's survey of the same territory. Unlike Darwin and Kropotkin, Huxley found the notion of ethics to be increasingly and oddly estranged from its origins in natural selection. For Huxley, in fact, mutual aid ultimately runs counter to the self-preservation intent of natural selection. In *Evolution and Ethics*—published 12 years after Darwin's death and so deprived of that colleague's direct and perhaps mitigating influence—Huxley explores what he viewed as a paradox. In the concept of ethics, which is "born of cosmic nature," he essentially sees natural selection as working against itself: "Cosmic nature is no school of virtue, but the headquarters of the enemy of ethical nature" (1897, pp. viii, 75). *Evolution and Ethics* is a 100-plus page essay of consternation over a contradiction that, a century later, Richard Dawkins (2006a) would explain, in part, by invoking genes and memes, defining a meme as "a unit of cultural transmission":

> We do not have to look for conventional biological survival values of traits like religion, music, and ritual dancing, though these may also be present. Once the genes have provided their survival machines with brains that are capable of rapid imitation, the memes will automatically take over . . . We have the power to defy the selfish genes of our birth and, if necessary, the selfish memes of our indoctrination . . . We are built as gene machines and cultured as meme machines, but we have the power to turn against our creators. We, alone on earth, can rebel against the tyranny of the selfish replicators [genes].
>
> (pp. 192, 200, 201)

For all his brilliance, however, Huxley did not have the ideas of genes and memes within his grasp, nor could he easily go as far as Darwin and Kropotkin (and, later, Gould, Wilson, and Nowak) in accepting cooperation as operating within the laws of natural selection to improve individual fitness. And so he struggles to understand the endurance of self-sacrificing ethics:

> I have termed this evolution of the feelings out of which the primitive bonds of human society are so largely forged . . . the ethical process. So far as it tends to make any human society more efficient in the struggle for existence with the state of nature, or with other societies, it works in harmonious contrast with the cosmic process. But it is none the less true that, since law and morals are restraints upon the struggle for existence between men in society, the ethical process is in opposition to the principle of the cosmic process, and tends to the suppression of the qualities best fitted for success in that struggle.
>
> (T.H. Huxley, 1897, p. 33)

Without Kropotkin's resolution of the double tendency of individual and collectivism—in which collectivism ultimately enhances individual freedoms —Huxley (1897) can explain an enduring ethical nature only by imagining a society that has eliminated individual strivings:

> I have endeavoured to show that, when the ethical process has advanced so far as to secure every member of the society in the possession of the means of existence, the struggle for existence, as between man and man, within that society is, ipso facto, at an end . . . In other words, the kind of evolution which is brought about in the state of nature cannot take place.
>
> (pp. 35–36)

But though he speculates that "the most highly civilized societies have substantially reached this position," he cannot accept the permanence of such a state given his vision of the workings of natural selection: "The universal experience of mankind testified then, as now, that, whether we look within us or without us, evil stares us in the face on all sides; that if anything is real, pain and sorrow and wrong are realities" (T.H. Huxley, 1897, pp. 36, 71).

On the evidence of *Evolution and Ethics*, Huxley is much closer to a "Nature, red in tooth and claw" (Tennyson, 1851, p. 80) vision of humans than either Darwin or Kropotkin. "Self-assertion . . . is the essence of the cosmic process," he writes, and this is a persistent theme within that work:

> Social progress means a checking of the cosmic process at every step and the substitution for it of another, which may be called the ethical process; the end of which is not the survival of those who may happen to be the fittest, in respect of the whole of the conditions which obtain, but of those who are ethically the best. As I have already urged, the practice of that which is ethically best—what we call goodness or virtue—involves a course of conduct which, in all respects, is opposed to that which leads to success in the cosmic struggle for existence.
>
> (T.H. Huxley, 1897, pp. 81–82)

An ethical human society, he concludes, is an "artificial world within the cosmos" (1897, p. 83).

And yet Huxley would have humans build that artificial society, struggling against the ways of the world. He believes, in the words of David Hume (1751/1983), that "there is . . . some particle of the dove, kneaded into our frame, along with the elements of the wolf and serpent" (p. 74):

> The conscience of man revolted against the moral indifference of nature . . . Laws and moral precepts are directed to the end of curbing the cosmic process and reminding the individual of his duty to the community . . . The cosmic process has no sort of relation to moral ends . . . Let us understand,

once for all, that the ethical progress of society depends, not on imitating the cosmic process, still less in running away from it, but in combating it.
(T.H. Huxley, 1897, pp. 59, 82, 83)

There is an irresistible parallel here to the thought of a modern scholar of public relations. In *Rethinking Public Relations* and related articles, Kevin Moloney characterizes the practices of public relations much as Huxley characterized the cosmic process. In asserting that "PR reflects and generates social competition, not harmony," Moloney uses such phrases as the "search for advantage and survival" in a "competitive environment" (2006, p. 14; 2005, p. 550). Like Huxley, however, Moloney (2006) is loath to accept this egoistic view of existence, and he recommends rebellion in the form of redress—"a subsidy, a transfer of PR productive resources from the resource rich to the resource poor":

A principal aim of [*Rethinking Public Relations*] is to argue for a PR system based on this idea of communicative equality, and for a funded, practical system of subsidy to ensure it . . . Communicative equality sets a minimum threshold for PR "voice," not a maximum. It does not limit free speech; it is a device to offer it to those not heard.

(p. 169)

For Huxley and Moloney, there is something within humans that rejects the inevitability of an egoistic status quo. Moloney, incidentally, has done more than merely recommend redress: At the risk of embarrassing him, I must note that as he and I were corresponding about an early draft of this book, he was donating his time and talents to a living-wage advocacy group in the United Kingdom.

Kropotkin's *Ethics: Origin and Development* is a direct response to Huxley's misreading, by Kropotkin's lights, of both Darwin and the evidence of history. Not altogether fairly, Kropotkin (trans. 1924/1992) charges that "Huxley . . . vacillates between the theories of coercion, utilitarianism, and religion, unable to find outside of them the source of morality" (p. 48). More to the point, he targets Huxley's narrow reading of the cosmic process:

The theory of evolution does not at all lead to the contradictions such as those to which Huxley was driven, because the study of nature does not in the least confirm the above-mentioned pessimistic view of its course, as Darwin himself indicated in his second work, "The Descent of Man."
(trans. 1924/1992, p. 13)

Far from casting mutual aid as a weakness that runs counter to individualistic self-preservation, Kropotkin (trans. 1924/1992)—like Darwin—maintains the opposite:

Without the continual growth of sociality, and consequently of the intensity and variety of sensations, life is impossible. Therein lies its essence. If that element is lacking life tends to ebb, to disintegrate, to cease. This may be recognized as an empirically discovered law of Nature.

(p. 20)

Earlier, in *Mutual Aid*, he states the case more bluntly:

We see that in the animal world, progressive development and mutual aid go hand in hand, while the inner struggle within the species is concomitant with retrogressive development.

(Kropotkin, 1902/1989, p. 296)

"The conceptions of . . . Huxley," he concludes, "are incomplete, one-sided, and consequently wrong" (Kropotkin, trans. 1924/1992, p. 13). The cosmic process need not be countered "by some extra-natural influence" (Kropotkin, trans. 1924/1992, p. 16).

Building upon Darwin, Kropotkin believes that our social instinct, which synthesizes individual and group needs, has been gathering strength over the eons. It is the source of our notions of ethics, and it is the increasingly powerful product, not the enemy, of natural selection:

It is already possible to conceive the history of mankind as the evolution of an ethical factor, as the evolution of an inherent tendency of man to organize his life on the basis of mutual aid, first within the tribe, then in the village community, and in the republics of the free cities,– these forms of social organization becoming in turn the bases of further progress, periods of retrogression notwithstanding . . . A striving for the general good is the distinguishing feature of every act which we call moral, and moral duty means being guided by the considerations of the general good.

(Kropotkin, trans. 1924/1992, pp. 17, 199)

New discoveries in neuroscience, in fact, add biological support for Kropotkin's fusion of the social instinct and ethics:

The link between empathy and our sense of right and wrong has support at the neural level . . . Brain areas active during moral judgments . . . include the amygdala, thalamus, insula, and upper brain stem. All these areas are involved, too, in perceiving someone else's feelings . . . An interconnected circuit running between the frontal lobe and the anterior temporal lobe (including the amygdala and the insular cortex) has been proposed as crucial for empathy.

(Goleman, 2006, p. 327)

Such support, however, is not with caveats. Again, though feminist philosopher Nel Noddings (2010) supports evolutionary biological explanations for social harmony, she also declares, "We would make a mistake to assume that, once we have uncovered the roots of morality in evolutionary events, we now have the whole story on morality" (p. 17).

Origins of cooperation

Kropotkin's theory of mutual aid expands the scientific foundation for envisioning cooperation as a means and social harmony as a legitimate goal of public relations. In tandem with Darwin's similar belief that natural selection favors intra-species cooperation over competition, the theory of mutual aid helps counter the notion that frameworks such as two-way symmetry, communitarianism, fully functioning society theory, and Isocratean rhetoric embrace an unrealistic, utopian ideal. Such frameworks may well have other flaws that call into question their legitimacy or practicality—but, in light of evolutionary biology, they are not excessively normative in seeking social harmony and positing cooperation as a powerful driver within human nature.

Traces of evolutionary biology, in fact, already seem to characterize discussions of the ways and means of public relations. Within public relations scholarship, challenges to social harmony frameworks often, consciously or otherwise, evoke natural selection to describe the inevitability of competitive, inharmonious views of relationships. Cameron, again, has defined public relations as the "strategic management of competition and conflict for the benefit of one's own organization—and when possible—also for the mutual benefit of the organization and its various stakeholders or publics" (Wilcox & Cameron, 2009, p. 7). Offering a different view of natural selection's impact on public relations, Brown (2003) holds that "Darwin's idea of adaptation was a useful way for public relations to frame its definition as adjustment" (p. 361). If we are to pursue such important injections of evolutionary biology into public relations, we should pursue them fully, casting wide the net to include the core belief of Charles Darwin and Peter Kropotkin that, in terms of sustainable human cultures, natural selection favors harmonious, not competitive, instincts and relationships. Indeed, a broader application of evolutionary biology within public relations research offers a scientific foundation for a goal of social harmony within public relations frameworks. Kropotkin (1902/1989), in fact, closes *Mutual Aid* with these words:

> In the practice of mutual aid, which we can retrace to the earliest beginnings of evolution, we thus find the positive and undoubted origin of our ethical conceptions; and we can affirm that in the ethical progress of man, mutual support—not mutual struggle—has had the leading part. In its wide extension . . . we also see the best guarantee of a still loftier evolution of our race.
>
> (p. 300)

With that closing declaration, Kropotkin reasserts his belief that Kant's (trans. 1836) enduring question regarding the origins of social duty—"Whence thy original? and where find we the root of thy august descent?" (p. 136)—could be answered, in the words of Darwin, "from the side of natural history" (Darwin, 1871/1998, p. 100).

Summary

Peter Kropotkin's analysis of mutual aid leads us to at least six important points for the understanding and practice of public relations:

1. Mutual aid is a more powerful instinct within social species than instincts of competition and conflict. Mutual aid has "the greatest importance for the maintenance of life, the preservation of each species, and its further evolution."
2. Mutual aid within social species is not antithetical to the processes of natural selection. Rather, cooperation is cultivated by natural selection; it is a strategic advantage for resource acquisition and survival.
3. The foundation of modern ethics—including public relations ethics—is the biological instinct, derived through natural selection, to harmonize individualistic and collectivist tendencies. Ethical behavior that accommodates the needs of others is, thus, not normative, idealistic, or contrary to human nature; it is, rather, the satisfying of an urge no less inherent, according to Darwin and Kropotkin, than hunger.
4. Individual autonomy cannot be sustained through disregard of others' needs. Conversely, social cooperation can be sustained only through honoring individual rights.
5. The social instinct for cooperation, derived through natural selection, engenders justice, which is an ongoing calibration of individual and collective rights. In free societies, a collectivist emphasis on justice ensures individual rights. Kropotkin's mutual aid philosophy thus addresses the seeming conflict within public relations between individual and collectivist tendencies.
6. Social cooperation does not mean invariable accommodation of publics with incompatible, or even hostile, values or intentions.

This point addresses six of the Nine Tenets of public relations' social harmony frameworks outlined in Chapter 1:

II. Cooperation is the relationship strategy best suited to resource acquisition. Evidence from evolutionary biology, philosophy, and rhetoric shows that, in general, cooperative relationships are more successful in sustained resource acquisition than relationships based on egoism, conflict, and competition.

III. Cooperative relationships are not merely normative, idealistic, or utopian. Rather, evidence from evolutionary biology, philosophy, and rhetoric shows that cooperation is a stronger instinct within human nature than the competing instincts of egoism, conflict, and competition.

IV. Justice begins in the social defense of resources, both our own and the resources of others. Based in self-interest, a quest for justice is not normative or contrary to human nature. Justice is inseparable from the processes of sustainable resource acquisition and thus is inherent within the processes of cooperation and public relations.

V. Biological and social tensions between individualism and collectivism are most sustainably resolved in favor of collectivism that defends individualism.

VI. Ethical behavior that accommodates the needs of others has enduring foundations in the biological and social origins of cooperation. Such behavior is not normative, idealistic, or contrary to human nature.

VII. Building relationships on the principles of cooperation and justice does not exclude the option of refusing to cooperate with hostile or destructive publics.

Chapter 6

Dawkins, Gould, and Wilson
The modern debate

A reassuring thing in the study of ethics is the agreement among Aristotle, Kant, and Mill that, above all else, humans seek happiness—and that to be happy, we must be ethical. On other matters, these philosophers can disagree so deeply that Mill (1863/1957) tears into Kant with a diatribe that begins "It is not my present purpose to criticize"—and then observes that Kant "fails, almost grotesquely" (p. 6) to prove the core elements of his philosophy. That three such different minds and such different approaches to ethics theory agree on the goal of human striving is heartening. They part company on ways and means, but all three philosophers agree that, in Kant's (trans. 1997) words, "happiness" is "the universal end" of humans (p. 43). That consensus—not to be taken for granted—gives powerful credibility to the shared belief, a belief that both Darwin (1887/1983) and Kropotkin (trans. 1924/1992), incidentally, echoed.

   A similar situation characterizes the current state of evolutionary biology: Three of the most honored and, in terms of publications, best-selling evolutionary biologists of the twentieth and twenty-first centuries—Stephen Jay Gould, Richard Dawkins, and Edward O. Wilson—profoundly disagree on the processes of evolution. To twist Mill's words, two of the three, in fact, seem to revel in having a *definite* purpose to criticize: In a notorious *New York Review of Books* article (to which we will return), Gould (1997a) writes, "Personal attack generally deserves silence by way of response" (para. 34)— but both he and Dawkins shun silence in personal attacks as well as responses. Like Darwin himself, Wilson has taken a higher road in response to personal criticism—which enhances the sting of his rare and understated retorts. And yet . . . Just as Aristotle, Kant, and Mill converge on happiness, Gould, Dawkins, and Wilson all champion the power of cooperation within evolutionary processes. Perhaps most telling, in the preface to the 30th anniversary edition of *The Selfish Gene*, Dawkins (2006a) speculates about what he might have titled that work had it been composed then, 30 years later, and concludes, "Another good alternative to *The Selfish Gene* [besides *The Altruistic Vehicle*] would have been *The Cooperative Gene*" (p. ix).

The central point of this chapter is simple and important: Three top evolutionary biologists—arguably, *the* three top evolutionary biologists of recent decades—who often bitterly disagree on fundamentals ranging from the workings of natural selection to the origins of human behavior do agree that humans are, increasingly, a cooperative species. Each of the three, as this chapter will show, believes that cooperation is a powerful drive within human nature that generally serves us more effectively than conflict. Again: That consensus—not to be taken for granted—gives compelling credibility to the shared belief. And the shared belief matters to the practice of public relations: As humans, our default position, particularly within our own overlapping networks and cultures, generally is not conflict and competition; it is cooperation.

For two reasons, the bulk of this chapter will review the areas of disagreement that provide such an effective backdrop for the consensus on cooperation. First, the disagreements help illuminate the ongoing debate of who, as humans, we are—and how we came to be who we are, how we came to be cooperators. To paraphrase Socrates in Plato's (trans. 1898) *Republic* (352D), this is no small matter we're examining: Rather, it's the revelation of what it means to be human. For public relations (or advertising or marketing or almost any profession), what could be a more important understanding? Second, just as with Aristotle, Kant, and Mill and their convergence on happiness, the identification of common ground in such a bare-knuckled debate should command our attention. For those reasons, this will be the longest and, perhaps, most important chapter in this book. After a review of the acrimonious disputes, the chapter will close with the biologists' general consensus that, in the words of Wilson's colleague Martin Nowak (Nowak & Highfield, 2011), "Previously, there were only two basic principles of evolution—mutation and selection . . . We must now accept that cooperation is the third principle . . . Cooperation is the master architect of evolution" (p. xviii).

Gould, Dawkins, and Wilson

Stephen Jay Gould (1941–2002) was the Alexander Agassiz Professor of Zoology at Harvard University, and, in his own words, was "an evolutionary and taxonomic biologist" (1990, p. 167) specializing in paleontology (Sterelny, 2007). (The professorship is named for the son of Darwin's opponent Louis Agassiz.) Gould wrote more than 20 books on evolution, many of them collections of his articles from the *New York Review of Books* and *Natural History Magazine*, culminating in the massive (the table of contents alone is 14 pages) *The Structure of Evolutionary Theory* (2002). As an author, Gould won a National Book Award (1981) and a Phi Beta Kappa Book Award (1983). In 2008, London's Linnean Society—the first group, in 1858, to hear of Darwin's and Wallace's theory of natural selection—posthumously awarded Gould the Darwin-Wallace Medal for "major advances in evolutionary biology" (Linnean Society of London, para. 1). In 1981, Gould was named a

MacArthur Foundation Fellow, the recipient of one of the foundation's "genius grants."

Richard Dawkins, also born in 1941, was the Charles Simonyi Professor for the Public Understanding of Science at the University Oxford, a position from which he retired in 2008. In his own words, he is an "ethologist" (ethology is the study of animal behavior) specializing in "zoology" (2006a, p. xxii). Dawkins has written more than 10 books on evolutionary biology, primarily three editions (as of 2016) of *The Selfish Gene*. He is a Fellow of the United Kingdom's Royal Society, arguably the world's leading scientific association, as well as the U.K.'s Royal Society of Literature. In 2006, Dawkins won the Lewis Thomas Prize for Writing about Science.

Edward O. Wilson, born in 1929, is a Pellegrino University Professor, Emeritus, at Harvard University. In his own words, he is a "myrmecologist" (Lenfield, 2011, p. 60); myrmecology is the study of ants. In 1990, Wilson won a Pulitzer Prize for General Nonfiction for *The Ants*, co-authored with Bert Hölldobler. In 1979, he won a second Pulitzer Prize for General Nonfiction for *On Human Nature*. Wilson (1975) coined the term *sociobiology* to signify "the systematic study of the biological basis of all social behavior" (p. 595) and, in 1975, wrote the first textbook for that new discipline. He has written more than 20 books on myrmecology, sociobiology, evolutionary biology, and related topics.

Units of selection

Of all of the achievements of *On the Origin of Species*, Darwin (1872) seemed most proud of natural selection—the "preservation of favourable individual differences and variations, and the destruction of those which are injurious" (p. 63). By the fifth edition of that work, Darwin had—at Wallace's urging (Irvine, 1955, p. 171)–adopted Herbert Spencer's phrase to describe natural selection: "the survival of the fittest."

But the fittest what? Fittest gene? Individual? Group? Species? More than any other dispute, the debate that surrounds this key question sends Gould, Dawkins, and Wilson to the barricades. "At stake," Dawkins (2012) explains, " is the level at which Darwinian selection acts" (p. 2).

For Dawkins (2006a), the answer is clear and narrow: The unit of selection is the gene, the selfish gene, a "replicator" (pp. 15, 19) that strives to send itself—via self-generated identical copies—into posterity. The correct word to emphasize in the title of *The Selfish Gene*, Dawkins (2006a) asserts, is *gene* (p. viii)—and he comes to this key point again and again in that book's early pages:

> I shall argue that the fundamental unit of selection, and therefore of self-interest, is not the species, nor the group, nor even, strictly, the individual.

> It is the gene, the unit of heredity . . . The basic unit of natural selection
> is best regarded not as the species, nor as the population, nor even as the
> individual, but as some small unit of genetic material which it is con-
> venient to label the gene.
>
> (pp. 11, 39)

Dawkins (2006a) even offers an argument-in-a-circle definition to ensure that
genes stand as the units of selection: "A gene is defined as any portion of
chromosomal material that potentially lasts for enough generations to serve
as a unit of natural selection"—a tautology that, later, he cheerfully acknowledges (p. 28).

Dawkins (2006a) also concedes that an "uneasy tension" troubles this vision
of natural selection: The gene as the true unit of selection versus Darwin's
logical focus on the individual organism (p. 234). (The concept of genetics
did not enter evolutionary theory until the rediscovery, in 1900, of Gregor
Mendel's earlier experiments in the 1850s and 1860s.) Dawkins' solution does
not flatter humans—or eagles or toadstools or even bedbugs, for that matter.
Each of those organisms, for Dawkins (2006a), is a "survival machine" (p. 44)
built by genes to increase their chances of launching copies into posterity.
Dawkins (2006a) deploys that particular phrase dozens of times throughout
The Selfish Gene:

> [Genes] merely change partners and march on. Of course they march on.
> That is their business. They are the replicators and we are their survival
> machines. When we have served our purpose we are cast aside. But genes
> are denizens of geological time: genes are forever.
>
> (p. 35)

As long as we understand that genes are the true units of selection, the drivers
and reasons for being of the vehicles, so to speak, Dawkins allows us to stretch
a point and think of individual organisms as units of selection.

That stretch, however, occurs within the persistent assertion of reductive
comparisons. Throughout *The Selfish Gene*, Dawkins (2006a) characterizes
individual organisms as "survival machines" (p. 35), "vehicles" (p. 254),
"robot vehicles blindly programmed to preserve the selfish molecules known
as genes" (p. xxi), "a colony *of genes*," referring to an individual body (p. 46),
and (my personal favorite) "gigantic lumbering robots" (p. 19). By my count,
the phrase *survival machine* appears 99 times in the third edition of *The Selfish
Gene*. When Dawkins (2006a) expresses personal "astonishment" (p. xxi) at,
himself, being a survival machine for selfish genes, Gould (2002) retorts, "I
can only regard this honest admission as a striking example of the triumph of
false consistency over legitimate intuition" (p. 619). Gould's sentence—
deliberately?—evokes a passage from Ralph Waldo Emerson that he had

quoted six years earlier in *Full House*: "A foolish consistency is the hobgoblin of little minds" (1996, p. 141).

Finally, Dawkins (2006a) painstakingly aligns his gene-centric view with traditional Darwinism:

> The selfish gene theory is Darwin's theory, expressed in a way that Darwin did not choose but whose aptness, I should like to think, he would instantly have recognized and delighted in. It is in fact a logical outgrowth of orthodox neo-Darwinism, but expressed as a novel image. Rather than focus on the individual organism, it takes a gene's-eye view of nature . . . [a] gene's-eye view of Darwinism.
>
> (pp. xv–xvi)

In other words, had Darwin only known of genes—and that was a concept he truly was envisioning (Irvine, 1955, pp. 171–175)—we might have avoided the uneasy tension between replicators and their robots as units of selection.

Gould (1997a) rejects this casting of Darwin's mantle over gene selection with language that typifies Gould/Dawkins clashes: It is "a hyper-Darwinian idea that I regard as a logically flawed and basically foolish caricature of Darwin's genuinely radical intent" (para. 8). Not that Gould (2002) supports Darwin's focus on the individual, however: "Supporters of hierarchy theory— and I am one . . .—are revising Darwinism into a multilevel theory of selection" (p. 136). Neuroscientist Donald Pfaff (Pfaff & Sherman, 2015) also supports the concept of multilevel selection.

Gould (2002) maintains that natural selection operates at six levels of entities, over time "banded together in a rising series of increasingly greater inclusion, one within the next" (p. 674). The six levels are genes, cells, organisms, demes (groups), species, and clades (a clade is a group of species with a common progenitor). Just as important, the processes of natural selection— because they are interacting with different materials—function differently at each level: "Hierarchical levels . . . cannot be reduced, one to the next below . . . New levels require an addition of principles; they neither deny nor contradict the explanations appropriate for lower levels" (Gould, 1990, p. 69). This multilevel theory of selection requires "unique explanatory principles emerging at each more inclusive plateau" (Gould, 1990, p. 218).

Gould's hierarchical approach, of course, offers the species as a unit of selection, an idea inherent in what is perhaps his greatest contribution to evolutionary biology, the concept of punctuated equilibrium—which, simply summarized, is evolution, particularly at the species level, by fits and starts rather than by gradual, steady accumulation of genetic variations over vast swathes of geologic time. Punctuated equilibrium will be discussed later in this chapter—and will, predictably, be fiercely disputed by Dawkins.

Gould's assertion that the processes of natural selection within one level of the hierarchy "cannot be reduced . . . to the next below" has become significant for continuing assessments of the prevalence and power of cooperation. Evolutionary biologists John Maynard Smith and Eörs Szathmáry (1997)identify eight key "evolutionary transitions" within the history of life, to date, on Earth, with each level engendering more complex workings of cooperation (p. 283). Their list begins with a self-replicating molecule preceding and enabling groups of such molecules and ending with early primate communities preceding and enabling human societies. In each level, "cooperation is instantiated and is necessary for each level of organic complexity"; each new level, in fact, displays "an intensification of cooperation" (Schloss, 2013, pp. 206, 209). "[A] very striking feature of the above major transitions," biologist Jeffrey Schloss (2013) asserts, "is that individual entities relinquish former capacities to survive and/or replicate on their own and come to require the aggregate" (p. 207). In the estimation of Gould (1990), Schloss (2013), and Clayton (2013), each new level also displays "property emergence"—the idea that "genuinely novel properties emerge in these complex systems," properties that are "irreducible" to previous levels (Clayton, 2013, p. 350). In this view of the hierarchy, human cooperation traces its origins almost to the beginning of life itself, yet its complexity and power are, by virtue of emergence, unique.

Dawkins (2006a) acknowledges hierarchical selection in general and species selection in particular—but only as "widely disseminated misunderstandings of Darwinism that originally provoked me to write [*The Selfish Gene*]" (p. viii). In comparatively restrained language, he states that species selection is "wrong . . . an erroneous assumption" (Dawkins, 2006a, p. 2).

Wilson embraces multilevel selection but, over his career, has placed increasing focus on group selection. In *The Social Conquest of Earth*, he writes:

> Substantial evidence now exists that human social behavior arose genetically by multilevel evolution . . . Selection at the individual level tends to create competitiveness and selfish behavior among group members— in status, mating, and the securing of resources. In opposition, selection between groups tends to create selfless behavior, expressed in greater generosity and altruism, which in turn promote stronger cohesion and strength of the group as a whole.
>
> (Wilson, 2012, pp. 273–274)

Wilson's individual-group conflict recalls Kropotkin's "double tendency" of humans toward both self-interest and cooperation (Chapter 5)—a conflict, again, that Kropotkin resolves by showing that, within societies, cooperation ultimately defends and subsumes self-interest. Chapter 9 of this book will examine David Hume's analysis of the same multilevel/double-tendency tensions, an inquiry that, from the perspective of philosophy, concurs with Kropotkin's later biological resolution in favor of cooperation.

Within multilevel selection, Wilson defends the presence and power of group selection more than either Gould or, certainly, Dawkins. "Hereditary altruists," he asserts, form groups so cohesive and cooperative that, within the processes of natural selection, they "outcompete" groups of self-interested individuals who battle one another for resources (Wilson, 2012, p. 166)—a point that Darwin (1871/1998) himself had made almost 150 years earlier (pp. 113, 137). "Human beings," Wilson (2012) declares, "are prone to be moral—do the right thing, hold back, give aid to others, sometimes even at personal risk—because natural selection has favored those interactions of group members benefitting the group as a whole" (p. 247). At the risk of breaking the thread of Wilson's focus on group selection, we should pause to appreciate this direct reference to an important theme of this book: Cooperation is not utopian, normative, or idealistic. In Wilson's estimation, cooperation is pure biology, the result of natural selection. "The instinct that binds [human groups] together," he states simply, "is the biological product of group selection" (Wilson, 2012, p. 57).

Both Wilson and Gould believe that Dawkins' gene-centric view of natural selection, which excludes group selection, suffers from confusion of effect and cause: A gene's ability to store traits favored by natural selection, they maintain, does not necessarily mean that the gene itself is the unit of selection. "One of the principles [of natural selection]," Wilson (2012) writes, "is the distinction between the unit of heredity, as opposed to the target of selection in the process that drives evolution" (p. 162). Gould (2002) is perhaps even clearer with his repeated portrayal, in *The Structure of Evolutionary Theory*, of the gene as bookkeeper: "[Dawkins'] false argument rests on a confusion of bookkeeping with causality . . . The error and incoherence of gene selectionism . . . can be summarized in a single statement illustrating . . .the central fallacy: Proponents of gene selectionism have *confused bookkeeping with causality*" (pp. 136, 632). Similarly, in Gould's (2002) reckoning, Dawkins "commits one of the classical errors in historical reasoning by arguing that because genes preceded organisms in time . . . genes must therefore control organisms" (p. 618).

Dawkins, again, is unmoved by the advocates of multilevel selection. Wilson's embrace of group selection, he laments, is a "weird infatuation" (Dawkins, 2008, p. 17) because anything beyond the gene is too ephemeral to be an enduring unit of selection:

> Genetically speaking, individuals and groups are like clouds in the sky or dust-storms in the desert. They are temporary aggregations or federations. They are not stable through evolutionary time . . . A population is not a discrete enough entity to be a unit of natural selection, not stable and unitary enough to be "selected" in preference to another population.
>
> (Dawkins, 2006a, p. 34)

In a particularly caustic review of Wilson's *Social Conquest of Earth* and its advocacy of multilevel selection, Dawkins (2012) characterizes group selection as a "poorly defined and incoherent view" and concludes, "Unfortunately one is obliged to wade through many pages of erroneous and downright perverse misunderstandings of evolutionary theory" (p. 1).

In one memorable sentence of that notorious review, Dawkins (2012) strikes two evolutionary biologists with one stone: "Biologists with non-analytical minds warm to multi-level selection: a bland, unfocussed ecumenicalism of the sort promoted by (the association may not delight Wilson) the late Stephen Jay Gould" (p. 2).

Wilson's above-the-fray response to the review noted that Dawkins' views were "archaic" (Dawkins, 2012, p. 4)—but, earlier, Gould typically had shown no reluctance to attack both Dawkins' influence and his intellect. "I haven't seen a picture of an animal in the leading journal of evolutionary ecology for years," he wrote in 1990 of his discipline's obsession with gene selection (Gould, 1990, p. 181). More than a decade later, in *The Structure of Evolutionary Theory*, he writes of "the fallacy of the selfish gene," calling it "a conceptual error . . .initiated by an error in reasoning" (2002, p. 613). Given these spates of conflict and vitriol, we might step back at this juncture to remember the focus of this chapter: These three distinguished evolutionary biologists, who disagree so dramatically and entertainingly on so much, do agree that cooperation, vis-à-vis egoism and conflict, generally offers profound competitive advantages in the struggle for resources and in the processes of natural selection.

I cannot resist a further digression at this point: Something about evolutionary biology seems to provoke venomous, eloquent, and highly enjoyable clashes among its disciples. There is Richard Owen's (1860) comment that Darwin's intellect was "not weighted or troubled with more than a discursive and superficial knowledge of nature" (p. 530)—and Huxley's parting shot, after successfully ridiculing Owen again and again: "Life is too short to occupy oneself with the slaying of the slain more than once" (Browne, 2002, p. 159). The aphorism attributed to former U.S. Secretary of State Henry Kissinger, among others, that academic politics are so bitter because the stakes are so low hardly applies here: From the vantage point of humans, the stakes of these evolutionary biology debates could scarcely be higher. But, for me, there remains guilty delight in reviewing the decades, dating at least to Darwin's generation, of *ad hominem* give and take. Cooperation no doubt is a more powerful force than egoism and conflict within species in general and humans in particular—but it would be foolish to deny the existence, productivity, and occasional pleasure of conflict. Of the three evolutionary biologists examined in this chapter, only Wilson approaches the general equanimity of Darwin, of whom one critic wrote, "He avoided controversy and practiced the British art of reticent and unprovocative statement" (Irvine, 1955, p. 102).

Kin selection

Stephen Jay Gould died before he could contribute his knowledge, passion, and wit to the kin selection debate that, beginning in 2010, ratcheted up the rhetoric of evolutionary biology. Since the mid-twentieth century, kin selection has been a primary explanation for what, again, has been termed "the problem of cooperation" (Axelrod, 2006, p. 3)—that is, the seemingly (though not actually) anti-Darwinian idea that some individuals are willing to help others even at a cost to themselves. The basic, gene-centric idea of kin selection—one that Gould (1977) tended to accept—is that close relatives (kin) will sacrifice to help one another because they share genes. Under the aegis of kin selection, an identical twin would be more likely, at some cost to herself, to aid her twin sister than to aid her spouse. The concept (some believe) rests on mathematical foundations: "For example, altruism will evolve if the benefit to a brother or sister is greater than two times the cost to the altruist ($R=1/2$) or eight times in the case of a first cousin ($R=1/8$)," with R signifying "the fraction of the genes shared between the altruist and the recipient due to their common descent" (Nowak, Tarnita, & Wilson, 2010, p. 1057). Kin selection is pivotal to a gene-centric view of natural selection; it can help explain the seemingly unselfish behavior of selfish genes.

By his own account, Wilson (2012) originally doubted kin selection, then embraced it as one of its foremost champions, including the theory in his Pulitzer Prize-winning *On Human Nature*. However, in an epochal article in *Nature* in 2010 [the prestigious journal co-founded in 1869 by Thomas Huxley], Wilson rejects kin selection as too flawed to accept as a force in evolution and as an explanation for cooperation. With evolutionary biologists Martin Nowak (a focus of Chapter 7 in this book) and Corina Tarnita as his co-authors, he examines the math of kin selection as well as its viability in the light of new studies and concludes, "Many empiricists, who measure genetic relatedness and use [kin selection] arguments, think that they are placing their considerations on a solid theoretical foundation. This is not the case" (Nowak, Tarnita, & Wilson, 2010, p. 1058–1059).

There may be a precise biological term for "and then all hell broke loose"— but the common expression suffices in this case. Dozens of evolutionary biologists protested, prompting *Nature*, in a subsequent issue, to publish a rebuttal article consisting of nothing but verbatim objections (as well as a response from Nowak, Tarnita, and Wilson). One protest, signed by dozens of evolutionary biologists, states, "We believe that [Nowak, Tarnita, and Wilson's] arguments are based upon a misunderstanding of evolutionary theory" (Abbot et al., 2011, p. E1). Another response charges that "Nowak et al. cherry-pick examples and . . . misrepresent relevant literature." That passage concludes, "Reports of the fall of [kin selection] theory have been greatly exaggerated" (Herre & Wcislo, 2011, p. E8).

Editors allowed Nowak, Tarnita, and Wilson to respond to the criticism in the same issue. "Several aspects of our paper are misrepresented," they wrote, adding that no one had successfully defended the mathematics of kin selection against their charges (2011, p. E9). Two years later, in *The Social Conquest of Earth*, Wilson (2012) added:

> The foundations of . . . kin selection have crumbled . . . The beautiful theory never worked well anyway, and now it has collapsed . . . Kin selection may occur, but there is no case that presents compelling explanation for its role as the driving force of evolution . . . Theorists . . .have argued that kin selection can be translated into group selection, even though that belief now has been disproved mathematically. More importantly, group selection is clearly the process responsible for advanced social behavior.
>
> (pp. 51, 175, 289–290)

Perhaps it was this advocacy of group selection that drew out Dawkins, although Wilson's (2012) concurrent reference to the author of *The Selfish Gene* as "a widely read champion of kin selection" (p. 171) may have irritated, given other honors that Wilson might have used to describe his fellow scientist.

Dawkins' review of *The Social Conquest of Earth* already has been cited above—but its most biting, personal comments are reserved for Wilson's rejection of kin selection. Accusing Wilson of "wanton arrogance" and a decades-long failure to understand the mechanics of kin selection, Dawkins (2012) closes the review with these words:

> As for the book under review, the theoretical errors I have explained are important, pervasive, and integral to its thesis in a way that renders it impossible to recommend. To borrow from Dorothy Parker, this is not a book to be tossed lightly aside. It should be thrown with great force. And sincere regret.
>
> (pp. 2, 4)

Wilson's calm response was that "the science in our argument has, after 18 months, never been refuted or even seriously challenged—and certainly not by the archaic version of [kin selection] from the 1970s recited . . .by Professor Dawkins" (Dawkins, 2012, p. 4). Wilson also corrected Dawkins' key assertion that the prominent scientists Robert Trivers and Steven Pinker had joined the rebuttals of the *Nature* article.

Additional areas of disagreement

Units of selection and kin selection are only the beginning of the debates that involve these three scientists. Gould and Dawkins, in fact, seem to take particular delight in disparaging the other's most significant contributions to current theories within evolutionary biology. For Gould, that would be punctuated equilibrium. For Dawkins, it would be the extended phenotype.

Punctuated equilibrium

Earlier, I defined punctuated equilibrium, perhaps too simply, as evolution, particularly at the species level, by fits and starts rather than by the gradual, steady accumulation of genetic variations over immense swathes of geologic time. Gould (2002) describes the concept in this way: "As a central proposition, punctuated equilibrium holds that the great majority of species . . .originate in geological moments (punctuations) and then persist in stasis [periods of virtually no change] throughout their long durations" (p. 766). In other words, evolution does *not* proceed as "a gradual accumulation of adaptations generated by organisms within a continuously evolving population" (1997a, para. 18). Gould (1997a) hastens to add that the "geological moments" of origin are vast expanses of time (para. 18). As a paleontologist, he supports punctuated equilibrium with evidence from the fossil record: "The fossil records of our evolutionary lineage [do] not support [a] story of continuous and inexorable advance" (1990, p. 212). Gould (2002), in fact, criticizes Darwin for a "strong, even pugnacious, defense of strict gradualism" (p. 151), which, of course, opposes the current fossil record and punctuated equilibrium. Gradualism was indeed, writes biographer Janet Browne (2006), "Darwin's underlying theme" (p. 67). Punctuated equilibrium strengthens Gould's (2002) belief that a species can be a unit of selection (pp. 644–646).

Dawkins (1996) counters punctuated equilibrium by holding that Darwin was not an extreme gradualist (p. 245), that Darwinian gradualism accommodates punctuation and stasis, and that Gould is overemphasizing a mundane idea. "The theory of punctuated equilibrium is a gradualist theory. . .," Dawkins (1996) asserts. "Gould has misled himself by his own rhetorical emphasis . . . The theory of punctuated equilibrium is a minor gloss on Darwinism" (pp. 244, 250). As for a fossil record that seemingly supports dramatic punctuated equilibrium, Dawkins (1996) holds that migration, not stasis and punctuation, can explain the lack of fossil evidence for gradual changes in organisms: "When we look at a series of fossils from any one place, we are probably not looking at an *evolutionary* event at all; we are looking at a *migrational* event, the arrival of a new species from another geographic area" (p. 240)—an opinion that Darwin shared (Irvine, 1955, p. 95).

Gould's response? Dawkins resents the success of punctuated equilibrium— which has, indeed, won widespread acceptance (Sterelny, 2007): "I should state upfront that I regard this discourse as rooted in little more than complex fallout from professional jealousy, often unrecognized and therefore especially potent" (Gould, 2002, p. 1000). One of Darwin's few attacks on his own critics was, in the *Autobiography* written only for "friends and family" (Browne, 2002, p. 427), to accuse Richard Owen, director of the British Museum, of becoming "my bitter enemy" because of "jealousy" at the success of *On the Origin of Species* (1887/1983, p. 61). In regard to Daniel Dennett, author of *Darwin's Dangerous Idea*, who has joined Dawkins in vigorously attacking punctuated equilibrium, Gould (2002) paraphrases a riposte from German philosopher Friedrich Schiller: *"Mit Dummheit kämpfen die Götter selbst vergebens"*—with stupidity, the gods themselves struggle in vain (p. 1009).

Wilson remains noncommittal on punctuated equilibrium, observing that several current theories explain the varying pace of evolution, but that there is "insufficient data to choose among them" (Ruse & Wilson, 1986, p. 175).

Extended phenotypes

In the 30th-anniversary edition of *The Selfish Gene*, Dawkins (2006a) concedes that his book *The Extended Phenotype* is "the book that, more than anything else I have achieved in my professional life, is my pride and joy" (p. 234). He adds, "It is probably the finest thing I shall ever write" (2006a, p. xvii). Careful readers of this chapter may, perhaps, already be speculating about how Gould might use this admission.

A phenotype, in Dawkins' (2006a) words, is "the bodily manifestation of a gene, the effects that a gene . . . has on the body" (p. 235). An extended phenotype extends beyond the body, beyond a single gene-driven organism:

> The phenotypic effects of a gene are normally seen as all the effects that it has on the body in which it sits. This is the conventional definition. But we shall now see that the phenotypic effects of a gene need to be thought of as *all the effects that it has on the world* . . . Examples that spring to mind are artefacts like beaver dams, bird nests and caddis houses [a caddis is a fly that, with materials from its immediate environment, builds a shell-like cover for itself].
>
> (Dawkins, 2006a, p. 238)

An extended phenotype can even encompass the bodies of other organisms as genes "reach outside their 'own' body to influence phenotypes in other bodies" (Dawkins, 2006a, p. 243). For Dawkins (2006a), however, the extended phenotype remains a gene-centric concept, with the gene "sitting at the centre of a radiating web of extended phenotypic power" (p. 265).

Gould and Wilson are of a different mind. Both see the extended phenotype, Dawkins' pride and joy, as a muted or perhaps unwitting acceptance of multilevel selection. Wilson's pronouncement of this acceptance is typically scholarly. With David S. Wilson (no relation), he writes, "Dawkins . . . envisioned selfish gene theory and the concept of extended phenotypes as arguments against group selection but, in retrospect, they are nothing of the sort" (Wilson & Wilson, 2007, p. 335). In *The Leafcutter Ants*, with Bert Hölldobler, Wilson observes, "There has been increasing acceptance of the view that the entire [ant] colony represents an extended phenotype of the queen and her mates on which evolutionary selection operates" (2011, p. 9).

Dawkins utterly rejects the idea that the extended phenotype is a backdoor to group selection. "Do groups have phenotypes, which might qualify them to count as gene vehicles?" he asks. "Convincing examples are vanishingly hard to find" (2012, p. 3).

Gould's response to the extended phenotype is a masterful passage of smash-mouth rhetoric. In one paragraph, he uses Dawkins' favorite work to undermine his most popular work—and caps the insult by using Dawkins' most significant contribution to modern digital culture, the meme (a term Dawkins created in *The Selfish Gene*):

> I do not know why Dawkins altered his view so radically. But may I suggest that he simply could not—because no one can after a proper analysis of the basic logic of the case—maintain full allegiance to the fallacious argument of strict gene selectionism . . . With such an admission, the selfish gene becomes an impotent meme.
>
> (2002, p. 641)

Adaptation

Many of the remaining disputes among Gould, Dawkins, and Wilson revolve around concept of adaptation, an idea that encompasses the Modern Synthesis, sociobiology, evolutionary psychology, and the role of culture in evolution. In *Sociobiology*, Wilson (1975) offers this definition of *adaptation*:

> In evolutionary biology, any structure, physiological process, or behavioral pattern that makes an organism more fit to survive and to reproduce in comparison with other members of the same species. Also, the evolutionary process leading to the formation of such a trait.
>
> (p. 578)

Gould's enduring concern with adaptation stems from a fusion of these two definitions: The idea that natural selection shaped all existing and useful features for their present functions. He ridicules that extreme position by comparing it to Dr. Pangloss' panegyric on the nose in Voltaire's *Candide*: "Our noses were made to carry spectacles, so we have spectacles" (Gould, 1990, p. 206). For Gould (1990), the inherent sin of extreme views of adaptation is "the confusion of current utility with historical origin" (p. 35). He scorns any theory that holds that, over eons, natural selection gradually (there's that word again) shaped all existing features precisely for their current uses. In her biography of Charles Darwin, Browne (2002) notes that Darwin himself struggled with the word *adaptation*, which "hinted at some form of purposeful strategy in animals and plants, the exact opposite of what he meant" (p. 59).

Gould (1991a) counters extreme views of adaptation with the concept of exaptation, which he defines as "a feature, now useful to an organism, that did not arise as an adaptation for its present role, but was subsequently co-opted for its current function" (p. 43). Exaptations, he adds, "were not built by natural selection for their current role" (Gould, 1991a, p. 47). Spandrels—yet another Gould coinage (with Lewontin, 1979)—are exaptations that began as by products of true adaptations:

> According to Gould . . .exaptations come in two types. In the first type, features that evolved by selection for one function are co-opted for another function . . . The feathers of birds first having evolved for thermal regulation but then later co-opted for flight is an example . . . In the second type, "presently useful characteristics did not arise as adaptations . . .but owe their origin to side consequences of other features" (Gould, 1991[a,] p. 53). Gould called such side effects of the organism's architecture "spandrels." The term *spandrels* is an architectural term that refers to the spaces left over between structural features of a building. The spaces between the pillars of a bridge, for example, can subsequently be used by homeless persons for sleeping, even though such spaces were not designed for providing such shelter.
>
> (Buss, Haselton, Shackelford, Bleske, & Wakefield, 1998, p. 539)

Centuries earlier, Aristotle anticipated exaptations with his concept of accidental final causes. In *Physics*, he wrote:

> Of the "ends" actually achieved, some are those we aimed at, but some are not. In this latter case our actions were as a fact making for the uncontemplated result just as much as if it had been intended; so that an action may actually "serve a purpose". . . which it was not intended to serve.
>
> (trans. 1934, 196b)

Though Dennett (1995) ridicules Gould for failing to offer a precise definition of spandrel and failing to understand the exact architectural nature of the term (p. 275), Dawkins and Wilson generally agree that current utility need not always be the result of careful grooming by natural selection over the eons. Wilson (2012) speculates that human consciousness was not designed for its current function of self-analysis (pp. 8–9), and Dawkins (2006a) confesses to being "dissatisfied" with colleagues who seek historic-fitness origins for every aspect of civilization (pp. 189–190). It is only when Gould uses the overemphasis on adaptation to attack what he views as excessively gradualist or biological explanations of human behavior that Wilson and Dawkins resist. Again, those flashpoints include the Modern Synthesis, sociobiology, evolutionary psychology, and the role of culture in evolution.

The Modern Synthesis

Julian Huxley, the grandson of Darwin's bulldog, Thomas Henry Huxley, coined the term *Modern Synthesis* to denote the integration of Mendelian genetics into Darwinian natural selection—and, consequently, the grouping of all biological disciplines within this enriched understanding of evolution (Gould, 2002, p. 503). Darwin's inability to explain the source of the variation necessary for natural selection had led the prominent botanist William Henry Harvey, in 1860, to assert a divine origin (Browne, 2002, p. 110). The science of genetics offers a source for variation, and the synthesis has become one of the core ideas in modern evolutionary biology. "No biologist would dream of disregarding the evidence" for it, Browne (2006) asserts (p. 153)—but in 1980, Gould pronounced it "dead" (p. 120). He actually accepted the Modern Synthesis so long as it remained a "pluralist" concept with flexible ideas about adaption. In publishing its death notice, however, he charged that the Modern Synthesis had "hardened" into an inflexible insistence on the linkage of steady, gradual adaptation to current usage:

> Under the orthodoxy of the "hardened" version of the Modern Synthesis, biologists became so accustomed to regarding all evolutionary change as adaptation directed by natural selection that they lost sight of the importance, or even the existence, of an undeniable corollary—that many (indeed most) features, as a consequence of quirky functional shift, do not reveal their original evolutionary context in their current utility.
>
> (2002, pp. 1232–1233)

Gould (2002) concedes that consigning the Modern Synthesis to the graveyard of biological ideas was excessive—but only, he adds, because it enraged some readers to the point of being unable to calmly digest his true concerns about the hardening (p. 1003).

Wilson quietly but clearly disagreed with Gould's obituary for the Modern Synthesis. Earlier, in the first chapter of *Sociobiology*, he wrote that one aim of sociobiology was "to reformulate the foundations of [sociology and the social sciences] in a way that draws these subjects into the Modern Synthesis" (1975, p. 4)—and that passage has remained in newer editions that follow Gould's announcement of the death of the synthesis. (The subtitle of *Sociobiology* is, in fact, "The New Synthesis.") Dawkins holds that Gould has no choice but to reject the Modern Synthesis because of its emphasis on gradualism. Gradualism, again, runs counter to Gould's belief in punctuated equilibrium, a theory that Dawkins (1996) characterizes with three words: "quite probably wrong" (p. 248). "All sensible evolutionists," he concludes, accept gradualism (Dawkins, 1996, p. 224).

Sociobiology

Edward O. Wilson essentially invented sociobiology, defining it and giving it a mission. As noted earlier in this chapter, in Wilson's eyes sociobiology is the exploration of the biological foundations of social behavior; its consequent mission, in part, is to pull the social sciences into the Modern Synthesis. Wilson's further definition of the discipline in the final chapter of *Sociobiology* may add clarity—but it prompts Gould to include sociobiology in the list of aspects of evolutionary biology that, for him, grossly distort the power and importance of adaptation. In Chapter 27, the final chapter of *Sociobiology*, Wilson (1975) writes:

> It is the task of comparative sociobiology to trace . . .human qualities as closely as possible back through time. Besides adding perspective and perhaps offering some sense of philosophical ease, the exercise will help to identify the behaviors and rules by which individual human beings increase their Darwinian fitness through the manipulation of society.
>
> (p. 548)

In the sentences that follow this passage, Wilson notes the need to examine a gray area between the gradualist adaptive origins and the cultural origins of modern human behavior—but this chapter-opening focus on historical/biological origins of current human qualities suffices to call down Gould's wrath.

"Most of *Sociobiology* wins from me the same high praise almost universally accorded it," Gould (1977) begins—before adding, "But Wilson's last chapter . . .leaves me very unhappy indeed" (p. 252). The sources of his unhappiness are related and predictable: A hardened view of adaptation, in his estimation, and an overemphasis on genes, particularly in the development of human behavior. Just as Darwin had delayed publicly analyzing the processes of natural selection within the human species until *The Descent of Man*, which followed *The Origin of Species* by 12 years, Wilson had largely delayed applying the principles of sociobiology to humans until the final chapter of *Sociobiology*. "Gould thinks these ideas are dangerous and ill-motivated as well as wrong," Sterelny (2007) summarizes in *Dawkins vs. Gould*. "They smack of hubris, of science moving beyond its proper domain, and incautiously at that" (p. 166). And then Sterelny (2007) adds—as if we couldn't guess—"Dawkins does not concur" (p. 166).

Gould's (1990) first objection to the application of sociobiological principles to humans addresses an overemphasis on adaptation—the familiar "confusion of current utility with historical origin . . . The false equation of one with the other is, in my view, the Achilles heel of human sociobiology" (p. 35). His second, related objection—aimed at both Wilson and Dawkins—is his longstanding rejection of genes as super-powerful free agents:

Wilson concludes with an extended speculation on the genetic basis of supposedly universal patterns in human behavior . . . I am disturbed by the erroneous idea that genes are discrete and divisible particles, using the traits that they build in organisms as weapons for their personal propagation . . . The bits have not meaning outside the milieu of their body, and they do not directly code for any bounded piece of morphology or any specific behavior.

(Gould, 1977, pp. 252, 269)

"Behavior that works," Gould (1990) writes elsewhere, "need not have a specific genetic ground" (p. 35).

Wilson, as we shall see in the forthcoming discussion of culture's role in developing modern humans, does not believe genes are the sole determinants of human behavior. But almost 40 years after the first edition of *Sociobiology*, he still asserted that "even the most complex forms of human behavior are ultimately biological" (2012, p. 288). Dawkins (2006a) —perhaps pleased to see Gould's ire directed elsewhere—finds *Sociobiology* to be "admirable," disputing only Wilson's contention in that book that kin selection is subsumed within group selection (p. 94). Dawkins, as we know, supports the first concept and rejects the second.

Evolutionary psychology

Both Wilson (2012, p. 169) and Gould agree that evolutionary psychology is, in words Gould (1997b) borrowed from Darwin, "descent with modification" from sociobiology (para. 24). Buss' (1995) description of the new science, in a *Psychological Inquiry* article cited more than 1,300 times by 2016, almost ensures a forthcoming attack from Gould: "A central premise of evolutionary psychology is that the main nonarbitrary way to identify, describe, and understand psychological mechanisms is to articulate their functions—the specific adaptive problems they were designed by selection to solve" (p. 6). The sentiment of the final 11 words, the words following the dash, escort almost everything Gould detests in sociobiology into evolutionary psychology. "This adaptationist premise is the fatal flaw of evolutionary psychology in its current form," Gould (1997b) declares in the *New York Review of Books* (para. 33).

In rejecting adaptationist evolutionary psychology, Gould (1997b) revives a concept that he, with Lewontin, had created to counter the Panglossian nose aspects of the Modern Synthesis:

Many, if not most, universal behaviors are probably spandrels, often coopted later in human history for important secondary functions . . . The human brain must be bursting with spandrels that are essential to human nature and vital to our self-understanding but that arose as nonadaptations, and are therefore outside the compass of evolutionary psychology . . .

(paras. 42, 43)

Just as with sociobiology, however, Gould doesn't reject the entire premise of evolutionary psychology—just its hardening into rigid determinism. Again like Aristotle (trans. 1934) in *Physics* (195b), Gould (1990) posits the idea of biological *potentiality* as an alternative to evolutionary psychology's tendency toward biological *determinism* (pp. 113–114; 1997, p. 251). Such a substitution, he maintains, could transform this evolution of sociobiology into "a fruitful science" (Gould, 1997b, para. 4).

Perhaps surprisingly, Wilson (2012) tips close to agreeing with Gould (and Aristotle) when he writes that "human nature is not the genes underlying it. They prescribe the developmental rules of the brain . . . Behaviors are learned, but the process is what psychologists call 'prepared'" (pp. 192, 194). A favorite word with Wilson (2012) is *springloaded*, signifying a biological predisposition to move, in terms of the structure of body and mind, in certain directions (pp. 47–48). Against this seeming acceptance of potentiality versus determinism, however, we must set Wilson's (2012) adaptation-oriented comments that "behavioral traits defining each species. . . are hereditary . . . Even the most complex forms of human behavior are ultimately biological" (pp. 158, 288). Dawkins, of course, was an early champion of evolutionary psychology, lending support even before the discipline had acquired that name. In *The Selfish Gene*, first published in 1976, Dawkins (2006a) wrote, "By dictating the way survival machines and their nervous systems are built, genes exert ultimate power over behaviour" (p. 60).

Gould's rejection of gene-centered evolutionary psychology did spark the now-familiar and entertaining fireworks, though not primarily from Wilson or Dawkins. In their response to Gould's charge, in the *New York Review of Books*, that they were narrow-minded Darwinian fundamentalists, David Dennett, author of *Darwin's Dangerous Idea*, and Robert Wright, author of *The Moral Animal*, entered the arena. "Gould labors to create a caricature of the 'strict' adaptationist, a type that occurs nowhere in nature and is explicitly disavowed, at length, by me [in] *Darwin's Dangerous Idea* and elsewhere," Dennett (1997) contends (para. 4). "Gould had failed to grasp basic principles of evolutionary psychology (and, apparently, hadn't actually read my book)," Wright (1997) adds (para. 2). Gould's (1997c) response? "Dennett may bluster, but Wright is more pathetic" (para. 6) He concludes by tweaking Huxley's attack on anti-evolutionist Richard Owen: "Life is just too short for occupying oneself with the slaying of the slain more than twice" (1997c, para. 8).

The role of culture in evolution

If social cultures play a role in the development of human behavior—particularly behavior that enhances the survival odds of related genes, individuals, groups, and species—then extreme, hardened forms of adaptation, socio-biology, and evolutionary psychology cannot be accurate. As Gould (1990) says of Wilson's relatively new discipline, "The central flaw in sociobiology results from this Darwinian premise: The behaviors that the theory purports to explain must be interpreted as adaptations of organisms" (p. 30)—with the definition of adaptation, again, skewing toward historical, biological origins of current features. Gould, Wilson, and Dawkins do agree, of course, that social cultures play a role in shaping human behavior. The comparatively mild disputes among the three involve the extent of social culture's role; whether culture's effects are narrowly adaptive; and how much the recognition of culture's role damages the concepts of sociobiology and evolutionary psychology.

Gould (1990) describes the interplay of culture and biology in the shaping of human behavior as a "dialectic" in which neither influence has priority or unmatched power (p. 153). He rejects the "stupefying sterility of nature-nurture arguments" and asserts that the only question in the argument is "the degree, intensity, and nature of the constraint exerted by biology upon the possible forms of social organization" and the related human behaviors (Gould, 1990, pp. 148, 113). And just as he insisted that each new level of the various units of selection renegotiates the processes of natural selection, he holds that cultural evolution "needs laws of its own" (Gould, 1990, p. 70), not those of any previous unit of biological selection.

In this general approach, Gould finds a surprising ally in Richard Dawkins, creator of the concept of the meme. For Dawkins (2006a), a meme is "a unit of cultural transmission, or a unit of *imitation*" (p. 192). (In Chapter 12, we will see Isocrates also emphasize the power of imitation/*mimesis* over human behavior and cultural-constructive processes.) "Examples of memes," Dawkins (2006a) continues, "are tunes, ideas, catch-phrases, clothes fashions, ways of making pots or building arches" (p. 192); Nowak (Nowak & Highfield, 2011) cites "the concept of Darwinian evolution" as a meme "leaping from the mind of one biologist to infect another" (p. 269). And while, for Dawkins (2006a), the gene reigns supreme in biologically sourced evolution, he acknowledges, as does Gould, the role of memes and cultures in human development: "I am an enthusiastic Darwinian, but I think Darwinism is too big a theory to be confined to the narrow context of the gene" (p. 190). Lest this seem to be too large a step toward Gould and away from the supremacy of genes, Dawkins (2006a) quickly notes the genetic origins of memes: "Once the genes have provided their survival machines with brains that are capable of rapid imitation, the memes will automatically take over" (p. 200). Finally, like Gould, Dawkins (2006a) believes that memes and their role in culture as a source of human evolution must operate within their own laws, not within those of biology:

> I think we have got to start again and go right back to first principles . . . The old gene-selected evolution, by making brains, provided the soup in which the first memes arose. Once self-copying memes had arisen, their own, much faster, kind of evolution took off. We biologists have

assimilated the idea of genetic evolution so deeply that we tend to forget that it is only one of many possible kinds of evolution.

(pp. 191, 194)

Martin Nowak (Nowak & Highfield, 2011) adds that, like genetic evolution, mimetic evolution both generates and is affected by cooperation (p. 11).

Gould's relative silence regarding Dawkins's concept of the meme and its role would seem to indicate agreement. Throughout his writings, his few references to memes seem to accept the concept but use it (with an attached pejorative) to ridicule Dawkins' pet beliefs. Examples include the extended phenotype as "an inadaptive meme" and, as we saw earlier, the selfish gene as "an impotent meme" (2002, pp. 632, 641).

Wilson (2012) initially appears to follow Dawkins in approaching Gould's understanding of the biology-culture dialectic—that is, a recognition that biology, via the brain's "complex inherited architecture" has made humans particularly susceptible to cultural influences and the interplay of genes and culture (p. 217). Both Wilson and Dawkins, in fact, agree that cultural influences can overpower—"smother," in Wilson's (2012) language—genetic influences (p. 197). In the estimation of Wilson, with co-author Charles J. Lumsden (1983), the two influences can intertwine to form "culturgens," or products of "gene-culture coevolution" (pp. 118, 121). And at this point, Gould (1990) asserts, the counterproductive hardening of the culturgen begins:

[Lumsden and Wilson's] analysis then traces the spread of each culturgen, considered independently, via the adaptive force of natural selection . . . [However], the adaptive analysis of culturgens cannot unlock their meaning, since most did not arise for adaptive reasons and are not, therefore, "items" for Darwinian analysis.

(pp. 120, 122)

Lumsden and Wilson's historical-biological analysis of culturgens has, for Gould, transformed those phenomena into new manifestations of Pangloss' nose. And Gould (1990) has one more attack: Wilson's advocacy of "gene-culture coevolution," he writes, is a corrective, a backpedaling response to the charge that *Sociobiology* "ignored culture for a crude form of genetic determinism" (p. 107). In Wilson's 2004 edition of the Pulitzer Prize-winning *On Human Nature*, he still held that "genes hold culture on a leash" (p. 167).

One important addendum before we turn, finally, to our three evolutionary biologists' analyses of cooperation: The scope and the passion of the debates among the three do not undermine their belief in the concept of evolution—of descent, with modification, over time. They disagree on the specific mechanics of the processes, but not on the fact of evolution itself. Their well-documented differences in no way defeat this mainstay idea of biology.

In the words of evolutionary biologist David Barash (2015), a professor of psychology and biology at the University of Washington:

> Changes in scientific insights have also provided opportunities for male-factors to sow undeserved doubt. Creationists point to the shifting intel-lectual dynamic between advocates of phyletic gradualism (evolution proceeds slowly) and punctuated equilibrium (sometimes it is rather fast), as showing that Darwinism is seriously in doubt. It isn't; specialists merely disagree as to the rates at which evolution by natural selection occurs, not *that* it occurs. Ditto for controversy over whether the meaningful unit of selection is the gene, the individual, or even the group.
>
> (para. 27)

In no way do I mean for this chapter to cast doubt on Charles Darwin's remark-able insights into our essence and origins.

The consensus on cooperation

In this chapter, we have taken a long, important, and, I hope, interesting path to a final consensus that we'll now explore: The best minds in modern evolu-tionary biology, who disagree so vocally on so much, agree that, as humans, we are cooperators. In the language of Wilson's colleague Martin Nowak, we are, in fact, "SuperCooperators" (Nowak & Highfield, 2011, p. 283). Our urge to cooperate, our willingness to make sacrifices to help others, is not utopian, normative, or idealistic. If we wish to, we can view and defend cooperation as purely materialistic, arising—according to the contentious trio of Gould, Dawkins, and Wilson—though some fusion of biology, culture, history, and sheer human reflection (a relatively recent human capacity) on what works and what doesn't.

Given his enduring advocacy of group selection and the title of *The Social Conquest of Earth*, Edward O. Wilson is the least surprising champion of cooperation among the three evolutionary biologists featured in this chap-ter. As he writes in *The Social Conquest of Earth*, "Colonies of cheaters lose to colonies of cooperators" (Wilson, 2012, p. 163). Humans, Wilson (2012) asserts, are one of our planet's few truly "eusocial" species, with that pre-cise biological term denoting a species that consists of communities of "group members containing multiple generations and prone to perform altruistic acts as part of their division of labor" (p. 16). Human eusociality is "based on cooperation among individuals or groups" (Wilson, 2012, p. 17). That cooper-ation, particularly as a species enters new or increasingly competitive environ-ments, is "more important" for survival than "competition among group members" (Wilson, 2012, p. 224). In this assertion Wilson again echoes the findings of Peter Kropotkin (Chapter 5): Mutual aid among humans is a more powerful force in survival of the fittest than mutual struggle. Once eusociality took root in human societies, "it could no longer be displaced by a solitary lifestyle" (Nowak & Highfield, 2011, p. 166).

For Wilson (2012), true altruism within humans not only exists: Stemming from biological, not idealistic, origins, altruism is an evolving cause of the continued survival and development of the species: "Authentic altruism is based on a biological instinct for the common good of the tribe, put in place by group selection, wherein groups of altruists in prehistoric times prevailed over groups of individuals in selfish disarray" (p. 251). Wilson (2012) further believes that, over time, altruism evolves from an unconscious instinct to a conscious ethical goal:

> Beyond the ordinary instincts of altruism, there is something more, delicate and ephemeral in character but, when experienced, transformative. It is *honor*, a feeling born of innate empathy and cooperativeness. It is the final reserve of altruism that may yet save our race.
>
> (p. 251)

In this belief, he concurs with the philosophers Aristotle (Chapter 8) and David Hume (Chapter 9) and the rhetorician Isocrates (Chapter 12): Over time, human altruism, without sacrificing its biological moorings, evolves into an ethical imperative. For Wilson, the cooperation inherent in our human nature is the key to the survival of our species.

Though not protracted, Stephen Jay Gould's strong endorsement of cooperation is extraordinary for two reasons: First, he agrees with (rather than eviscerates) another evolutionary biologist; and, second, he—Stephen Jay Gould —presents cooperation as a possible example of his bête noir, as an example of gradualist, biological adaptation. Earlier, in Chapter 5, we saw Gould endorse Kropotkin's (1902/1989) philosophy of mutual aid, with its core tenet that "besides the law of Mutual Struggle there is in Nature the law of Mutual Aid, which, for the success of the struggle for life, and especially for the progressive evolution of the species, is far more important than the law of mutual contest" (p. xxxviii). Again, of that belief Gould (1991b) concludes, "The central logic of Kropotkin's argument is simple, straight-forward, and largely cogent . . . In fact, I would hold that Kropotkin's basic argument is correct" (pp. 334, 338). Shunning an unrealistic idealism, however, Gould (1990) further agrees with Kropotkin that the comparative strength of cooperation does not mean the dawn of "a nirvana of self-benefiting cooperation" (p. 228). Gould (1990) sees " no intrinsic bar to a decent life for all, but I doubt that we will ever escape sacrifice, struggle, and compromise" (p. 228). Recognizing the superior power of the cooperative aspects of human nature, in other words, does not mean a utopian cessation of conflict and competition.

Gould's case for cooperation includes one of the most remarkable concessions in this chapter, perhaps in this entire book. Gould's acutely sensitive resistance to viewing any aspect of the human body or human behavior as a clear, case-closed example of adaptation leads him to attack such staples of evolutionary biology as the Modern Synthesis, sociobiology, and evolutionary psychology, as well as isolated examples of supposed adaptation. The shadow of Pangloss' nose, so to speak, darkens his every consideration of adaptation. And yet—for Gould (1977), the human cooperative instinct may well be a biological/historical adaptation:

> Our selfish and aggressive urges may have evolved by the Darwinian route of individual advantage, but our altruistic tendencies need not represent a unique overlay imposed by the demands of civilization. These tendencies may have arisen by the same Darwinian route via kin selection. Basic human kindness may be as "animal" as basic human nastiness.
>
> (p. 266)

As if stunned at this concession to strict adaptation, Gould (1977) quickly adds, "But here I stop—short of any deterministic speculation that attributes *specific* behaviors to the possession of specific altruist or opportunist genes" (p. 266).

Gould's characterization of selfishness as "nastiness," as contrasted with kindness, may supply additional evidence for Wilson's, Hume's, and others' belief that biological instincts have evolved into ethical judgments. Given his career-long antipathy toward most supposed examples of adaptation, we might think that Gould's case for cooperation is the most compelling from our three evolutionary biologists. But that distinction surely goes to Richard Dawkins, author of *The Selfish Gene*.

The progressive editions of *The Selfish Gene* document Dawkins' increasing appreciation of the power and presence of cooperation within evolution. In the preface to the first edition in 1976, Dawkins (2006a) writes, "We are survival machines—robot vehicles blindly programmed to preserve the selfish molecules known as genes" (p. xxi). As we know, Dawkins still holds that belief—but, from the evidence of the second and third editions, his focus on selfish genes has become increasingly enriched by the idea that cooperation often is a more effective path toward self-preservation than the competing routes of egoistic conflict and competition. In the second edition in 1989, for example, Dawkins adds a chapter titled "Nice Guys Finish First," a title that he did not mean ironically. In that chapter, Dawkins (2006a) carefully examines then-new findings in biology and game theory (Chapter 7) and concludes, "Without departing from the fundamental laws of the selfish gene, we can see how cooperation and mutual assistance can flourish ... Even with selfish genes at the helm, nice guys can finish first" (pp. 224, 233). Finally, in 2006, in the 30th anniversary edition of *The Selfish Gene*, Dawkins (2006a), as we know, asserts that self-interest directly engenders cooperation, noting that perhaps a better title for *The Selfish Gene* might have been *The Cooperative Gene* (p. ix). In his preface to the 30th-anniversary edition, he notes that his book now "devotes more attention to altruism" and its explanations than to selfishness (Dawkins, 2006a, p. viii). In the words of science writer Kim Sterelny (2007), *The Selfish Gene* has become "a response to a pressing evolutionary problem. How could cooperation have evolved?" (p. 51).

Dawkins, however, remains steadfast in his focus on genes. As noted earlier, he acknowledges that a human individual is, remarkably, an *Altruistic Vehicle* motivated by the *Cooperative Gene* (both phrases, again, are in his opinion more accurate titles for the book)—but altruism and cooperation are not antithetical to the self-interest of genes that seek eternal life. Rather, cooperation enhances the quest for immortality:

> A gene that cooperates well with most of the other genes that it is likely to meet in successive bodies, i.e. the genes in the whole of the rest of the gene pool, will tend to have an advantage . . . Selection has favoured genes that cooperate with others. In the fierce competition for scarce resources, in the relentless struggle to eat other survival machines, and to avoid being eaten, there must have been a premium on central coordination rather than anarchy within the communal body.
>
> (Dawkins, 2006a, pp. 39, 49)

This conclusion hearkens back to Kropotkin's double tendency (Chapter 5) and the idea that cooperation actually promotes individual interests—and it looks toward a similar assertion that we find in the philosophy of David Hume (Chapter 9).

Summary

Near the beginning of *Antidosis*, one of his longest essays, Isocrates warns his readers of the voyage to come and invites them to take breaks—to set aside the essay, occasionally, and to relax. This chapter, the longest in this book, did not offer a similar courtesy—but it will, at least, offer a very brief summary. A lengthy analysis of decades of work from, arguably, the three top evolutionary biologists of the late-twentieth and early-twenty-first centuries leads us to at least four important points for the understanding and practice of public relations:

1. There is powerful consensus among modern evolutionary biologists that humans are a cooperative species. Cooperation, not egoistic conflict and competition (which indeed exist), is our default position.
2. Modern evolutionary biologists concur that cooperation is not utopian, normative, or idealistic. Developed by natural selection, its origins are biological. The basis of social harmony frameworks of public relations can be purely materialistic, with no trappings at all of idealism.

3. Modern evolutionary biologists concur that cooperation does not inhibit self-interest. Rather, cooperation generally is the most successful path to long-term self-interest.
4. In the words of evolutionary biologist Richard Dawkins, author of *The Selfish Gene*, "nice guys finish first"—with *nice* denoting the initial and consistent enactment of cooperation within relationships.

These four points address three of the Nine Tenets of public relations' social harmony frameworks outlined in Chapter 1:

II. Cooperation is the relationship strategy best suited to resource acquisition. Evidence from evolutionary biology, philosophy, and rhetoric shows that, in general, cooperative relationships are more successful in sustained resource acquisition than relationships based on egoism, conflict, and competition.
III. Cooperative relationships are not merely normative, idealistic, or utopian. Rather, evidence from evolutionary biology, philosophy, and rhetoric shows that cooperation is a stronger instinct within human nature than the competing instincts of egoism, conflict, and competition.
V. Biological and social tensions between individualism and collectivism are most sustainably resolved in favor of collectivism that defends individualism.

Chapter 7

The evolution of game theory

Theories of evolution evolve, and surely one of the most remarkable examples of that truth is the history of Richard Dawkins' *The Selfish Gene*. In beginning my research for this book several years ago, I initially thought *The Selfish Gene* would run counter to the idea that evolutionary biology would argue in favor of public relations' social harmony frameworks. Had I read only the first edition of that work, published in 1976, my early concern would have been near the mark. In that first edition, key passages would have steered us toward public relations frameworks typified by adversarial society theory and egoistic versions of contingency theory, frameworks characterized by competition and conflict. As we saw in Chapter 6, in that first edition, Dawkins (2006a) wrote: "We are survival machines—robot vehicles blindly programmed to preserve the selfish molecules known as genes" (p. xxi). In his second edition in 1989, however, Dawkins (2006a) added a chapter titled "Nice Guys Finish First," in which he declared: "Without departing from the fundamental laws of the selfish gene, we can see how cooperation and mutual assistance can flourish . . ." (p. 225). Again, in the 30th anniversary edition of *The Selfish Gene*, Dawkins (2006a) asserts that self-interested genes directly engender cooperation, noting that perhaps a better title for *The Selfish Gene* might have been *The Cooperative Gene* (p. ix).

What led to this evolution of thought? By Dawkins' (2006a) own admission, it was game theory—particularly the computer-based Prisoner's Dilemma games of Robert Axelrod, a professor of political science and public policy at the University of Michigan (pp. xvii). For Dawkins, those games demonstrated the remarkable power of cooperation vis-à-vis competition in the processes of evolution and survival.

This chapter will review the game-theory findings of Axelrod and more recent successors, including Martin Nowak, C. Daniel Batson and Nadia Ahmad, and Johan Almenberg and Anna Dreber—and will take a quick look back at the pioneering pre-Axelrod work of evolutionary biologist Robert Trivers. These scholars' findings indicate that the cooperation inherent in Isocratean rhetoric, fully functioning society theory, and public relations' other social harmony frameworks, far from being overly idealistic and utopian, is a powerful fact, not an aberration, in the ongoing survival and evolution of humans. Given the impossibility of directly observing the growth of cooperation within the eons of human evolution, game theory, according to Nowak, Edward O. Wilson, and their colleague Corina E. Tarnita (2011), affords the best opportunity for studying how cooperation, via natural selection, might have developed (p. E9). Game theory helps prove that cooperation is not merely aspirational; it is an inherent human instinct, increasingly developed through natural selection operating in both the biological and cultural spheres (Dawkins, 2006a; Nowak & Highfield, 2011; Pinker, 2011).

The Prisoner's Dilemma

Evolutionary biologists (Trivers, 1971; Dawkins, 2006a; Nowak & Highfield, 2011), economists (Ostrom, 1990; Almenberg & Dreber, 2013), political scientists (Axelrod, 2006), psychologists (Batson & Ahmad, 2001), and others have turned to game theory in general and the Prisoner's Dilemma in particular to study the "social dilemma" (Hauert, 2013, p. 115) of "how cooperation can emerge among egoists without central authority" (Axelrod, 2006, p. viii). The Prisoner's Dilemma—which, like all games in game theory, involves "strategic interaction" (Almenberg & Dreber, 2013, p. 133)—posits a scenario in which two culpable partners have been captured by authorities and are interrogated separately. If each partner cooperates with the other and refuses to confess, they each earn a sentence of, say, one year. However, if one partner defects (blames the partner) and the other partner cooperates (refuses to confess), the defector is set free and the cooperator receives a three-year sentence. If both defect, each receives a two-year sentence. The length of these sentences can be changed as long as a defection/cooperation decision earns the conjoined best and worst sentences. In the middle are mutual cooperation, earning the best combined sentencing for both, and mutual defection, earning the worst. In the Prisoner's Dilemma experiments that we will examine, success is more generally paid out in points or offspring awarded. According to Harvard Psychology Professor Steven Pinker (2011):

> The Prisoner's Dilemma has been called one of the great ideas of the 20th century, because it distills the tragedy of social life into such a succinct formula . . . Our species was born into the dilemma because our ultimate interests are distinct, because our vulnerable bodies make us sitting ducks for exploitation, and because the enticements to be the exploiter rather than the exploited will sentence all sides to punishing conflict.
>
> (pp. 533, 694)

Games such as the Prisoner's Dilemma consist of three elements: Players, possible actions, and prescribed payoffs or punishments (Almenberg & Dreber,

2013). In the words of Nowak (Nowak & Highfield, 2011), the Prisoner's Dilemma is "the ultimate dilemma of cooperation. We all encounter the Dilemma in one form or another all the time in everyday life" (p. 8).

The Prisoner's Dilemma and the work of Axelrod have not received extensive mention in public relations research, a notable exception being Murphy's (1991, 2000) late twentieth-century work. Murphy's assessment of game research, including some of Axelrod's work with the Prisoner's Dilemma, ultimately suggested a mixed-motive model to modify the two-way symmetry approach of excellence theory (J.E. Grunig & White, 1992), and it further became a basis for contingency theory (Cancel, Cameron, Sallot, & Mitrook, 1997). Willis' (2012) analysis of the work of Nobel Prize-winning economist Elinor Ostrom includes her game theory findings that face-to-face communication among players increases cooperation in competitive games such as the Prisoner's Dilemma—an important point to which we will return. Much of what follows will focus on Axelrod's research, which so influenced Dawkins, and on Nowak's elaborate follow-ups to that research—but it would be unfair to bypass the work of Robert Trivers, who, a decade before Axelrod, had used the Prisoner's Dilemma to identify the key catalyst of reciprocity within the evolution of cooperation. It was Trivers, writes evolutionary biologist David Barash (2016), who in 1971 "came up with an elegant demonstration of how reciprocity could in fact be evolutionarily stable" (para. 5). And what accounted for such elegance? Trivers "introduced evolutionary biologists to the elegant albeit frustrating logic of the Prisoner's Dilemma" (Barash, 2016, para. 5). Axelrod does note Trivers' work several times his *Evolution of Cooperation*, the work that so influenced Dawkins.

The bulk of this chapter is divided into chronological phases of the Prisoner's Dilemma, beginning with the rudimentary model that inspired Axelrod and continuing into Martin Nowak's twenty-first-century experiments.

Phase 1: The one-off Prisoner's Dilemma

If the Prisoner's Dilemma (PD) lasts only one round, as a true Prisoner's Dilemma would play out, conventional wisdom recommends defection (Nowak & Highfield, 2011, p. 29). The defector either goes free or earns a two-year sentence; he or she definitely avoids the three-year sentence of a betrayed cooperator.

The inevitability of defection was, until recently, the position of economic theorists in regard to one-off PD games: "The theoretical predictions of game theory are based on the assumption that individuals choose actions in order to maximize their own utility" (Almenberg & Dreber, 2013, p. 134.) However, Almenberg and Dreber's (2013) review of game-theory experiments found that "we can reject. . . the notion that individuals only seek to maximize their own material payoffs in games" (p. 134). Their state of the studies report, in fact, undermines the theory of maximized individual utility:

Players do not always defect in a one-shot PD. Many individuals act in a way that strongly indicates a concern for the wellbeing of the other player. They are willing to forgo part of their material payoff in order to benefit the other player . . . The experimental research shows that cooperation is frequent even when this is not an [advisable] strategy in terms of the material payoffs . . .

(2013, pp. 138, 146)

Almenberg and Dreber (2013) conclude, "This shows that a simple theoretical economic model is which individuals are only concerned with maximizing their own material payoffs does a bad job of predicting actual behavior" (p. 138).

Economists increasingly are rebelling against the notion that narrow, powerful egoistic interests motivate human decision making. Elinor Ostrom, co-winner of the 2009 Nobel Prize for Economics, used a variant of the Prisoner's Dilemma, a community "commons" game in which participants can either cooperate or defect in pursuit of an important shared goal, to show that "societies and groups regularly devise autonomous rules and enforcement mechanisms that stop the degradation of nature. These conclusions are in stark contrast to traditional commons theory" (Willis, 2012, p. 117). In *Misbehaving: The Making of Behavioral Economics*, economist Richard Thaler (2015) attacks the notion that, in economic matters, humans generally function as a species he calls "Econs" (p. 4), motivated by narrowly defined, self-aggrandizing self-interests. In debunking the existence of pure Econs, Daniel Kahneman (2011), winner of the 2002 Nobel Prize for Economics, asserts that psychologists and traditional economists often "seem to be studying different species"; unlike Econs, humans "are sometimes generous and often willing to contribute to the group to which they are attached" (p. 269). Kahneman (2011), in fact, believes that economic decisions often are instinctive rather than deliberate, generated by our brain's "System 1" (instinct) rather than System 2 (deliberation) (pp. 20–21), a finding echoed by science journalist Daniel Goleman (2006), whose compilation of neuroeconomic research shows that economic decisions are significantly affected by the brain's "low road" (instinct) as opposed to its "high road" (deliberation) (pp. 15–16). "Our species is not *Homo oeconomicus*," concludes Edward O. Wilson (2012). "We are *Homo sapiens*, imperfect beings, soldiering on with conflicted impulses" (p. 251). For public relations and marketing, these findings certainly push back against economist Milton Friedman's (2002) contention, in *Capitalism and Freedom*, that "there is one and only one social responsibility of business—to use its resources and engage in activities designed to increase its profits" (p. 133).

Darwin, as we know, cites instinct in resisting the supposedly inevitable human logic of self-interested defection when, in *The Descent of Man* (1871/ 1998), he writes:

> That feeling of dissatisfaction, or even misery, which invariably results, as we shall hereafter see, from any unsatisfied instinct, would arise, as often as it was perceived that the enduring and always present social instinct had yielded to some other instinct, at the time stronger, but neither enduring in its nature, nor leaving behind it a very vivid impression . . .
>
> (p. 101)

Darwin (1871/1998) asserts that we would learn from such disappointments and would modify our antisocial behavior—in this case, a tendency to defect (p. 117).

Furthermore, in *The Better Angels of Our Nature*, Pinker (2011) reviews the one-off PD research of Batson and Ahmad (2001), which found that "when the participant read a personal note from her otherwise anonymous partner and was induced to feel empathy for her, her rate of cooperating jumped from 20 percent to 70 percent" (p. 585). Another experiment showed a downturn in defection when written instruction were "adorned with drawings that vaguely resembled eyes," suggesting that someone was watching (Almenberg & Dreber, 2013, p. 143). A similar experiment found that "people are significantly less selfish in laboratory experiments when surreptitiously primed to believe that supernatural agents are watching them. . ." (D.D.P. Johnson, 2014, p. 179). "Willful selfishness may not be so obvious or primary as it seems. . .," conclude Coakley and Nowak (2013). "No wonder, then, that economists are constantly surprised by what they see as 'fuzzy thinking' in human game playing" (pp. 10, 10–11). In sum, one-off PD studies indicate a surprising social instinct for cooperation even at our own possible expense.

Phase 2: The iterated PD game

The PD research that helped modify Dawkins' ideas about cooperation began with a computer-hosted tournament in the 1980s. Axelrod (2006) invited players around the world to create computer programs that contained strategies for winning an iterated PD game of several rounds. Scholars have noted that iterated PD games, as opposed to one-off versions, better mimic the real world with its probability of repeated encounters/social dilemmas with recognized players (Dawkins, 2006a; Nowak & Highfield, 2011). Fourteen "players" (designed programs) entered the game.

To his first tournament, Axelrod added a program he titled Random, which cooperated and defected randomly, without pattern. Each of the 15 programs played each of the other programs (including a twin of itself) for 200 iterations, and the process was repeated five times. Each program had access to the previous history of the game; in other words, it could remember how its opponents had behaved—and memory, of course, is essential for the concepts of direct reciprocity and, particularly, indirect reciprocity within relationships (Dawkins,

2006a, p. 187; Wilson, 2012, p. 20). When overall points were totaled, Axelrod (2006) found these results:

- To his "considerable surprise" (p. viii), the simplest program in the tournament, Tit for Tat, won. Tit for Tat always cooperated on the first move and then mimicked the opponent's previous move—so Tit for Tat was "nice, forgiving, and retaliatory" (p. 46). In PD games, a "nice" program is one that cooperates on its first move. A "forgiving" program "is swift to overlook old misdeeds . . . It raps a defector over the knuckles instantly but, after that, lets bygones be bygones" (Dawkins, 2006a, p. 212). A "retaliatory" program meets defection with defection (but, as in the case of Tit for Tat, may be willing to make a forgiving overture).
- "Tit for Tat never once scored better in a game than the other player! In fact, it can't . . . Tit for Tat won the tournament, not by beating the other player, but by eliciting behavior from the other player which allowed both to do well" (p. 112). From this phenomenon, Axelrod drew a perhaps surprising maxim: "Don't be envious . . . There is no point in being envious of the success of the other player, since in an iterated Prisoner's Dilemma of long duration the other's success is virtually a prerequisite of your doing well for yourself" (pp. 100, 112). These particular findings bear repeating: In the game of cooperation and defect—which Nowak (Nowak & Highfield, 2011), Pinker (2011), and Dawkins (2006a) contend is an everyday reality for humans—we succeed, in the long run, only if the other succeeds. Isocrates (Chapter 12) also embraced this philosophy, using the Greek term *sophrosyne*, moderation of wants, for the concept.
- In the course of the tournament, nice programs (programs that open with cooperation) significantly outperformed defector programs. The top eight programs in the tournament, led by Tit for Tat, were nice programs (p. 33).
- The losing programs were, comparatively, too eager to defect to try to gain competitive advantage; did not sufficiently forgive defections; and were too pessimistic about the probability of cooperative moves from opponents (p. 40). Regarding forgiveness, primatologist Frans de Waal has noted that "in most primate species, after two animals have fought, they will reconcile" (Pinker, 2011, p. 516)—and Goleman (2006) observes that forgiveness has biological advantages: "It lowers our blood pressure, heart rate, and levels of stress hormones" (p. 308).

For a second tournament, Axelrod (2006) secured 62 entries from six nations (p. 43) and once again added Random for a total of 63. He provided the results of the previous tournament to all participants. As in the first tournament, each program played every other program, including Random and a twin of itself. Once again, the simplest program, Tit for Tat, won. Of the top 15 programs, 14 were "nice"—again, meaning that they began with cooperation (Axelrod, 2006, p. 44). From the two tournaments, Axelrod (2006) concludes that "cooperation can indeed emerge in a world of egoists without central authority" (p. 20) and that, in addition to niceness, four properties tend to ensure the success of cooperation (pp. 110–123):

1. Avoidance of unnecessary conflict by cooperating as long as the other player does.
2. Provocability in the face of an uncalled for defection by the other.
3. Forgiveness after responding to a provocation.
4. Clarity of behavior [simplicity] so that the other player can adapt to your pattern of action.

Significantly, to mimic the processes of biological evolution, Axelrod reran the second tournament, awarding extra copies/offspring (successful reproduction) instead of points. Again, the cooperative Tit for Tat program won: "By the one-thousandth generation it was the most successful [program] and still growing at a faster rate than any other [program]" (Axelrod, 2006, p. 53).

Finally, Axelrod (2006) divided the large 63-program tournament into smaller tournaments, pitting Tit for Tat against six smaller groups, "each with a very different distribution of the types of [programs] participating" (p. 48). Tit for Tat won five of those competitions and finished second in the sixth (Axelrod, 2006, p. 48)—and in the sixth, a competing nice/cooperative program won (Dawkins, 2006a, p. 216). Of the highly cooperative Tit for Tat's success in the several computer-based tournaments that Axelrod (2006) ran, he concludes, "What can be said for the empirical successes of Tit for Tat is that it is a very robust [program]; it does very well over a wide range of environments" (p. 53). In the course of his PD tournaments, Axelrod (2006) found niceness to be "the single best predictor of how well a [program] performed" (p. 113). Dawkins (2006a) terms niceness the "most important category" (p. 212) that Axelrod identified—and acknowledges that it led to his conclusion, in the second edition of *The Selfish Gene*, that "nice guys finish first" (p. 202).

Evolutionary biologists and economists repeatedly use the term "shadow of the future" to describe the relevance of the iterated PD versus its one-off version (Axelrod, 2006; Dawkins, 2006a; Nowak & Highfield, 2011; Almenberg & Dreber, 2013). As Dawkins (2006a) explains, when a player doesn't know the termination date for a relationship, "the nicer, more forgiving, less envious he will be"; conversely, in a one-off game or a tournament with a defined and short shadow of the future, "the nastier, and less forgiving will he be" (p. 225). Again, however, new research is challenging that second assertion: Although they found surprising levels of cooperation in one-off PDs, economists Almenberg and Dreber (2013) downplay the relevance of shadowless one-off PDs because "humans have not evolved in settings where this is a meaningful notion" (p. 142). The iterated PD is more relevant to human experience.

Even beyond their focus on the success of initial cooperation, Axelrod's findings might pose an additional challenge for egoistic, conflict-oriented versions of contingency theory, with its 80-plus variables that affect an organization's stance vis-à-vis a particular public (Cancel, Cameron, Sallot, & Mitrook, 1997): In virtually all of Axelrod's tournaments, the simplest program won. An uncomplicated preference for cooperation—"avoidance of unnecessary conflict" (Axelrod, 2006, p. 20)—defeated more complex, stance-calculating programs in each iterated tournament. Furthermore, the simplicity of Tit for Tat—"clarity of behavior," in Axelrod's (2006, p. 20) words— allowed other players to quickly and easily adjust their own behavior to form mutually beneficial relationships; confusion about the strategy of the "other" was minimized. In fact, stances of cooperation and conflict, according to Dawkins (2006a), rarely involve conscious deliberation: "It is important to realize that we are not thinking of the strategy as being consciously worked out by the individual. Remember that we are picturing the animal as a robot survival machine with a pre-programmed computer. . ." (p. 69). In Dawkins' (2006a) estimation, many of the failed egoistic/defect-oriented programs in Axelrod's tournaments "tried to be too cunning" (p. 213). In contrast, cooper-ation, simplicity, and clarity/predictability seemingly generated productive reputation and consequent success, a combination that Nowak and Sigmund affirm in Phase 6 below.

Dawkins' (2006a) strongest endorsement of Tit for Tat and its "nice guys finish first" performance record is his declaration that the nice, forgiving program eventually establishes what is essentially an "evolutionarily stable strategy" (ESS) (p. 69). The term was coined by evolutionary biologist John Maynard Smith to signify a strategy so successful that it spreads to dominate a culture, impervious to sustained invasion by other strategies: "Although Tit for Tat is strictly speaking not a true ESS, it is probably fair to treat some sort of mixture of basically nice but retaliatory 'Tit for Tat-like' strategies as roughly equivalent to an ESS in practice" (Dawkins, 2006a, pp. 216–217). Dawkins notes that, in Axelrod's experiments, "Always Defect" programs were unable to achieve an ESS when pitted against nice, forgiving pro-grams, and he speculates that Axelrod, in conducting the version of his second tournament that paid with offspring (identical programs as progeny), was try-ing to discover if Tit for Tat could establish something near an ESS. "Eventually, after about 1,000 generations, there were no further changes in proportions, no further changes in climate," Dawkins (2006a) writes. "Stability [for Tit for Tat] was reached" (p. 216).

Phase 3: The primordial chaos PD game

Inspired by Axelrod's findings and the dramatic gains in computer abilities in the years after Tit for Tat's early successes, Martin Nowak, director of Harvard University's Program for Evolutionary Dynamics, modified Axelrod's tournament. Describing himself as a "professor of mathematical biology," Nowak is scarcely an idealist about the subject of his studies. "Humans are selfish apes . . .," he has written. "We are motivated by self-interest alone"— and yet his game theory studies have led him to the conclusion that "cooperation can emerge out of nothing more than the rational calculation of self-interest" (Nowak & Highfield, 2011, pp. xiii, 29). Whereas Axelrod worked with designed, glitch-free programs, Nowak and his colleague Karl Sigmund designed a PD computer tournament in which, first, computers randomly generated cooperate/defect programs in "primordial chaos" (Nowak & Highfield, 2011, p. 35) to see which variations would, over generations, survive and succeed and, second, those programs occasionally made mistakes to simulate the messiness and mistakes of real life (and to simulate the random mutations essential to natural selection and evolution). Such mutations generated new programs and strategies. Successful programs were rewarded with comparatively more identical offspring.

Nowak and Sigmund's primordial chaos approach to player/program design, enhanced by programed random variations that generated new players and strategies, addressed Dawkins' sole concern with Axelrod's earlier findings: The limitation of dealing with submitted programs rather than with a wider, real-world variety of naturally occurring players and strategies. "Is there an objective way," Dawkins (2006a) asked, "in which we can judge which is the truly best strategy, in a more general and less arbitrary sense?" (p. 215). Nowak and Sigmund's primordial chaos with variations game addressed that concern.

In repeated runnings of the multigenerational game, Nowak and Sigmund consistently found the same results (Nowak & Highfield, 2011, pp. 34–37):

- Always Defect programs dominated for the first 100 generations.
- Tit for Tat then would assume dominance.
- Eventually, the even nicer Generous Tit for Tat (which forgives every third defection) would overtake Tit for Tat.
- After the overall population became complacently and consistently nice and generous, a random mutation of defection could trigger a serious setback for the Generous Tit for Tat culture: "A population of nice players who always cooperate is dry tinder for an invasion by any lingering or newly emerged defector. In this way, the cycle starts anew" (Nowak & Highfield, 2011, p. 36).
- However, "the good news is that a reasonably nice strategy dominates the tournament" (Nowak & Highfield, 2011, p. 37). Nice programs, again, begin with cooperation.

The early dominance of Always Defect programs helps address another of Dawkins' concerns regarding game theory, a concern familiar to public relations scholars and practitioners: Power disparities in relationships. In *The*

Selfish Gene, Dawkins (2006a) writes, "So far we have considered only . . . 'symmetric' contests. This means we have assumed that the contestants are identical in all respects except their fighting strategy" (p. 77). Relationships, however, are rarely built among equal partners. Nowak and Sigmund's findings in their primordial chaos games do not remove concerns of power disparities in relationships, of course—but they do show that selfishness and an initial ability to exploit are, eventually, counterproductive. Their findings, in fact, echo the much earlier conclusions of Isocrates (trans. 1929/1992), who recognized the ultimate outcome of abuses of asymmetric power:

> Those who prefer the way of injustice, thinking it the greatest good fortune to seize something that belongs to others, are in like case with animals which are lured by a bait, at first deriving pleasure from what they seize, but the moment after finding themselves in desperate straits . . . Arrogance and insolence have been the cause of our misfortunes while sobriety and self-control [*sophrosyne*] have been the source of our blessings.
>
> (*On The Peace*, 34, 119)

Phase 4: The self-aware PD game

Nowak's next variation of the iterated Prisoner's Dilemma once again began with primordial chaos and rewards of offspring to successful randomly generated programs—but this version allowed programs to be "self-aware" of their previous behaviors:

> We now wanted to look at strategies that also take into account the player's own moves . . . Put yourself in the position of a contestant in one of our tournaments. You might be less annoyed with a fellow player who had defected if you had defected too. Equally, you might be more angry with him if you had cooperated.
>
> (Nowak & Highfield, 2011, p. 42)

In this self-aware version, Generous Tit for Tat did not prevail. Instead, the winner was a different "cooperative strategy" named Win Stay/Lose Shift, which cooperated after players made the same move—either joint cooperation or joint defection; if the players made different moves, however, Win Stay/Lose Shift defected (Nowak & Highfield, 2011, p. 45). "Overall, Win Stay/Lost Shift can cope better with mistakes," Nowak and Sigmund concluded, "because it actively seeks good outcomes, trying to restore cooperation after mutual defection, though it will try to exploit unconditional cooperators" (Nowak & Highfield, 2011, p. 48).

Phase 5: The alternating PD game

Nowak and Sigmund next determined that a shortcoming within the ability of a PD game to imitate reality was its "Rock Scissors Paper" (Nowak & Highfield, 2011, p. 35) rule of having each player commit to a decision at the same time. In the Alternating Prisoner's Dilemma players take turns in making a cooperate/defect decision. Within a single game, thus, a player's first decision could be in response to the other player's prior decision to defect or cooperate.

In this version of the multigenerational PD, Nowak and Sigmund again noted "a tendency to evolve toward cooperation" (Nowak & Highfield, 2011, p. 46). However, in this more-realistic PD, Generous Tit for Tat regained ascendancy over Win Stay/Lose Shift. The two successful programs have much in common: Both are "nice," meaning that neither is the first to defect, and each has a "sprinkling of forgiveness" with a policy of occasionally forgiving defections (Nowak & Highfield, 2011, p. 47). Overall, the randomly generated programs winning these complex tournaments, including the Alternating PD, were more inclined to forgive than the Tit for Tat program that triumphed in Axelrod's earlier competitions (Pinker, 2011, p. 541).

Phase 6: The reputation/indirect reciprocity PD game

Nowak and Sigmund's next variation—significant for public relations—was to study what would happen when players knew the reputation of the other players whom they had not yet played. In this complex multigenerational variation, in each encounter one program has the option to help the other—somewhat to its own cost. To avoid a direct reciprocity situation of Player B helping Player A because the reverse had happened earlier, Nowak disallowed repeat engagements: No two players met twice. Initially, the known reputation of each program is zero, and it "rises whenever that player helps others. Equally, it falls when the player withholds help" (Nowak & Highfield, 2011, p. 59). To mimic the real world, Nowak and Sigmund created occasional imperfections in the players' knowledge of other players' reputations: "As a result of this, different people [held] different views about the reputation of the same person" (Nowak & Highfield, 2011, p. 61).

In this first version of the Reputation PD game, cooperation and the power of reputation built by cooperation prevailed:

> If the cost-to-benefit ratio of cooperation is sufficiently low, and the amount of information about the co-player's past sufficiently high, cooperation based upon discrimination—favoring good reputations—can emerge . . . If there is enough transfer of information about who did what to whom from person to person, then natural selection favors strategies that base their decision to cooperate (or defect) on the reputation of the

recipient . . . As one would expect, Bad Samaritans with a poor reputation receive less help.

(Nowak & Highfield, 2011, p. 60)

Nowak and Sigmund then tweaked the game by introducing random mistakes to mimic the biological mutations essential to natural selection and evolution. In this version, they found more ebb and flow regarding the dominance of cooperation and defection—but they also identified a marked tendency: "Importantly, we found that natural selection favored strategies, called Discriminating Strategies, that pay attention to the reputations of others. These strategies prefer to interact with people who have a good reputation," which is based on a history of cooperation, or indirect reciprocity. (Nowak & Highfield, 2011, p. 62)

Noting complementary PD studies in Japan that showed that reputation is not harmed when we defect against known defectors (Nowak & Highfield, 2011, pp. 65–66), Nowak and Sigmund concluded, "We cooperate more with those who have a good reputation. As a result, people who started off by being generous ended up with a higher payoff. We like to give to those who have given to others. Give and you shall receive!" (Nowak & Highfield, 2011, p. 64). In the words of E.O. Wilson (2012), "The currency of favor is paid by direct reciprocity and indirect reciprocity, the latter in the form of reputation and trust" (pp. 53–54).

In his own analysis of PD games, Pinker (2011) found that indirect reciprocity is fueled by "reputation and gossip . . . People avoid hits to their reputations as well as to their bodies and bank accounts" (pp. 535, 682). In a variation of the Prisoner's Dilemma known as the Dictator Game, in which one player decides how much money to share with another player, researchers found that such donations dropped by 50 percent when the recipient could not identify the donor (Nowak & Highfield, 2011)—and thus could not assess and discuss with others the donor's reputation. In contrast, Almenberg and Dreber (2013) found that generosity increased when the giving player in Dictator Games believed he or she was being observed, even indirectly, a phenomenon they attribute to an inherent "reputation mechanism" within humans (p. 143).

Nowak (Nowak & Highfield, 2011) has written that, through such research, he and research colleague Karl Sigmund "discovered another mechanism for the evolution of cooperation, one that relied on reputation" (p. 66). Nowak and Sigmund may have proven, via PD experiments, the intertwining of reputation, indirect reciprocity, and cooperation, but, as we shall see, their results were anticipated in the philosophy of David Hume and the rhetoric of Isocrates—and certainly in the findings of Charles Darwin (1887/1983):

> If [an individual] acts for the good of others, he will receive the appro-
> bation of his fellow men and gain the love of those with whom he lives;

and this latter gain undoubtedly is the highest pleasure on this earth. By degrees it will become intolerable to him to obey his sensuous passions rather than his higher impulses, which when rendered habitual may be almost called instincts.

(p. 55)

Regardless of its provenance, however, the key point for public relations is clear: Cooperation—known cooperation, that is, particularly in the form of indirect reciprocity—builds reputation, which leads to a competitive advantage in resource acquisition.

Phase 7: The spatial PD game

In this brutal tweak of the PD game, Nowak mimicked the power of social networks by allowing players to interact only with their eight neighbors in a chessboard-like arrangement; in turn, those eight neighbors were affected by their interactions with their own neighbors. The brutality stems from a severe challenge to cooperative programs: Nowak allowed only pure coopera-tors and pure defectors; in other words, the proven policies of forgiveness and of retaliation against consistent defectors were barred. By the rules of the traditional PD, this meant defectors always outscored cooperators in individual interactions when those two strategies met. In various versions of this Spatial PD game, Nowak (Nowak & Highfield, 2011) tweaked the percentages and distributions of defectors and cooperators (pp. 75–76). In later research, Nowak (2013) has used the term "network reciprocity" for such games (p. 103).

The results surprised Nowak. Over the generations, clusters of disadvan-taged cooperators survived even in those harsh environments:

> Before my eyes, a complex variety of patterns blossomed. Cooperators and defectors could coexist with each other ... These clusters of cooperators and defectors could keep on growing. Yet, though the actual pattern was fluid and changing all the time, the relative abundance of cooperators always fluctuated around the same level, a mysterious 31.78 percent.
>
> (Nowak & Highfield, 2011, pp. 76, 78)

If the "primordial soup" that gave rise to life consisted only of pure defectors and cooperators, then spatial interactions could create "primordial pizzas" in which pepperoni-like clusters of cooperation could survive, awaiting mutations that could enhance cooperation with the powerful forces of forgive-ness and retaliation (Nowak & Highfield, 2011, pp. 75, 79–80): "Clusters of cooperation can prevail, even if besieged by defectors" (Nowak & Highfield, 2011, p. 80). John Hedley Brooke (2013), the former Andreas Idreos professor of science and religion at Oxford, points out that spatial considerations certainly influenced the varied receptions of Darwin's *On the Origin of Species*: "Geographic parameters played a key role in shaping receptivity to Darwinian ideas, making them seem less natural in some constituencies than others" (p. 41).

Earlier, Axelrod's (2006) variations of his second iterated PD tournament had shown similar results:

> The beginning of the story is that cooperation can get started even in a world of unconditional defection. The development *cannot* take place if it is tried only by scattered individuals who have virtually no chance to interact with each other. However, cooperation can evolve from small clusters of individuals who base their cooperation on reciprocity and have even a small proportion of interactions with each other.
>
> (p. 21)

Because Axelrod did allow cooperative programs to retaliate and forgive, his game might have had stronger real-world implications than Nowak's harsh version. Similarly, in his own analysis of PD research, Pinker (2011) concludes that spatial relationships are conducive to cooperation:

> Subsets of players who are stuck with playing against each other—say because they are neighbors who cannot move—tend to be more forgiving than ones who can pick up and choose a neighborhood in which to find partners. Cliques, organizations, and other social networks are virtual neighborhoods because they force groups of people to interact repeatedly, and they tilt people toward forgiveness, because mutual defection would be ruinous to everyone.
>
> (p. 535)

Pinker (2011) also notes the power of a reputation for cooperation within such social networks (p. 535) and the ability of technology to build new networks that transcend physical proximity (p. xxvi). "If people belong to many groups and can switch in and out of them," he writes, "they are more likely to find one in which they are esteemed, and an insult or slight is less consequential" (Pinker, 2011, p. 516).

Phase 8: The group selection PD game

Darwin, in *The Descent of Man*, introduces the notion of the natural selection of groups as opposed to individuals. In the decades since, evolutionary biologists and psychologists have divided over the idea: Dawkins (2006a) and Pinker (2012) tend to reject it; Gould (2002), Wilson (2012), and Nowak (Nowak & Highfield, 2011) tend to support it as part of selection at many levels, including groups. In a group selection PD designed by Nowak and Arne

Traulsen, players cooperated and defected within a group—and were paid with successful reproduction. As cooperation inevitably took hold, as in previous PD versions, players who cooperated reproduced at higher rates (Nowak & Highfield, 2011, p. 88).

To create competition, Nowak and Traulsen had groups split when they grew, through reproduction of individual members, past a certain point. But they also allowed only a finite number of groups, so each new group meant the elimination of the weakest group in the pool. Just as with other PD games, the results of the Group Selection game tended to favor groups with cooperative members:

> Defectors can win within a group, but at the level of the group, groups of cooperators can triumph over groups of defectors . . . We observed that groups in which cooperation emerges are more likely to stick around longer than those with exclusively selfish behavior.
>
> (Nowak & Highfield, 2011, p. 89)

As we know, this finding echoes Darwin's (1871/1998) own assessment in *The Descent of Man*:

> A tribe including many members who, from possessing in a high degree the spirit of patriotism, fidelity, obedience, courage, and sympathy, were always ready to aid one another, and to sacrifice themselves for the common good, would be victorious over most other tribes; and this would be natural selection.
>
> (p. 137)

Coakley and Nowak (2013) have a succinct summary for the findings of these various cooperation/defect games: "Empirical evidences in laboratory conditions are also now mounting up. . . [that] adult humans are now more inclined, in social situations, to 'cooperate' than to 'defect'" (p. 25). But do these findings translate from the laboratory to the real world? In asking a similar question—whether Axelrod's game-theory findings operate in the real world—Dawkins (2006a) had an even more succinct response: "The answer is yes, of course they do" (p. 229).

Palenchar's question

According to Nowak and Traulsen's group selection games, successful groups are characterized by increasing levels of individual cooperation within the group, a quality preserved and expanded by natural selection. But what about the next level in the hierarchy (albeit disputed) of units of selection? Do groups cooperate with groups? Is there a biological impetus toward inter-group cooperation, or does defection prevail at that level? Game theory, as we have seen, tends to focus on individual transactions. After I had presented an earlier summary of these game theory findings at the Barcelona 2015 public relations conference, one of my favorite public relations scholars, Michael Palenchar, posed that question: What does game theory—or, by extension, evolutionary biology—say about intergroup cooperation and defection (which, after all, is much closer to the modern practice of public relations than individual relationships). My gratitude that someone actually had been listening may have overwhelmed my ability to answer satisfactorily, but I gave it a try: A culture, I said, is a coalition of groups—what justice philosopher John Rawls (2001) refers to as "a social union of social unions" (p. 142)—so cooperation must exist. And if genetic cooperation is ascendant within successful groups, wouldn't such behavior inevitably affect intergroup transactions? And Isocrates firmly believed that individual values controlled intergroup relations. It was the beginnings of an answer—but it was sadly lacking in what evolutionary biologists had to say about the matter. Michael politely let me escape with that effort, but it was a good question, and I set out to answer it. There are at least three biologically supported reasons, I've discovered, for believing that intergroup interactions can mimic the cooperative individual interactions of the Prisoner's Dilemma:

1. *Intra*group cooperation positively influences *inter*group cooperation.
2. Increasing contact among groups reduces intergroup friction.
3. Genetic variation *within* societies tends to exceed genetic variation *between* societies.

In brief, however, the answer is yes: Game theory findings apply to groups as well as individuals. In Nowak's (Nowak & Highfield, 2011) words, "Natural selection can act both on individuals and on groups of individuals. It is even possible for selection to occur between groups of groups" (p. 84). If cooperation is, with variation and natural selection, one of the three inherent aspects of evolution, as Nowak (Nowak & Highfield, 2011) concludes, then it indeed operates at the intergroup level (p. xviii).

Edward O. Wilson (2012) believes that the evolutionary increase of intragroup cooperation positively influences intergroup cooperation in two ways: Initially, the decline of genetically driven selfish behaviors (as cooperators outperform defectors in the real world) liberates human genome "to create more complex forms of social organization" (p. 142). Second, the success of cooperative groups against individualistic groups, a tendency that Darwin (1871/1998) himself noted (p. 137), tends to drive humans to "greater and wider instinctive cooperation" (Wilson, 2012, p. 249).

A more powerful reason, perhaps, for believing that the dynamics of intergroup cooperation can mimic those of intragroup cooperation is the increasing contact among different groups, driven in our era by unprecedented levels of travel and communication. But even before these advances, Darwin himself, in *The Descent of Man* (1871/1998), noted the evolutionary growth of inter-group cooperation:

> As man advances in civilization, and small tribes are united into larger communities, the simplest reason would tell each individual that he ought to extend his social instincts and sympathies to all the members of the same nation, though personally unknown to him. This point being once reached, there is only an artificial barrier to prevent his sympathies extending to the men of all nations and races.
>
> (p. 126)

Wilson (2012) concurs, holding that human cultures are based on "cooperation among individuals *or groups*" (p. 17, emphasis added)—and he appends the related point that increasing contact lessens intergroup competition (p. 293), a finding that Pinker's (2011) research confirms (p. 585).

In fact, Steven Pinker's entire 800-plus page *Better Angels of Our Nature* devotes itself to explaining declining levels of violence, over the centuries, both within and between groups. One powerful driver of that reduction is the focus of "the new science of sympathy" (Pinker, 2011, p. 590), which shows that, far from breeding contempt, familiarity breeds cooperation—or at least a degree of identification (a Burkean idea explored more thoroughly in Chapter 13) that leads to a reduction of intergroup violence. Pinker (2011) cites studies from philosopher Peter Singer and economist Jeremy Rifkin that reveal, over the eons, sweeping trends toward "intensification and extension of empathy to more diverse others across broader temporal and spatial domains" (pp. 648, 572). Pinker (2011) himself concludes, "When our circle of empathy expands . . . our circle of forgivability expands with it" (p. 541).

The expanding circle of empathy seems to generate a quality related to forgiveness: Tolerance. Increased contact with traditional "others" has been shown to increase tolerance (Pinker, 2011, p. 590; Burge, 2013, pp. 278–279), and Goleman (2006) observes that "studies that track the time course of across-the-divide friendships show that the closeness itself leads to a reduction in prejudice" (p. 303). But what of war, the ultimate act of intolerance in intergroup relations? Pinker (2011) notes that despite modern headlines, the frequency of war has, over the centuries, been decreasing, and both Richard Dawkins (2006a) and Robert Axelrod (2006) cite World War I's informal two-year truce in areas of the trench warfare between British and German soldiers. As each side avoided inflicting unnecessary harm on the other in the stalemate, "something like Tit for Tat could be expected to grow up, and it did," in Dawkins' (2006a) words. "Mutual cooperation. . .," he adds, "was highly desirable from the point of view of the individual soldiers on both sides" (p. 226). In assessing that same prolonged episode in history, Axelrod (2006) is equally explicit: "The historical situation in the quiet sectors along the Western Front was an iterated Prisoner's Dilemma . . . At the local level, along the front line, mutual restraint was much preferred to mutual punishment" (pp. 75, 77). Groups will cooperate with groups, then, when the relative merits of cooperation and defection become clear and the shadow of the future seems to stretch beyond the horizon. If we could depart from evolutionary biology for just a moment, Scottish philosopher David Hume (1739/1968) believed, as we shall see in Chapter 9, that sheer self-interest in the processes of resource acquisition would lead to intergroup cooperation: "The advantages. . .of peace, commerce, and mutual succour, make us extend to different kingdoms the same notions of justice, which take place among individuals" (pp. 567–568).

Finally, Wilson (2012) is fond of pointing out that genetic diversity within societies tends to be greater than genetic differences between societies—and that as intragroup diversity increases, intergroup diversity decreases (p. 100): The strange becomes increasingly familiar. In biological terms, more distinguishes us internally than separates us externally. Given emigration patterns, Wilson (2012) even has speculated that "the population of Stockholm could come to be the same genetically as that in Chicago or Laos" (p. 95). Philosopher John Rawls (1999) underscores the current diversity within nations that have achieved sustainable levels of social cooperation: "Historical conquests and immigration have caused the intermingling of groups with different cultures and historical memories who now reside within the territory of most contemporary democratic governments" (p. 24). Wilson (2012) caps his own observations on this internal diversity with a review of the work of psychologist Richard W. Robins (2005) of the University of California, Davis, who found during his research in Burkina Faso that "there is a core to human mentality and social behavior that cuts across nations, cultures, and ethnic groups" (p. 62).

This, then, would be my more deliberate answer to Michael Palenchar's excellent question: Is there evidence that cooperation also can prevail in intergroup relationships? I believe that the answer is a qualified yes, for reasons of genetics and increasing contacts between groups. And given the rate of progress of studies in evolutionary biology, if we ask the question again in 10 years, we will have a much richer answer. Additional affirmations from philosophy and rhetoric will appear in later chapters.

Conclusion

Richard Dawkins himself—author of *The Selfish Gene*—has written the best conclusion for this chapter: "Nice guys finish first"—in virtually every reality-mimicking tweak of the Prisoner's Dilemma. In fact, in a preface to the 2006 revised edition of Axelrod's 1984 classic *The Evolution of Cooperation*, Dawkins (2006b) writes, "The world's leaders should be locked up with this book and not released until they have read it. This would be a pleasure to them and might save the rest of us" (p. xvi). And, again, in *The Selfish Gene* (2006a), he declares, "It is natural to ask whether [Axelrod's] optimistic conclusions—about the success of non-envious, forgiving niceness—also apply in the world of nature. The answer is yes, of course they do" (p. 229).

Evolutionary biologists including Dawkins, Darwin, Kropotkin, Axelrod, Gould, Wilson, and Nowak—who, as we know, have profound disagreements among themselves regarding matters such as group selection in the processes of evolution—*do* agree that cooperation is an inherent survival instinct groomed by the processes of evolution and at work in the mechanics of what it means to be human. Our selfish desire to survive, in fact, leads us to cooperate. According to Nowak (Nowak & Highfield, 2011):

> Our breathtaking ability to cooperate is one of the main reasons why we have managed to survive in every ecosystem on Earth . . . Our ability to cooperate goes hand in hand with succeeding in the struggle to survive, as surmised more than a century ago by Peter Kropotkin . . . Previously, there were only two basic principles of evolution—mutation and selection . . . For us to understand the creative aspects of evolution, we must now accept that cooperation is the third principle . . . Cooperation is the master architect of evolution.
>
> (pp. xiv, xvi, xviii)

Summary

The game theory findings of Axelrod, Nowak, and others lead us to at least seven important points for the understanding and practice of public relations:

1. Game theory affirms that the cooperation inherent in public relations' social harmony frameworks, far from being overly idealistic or utopian, is a powerful, inexorable fact in the ongoing survival and evolution of humans.
2. The practical strategy of cooperation, as opposed to egoistic conflict and competition, is not aberrant. It consistently arises from the "primordial chaos" of computer programs that randomly generate cooperate/defect strategies, and it consistently grows to dominate such multigenerational experiments as, essentially, an evolutionarily stable strategy.
3. In the competition for resources, the most effective tactics, over time, are niceness (beginning a relationship with cooperation), forgiveness, and a lack of envy. Game theory experiments show that, in the social competition for resources, individuals succeed over time only if their relationship partners also succeed.
4. Vigilance within relationships is required. A relationship strategy that never retaliates against defection cannot be an evolutionarily stable strategy.
5. Consistent enactments of indirect reciprocity build reputation. A reputation built upon cooperation produces more benefits than one built upon conflict.

6. Simplicity, predictability, and the clarity of cooperate/defect behaviors are keys to successful resource acquisition. Complex cooperate/defect strategies can baffle relationship partners and do not fare well in Prisoner's Dilemma games. An uncomplicated preference for cooperation—"avoidance of unnecessary conflict," in Axelrod's words—consistently defeats more complex, stance-calculating programs in iterated Prisoner's Dilemma tournaments.
7. Traditional public relations practices such as boundary spanning, coorientation, and the reflective paradigm's inclination to move beyond organizational walls are essential for intergroup cooperation. Increasing contact and understanding among groups can increase the cooperation that generates resources.

These seven points address five of the Nine Tenets of public relations' social harmony frameworks outlined in Chapter 1:

II.   Cooperation is the relationship strategy best suited to resource acquisition. Evidence from evolutionary biology, philosophy, and rhetoric shows that, in general, cooperative relationships are more successful in sustained resource acquisition than relationships based on egoism, conflict, and competition.
III.   Cooperative relationships are not merely normative, idealistic, or utopian. Rather, evidence from evolutionary biology, philosophy, and rhetoric shows that cooperation is a stronger instinct within human nature than the competing instincts of egoism, conflict, and competition.
VII.   Building relationships on the principles of cooperation and justice does not exclude the option of refusing to cooperate with hostile or destructive publics.
VIII. Acts of cooperation and justice are the most effective builders of a positive reputation. A positive reputation is a powerful, productive force within the processes of public relations and resource acquisition.
IX.   Public relations practitioners can take specific actions, drawn from evolutionary biology, philosophy, and rhetoric, to build and enhance relationships built upon cooperation and justice.

Philosophy, public relations, and cooperation

Chapter 8

Introduction to Part III

Philosophical materialism, cooperation, and justice

This short chapter takes us across the gulf dividing what British scientist and novelist C.P. Snow (1961) called "the two cultures"—the separate worlds of "scientists" and "literary intellectuals," including philosophers (p. 4). Despite the separation that Snow documents and laments, I hope I can demonstrate that elements of philosophy join elements of evolutionary biology in a consilience of cooperation, a union of the two cultures, that strongly supports the social harmony frameworks of public relations. In fact, the broad disciplines of philosophy and rhetoric made strong, objective cases for the power of cooperation over egoistic conflict and competition well before science began to provide biological explanations for that reality. Part III of this book primarily addresses the inherency of justice within cooperation—theories of justice having been the province of philosophy since at least Plato's *Republic* (trans. 1930/1989), which begins in earnest with Glaucon's desire to hear, from Socrates, "an encomium on justice in and by itself" (358D).

However, this introductory chapter will also touch on the concept of philosophical materialism and its relationship to cooperation, justice, ethics, and the power of habit. Philosophical materialism positions itself against idealism, embracing a "demonstrably *is*" approach to reality as opposed to a more ethereal "*ought*." In the language of theories, materialism skews toward the practical while idealism can skew toward the normative. Materialism privileges the tangible. Peter Angeles' *Dictionary of Philosophy* (1981) offers this definition of various aspects of materialism:

> Nothing but matter in motion exists . . . Matter and the universe do not in any way possess characteristics of mind such as purpose, awareness, intention, goals, meaning, direction, intelligence, willing, striving . . . Every change (event, activity) has a material cause, and material explanations of phenomena are the only correct explanations . . . Values do not exist in the universe independently of the activities of humans.
>
> (p. 160)

In philosophical materialism, adds Frost (1962), "everything in nature must be explained mechanically, without the aid of forms, ideas, universals" (p. 31). Conversely, idealism "may escape strict determinism and make possible freedom and morality" (Frost, 1962, p. 50). The difference may be more familiar when cast as Bertrand Russell's (1945) contrast between "idealism" and "empiricism" (p. 542).

For me, personally, this seems to be an unnecessarily gloomy approach (and one that, as we shall see, some public relations scholars have resisted)—but it has the advantage of aligning with this book's strict avoidance of normative, idealistic support for the social harmony frameworks of public relations. Just as Part II of this book adopted the empirical approach of evolutionary biology to explore the ascendancy of cooperation over egoistic conflict, this new section will ground the linkage of public relations, cooperation, and justice in materialism, rather than idealism. Again, the social harmony frameworks of public relations need not be grounded in "we wish" and "if only." Instead, we can dispassionately examine evidence from a variety of disciplines to conclude that, as humans, we do a better job of resource acquisition within just, cooperative relationships than within those built on narrowly self-serving competition and conflict.

Public relations scholars have embraced a range of mixtures of materialism and idealism. In "The Effect of Worldviews on Public Relations," for example, J.E. Grunig and White (1992) readily acknowledge that the two-way symmetrical model of excellence theory is both "normative" and "idealistic" (pp. 55, 56). In "Toward the Philosophy of PR," L.A. Grunig (1992) notes that "positive relativism" can employ both approaches toward the discipline. In his application of Pierre Bourdieu's fields theory to public relations, Ihlen (2009) writes that Bourdieu rejects the "classic antagonism concerning idealism and materialism," offering instead a concept of social relationships that "made the opposition between subjectivism and objectivism obsolete" (pp. 64, 65). More in keeping with the approach of this chapter, Frandsen and Johansen (2010) assert, "The development within the field of strategic management can be described as a long and complex journey, moving away from a position that can be described as *normative idealism* to a position that can be described as *critical realism*" (p. 298). As we shall see in the approaches to justice from David Hume and John Rawls, Part III of this book follows the trajectory noted by Frandsen and Johansen and views the relationship of public relations and justice through a materialistic lens of critical realism—yet still moves directly to the conclusion that effective public relations involves the pursuit and advocacy of cooperation and justice.

A materialistic view of justice

As the forthcoming two chapters will document, both David Hume and John Rawls are preeminent philosophers of justice—and each, as we shall see, offers not an aspirational, normative concept of justice, but, rather, one grounded in human self-interest and resource acquisition. Both discussions of justice align with Peter Kropotkin's (trans. 1924/1992) conclusion (Chapter 5) that justice is an inevitable outgrowth of human cooperation, which itself is derived and strengthened through the processes of natural selection:

> In the same instinct [mutual aid] we have the origin of those feelings of benevolence and of that partial identification of the individual with the group which are the starting-point of all the higher ethical feelings. It is upon this foundation that the higher sense of justice, or equity, is developed . . . In proportion as mutual aid becomes an established custom in a human community, and so to say instinctive, it leads to a parallel development of the sense of *justice*, with its necessary accompaniment of the sense of *equity* and equalitarian self-restraint.
>
> (pp. 16–30)

We should recall that Kropotkin, like Charles Darwin, did not view cooperative mutual aid as a noble goal of our species. Rather, it was our species' most effective survival strategy, prevailing over competitive and conflict-ridden relationships. Perhaps the only fact on which the six key evolutionary biologists of Part II agree—besides the basic existence of natural selection—is that cooperative relationships generate more resources than egoistic relationships. For Kropotkin, natural selection engenders self-interested cooperation, which, in turn, engenders self-interested justice.

Announcing that a quest for justice—whatever its source—is or should be a goal of public relations is hardly a new or bold idea. Even within the current "paradigmatic variety" (Edwards, 2012, p. 7) that characterizes the envisioning and enactment of public relations, the championing of justice frequently appears, as we shall see, as a core value for the discipline. However, as Heath (2006) notes, critics of public relations do hold that the profession includes

> a penchant for deception and other base acts: promoting one vested interest against other interests, engaging in irresponsible advocacy, controlling information to the advantage of an interest, lying, spinning, and otherwise betraying the public interest and trust . . .
>
> (p. 94)

Curtin and Gaither (2005) further observe that the inevitable presence of power disparities in relationships complicates traditional notions of justice and fair play:

> The basic problem remains, however: These [idealistic] approaches assume that power, while perhaps not absent from relationships, can be controlled and ultimately set aside in the name of a greater social good

by relying on a utopian vision 'of noncoerced consensus in an ideal communication community' (Weber, 2002, p. 309).

(pp. 95–96)

Fortunately, the materialistic approaches of Hume and Rawls will show that we need not retreat to idealism and utopianism to see a form of justice, albeit imperfect, as deeply embedded within human nature and actually conducive to the resource acquisition aims of public relations. The research of the evolutionary biologists of Part II already has shown the unsustainability of the "irresponsible advocacy" that, according to the critics Heath cites, characterizes some enactments of public relations.

In public relations as in other professions, ethics involves the identification of "values that members of the profession are encouraged to internalise" (Harrison, 2004, p. 2). Envisioning justice and the pursuit of justice as a core value within public relations is a pervasive, if broadly defined, idea within the discipline. Isocratean rhetoric, posited by Heath (2000) and Marsh (2001) as a formative antecedent of modern public relations, is founded on the intertwined values of justice and moderation (Poulakos, 1997). L.A. Grunig, Toth, and Hon (2000) include justice as one of the key "feminist values in public relations" (p. 49). Holtzhausen (2000) has observed that although justice is a core value within postmodern approaches to public relations, the tendency of postmodernism to resist metanarratives prevents a single, widespread definition or standard enactment of that value. Curtin and Boynton (2001) have charted the history of justice as a key element within deontological and other approaches to public relations ethics. Leichty (2003) positions the "justice principle" as one of the "foundational beliefs" in public relations, but he notes that attitudes toward and enactments of justice differ among various approaches to the discipline (p. 279). Both Nel (2001) and Simmons and Walsh (2012) have asserted that organizational justice can provide a "basis for planning, framing and evaluating organizational communication and processes that would help PR focus on the frames and drivers of fairness" (Simmons & Walsh, 2012, p. 141); organizational justice "tends to use the terms justice and fairness interchangeably. . .and focuses on studying what people perceive to be fair, rather than normative criteria" (Simmons & Walsh, 2012, p. 143). McKie and Munshi, in *Reconfiguring Public Relations: Ecology, Equity and Enterprise* (2007), define the equity specified by their book's title "in a broad sense to encompass issues of diversity, democracy, politics, and justice" (p. 25). Finally, Bowen (2010) notes that viewing public relations even "as the management of competition and conflict can be supported through the moral philosophy of justice," though she adds this counterbalance:

The evidence. . . suggests that only the highest level decision makers within the public relations profession actively consider concepts of justice in their decision making and that those at lower levels of responsibility most often consider creating advantage through persuasive advocacy.

(p. 575)

This reported absence of justice as a core value at most levels of public relations suggests a lack of universality of this concept within the profession. Roberts' (2012) finding that the word *justice* itself does not appear in standard public relations ethics codes underscores this lack of universality. Roberts (2012) concludes that public relations has no settled definition of justice and no inherent commitment to such a value: "Philosophers' and practitioners' concepts of justice vary widely, and. . . not everyone sees the need to balance justice against other considerations" (p. 167). Indeed, justice would not seem to be a primary value within one prominent definition that casts public relations as a contributor an adversarial society, in which "truth is not so important as the obligation of opposing counsel to create scenarios that conflict with those of their opponents" (Barney & Black, 1994, p. 244). Despite its popularity with some public relations scholars, then, a quest for justice may appear excessively normative for the day-to-day realities of public relations practice.

As Holtzhausen (2000) and Marsh (2013) note, the concept of justice within public relations has a variety of definitions. Legal scholar Peter Koller (2009) maintains that "four kinds of justice" can characterize "social relationships":

1. transactional justice applying to exchange relationships;
2. political justice concerning power relationships;
3. distributive justice dealing with communal relationships; and
4. correctional justice focusing on wrongness relationships. (p. 188)

The three chapters of Part III of this book will focus on the transactional justice of exchange relationships, the definition that seems to fit best with a practical resource-acquisition vision of public relations. Transactional justice "demands that. . . transactions occur in a way which makes sure that, in general, they are to the benefit of all parties involved, so that none of them has a legitimate reason to complain about the outcome" (Koller, 2009, pp. 188–189). Koller (2009) holds that such transactions "are between independent parties who agree on a mutual transfer of certain goods or services" (p. 188). Again, the forthcoming chapters on David Hume and John Rawls will offer decidedly materialistic explanations for the existence of transactional justice.

A materialistic view of ethics

If, as philosophers dating at least to Plato assert, a value such as justice is part of a larger system of ethics, we also can take a non-idealistic approach to that larger field: Kropotkin's (trans. 1924/1992) praise of Darwin, in Chapter 4, already has made a case for the materialistic origins of ethics:

> Darwin pointed out that the social instinct. . . has been developed by
> natural selection for its own sake, as it was useful for the well-being and
> the preservation of the species . . . Nature has thus to be recognized as
> the first ethical teacher of man. The social instinct, innate in men as well
> as in all the social animals,— is the origin of all ethical conceptions and
> all the subsequent development of morality.
>
> (pp. 37, 45)

Decades earlier, Darwin (1871/1998) had written, "Ultimately our moral sense
or conscience becomes a highly complex sentiment—originating in the social
instincts" (p. 137)—and, again, in the pages of his notebooks, he had laughed
at his audacity, declaring, "Oh you Materialist!" (Barrett et al., 1987, p. 291).

Darwin (1871/1998) even rejected idealistic utilitarianism (with its
calculation of the greatest happiness for the greatest number) as a direct
motivation for altruistic—or, in his words, "sympathetic"—behavior (p. 110).
In *The Descent of Man* (1871/1998), he concludes:

> Under circumstances of extreme peril, as during a fire, when a man endea-
> vors to save a fellow-creature without a moment's hesitation, he can hardly
> feel pleasure; and still less has he time to reflect on the dissatisfaction
> which he might subsequently experience if he did not make the attempt.
> Should he afterwards reflect over his own conduct, he would feel that there
> lies within him an impulsive power widely different from a search after
> pleasure or happiness; and this seems to be the deeply planted social
> instinct.
>
> (p. 124)

For Darwin, the impulse to aid another, even at a potential cost, is pure materialistic instinct.

Within Western materialistic philosophy, Friedrich Nietzsche (1844–1900)
is an unusual champion of the power of cooperation over egoistic conflict
and competition—unusual because, like Freud (Chapter 3), Nietzsche believes
that cooperation (although triumphant) is alien to original human nature
and has debased our species. In particular, Nietzsche (trans. 1913/2003)
believes that social altruism is a manifestation of the victory of debased
"slaves" over the "egoistic. . . aristocratic [master] races" (pp. 17, 11, 23)—
the races of Nietzsche's favored "blond brute" who is driven by "the Will to
Power" and "the ecstasies of victory and cruelty" (pp. 22, 51, 23). In *The
Genealogy of Morals*, Nietzsche (trans. 1913/2003) writes:

> To-day the prejudice is predominant, which, acting even now with all the
> intensity of an obsession and brain disease, holds that "moral," "altruistic,"
> and *"désinteressé"* [disinterested] are concepts of equal value . . . The
> *revolt of the slaves* begins in the sphere of *morals*; that revolt which has

behind it a history of two millennia, and which at the present day has only moved out of our sight, because it—has achieved victory.

(pp. 11, 17)

In Nietzsche's view, the perverse victory of altruism over egoism involves a sublimation of our inherent cruelty. If we can no longer bring ourselves to be cruel to others, we will be cruel to ourselves by denying our will to power and cruelty:

> I regard the bad conscience as the serious illness which man was bound to contract under the stress of the most radical change which he has ever experienced—that change, when he found himself finally imprisoned within the pale of society and of peace . . . It is only the bad conscience, only the will for self-abuse, that provides the necessary conditions for the existence of altruism as a *value* . . . Man . . . invented the bad conscience so as to hurt himself after the *natural* outlet for this will to hurt, became blocked.
>
> (Nietzsche, trans. 1913/2003, pp. 56, 59, 62–63)

From one of the leading philosophers of Western civilization, this is hardly an idealistic addition to the consilience of cooperation, and that is why I include it. Nietzsche despises peaceful social cooperation—even as he acknowledges its victory over egoism and narrow self-interest within human nature. Forecasting the later misgivings of Freud, Nietzsche (trans. 1913/2003) laments, "The very essence of all civilisation is to train out of man, the beast of prey" (p. 23).

Nietzsche has a similarly materialistic assessment of the origins of justice. Like Hume (Chapter 9), he attributes the origins of sociality in general and justice in particular to commerce:

> It is then in this sphere of the law of contract that we find the cradle of the whole moral world of the ideas . . . The feeling of "ought," of personal obligation . . . has had, as we saw, its origin in the oldest and most original personal relationship that there is, the relationship between buyer and seller, creditor and owner . . . There has not yet been found a grade of civilisation so low, as not to manifest some trace of this relationship. Making prices, assessing values, thinking out equivalents, exchanging— all this preoccupied the primal thoughts of man . . . Sale and purchase, together with their psychological concomitants, are older than the origins of any form of social organisation and union . . . Man soon arrived at the great generalisation, "everything has its price, all can be paid for," the oldest and most naive moral canon of justice, the beginning of all "kindness," of all "equity," of all "goodwill."
>
> (Nietzsche, trans. 1913/2003, pp. 41, 44, 45)

If public relations, at some level, involves the process of securing necessary resources, then even Nietzsche (albeit bitterly) would argue that we inevitably operate within a realm that involves concepts of equity and kindness.

Ethics and habit

In Chapter 9, David Hume (1739/1968) will argue that justice becomes an inherent, natural value within humans only after eons of existence as a practical, materialistic, "artificial" value (p. 484). Aristotle (trans. 1984b), of course, offers a similar view, holding that virtue is not intrinsic within human nature; it is, rather, developed by habit:

> Moral excellence comes about as a result of habit . . . It is also plain that none of the moral excellences arises in us by nature; for nothing that exists by nature can form a habit contrary to its nature . . . Neither by nature, then, nor contrary to nature do excellences arise in us; rather we are adapted by nature to receive them, and are made perfect by habit . . . Men become builders by building and lyre-players by playing the lyre; so too we become just by doing just acts . . . In our transactions with other men we become just or unjust . . . It makes no small difference, then, whether we form habits of one kind or of another from our very youth; it makes a very great difference, or rather *all* the difference.
>
> (1103a, 1103b)

In short, we are not naturally good. For Aristotle (trans. 1984b), moral excellence (clearly including a quest for justice) is a choice, not an idealistic default position within human nature: "Again, we feel anger and fear without choice, but the excellences are choices or involve choice" (1106a).

Darwin (1871/1998), as we have seen, asserts that some human qualities now accepted as virtues actually have self-interested, biological origins—but he does concur with Aristotle on the power of habit:

> The so-called moral sense is aboriginally derived from the social instincts, for both relate at first exclusively to the community . . . Ultimately our moral sense or conscience becomes a highly complex sentiment— originating in the social instincts, largely guided by the approbation of our fellow-men, ruled by reason, self-interest, and in later times by deep religious feelings, and confirmed by instruction and habit.
>
> (pp. 128, 137)

Later, in his *Autobiography*, he added, "By degrees it will become intolerable to [an individual] to obey his sensuous passions rather than his higher impulses, which when rendered habitual may be almost called instincts" (1887/1983, p. 55).

Modern neuroscience actually offers substantial evidence that Aristotle and Darwin are correct—at least in regard to the power of habit. Donald Pfaff (Pfaff & Sherman), originator of altruistic brain theory (Chapter 3), notes that recent research "has shown that if we practice morality the brain will actually develop pathways that reinforce that behavior. . . . Creation of such 'neural niches' allows transitory events, such as training in empathic behavior, to be turned into temperamental traits" (pp. 51, 167). Psychologist and science journalist Daniel Goleman (2006) offers this explanation of such pathways:

> Neuroscientists use the term "neural scaffolding" to describe how once a brain circuit has been laid out, its connections become strengthened with repeated use—like a scaffold being erected at a building site. Neural scaffolding explains why a behavioral pattern, once it is established, requires effort to change. But with new opportunities—or perhaps just with effort and awareness—we can lay down and strengthen a new track.
>
> (p. 161)

Ben Franklin (1818/1888) knew as much when, in order to achieve "moral perfection," he developed his list of 13 virtues and proudly set out to embed them by practicing them—adding "Humility" to his original list of 12 at the urging of a friend (pp. 101, 112).

But if moral excellence is, as Aristotle maintains, a choice, why choose it? Why strive, for example, for justice? Doesn't that take us to idealism? Aristotle's answer, instead, takes us more toward self-interest and teleology: As he writes in *Generation of Animals* (trans. 1984a), "Everything then exists for a final cause" or purpose (778b). For Aristotle (trans. 1984b), ethics is the process of discerning and achieving the "chief good" in life (1094a). In *Outlines of the History of Ethics*, Sidgwick (1902/1988) approvingly paraphrases Aristotle in holding that "the primary subject of ethical investigation is all that is included under the notion of what is ultimately good or desirable for man" (p. 2). Aristotle (trans. 1984b) posits that this ultimate goal or "chief good" is "happiness" (1095a)—or, in Greek, *eudaimonia*, a word, Rackham (1926/2003) laments, that in English we diminish by translating merely as happiness. *Eudaimonia*, Rackham explains, additionally denotes "a kind of activity" consonant with and productive of happiness (p. 10). Similarly, Gregory Vlastos (1991) attributes to Plato what he terms "the Eudaemonist Axiom," which is "that happiness is desired by all human beings as the ultimate end (*telos*) of all their rational acts" (p. 203). For Aristotle (trans. 1984b), happiness and moral excellence are inseparable: "Happiness [*eudaimonia*] is an activity of soul in accordance with complete excellence" (1102a).

Aristotle thus provides yet another materialistic foundation for justice, self-control, and other virtues associated with cooperation. We are not naturally good, he tells us. Rather (like all objects in Aristotle's worldview) we innately strive toward a particular end, which, in our case, is the rich, full, happy life: *eudaimonia*. And that state is attainable only by enacting virtues that can be built and strengthened only by habit. Like his contemporaries Plato and Isocrates, Aristotle (trans. 1984b) lists justice as key among those indispensable virtues. If Aristotle is correct about power of habit—and philosophers from Plato to Mill as well as modern neuroscientists do agree—then enacting cooperation and justice within public relations would strengthen those aspects of ourselves, enabling us to become, in theory, even more cooperative and just. Aristotle would add that in doing so, we even increase our personal chances of happiness, of *eudaimonia*.

Within philosophy—and certainly within theology—there are of course idealistic approaches to cooperation and justice, theories that seek nonphysical explanations for human attributes and behavior. In Plato's *Republic* (trans. 1930/1989), for example, Socrates declares, "Philosophers are those who are capable of apprehending that which is eternal and unchanging" (484B)—a definition that draws this protest from twentieth-century philosopher Karl Popper (1966): "Plato gives the term *philosopher* a new meaning, that of . . . a seer of the divine world" (p. 145). For Plato (trans. 1930/1989), eternal and unchanging concepts are ideas, or forms, in God's mind, and he offers a familiar example:

> Now God, whether because he so willed or because some compulsion was laid upon him not to make more than one couch in nature, so wrought and created one only, the couch which really and in itself is. But two or more such were never created by God and never will come into being . . . If he should make only two, there would again appear one of which they both would possess the form or idea, and that would be the couch that really is in and of itself, and not the other two.
>
> (597C)

The best philosophers, Plato (trans. 1930/1989) concludes, are able to discover this "first principle itself" (533C), this original couch. Plato's sense of the transcendent forecasts Kant's (trans. 1836) idealism in attributing a human sense of duty to a divine source. This book, however, avoids such idealistic approaches because of their association with normative, aspirational, and even utopian worldviews of public relations. Again, we can adopt a strict materialistic, empirical, critical-realism approach to human behavior—and we can still assert that public relations logically should be a striving toward social harmony.

Summary

Even this brief examination of philosophical materialism leads us to at least two important points for the understanding and practice of public relations:

1. We do not need philosophical idealism to defend the social harmony frameworks of public relations. Philosophical materialism, grounded in empiricism and even, sometimes, in pessimism, clearly offers firm foundations for the discipline's social harmony frameworks.
2. Habit is both essential and effective in forming the values inherent in ethical behavior. Enacting cooperation and justice within public relations can strengthen the commitment to and the prevalence of those values.

These two points address two of the Nine Tenets of public relations' social harmony frameworks outlined in Chapter 1:

III. Cooperative relationships are not merely normative, idealistic, or utopian. Rather, evidence from evolutionary biology, philosophy, and rhetoric shows that cooperation is a stronger instinct within human nature than the competing instincts of egoism, conflict, and competition.
IX. Public relations practitioners can take specific actions, drawn from evolutionary biology, philosophy, and rhetoric, to build and enhance relationships built upon cooperation and justice.

Chapter 9

David Hume and the origins of justice

In his concept of justice as fairness, philosopher John Rawls is adamant that without justice, social cooperation is impossible. Before Rawls, however, eighteenth-century Scottish philosopher David Hume pushed the linkage of justice and cooperation even further: Justice not only is essential to social cooperation; justice engenders the society sustained by cooperation. For Hume, justice predates and creates society—and, fortunately for our materialistic, utopia-shunning viewpoint in this book, the justice that begets society and cooperation begins, for Hume, not with altruism but with pure human self-interest. Ideally, this chapter will demonstrate that, far from being a normative ideal, justice—as defined by Hume—is inextricably embedded within resource dependency theory, that staple of so many approaches to public relations. In Hume's estimation, to work for the sustainable transfer of resources is unavoidably to work for justice. Additionally, Hume believed a respect for justice to be the primary foundation of a positive reputation—an idea, as we shall see, not far afield from evolutionary biology's association of reputation with indirect reciprocity. Far from being utopian, then, some measure of a quest for justice seems both inevitable and advisable within the practice of public relations. Through the philosophy of David Hume, I'll strive to continue to show the practical, as opposed to merely normative, status of justice as a core value of public relations.

For a moment, however, we must hearken back to how we are defining justice and what we mean by resource dependency theory. Again, of the four forms of social-relationship justice described by Koller (2009)—transactional, political, distributive, and correctional—this chapter will focus on the transactional justice of exchange relationships. Transactional justice "demands that . . .transactions occur in a way which makes sure that, in general, they are to the benefit of all parties involved, so that none of them has a legitimate reason to complain about the outcome (Koller, 2009, pp. 188–189). Koller (2009) holds that such transactions "are between independent parties who agree on a mutual transfer of certain goods or services" (p. 188). As we shall see below, however, Hume gradually expands this concept of justice into what we now recognize as John Rawls' pervasive "justice as fairness" concept of social justice. As for resource dependency theory, here again are its three basic tenets:

1. To fulfill their values-driven goals, organizations and other entities need resources such as raw materials, fair media coverage, and employee dedication and commitment.
2. Some of those key resources are not controlled by the organization or entity.
3. To acquire those resources, organizations and other entities build productive relationships with the publics that control the resources. (Guth & Marsh, 2017, p. 19)

Hume's theory of justice directly addresses this core concept in public relations.

Because the bulk of this chapter will focus on Hume's concept of justice and its inherent relationship to resources, we should note that few scholarly works in public relations have cited Hume's influence. J.E. Grunig (1993) cites Hume's importance in the analysis of human thought and Pieczka (1996) his pioneering idea that public opinion is the foundation of government. Lawniczak (2009) casts Hume as a progenitor of modern economics— increasingly so, perhaps, as economists begin, like Hume (1739/1968), to believe that we may be governed more by emotion than rationality (p. 415). Moore (2012) recalls Hume's attack on the primacy of reason, and Everett and Johnston (2012) touch on his indictment of inductive processes. L'Etang (1996) does note that Hume's concept of justice includes the idea of reciprocity, a point to which this article will return below. A search of Google Scholar, in 2016, revealed no works besides the earlier journal-article version of this chapter that included the terms *public relations* and *Hume* in their title.

Hume's philosophy of justice: An overview

David Hume (1711–1776) was a Scottish philosopher, historian, and diplomat. Today, he is known best for his philosophical skepticism about the reliability of two staples of modern logic: Causality and inductive reasoning. Accordingly, he believed that "reason" functioned primarily as "the slave of the passions" (1739/1968, p. 415). Hume's general skepticism is significant for public relations because, historically, scholars have viewed him as a pleasant—*le bon David* (Edmonds & Eidinow, 2006, p. 3)—but steely-eyed realist, a philosopher highly unlikely to lead modern public relations scholars into unrealistic visions of self-sacrifice and utopian justice: Hume (1739/1968), in fact, challenged the intrinsic morality of quests for justice. Of Hume's philosophy, Steven Pinker (2011) writes, "It begins with skepticism" and remains fully cognizant of "the history of human folly, and our own susceptibility to illusions and fallacies" (p. 180). Hume's hard-nosed concept of justice and its relation to the possession and exchange of resources remains a powerful idea in modern philosophy: "[Hume's] notion of justice as dealing *with conflicting claims regarding possessions* in *circumstances of scarcity* becomes a pervasive theme throughout modern discussions" (Lebacqz, 1986, pp. 18–19); that description already touches on resource dependency theory, a point to which we will return. Extending to religious matters, Hume's skepticism played a significant role in dashing his wish to hold a Chair of Ethics professorship at Edinburgh University (Baillie, 2000). In fact, the philosopher and economist Adam Smith, author of *The Wealth of Nations* and one of Hume's greatest friends, was excoriated for his written praise of Hume's character after his death:

> A single, and as I thought, a very harmless Sheet of paper, which I happened to write concerning the death of our late friend, Mr. Hume, brought upon me ten times more abuse than the very violent attack I had made upon the whole commercial system of Great Britain.
>
> (Baillie, 2000, p. 9)

In comparing Hume with Darwin, historian Anthony Gottlieb (2016) concludes:

> He argued that the study of the mind and of morals should be pursued by the same empirical methods that were starting to cast new light on the rest of nature. Philosophy, for Hume, was thus not fundamentally different from science. This outlook is much more common in our time than it was in his.
>
> (para. 6)

In this overview section, I'll sketch Hume's beliefs regarding the origins and maintenance of justice. Following the overview, additional sections will offer textual evidence for Hume's specific beliefs and will link them to resource dependency theory, reputation, reciprocity, and other touchstones of modern public relations.

We can liken Hume's concept of justice to a four-square box (Figure 9.1), with respective quadrants devoted to human nature (in particular, self-interest), property, justice, and society. Primary among the quadrants—the first cause, so to speak—is human nature; each quadrant, however, helps shape and sustain the others.

In brief, Hume maintains that justice is born in the self-interested human need for stable and transferable property; *stable* in this sense denotes reliable, sustainable ownership. The relationship between justice and property is symbiotic: Without a desire for property (including intangible property, such as reputation), there is no human impetus for justice—and without justice, there can be no stable and transferable property. The provenance of justice, for

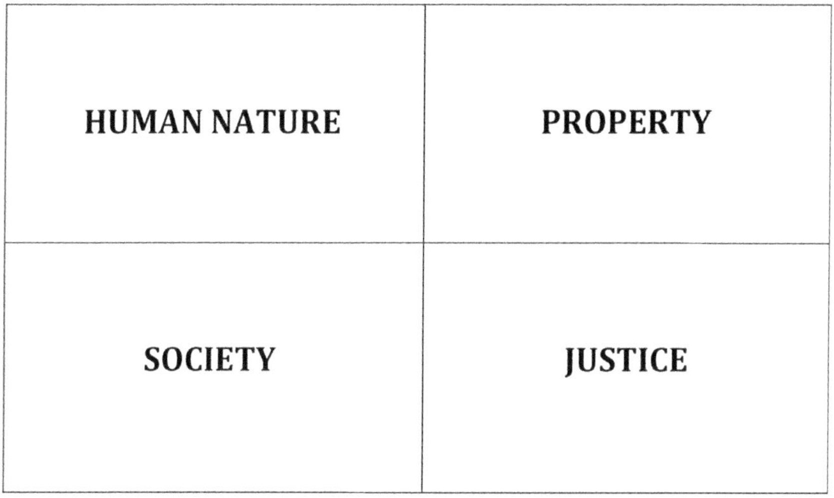

HUMAN NATURE	PROPERTY
SOCIETY	JUSTICE

Figure 9.1 Origins and maintenance of justice (Hume)

Hume, is the need for reliable property; the provenance of enduringly stable and transferable property is pervasive and sustained justice.

One source of possible frustration for scholars is that Hume defines his concept of justice more by origin and effects than by a traditional dictionary definition. "Hume does not offer a direct definition of justice," Lebacqz (1986) concedes. "However, from his discussion it can be seen that justice has to do with 'separating' and respecting claims about private property" (p. 18). Other scholars have noted the same lack of definition but, like Lebacqz, have underscored Hume's close association of justice with property and property exchange (Miller, 1976; Harrison, 1981; Gauthier, 1998; Baier, 2010). Hume, in fact, elaborately demonstrates that imaginary societies with no need for stable property and the exchange of property—such as societies characterized by a super-abundance of resources—would require no traditional concepts of justice (Gauthier, 1998). Rawls (1971) makes much the same point in *A Theory of Justice* (p. 128) and Johan Almenberg and Anna Dreber (2013), the economist/game theorists cited in Chapter 7, concur while noting the unreality of that situation: "If a resource is unlimited in supply, there is no conflict between your material well-being and mine. But resources are usually limited in supply" (pp. 132–133).

Though Hume's early efforts to describe justice in *A Treatise of Human Nature* and *An Enquiry Concerning the Principles of Morals* clearly focus primarily on basic property rights, in his later *History of England* he expands his concept of justice to include fairness in additional realms. In *The Cautious*

Jealous Virtue, a study of Hume's concept of justice, Baier (2010) writes, "Hume in his *History* has enlarged his conception of justice to include fair trials, fair return on labor, a fair chance at some station in life, a fair account of one's character, as well as protection of one's property rights" (pp. 97–98). Later philosophers, particularly Rawls, would emphasize that a sustainable system of resource exchange must be fair and cognizant of the have-nots in society. But even Rawls (1971), in *A Theory of Justice*, directly agrees with Hume regarding the origins of justice within self-interest and property:

> Hume's account of [the originating circumstances of justice] is especially perspicuous and [Rawls'] preceding summary [of those circumstances] adds nothing essential to his much fuller discussion . . . The circumstances of justice obtain whenever mutually disinterested persons put forward conflicting claims to the division of social advantages under conditions of moderate scarcity. Unless these circumstances existed there would be no occasion for the virtue of justice, just as in the absence of threats of injury to life and limb there would be no occasion for physical courage.
>
> (pp. 127–128)

Rawls both endorses and expands Hume, elaborating the concept of fairness inherent in Hume's theory of justice. We can, thus, extend Rawls' general idea of justice as fairness (2001) to Hume's idea of justice, particularly as Hume did enlarge his concept beyond property to the fairnesses emphasized by Baier (2010). Indeed, as we shall see, Hume believed that the foundation of justice could grow from these origins rooted in self-interest to moral underpinnings.

Through the notion of stable and transferable property, then, Hume's concept of justice embeds itself within resource dependency. For Hume, to work for the stability and the fair transfer of property (or owned resources) in general or in particular is, intentionally or not, to work for transactional justice. And conversely, to work for transactional justice is to strengthen the stability and fair transferability of property, both in general and in particular cases. According to Hume, to work for a just society—Heath's (2006) fully functioning society, perhaps—is, in part, to work for the increased sustainability of a fair, broad, and secure system of resource acquisition and exchange, a system essential to many (surely most) concepts of public relations.

A final extension of Hume's theory of justice—again shared by Rawls (1971; 2001) and philosophers ranging from Thomas Hobbes (1651/1985) in the seventeenth century to Robert Nozick (1974) in the twentieth century—holds that the overall scarcity of resources and the consequent need for transferable property helps drive the formation of societies with laws: Without property (transferable resources) and transactional justice, there can be no enduring society. This extension links Hume's theory of justice to the reflective paradigm of public relations, which, again, holds that the ultimate resource sought by public relations practitioners is the social legitimacy of the entities they represent (van Ruler & Verčič, 2005). There can be no social legitimacy without society—and, in Hume's view, there can be no society without justice. A quest for justice, thus, helps establish the venue (society) within which exists the ultimate resource (social legitimacy) in the reflective paradigm.

In yet another link to modern public relations, Hume notes that an individual's respect for others' property—i.e., an individual's personal enactments of transactional justice—does more than any other element to enhance his or her reputation. This idea will be developed below.

The forthcoming fleshing out of Hume's theory of justice offers evidence for this overview and includes seven broad topics and their connection to public relations:

1. Human self-interest leads to a desire for stable property.
2. Personal security necessitates acquiring resources held by others.
3. Justice is derived from the need for stable, transferable property.
4. Through habit and custom, justice becomes a value with moral foundations.
5. Respect for property and justice builds reputation.
6. Property and justice lead to the formation of society.
7. Concepts of justice can vary from society to society.

Again, viewing property as, in part, transferable resources make clear the link between Hume's philosophy and the core concept of resource dependency theory. Finally, all of this is wrapped in Hume's (1751/1983) skepticism and his pioneering efforts to apply scientific empiricism to a study of human nature and society:

> Men are now cured of their passion for hypotheses and systems in natural philosophy [i.e., science, in the eighteenth century], and will hearken to no arguments but those which are derived from experience. It is full time they should attempt a like reformation in all moral disquisitions; and reject every system of ethics, however subtle or ingenious, which is not founded on fact and observation.
>
> (p. 16)

Philosophy professor Don Ross (2011) has noted the similarity of Hume's empirical conclusions about social cooperation to the findings of the modern game theorists reviewed in Chapter 7 of this book:

> Hume, whose game-theoretic intuitions were astonishingly well developed in their completeness, clarity, and reliability, repeatedly explained moral rules governing social conduct as explicit regimentations of what we now

recognise as equilibrium behaviour in coordination games and other collective action problems . . . It grounded the social order in "natural" evolution
rather than "artificial" normative construction.

(p. 122)

Human self-interest leads to a desire for stable property

Property, Hume (1751/1983) asserts, is "any thing, which it is lawful for [an
individual], and for him alone, to use" (p. 30.) As a stable entity, it is "a constant possession, secur'd by the laws of society. . ." (1739/1968, pp. 504–505).
Such property need not be tangible but also "may extend to services and
actions, which we may exchange to our mutual interest and advantage"
(Hume, 1739/1968, p. 520). A cornerstone of *A Treatise of Human Nature*
is Hume's (1739/1968) belief that human self-interest triggers the desire
for property:

> But 'tis certain, that self-love, when it acts at its liberty, instead of engaging
> us to honest actions, is the source of all injustice and violence . . . This
> avidity alone, of acquiring goods and possessions for ourselves and our
> nearest friends, is insatiable, perpetual, universal, and directly destructive
> of society. There scarce is any one, who is not actuated by it; and there is
> no one, who has not reason to fear from it, when it acts without any restraint,
> and gives way to its first and most natural movements.
>
> (pp. 480, 491–492)

Hume maintains that this inherent selfishness gives rise both to property and,
as we shall see, to justice. This bleak view of human nature helps allay,
perhaps, concerns that envisioning public relations as, in part, a quest for justice
idealizes human nature and is improbably normative.

It is worth a quick digression, I hope, to note how Hume's belief in our
insatiable acquisitiveness ties to ideas expressed earlier in this book. In *The
Descent of Man*, for example, Darwin (1871/1998) declares, "The wish for
another man's property is perhaps as persistent a desire as any that can be
named" (p. 116). Though Darwin does not mention Hume by name in the main
text of either *Origin* or *Descent* (excluding endnotes and references), his pre-
Origin notebooks mention Hume several times, often specifying particular
essays to be reviewed.

Darwin's self-professed bulldog, Thomas Henry Huxley, was more effusive.
Huxley particularly admired Hume, even publishing a book on his life and
philosophy in 1879. Early in that work, he acknowledges that the dispassionate
subtitle of Hume's *A Treatise of Human Nature* had won his heart: *Being an
Attempt to Introduce the Experimental Method of Reasoning into Moral
Subjects* (T.H. Huxley, 1900, p. 51). In his volume on Hume, Huxley (1900)

even asserted—as had Plato millennia earlier (Yunis, 2003)—that philosophy was simply an extension of science and that Hume had helped to solidify that relationship: "Philosophy lies in the province of science, and not in that of letters . . . The laboratory is the fore-court of the temple of philosophy" (p. 43). Huxley (1900) praised Hume's scientific ability to "support the cause of righteousness in a cool, reasonable . . .fashion" (p. 196). We should recall that Huxley's standards for scientific rigor were so high that he initially accepted Darwin's theory of natural selection only conditionally, believing it, of course, to be true but withholding final endorsement until proof, not deduction, was produced. Peter Kropotkin (trans. 1924/1992) describes Hume's approach to philosophy in a similarly approving manner: "The bases of all knowledge rest on natural science, and its methods should be adopted in other sciences" (p. 198). Thus, the skeptical empiricists whom we examined in the previous section of this book champion Hume, including his belief that a quest for justice is not normative; it is, rather, an inalienable part of human nature.

Echoing Hume's belief that justice enables society, Huxley (1897), in *Ethics and Evolution*, writes:

> One of the oldest and most important elements in [ethical] systems is the conception of justice. Society is impossible unless those who are associated agree to observe certain rules of conduct towards one another; its stability depends on the steadiness with which they abide by that agreement; and, so far as they waver, that mutual trust which is the bond of society is weakened or destroyed.
>
> (p. 56)

We will return to this point below.

Personal security necessitates acquiring resources held by others

"Nature," Hume 1739/1968) writes, "seems, at first sight, to have exercis'd . . . cruelty . . . towards man, in the numberless wants and necessities, with which she has loaded him, and in the slender means, which she affords to the relieving [of] these necessities" (p. 484). Humans address these personal wants and necessities, he continues, through a system of resource exchange:

> Different parts of the earth produce different commodities; and not only so, but different men both are by nature fitted for different employments, and attain to greater perfection in any one, when they confine themselves to it alone. All this requires a mutual exchange and commerce; for which reason the translation [transfer] of property by consent is founded on a law of nature . . .
>
> (Hume, 1739/1968, p. 514)

"'Tis by society alone," Hume (1739/1968) maintains, that individuals are able to exchange property and prosper (p. 485), and he adds, "Possession and property shou'd always be stable, except when the proprietor consents to bestow them on some other person" (p. 514). Such an analysis seems perfectly consonant with resource dependency theory.

Justice is derived from the need for stable, transferable property

In nascent societies, Hume (1739/1968) holds, the self-interested need for stable, transferable property leads to "abstinence from the possessions of others"—and from this beginning, "there immediately arise the ideas of justice and injustice. . ." (p. 490). Hume's (1739/1968) unflattering view of human nature surfaces again in his stark summation that " *'tis only from the selfishness and confin'd generosity of men, along with the scanty provision nature has made for his wants, that justice derives its origin"* (p. 495). In *A Treatise of Human Nature*, Hume (1739/1968) repeatedly returns to this idea that justice per se does not originate in basic human nature but, rather, is a social convention derived from the self-interested need for stable property:

> The chief impediment to . . .society and partnership lies in the avidity and selfishness of [humans'] natural temper; to remedy which, they enter into a convention for the stability of possession, and for mutual restraint and forbearance . . . Those moral rules concerning . . . justice . . .arise merely from human conventions, and from the interest, which we have in the preservation of peace and order.
>
> (pp. 503, 569)

Hume's insistence on this non-idealistic origin of justice greatly appealed to Kropotkin, who, as we saw in Chapter 5, fervently rejected Kant's belief in the divine origin of social obligations, or duty. "The idea of justice presented itself to Hume chiefly under the guise of square dealing in order to protect the rights of property," Kropotkin (trans. 1924/1992) explains, "and not at all in the broader sense of equity" (p. 200).

Hume's (1739/1968) concept of the origins of justice touches on another staple of modern public relations theory and resource exchange (and, as we have seen, of evolutionary biology)—the norm of reciprocity (J.E. Grunig & White, 1992; Coombs, 1993; Culbertson & Knott, 2004): "Justice establishes itself by a kind of convention or agreement; that is, by a sense of interest, suppos'd to be common to all, and where every single act is perform'd in expectation that others are to perform the like" (p. 498). Gouldner (1960) offers a concise modern definition of the norm of reciprocity:

> Specifically, I suggest that a norm of reciprocity, in its universal form, makes two interrelated, minimal demands: (1) people should help

thosewho have helped them, and (2) people should not injure those who have helped them.

(p. 171)

Coombs and Holladay (2012), however, note that, within public relations, the norm of reciprocity does not obviate potentially unjust power disparities within organization-public relations. Although the game theorists of evolutionary biology demonstrate the ultimately self-defeating nature of power abuse in human transactions (Chapter 7), that eventuality may be scant consolation for current sufferers. In *The Selfish Gene*, Dawkins (2006a) starkly describes both the inevitability of self-interest as well as the consequences of failed reciprocity:

> To a survival machine, another survival machine (which is not its own child or another close relative) is part of its environment, like a rock or a river or a lump of food. It is something that gets in the way, or something that can be exploited. It differs from a rock or a river in one important respect: it is inclined to hit back. This is because it too is a machine that holds its immortal genes in trust for the future, and it too will stop at nothing to preserve them.
>
> (p. 66)

Hume believes that justice and reciprocity are born in our species' desire to avoid a property-focused, Hobbesian war of all against all.

Through habit and custom, justice becomes a value with moral foundations

Because of his firm belief that "the rules of justice are establish'd merely by interest," Hume (1739/1968) denies the existence of an original, idealistic yearning for justice per se within human nature:

> We must allow, that the sense of justice and injustice is not deriv'd from nature, but arises artificially, tho' necessarily from education, and human conventions . . . To avoid giving offence, I must here observe, that when I deny justice to be a natural virtue, I make use of the word, *natural*, only as oppos'd to *artificial* . . . Tho' the rules of justice be *artificial*, they are not *arbitrary*.
>
> (pp. 497, 483–484)

For Hume, "Something is artificial if it is the product of convention, that is, of human rules and/or institutions. So 'artificial' is a purely descriptive term, with no pejorative connotations" (Baillie, 2000, p. 153). Still, perhaps troubled by the negative connotations of *artificial*, Hume downplayed the distinction between artificial and natural virtues in the *Enquiry* (1751/1983), which followed the *Treatise* (1739/1968) by 12 years (Bourke, 1968). Hume (1777) believed that, of all his writings, the *Enquiry* was "incomparably the best" (p. 16).

Through habit, custom, and education, however, Hume (1739/1968) holds that the value of justice gradually becomes integrated into human nature: "Nothing causes any sentiment to have a greater influence upon us than custom, or turns our imagination more strongly to any object" (p. 556). A quest for justice, then, can become part of human nature when individuals are "train'd up according to a certain discipline and education" (Hume, 1739/1968, p. 479). As we saw in Chapter 8, Aristotle (trans. 1984b) makes much the same point in *Nicomachean Ethics*, declaring, "Moral excellence comes about as a result of habit . . . It is also plain that none of the moral excellences arises in us by nature" (1103a).

Just as Darwin (1871/1998) later held that the social instinct within humans is "confirmed by instruction and habit" and that unsocial behavior is, afterward, "judged by the ever-enduring social instinct," leading to "dissatisfaction, or even misery" (pp. 137, 117, 101), Hume (1751/1983) asserts that "where mutual regard and forbearance serve. . . no manner of purpose, they would never direct the conduct of any reasonable man. The headlong course of the passions would be checked by no reflection on future consequences" (p. 26). Rather than this being the case, however, Hume believes that habit strengthens our ability to resist the calling of selfish passions.

Hume (1751/1983), in fact, creeps eerily close to Darwin's revolutionary concept of natural selection in flirting with the idea that justice and transferable property themselves might be offshoots of "some internal sense or feeling, which nature has made universal in the whole species" (p. 15). He tosses the idea aside, however, because identifying the origins of such deep-seated yearnings seems too difficult:

> But who is there that ever heard of such an instinct? Or is this a subject, in which new discoveries can be made? We may as well expect to discover, in the body, new senses, which had before escaped the observation of all mankind . . . It is needless to push our researches so far as to ask, why we have humanity or a fellow-feeling with others.
>
> (Hume, 1751/1983, pp. 32, 43)

Is this a subject in which new discoveries can be made? A century later, Darwin would answer that question, placing the social instinct deeper, surely, than Hume ever imagined. But Darwin (1872) did actually believe, also, that "changed habits produce an *inherited* effect," a belief later condemned as Lamarckianism—that is, the notion that "the increased use or disuse of parts," for example, in a parent would affect the appearance and structure of offspring (p. 8). More recently, the science of epigenetics indicates that an organism's interaction with physical and cultural environments can turn on or turn off genetic behaviors, the result of which could indeed shape offspring (Wilson, 2012)—thereby providing an angle for the possible accuracy of Darwin's comment. If habits shape cultures or physical environments, those spheres, via epigenetics, might be able to shape biology.

In a mature society typified by the generally peaceful and systematic exchange of resources, Hume (1739/1968) thus believes that justice gradually secures two foundations:

> Upon the whole, then, we are to consider this distinction betwixt justice and injustice, as having two different foundations, *viz.* that of *interest*, when men observe, that 'tis impossible to live in society without restraining themselves by certain rules; and that of *morality*, when this interest is once observ'd, and men receive a pleasure from the view of such actions as tend to the peace of society, and an uneasiness from such as are contrary to it. 'Tis the voluntary convention and artifice of men, which makes the first interest take place; and therefore those laws of justice are so far to be consider'd as *artificial*. After that interest is once establish'd and acknowledg'd, the sense of morality in the observance of these rules follows *naturally*, and of itself . . .
>
> (p. 533)

In essence, though it cannot escape its origins in self-interest, justice over time can become a virtue with moral foundations: "*Self-interest is the original motive to the* establishment *of justice: but a* sympathy *with public interest is the source of the* moral approbation, *which attends that virtue*" (Hume, 1739/1968, pp. 499–500). Hume, therefore, certainly would argue that justice might begin as an unavoidable instrumental/means-to-an-end value of public relations but that, over time, it might grow stronger, moving from being only an artificial, situational value to becoming a deeply felt moral value.

Just as he praised Hume for locating the origins of justice within self-interest, Kropotkin (trans. 1924/1992) acknowledged the widening base for justice that Hume proposed: "[Hume] recognized that man is guided in his actions by self-love, but he claimed that man also develops a sense of duty toward others" (p. 202). While Pinker (2011) contends that "the ultimate goal [of empathy] should be policies and norms that become second nature and render empathy unnecessary" (p. 592), Hume describes the reverse of that process in the evolution of justice: Policy and norms born of sheer self-interest lead to empathy, rather than vice versa. Daniel Goleman (2006) cites neuroscientific research in using the term "neural scaffolding" to describe a Humean/habit process in which "once a brain circuit has been laid out, its connections become strengthened with repeated use," thereby gradually creating "a behavioral pattern" (p. 161).

Respect for property and justice builds reputation

Another way in which the increasing moral approbation of justice affects public relations is its impact on the concept of reputation management. As respect
for justice becomes a moral expectation within a maturing society, Hume
believes that compliance with that value would be indispensable in helping
an individual to establish a positive reputation. The individual's consequent
benefit from that reputation would, in turn, reinforce his or her veneration for
justice and its origins in stable property:

> What farther contributes to encrease their [the rules of justice] solidity,
> is the interest of our reputation, after the opinion, *that a merit or demerit
> attends justice or injustice*, is once firmly establish'd among mankind.
> There is nothing, which touches us more nearly than our reputation, and
> nothing on which our reputation more depends than our conduct, with
> relation to the property of others. For this reason, every one, who has any
> regard to his character, or who intends to live on good terms with mankind,
> must fix an inviolable law to himself, never, by any temptation, to be
> induc'd to violate those principles, which are essential to a man of probity
> and honour.
>
> (Hume, 1739/1968, p. 501)

This focus on justice as the builder of reputation is a continuing theme for
Hume (1751/1983), who in the later *Enquiry into the Principles of Morals*
pledges to "consider every attribute of the mind, which renders a man an object
either of esteem and affection, or of hatred and contempt; every habit or
sentiment or faculty, which. . . may enter into any panegyric or satire of his
character" (p. 16). The first two attributes he identifies are "benevolence and
justice. The explication of them will probably give us an opening by which
others may be accounted for" (Hume, 1751/1983, p. 16). In statements, thus,
that are highly significant for envisioning public relations as, in part, a quest
for justice, Hume (1739/1968) concludes that the relationship-oriented concepts of "publick praise and blame encrease our esteem for justice" (p. 500).
Desire for a good reputation, in other words, might help justice gain a moral
foundation—not merely one of self-interest—within public relations.

In connecting benevolence to reputation, Hume (1751/1783) frequently uses
the phrase "disinterested benevolence," which suggests the concept of indirect
reciprocity—a concept that the game theory experiments of Nowak and others
consistently link to a good reputation:

> Nothing can bestow more merit on any human creature than the sentiment
> of benevolence in an eminent degree; and *that* a *part*, at least, of its merit
> arises from its tendency to promote the interests of our species, and bestow
> happiness on human society.
>
> (pp. 92, 20)

Hume (1751/1783) quickly reminds readers, however, that his object is dispassionate analysis, not advocacy: "It is not my present business to recommend generosity and benevolence, or to paint, in their true colours, all the genuine charms of the social virtues" (pp. 17–18). That attitude, which so appealed to Huxley and Kropotkin, serves our ends as well: Hume is not advocating a particular stance in human relationships; he is, rather, analyzing effective motivations and behaviors in a manner that won the admiration of later evolutionary biologists.

Still, Hume (1751/1783) does add that, beyond self-interested protection of property and the establishing of a productive reputation, humans have a genuine interest in cooperating with one another:

> There is some benevolence, however small, infused into our bosom; some spark of friendship for human kind; some particle of the dove, kneaded into our frame, along with the elements of the wolf and serpent. Let these generous sentiments be supposed ever so weak; let them be insufficient to move even a hand or finger of our body; they must still direct the determinations of our mind, and where every thing else is equal, produce a cool preference of what is useful and serviceable to mankind, above what is pernicious and dangerous.
>
> (p. 74)

Such passages led Kropotkin (trans. 1924/1992) to declare, "Hume ascribed a special importance to sympathy. It softens our narrowly selfish tendencies, and, together with the general, natural benevolence of man, overcomes them" (pp. 202–203). However, praising the ever-present skepticism and empiricism that undergirds Hume's writings, Kropotkin (trans. 1924/1992) adds that Hume "had the most independent mind of the eighteenth century" (p. 197).

Evolutionary biologists, psychologists, and rhetoricians have made much the same claims regarding a fusion of justice and reputation—further consilience among the different disciplines. Long before Hume, Isocrates (trans. 2000) declared, "The more ardently someone wants to persuade his audience, the more he will strive . . .to have a good reputation among the citizens" (*Antidosis*, 278). For Isocrates, as I hope to demonstrate in Chapter 12, reputation was inextricably linked to a life built on moderation and justice (Poulakos, 1997). A century after Hume, Charles Darwin (1887/1983), in his *Autobiography*, writes, "If [an individual] acts for the good of others, he will receive the approbation of his fellow-men and gain the love of those with whom he lives; and this latter gain undoubtedly is the highest pleasure on this earth" (p. 55). Pinker (2011), a Harvard professor of psychology, asserts that "the drive to present the self in a positive light was one of the major findings of twentieth-century social psychology" (p. 490). If enacting justice, then, leads to positive reputation, and a positive reputation enhances the processes of resource acquisition—then a quest for justice would seem to be inherent within public relations.

Property and justice lead to the formation of society

Hume's belief that respect for justice and property leads to enhanced reputation and social approbation is, of course, relevant to social-theory approaches to public relations (Ihlen, van Ruler, & Fredriksson, 2009). It is particularly relevant to the reflective paradigm, which focuses on an entity's social legitimacy (Holmström, 2004), and to the role of reputation in developing social capital (Ihlen, 2009; Luoma-aho, 2009). Social theory tends to take a macro-level/societal view of public relations, as opposed to meso-level/organizational approaches or micro-level/individual approaches (McKie & Munshi, 2007; Ihlen, van Ruler, & Fredriksson, 2009). Thus Hume's belief that the intertwined forces of resource dependency and justice create society is significant for a growing body of public relations research: In essence, the indispensable element of social theory—society—has its origins in justice.

Of justice's role in the creation of societies and international relations, Hume (1739/1968) writes:

> But tho' it be possible for men to maintain a small uncultivated society without government, 'tis impossible they shou'd maintain a society of any kind without justice . . . The advantages, therefore, of peace, commerce, and mutual succour, make us extend to different kingdoms the same notions of justice, which take place among individuals.
>
> (pp. 541, 567–568)

Governments within societies, Hume (1739/1968) adds, finds their origins in the same primal force that creates justice and the desire for personal property: "The original sanction of government. . . is *interest*. . ." (p. 555). Again, the quest for justice within public relations, from Hume's perspective, may ultimately become altruistic, but it has its origins in self-interest: For Hume, justice is neither normative nor aspirational. In his work on Hume, Huxley (1900) echoes Hume's assessment of justice, self-interest, and society: "As for justice, the very existence of the virtue implies that of society; public utility is its sole origin" (p. 197).

Significantly, Hume—like Darwin and the game theorists and like, as we shall see, Isocrates—believes that just relationships can unite groups and even transcend national boundaries. In other words, such relationships operate at both intergroup and intragroup levels:

> Suppose that several distinct societies maintain a kind of intercourse for mutual convenience and advantage, the boundaries of justice still grow larger, in proportion to the largeness of men's views, and the force of their mutual connexions. History, experience, reason sufficiently instruct us in this natural progress of human sentiments, and in the gradual enlargement of our regards to justice, in proportion as we become acquainted with the extensive utility of that virtue.
>
> (Hume, 1751/1983, p. 26)

Hume (1739/1968) further believes that this increased commerce can lead us to discover the "great resemblance among all human creatures," which in turn will allow us, with increasing ease, to "enter into the sentiments of others; and embrace them with facility and pleasure" (p. 318). Pinker (2011) calls this "the pacifying effect of commerce between individuals and nations" (p. 635). Even earlier, Kant (trans. 1795/1897) noted that "commerce" itself can lead to "perpetual peace" (p. 29).

As justice is codified into laws, it extends its power to build society by, conversely, *regulating* empathy and cooperation. Applying contingency theory, we would say that codified justice ideally prevents radical accommodation in individual cases in which, contrary to law, we might feel excessive empathy and wish to forgive individual transgressions. In doing so, we would undermine the very concept, justice that springs from self-interest and supports society:

> Were men, therefore, to take the liberty of acting with regard to the laws of society, as they do in every other affair, they wou'd conduct themselves, on most occasions, by particular judgments, and wou'd take into consideration the characters and circumstances of the persons, as well as the general nature of the question. But 'tis easy to observe, that this wou'd produce an infinite confusion in human society, and that the avidity and partiality of men wou'd quickly bring disorder into the world, if not restrain'd by some general and inflexible principles.
>
> (Hume, 1739/1968, p. 532)

Hume's point here is similar to one Isocrates will make about social harmony: Unfettered cooperation is counterproductive. As Pinker (2011) asserts, "Empathy can subvert human well-being when it runs afoul of a more fundamental human principle, fairness" (p. 590). Hume thus seems very aware of Aristotle's key point, in *Nicomachean Ethics*, that extremes (excess or deficiency) of any emotion can be unethical

Concepts of justice can vary from society to society

As we note in Chapter 8, postmodern approaches to public relations discourage a standard concept of justice that applies to all times and all cultures: "There is first a multiplicity of justices," write Lyotard and Thébaud (1985), "each of them defined in relation to the rules specific to each game" (p. 100). Similarly, justice is not a one-size-fits-all concept for Hume (1751/1983):

> In general, we may observe, that all questions of property are subordinate to the authority of civil laws, which extend, restrain, modify, and alter the rules of natural justice, according to the particular *convenience* of each community. The laws have, or ought to have, a constant reference

to the constitution of government, the manners, the climate, the religion, the commerce, the situation of each society.

(p. 29)

Though justice can vary from society to society, within a single, mature, successful society the rules of justice are clear and much less variable: "'Twas, therefore, with a view to this inconvenience [inconsistency of application], that men have establish'd those principles, and have agreed to restrain themselves by general rules, which are unchangeable by spite and favour" (Hume, 1739/1968, p. 532). Hume's concept of justice, thus, meets the stability required of resource dependency theory, but it also encompasses a postmodern need to respect and reflect the diversity of human experience.

The philosophy of David Hume helps us address a key question that runs throughout this book: If the value of justice deserves consideration as an essential element of common ground amid the diversity of approaches to public relations, does that bit of ground exist only in Utopia, founded merely on a wishful appeal to the better angels of our natures? Hume's concept of justice brushes aside such normative optimism and anchors transactional justice in a stark depiction of self-interest, economic necessity, and desire for positive reputation. To use the language of Kenneth Burke (1950/1969), cited frequently by Robert Heath (2009), the origins of justice for Hume dwell in "the Scramble, the Wrangle of the Market Place, the flurries and flare-ups of the Human Barnyard, the Give and Take, the wavering line of pressure and counterpressure, the Logomachy, the onus of ownership, the Wars of Nerves, the War" (p. 23). For Hume, justice as a virtue enters human nature—and, perhaps, public relations—only after it has endured as an indispensable defender of self-interest, stable and transferable resources, and positive reputation.

The goal of this chapter has been to show that Hume's concept of justice is inextricably embedded within resource dependency theory and the desire for a positive reputation. Resource dependency theory and the concept of reputation management, of course, span a wide variety of explanations and enactments of public relations. Hume's circular notion that justice helps create property and reputation—and that property and reputation help create and maintain justice thus may find a parallel within public relations: To work for reliable and stable resource exchange is, intentionally or not, to work for justice and reputation—and to work for justice and reputation is, in part, to work for reliable and stable resource exchange.

What, then, might this mean for the enactment of public relations ethics? If Hume is correct, then a forsaking of the value of transactional justice damages the resource acquisition and reputational foundations of the profession; indeed, a shunning of justice, in Hume's view, damages the foundations of society. Pinker (2011) asserts that violence often is a perverted form of justice that has been denied through conventional channels (p. 495). In the terminology of *Ethics and Corporate Social Responsibility* (Sims, 2003), honoring justice as a core value of public relations therefore would seem to be on the "must do" rather than the "nice to do" (p. 144) list within the discipline.

Summary

David Hume's analysis of justice leads us to at least five important points for the understanding and practice of public relations:

1. Envisioning transactional justice as a core value of public relations is not idealistic or normative. Rather, it seems unavoidable. If the exchange of resources truly is indispensable to the practice of public relations, then enacting justice—which (Hume holds) was created by the self-interested need for stable and transferable property—is inevitable. Deliberately working for transactional justice ensures the continued effectiveness of public relations.
2. Respect for transactional justice—that is, respect for the sanctity of others' property and the social norms of resource exchange—builds reputation. For Hume, nothing is more powerful in the building of a positive reputation than enactments of justice.
3. Another powerful driver of reputation is benevolence, which Hume characterizes as a disinterested passion for the wellbeing of others. This reflects game theory findings that establish indirect reciprocity as a significant creator of positive reputation.
4. A quest for justice does not imply unfettered cooperation and benevolence, which would be detrimental to the overall fairness of society. The transactional justice that Hume envisions and that he expands into a broader "justice as fairness" concept both creates social cooperation and, ideally, prevents cooperative excesses that would favor particular individuals or groups.
5. As a creator of sustainable societies, justice is essential to social theories of public relations and particularly to the reflective paradigm, which emphasizes the maintenance of an entity's social legitimacy. Hume would argue that nothing does more to establish social legitimacy than a respect for justice, with its inherent honoring of others' property.

These five points address four of the Nine Tenets of public relations' social harmony frameworks outlined in Chapter 1:

IV.   Justice begins in the social defense of resources, both our own and the resources of others. Based in self-interest, a quest for justice is not normative or contrary to human nature. Justice is inseparable from the processes of sustainable resource acquisition and thus is inherent within the processes of cooperation and public relations.

VII. Building relationships on the principles of cooperation and justice does not exclude the option of refusing to cooperate with hostile or destructive publics.

VIII. Acts of cooperation and justice are the most effective builders of a positive reputation. A positive reputation is a powerful, productive force within the processes of public relations and resource acquisition.

IX.   Public relations practitioners can take specific actions, drawn from evolutionary biology, philosophy, and rhetoric, to build and enhance relationships built upon cooperation and justice.

Chapter 10

John Rawls and justice as fairness

In this book, all roads lead to twentieth-century American philosopher John Rawls. Such a roadmap might have surprised him because, as we shall see, in his "justice as fairness" philosophy he all but ignored evolutionary biology; he misunderstood game theory findings; and he belittled rhetoric. Yet the core topics of his major works, *A Theory of Justice* and *Justice as Fairness: A Restatement*, are the touchstones of this book: Self-interest, property/resources, cooperation, justice, reciprocity, reputation, relationships, reflection, rhetoric, legitimacy, power disparities, society, and more. Like Hume, Rawls—particularly in *Justice as Fairness*—begins with practical, materialistic self-interest, which inevitably creates justice; justice, in turn, catalyzes cooperation, which helps to build an enduring society—or, regrettably, an inadequate form of justice may fail to do so. Rawls' decades-long quest was to discover which form of the inevitable justice best creates and sustains a society.

Rawls' philosophy (as he noted himself) thus offers a continuation of Hume's analysis of justice. In *A Treatise of Human Nature* and the later *Enquiry Concerning the Principles of Morals*, Hume sought to establish who, as humans, we are, which led to his assessments of self-interest, justice, and society. Rawls asks what kind of justice is most effective and how we might determine that and then promote it. In other words, Rawls strives to see what form of justice best allows the prior self-interest to lead to cooperation and, consequently, a stable society.

John Rawls (1921–2002) was the James Bryant Conant University Professor at Harvard University. He published *A Theory of Justice* in 1971 and *Justice as Fairness: A Restatement* in 2001. Echoing many similar accolades, American philosopher Ronald Dworkin (2003) calls Rawls "the most influential political philosopher of his time" (p. 7). Rawls scholar Percy Lehning (2009) adds, "*A Theory of Justice* is generally considered to be the most influential philosophical work since the Second World War" (p. 239).

In this chapter, for two important reasons I'll rely more on Rawls' final work, *Justice as Fairness: A Restatement*, than on the earlier *A Theory of Justice*: First, *Justice as Fairness* is Rawls' ultimate explanation of his philosophy, following *A Theory of Justice* by 30 years; second, and more important, in this later work Rawls presents justice as fairness as a purely political, not a moral, construct. Just as we have avoided idealism, aspiratio-nal values, and normative ethics in earlier chapters, we can do so here. (Such concepts certainly do support the notion of public relations as a quest for cooperation and justice, but—to avoid charges of unrealistic utopianism—I have tried, throughout this book, to keep our focus solely on evidence of an empirical or philosophically materialistic nature.) In *Justice as Fairness*, Rawls does *not* consider what kind of justice is moral. Rather, he focuses on what kind of justice succeeds in catalyzing sustainable cooperation in a "property-owning democracy" (Rawls, 2001, p. 140). In the preface to *Justice as Fairness*, editor Erin Kelly (2001), who helped Rawls complete the book, writes that Rawls' final work is "a *political* conception" and is not "part of a more 'comprehensive' moral, religious, or philosophical doctrine" (p. xi).

Readers of this chapter may be familiar with the general outline of Rawls' philosophy: In a thought experiment, we enter a so-called "original position" by passing through a "veil of ignorance" that removes our personal characteristics and our knowledge of all but the basics of our previous society. As literal equals in the original position, we debate the merits of different philosophies of justice that, when we return, ideally will govern our society. But Rawls (2001) adds this kicker: Because the veil has stripped us of our identities, we don't know what our positions will be in the society to which we return; we don't know whom we're representing in the original position (pp. 85–86). We might return to our previous society as healthy millionaires or as individuals born into poverty with learning disabilities. Rawls believes that while in the original position we would act on self-interest and protect ourselves by choosing a form of justice that he terms "justice as fairness." The principles of justice as fairness include "the difference principle," which holds that people with unearned advantages related to natural endowments (such as intelligence), favorable socioeconomic circumstances of birth, and general good fortune justify those unearned advantages by assisting the less fortunate. After all, as we return from the original position to society, those unfortunate individuals could be us. Though he includes no notion of malevolent forces in the original position, Rawls (1971) notes that the justice as fairness principles "are those a person would choose for the design of a society in which his enemy is to assign him his place" (p. 152).

The difference principle does indeed strike some as too idealistic (Rawls, 2001)—but Rawls persistently replies with this question: What form of justice, then, would work better? We certainly can debate the merits of justice as fairness and the difference principle—but given the realistic view of Hume and Rawls (and others such as Thomas Hobbes [1651/1985] and Robert Nozick [1974]) that *some* form of justice is needed to defend personal property, what form would work better? In a world that, via new technologies, offers increasing voice and means of unity and activism to the disadvantaged, what form of justice will best promote cooperation and social stability among disparate groups with different levels of initial advantage? What form will best defend our self-interest in stable and transferable property? Rawls maintains that justice as fairness, with its difference principle, asks us to do what is in our own best interests.

An application of Rawls' justice as fairness philosophy to public relations frameworks and resource dependency theory clusters around 12 basic Rawlsian beliefs and proposals:

1. Self-interest leads to a desire for stable property, which creates a need for justice.
2. Justice enables and sustains social cooperation.
3. Challenges to establishing justice include social pluralism and existing inequalities.
4. For a property-owning democracy to survive, these challenges must be resolved through overlapping consensus.
5. Overlapping consensus requires publicity and, ultimately, legitimacy.
6. To address challenges to justice, Rawls proposes the original position thought experiment.
7. Justice as fairness, with its inherent justice principles, emerges from the original position.
8. The difference principle is key for the enactment of the justice principles.
9. Reciprocity is at the heart of the difference principle (and thus of cooperation and society).
10. Enactments of reciprocity build reputation.
11. Enactments of the justice principles lead to cooperation.
12. Justice as fairness enables cooperation enables and sustains society.

Of all the individual viewpoints summarized in this book (from Isocrates through the modern evolutionary biologists and game theorists), Rawls offers the best synthesis of how a desire for secure and transferable resources leads to justice and cooperation and, thus, to a stable society—or, as we might say, to a fully functioning society. In a *Theory of Justice*, in fact, Rawls (1971) defines society as "a cooperative venture for mutual advantage" (p. 4). With some consolidation, these 12 Rawlsian beliefs and proposals guide the organization of much of the rest of this chapter.

Self-interest, property, and justice

As we saw in the previous chapter, Rawls (1971) openly acknowledges his debt to David Hume's analysis of self-interest, property, and justice:

> Hume's account of [the originating circumstances of justice] is especially perspicuous and [Rawls'] preceding summary [of those circumstances]

adds nothing essential to his much fuller discussion . . . The circumstances of justice obtain whenever mutually disinterested persons put forward conflicting claims to the division of social advantages under conditions of moderate scarcity. Unless these circumstances existed there would be no occasion for the virtue of justice, just as in the absence of threats of injury to life and limb there would be no occasion for physical courage.

(pp. 127–128)

This concept of the "moderate scarcity" of the resources we need to survive—clearly related to resource dependency theory—is repeated throughout both *A Theory of Justice* and *Justice as Fairness*. In *A Theory of Justice*, Rawls (1971) even refers to the notion as "Hume's conditions of moderate scarcity" (p. 146).

For Rawls (2001), a basic concept of justice, a justice that ensures property rights, logically works best within some form of "property-owning democracy" (p. 140). Whatever form of government we have, however, Rawls (evoking Immanuel Kant's view of humans as rights-possessing ends, not means) specifies certain primary goods to which, ideally, all humans should have equal and unfettered access. These primary goods are "things citizens need as free and equal persons living a complete life"; such goods enable citizens to "advance their permissible conceptions of the good" (Rawls, 2001, pp. 58, 61). Rawls (2001) lists five such goods, including equal opportunity to hold things of "exchange value" (pp. 58–59). Thus, among the "equal basic liberties" that he believes would emerge from the original position is "the right to hold and have the exclusive use of personal property" (Rawls, 2001, p. 114). Ownership of that property within a society would be wide but not equal (Rawls, 1971, p. 280). Just as with Hume, for Rawls a desire for stable property not only leads to social cooperation through justice; the reverse of the process occurs. The benefits of social cooperation strengthen the justice that helped create it and strengthen the opportunities for the productive use of property. In Rawls' (2001) words, "Social cooperation. . . is always productive, and without cooperation there would be nothing produced and so nothing to distribute" (p. 61). In an assessment that echoes Peter Kropotkin's (Chapter 5) belief that democratic collectivism is the best defense of individualism, Rawls scholar Percy Lehning (2009) concludes:

> More than anything else, Rawls considers society as a fair system of cooperation . . . The idea that is that social cooperation makes possible for all a better life than anyone would have if each were to live solely by his own efforts.
>
> (p. 26)

For both Hume and Rawls, the self-interested and stable ownership of property is the foundation of such cooperation.

To belabor the obvious: Resource dependency theory, with its focus on stable, transferable property, is inherent in the concept of public relations. If property, including property exchange, and justice have a symbiotic created/creator relationship, then the promotion of justice is inevitably a core function of public relations.

Justice: Cooperation and challenges

For Rawls (2001), justice is the indispensable catalyst of social cooperation; it is a conduit from self-interest to stable society. Justice is "the first virtue of social institutions"; its function is to create "the basic structure of society" (pp. 3, 39). In moving from moral justice, in *A Theory of Justice*, to the more instrumental concept in *Justice as Fairness*, Rawls (2001) emphasizes that he speaks of "political justice" (p. 39): He is seeking what *will* work in the real world, not what *should* work in a morally perfect sphere such as Kant's kingdom of ends.

Rawls (2001) may momentarily confuse us as he declares, more than once, that he does not consider society—particularly a property-owning democracy —to be a community: "It is a serious error not to distinguish between the idea of a democratic political society and the idea of community" (p. 21). To distinguish the two concepts, he introduces a term that he clearly favors: "reasonable pluralism" (p. 4), which appears more than two dozen times in *Justice as Fairness*. He often expands the phrase to "the fact of reasonable pluralism" (p. 9). Reasonable pluralism entails a level of civil dissent not found, for Rawls, within a community. Although he never specifies a precise definition of the phrase, he does consistently link reasonable pluralism to a "diversity of reasonable comprehensive doctrines," particularly in the area of "religious and philosophical conceptions of the world" and related "moral and aesthetic values to be sought in life" (Rawls, 2001, pp. 3, 40). *Reasonable* denotes a willingness to seek a "common ground" characterized by public discussion and the creation of a "wide reflective equilibrium" of agreement (Rawls, 2001, pp. 1, 31). In a democracy, reasonable pluralism is fed by "burdens of judgment" (Rawls' [2001, p. 35] penchant for cryptic terms can be frustrating), which are sources of legitimate social disagreement. Such burdens include conflicting and complex "evidence" in a social debate; the relative importance of various bits of evidence; the occasional vagueness of our own engaged beliefs; our differing life experiences; and clashes of key related values (Rawls, 2001, pp. 35–36).

Rawls views reasonable pluralism as a beneficial challenge to *any* concept of social justice, not simply his justice as fairness philosophy. Reasonable pluralism is inseparable from the property-owning democracies within which justice—and public relations—function: "There is no politically practicable way to eliminate this diversity except by the oppressive use of state power" (Rawls, 2001, p. 84). For any democratic concept of social justice to prevail, it must (as we shall see below) achieve an "overlapping consensus" (Rawls, 2001, p. 33) within reasonable pluralism—something that surely sounds like a function of public relations. Given his analysis of reasonable pluralism, we cannot conclude that Rawls has an overly idealistic vision of a peaceful, gullible society that will passively accept any form of proposed justice.

A second challenge to any socially unifying concept of justice is the "fact," as Rawls might say, of social inequalities. Again and again in both *A Theory of Justice* and *Justice as Fairness*, Rawls (2001) emphasizes three enduring areas of undeserved (or unearned) inequality:

(a) [individuals'] social class of origin: the class into which they are born and develop before the age of reason;
(b) their native endowments (as opposed to their realized endowments); and their opportunities to develop these endowments as affected by their social class of origin; [and]
(c) their good or ill fortune, or good or bad luck, over the course of life (how they are affected by illness and accident; and, say, by periods of involuntary unemployment and regional economic decline).

(p. 55)

Rawls (2001) calls these three areas "social, natural, and fortuitous contingencies" (p. 55). They are not, he repeatedly emphasizes, the equivalent of disadvantages or inequalities brought on by personal actions for which the perpetrator clearly bears personal responsibility.

Rawls (2001) does specifically link these three areas of inequality to property: The "least advantaged" face additional hurdles in their quest for the primary goods—one of which, again, is things of "exchange value" (pp. 57, 58–59). Unaddressed, these three areas of inequality can threaten social stability. But if the winners of the "natural lottery" (Rawls, 1971, p. 104) that distributes unearned advantages and disadvantages in these three areas are willing to address issues of basic fairness, they can benefit by helping to create "a culture that inhibits the wastes of endless self- and group-interested bargaining and offers some hope of realizing social concord and civic friendship" (Rawls, 2001, p. 126). Justice, including a respect for fair access to the resources inherent in the concept of public relations, can increase the stability and transferability of those resources.

Overlapping consensus, publicity, and legitimacy

As we have seen, if a concept of justice is to gain favor and stability within a property-owning democracy, a supportive "overlapping consensus" of opinion must be achieved (Rawls, 2001, p. 32). Because of reasonable pluralism, unanimity on a governing form of social justice is impossible. The best we can hope for is overlapping consensus: "By this we mean that the political conception is supported by the reasonable though opposing religious, philosophical, and moral doctrines that gain a significant body of adherents and endure over time" (Rawls, 2001, p. 32). Near the end of *Justice as Fairness*, Rawls (2001) devotes an entire section to showing that creation of an overlapping consensus is not "utopian" (p. 192). His argument is predictably complex, but it rests on a sentiment reminiscent of a quotation often attributed to Winston Churchill: "Democracy is the worst form of government—except for all the others." He concludes his defense of overlapping consensus in a property-owning democracy by declaring, "[The] political values that, under the reasonably favorable conditions that make democracy possible, normally outweigh whatever values may oppose them. With this we have an overlapping consensus" (Rawls, 2001, p. 194). Overlapping consensus creates "a public basis of justification" (Rawls, 2001, p. 89) for a concept of justice.

If an overlapping consensus is to justify a particular concept of justice, that justification, Rawls (2001) maintains, must be preceded by "mutual recognition by citizens" of three things: The basic principles of justice; the fair process by which those principles came to be; and the fact that social institutions support those principles (p. 121). It's a pity that in his two primary works Rawls never used the phrase *public relations* or even referred to that discipline, because it would seem to be indispensable in achieving these mutual recognitions so essential to social justice. Because democracy and justice do rely on "a vigorous and informed citizen body," Rawls (2001) does refer to the desired establishment of these three mutual recognitions by "publicity" (pp. 144, 121). In his preface to *Justice as Fairness*, Rawls (2001) writes that "publicity" is essential to social acceptance of the difference principle (p. xvii). Though not in *Justice as Fairness* itself, Rawls was highly aware of Jurgen Habermas' (1989) concerns regarding the decline of a "bourgeois public sphere" (p. xviii) for civil and civic discourse. Rawls defended his means of achieving overlapping consensus in a lengthy 1995 *Journal of Philosophy* article titled "Political Liberalism: Reply to Habermas."

Percy Lehning (2009) asserts that "what makes Rawls a major philosopher is not the broad scope of his ambition, but rather the depth of his perception" (p. 240). One of the ironies of this chapter is that Rawls' keen but narrow focus on justice led him to the rejection, mischaracterization, or casual treatment of supporting evidence from the areas of evolutionary biology, game theory, and rhetoric. His comments in the previous paragraph would seem to pave a direct route to Isocrates' belief that rhetoric is "the values-driven discourse of responsible citizenship" (Marsh, 2013, p. 12); or Quintilian's emphasis on "the good man speaking well" (*Institutio Oratoria*, XII.1.1); or I.A. Richards' (1936/1965) belief that rhetoric should be "the study of misunderstandings and its remedies" (p. 3), or Kenneth Burke's (1950/1969) concept of identification. However, in *Justice as Fairness*, Rawls (2001) contrasts acceptable means of publicity and public reasoning with "mere rhetoric or artifices of persuasion" (p. 92), which lack legitimacy in the construction of overlapping consensus. Rawls' use of "mere rhetoric" surely refers to Wayne Booth's (1988) earlier and well-known description of "mere rhetoric" as "words or other symbols. . . used to deceive or to obscure issues or to evade action" (p. 109).

By whatever term we employ—publicity, public relations, rhetoric, or something else altogether—some form of strategic communication is, for Rawls (2001), indispensable in the achievement of overlapping consensus and, ultimately, "legitimacy" (p. 90). Legitimacy is, ideally, the product of public reason and is essential to any uniting theory of justice (Rawls, 2001, pp. 90, 92). It is the product of "public civility" rather than asymmetrical "coercive" means (Rawls, 2001, pp. 92, 90). Two connections to public relations and public relations history are irresistible here. Social legitimacy, again, is the primary aim of the reflective paradigm of public relations; Rawls is describing that general framework in his analysis of overlapping consensus. And as we will see in the next chapter, Isocrates, Aeschylus, and other forerunners of modern public relations positioned the persuasive aspects of rhetoric (*peitho*) as a peaceful alternative to the concept of force (*bia*).

The original position

Rawls (2001) is probably best known to public relations scholars for the phrase "veil of ignorance," but in his famous thought experiment that leads to the justice as fairness philosophy, the real action happens in the "original position":

> In the original position, the parties are not allowed to know the social positions or the particular comprehensive doctrines of the persons they represent. They also do not know persons' race and ethnic group, sex, or various native endowments such as strength and intelligence . . . We express these limits on information figuratively by saying the parties are behind a veil of ignorance.
>
> (p. 15)

Because we don't know whom we represent in the original position, we don't know who we will be when we return to our previous society. As noted above, Rawls believes that, in the original position, we would design safeguards to ensure help if we lose the "natural lottery" and return to society as someone plagued by one or more of the three areas of undeserved inequalities. We would design a system of justice as if our worst enemy were going to select our status within the society that adopts that system of justice. Though in *Justice as Fairness* Rawls generally avoids a discussion of the morality of this approach, Harvard Professor of Psychology Steven Pinker (2011) feels no such restriction: "The mindset that we adopt when we don moral spectacles is the mindset of the victim" (p. 496).

One point worth noting: In the original position, there are no power disparities among the participants. "By situating the parties symmetrically," Rawls (2001) writes, "the original position respects the basic precept of formal equality" (p. 87). This hardly continues, of course, as justice as fairness travels back into a property-owning democracy—but at least its origins address a challenge of increasing concern in public relations. We will return to power disparities again in our discussion of the difference principle.

Viewed from the perspective of recent advances in neuroscience and evolutionary biology, the nature and mission of the original position may not seem as farfetched as, perhaps, we once thought: Donald Pfaff's altruistic brain theory (Chapter 3), for example, explains the neurological processes—corollary discharge, mirror neurons, and more—by which we physiologically identify with the plight of the other. In describing residents of a "protected nest," an inherent characteristic of our planet's few truly eusocial species (including humans), Edward O. Wilson (2012) writes, "They must share food, both vegetable and animal, in ways that are acceptable to all. Otherwise, the bonds that bind them will weaken" (p. 43). Further, the game theory experiments detailed in Chapter 7 show humans' willingness to sacrifice in order to help others. Rawls (2001), in facts, notes that among the equals of the original position, envy lacks an effective toehold (pp. 88, 180). One of the characteristics of the Tit for Tat strategy that dominates iterated Prisoner's Dilemma experiments (Chapter 7) is its lack of envy. Based on the success of Tit for Tat in his own iterated Prisoner's Dilemma tournaments, Robert Axelrod (2006) concludes, "Don't be envious . . . There is no point in being envious of the success of the other player, since in an iterated Prisoner's Dilemma of long duration the other's success is virtually a prerequisite of your doing well for yourself" (pp. 100, 112). Still, Rawls (1971) reminds us that "in the original position. . . the parties are mutually disinterested rather than sympathetic" (p. 187). This is reassuring for our non-idealistic approach in this book: The justice as fairness principles emerge from a place of self-interest.

Given the nature of the original position, the justice principles emerge from a place of "uncertainty," as Rawls (1971) emphasizes, particularly in *A Theory of Justice* (p. 172). This particular quality—uncertainty—will, in the next few chapters, lead us to the rhetoric of Isocrates. Isocrates (trans. 2000) rejects Plato's belief that divine truth and certainty can be discovered through an arduous dialectical process, and he positions civic rhetoric as a means of coping with the resultant uncertainty:

> Since human nature cannot attain knowledge that would enable us to know what we must say or do, after this I think that the wise (*sophoi*) are those who have the ability to reach the best opinions (*doxai*) most of the time, and philosophers are those who spend time acquiring such an intelligence as quickly as possible.
>
> (*Antidosis*, 271)

Justice as fairness: Two principles

Rawls believes that general notions of fairness and definite notions of self-interest would, within the discussions in the original position, lead us to two principles that characterize justice as fairness. In his words, these "two principles of justice" are:

1. Each person has the same indefeasible claim to a fully adequate scheme of equal basic liberties, which scheme is compatible with the same scheme of liberties for all; and
2. Social and economic inequalities are to satisfy two conditions: first, they are to be attached to offices and positions open to all under conditions of fair equality of opportunity; and second, they are to be to the greatest benefit of the least-advantaged members of society (the difference principle).

(Rawls, 2001, pp. 42–43)

Rawls essentially maintains that representatives within the original position would create these two principles of justice to allow individual and societal socioeconomic success and advancement, thus protecting such things as individual initiative—and to protect the undeservedly disadvantaged, particularly because the veil of ignorance has temporarily removed their knowledge of their place within society. Representatives probably would reject equal distribution of resources, because, Rawls (2001) asserts, strict equality in a property-owning democracy would, in all likelihood, stifle individual initiative and societal economic progress (pp. 123, 151). Rawls (2001) holds that adherence to the two principles of justice would help create "a fair system of social cooperation between free and equal citizens from one generation to the next" (p. 133).

Of the two principles, Rawls (2001) asserts, the first has priority. The second can be satisfied only within the context of the first: Enactment of the difference principle, for example, cannot occur at the expense of any part of "a fully adequate scheme of equal basic liberties" for all citizens. Those equal basic liberties include such things as "the right to vote. . . freedom of speech. . . the right to hold (personal) property" and more (Rawls, 1971, p. 61). However, there is no hierarchy of basic liberties, and no single liberty is absolute because there may be clashes among them (Rawls, 2001, pp. 44, 104, 111). Sounding Aristotelian as he recommends an avoidance of excess or deficiency for each liberty, Rawls (2001) concludes:

The priority of these liberties is not infringed when they are merely regulated, as they must be, in order to be combined into one scheme. So long as what we may call "the central range of application" of each basic liberty is secured, the two principles are fulfilled . . . In cases of conflict we look for a way to accommodate the more significant liberties within the central range of each.

(pp. 111, 113)

The difference principle: An overview

Throughout *Justice as Fairness* (2001), Rawls describes the difference principle—part of the second justice principle—in various ways:

* Existing inequalities must contribute effectively to the benefit of the least advantaged. Otherwise, the inequalities are not permissible. (p. 62)
* The more advantaged are not to be better off at any point to the detriment of the less well off. (p. 124)
* Social institutions are not to take advantage of contingencies of native endowment, or of initial social position, or of good luck or bad luck over the course of life, except in ways that benefit everyone, including the least favored. (p. 124)

Rawls' difference principle thus directly addresses his three areas of unearned disadvantage. Just as significant, however, he adds that the principle ideally should not hamper the initiative of the winners of the "natural lottery": They are encouraged to "educate their endowments" and "to contribute to others' good as well as their own" (Rawls, 2001, pp. 74, 75); by benefiting themselves, they benefit others. Additionally, justice as fairness "does not say that we never deserve. . . the social position or the offices we may hold" (Rawls, 2001, p. 78); it is not meant to downplay the hard work of those who have educated their endowments, as Rawls puts it. Rawls (2001) positions the difference principle as a balance (not an extreme) between equality and efficiency (p. 123) and between altruism and mutual advantage (p. 77).

Both in origin and enactment, the difference principle addresses power disparities within relationships—again, an enduring concern within critical studies of public relations. In the original position, the difference principle is created by literal equals, and in enactment, it strives to ensure "that citizens similarly gifted and motivated have roughly an equal chance of influencing" whatever issue is at hand (Rawls, 2001, p. 46). If those citizens are not similarly gifted, and the disparity lies within one of the three areas of unearned disadvantage, then a justice as fairness culture works to address that arbitrary distribution of assets. As Harvard Professor of Government Michael J. Sandel (2009) notes, "If the runners start from different starting points, the race is hardly fair" (p. 153). And once again: In the justice as fairness philosophy, such action is not altruism (although, as Hume notes, it may become so over time). Rather, it is, in part, the enactment of self-interest in creating a stable society for the preservation of stable property. "What is essential for an overlapping consensus," Rawls (2001) asserts, "is stability with respect to the distribution of power" (pp. 192–193).

Regardless of that materialistic origin, could the difference principle truly work in public relations? Practitioner and professor Kevin Moloney poses that very question in *Rethinking Public Relations*. In that work, Moloney (2006) asks, "Can. . . general statements about a polity theorised as tolerant of and supportive of people associating to further their interests, facing few or many external obstacles to their combination, be made specific to public relations?" (pp. 79–80). His answer is bundled into his "normative theory of equalising PR resources":

> Differences in communicative resources of organisations and groups needed for PR should be made equal by all meeting the threshold for effective messaging in the pluralist competition over values, behaviours, ideas, resource allocations and reputations that exists in market, capital-ist, liberal democracies. Looked at in terms of PR-specific theory, this equalisation takes Gandy's (1982) concept of big business providing information subsidies to journalists through their PR productions, and expands the concept of subsidy out of the realm of resource-rich busi-nesses to all interests that do not come up to a minimum level of PR operational capacity.
>
> (Moloney, 2006, p. 79, 80)

The subsidy, he adds, could be "public or private" (Moloney, 2006, p. 9). Such a passage could be grafted into Rawls' philosophy with no thematic violations; in *A Theory of Justice*, Rawls (1971) acknowledges that freedoms of expression "lose much of their value whenever those who have greater private means are permitted to use their advantages to control the course of public debate" (p. 225). But could such assistance, particularly private, really be enacted within public relations? As I noted earlier, in Chapter 5, Kevin Moloney donates his time and talents to a living-wage advocacy group in the United Kingdom. The difference principle is not merely normative in public relations.

The difference principle: Reciprocity and reputation

Beyond portraying the difference principle as a means of achieving stability in societies characterized by inequalities and reasonable pluralism, Rawls (2001) further defines it in terms familiar to the disciplines of public relations and evolutionary biology—as a function of reciprocity: "As a principle of reciprocity, the difference principle rests on our disposition to respond in kind to what others do for (or to) us. . ." (p. 127). But what have the less fortunate done for the fortunate? With the difference principle, how is the relationship between the winners and the losers in the "natural lottery" truly a reciprocal, two-way process? For Rawls (2001), native endowments and the other categories of unearned advantages are "a common asset" (p. 75) for a society, pooled while we were in the original position. Without the difference principle, the less fortunate—moving as equals in the original position back into society—have contributed more to that pool than they have withdrawn. With the difference principle, those who withdrew—through no action or fault of their own—a more-than-equal share of advantages repay those who—through no action or fault of their own—withdrew a less-than-equal share. Lehning (2009) believes reciprocity to be "the most important moral psychological assumption underlying Rawls' theory of justice" (p. 138).

If we loosen, just a bit, the focus on unearned advantages and disadvantages, Rawls shows that we easily find existing enactments of the reciprocal difference principle in our current societies. In one instance, he offers an orchestra as an illustration (Rawls, 2001, p. 201): The lesser players allow the better players to assume leading (and better-paying) roles, knowing that the leaders' success will help ensure the success of the orchestra and all its members. In turn, the leaders themselves are well served by assisting the lesser players, thus further improving the orchestra and their own reputations and job security. Just as Rawls suggests in his two principles of justice, leadership positions within the orchestra—for example, first chair in the violin section—are open to all who audition. If the orchestra's top musicians achieved their leadership roles with the assistance of unearned advantages such as physical dexterity, intelligence, and parents who could afford to pay for music lessons, this indeed is an example of the difference principle. However, the example does weaken if the leading musicians achieved their top positions despite severe disadvantages and with little or no assistance.

Rawls (2001) also cites American professional sports leagues as a version of the difference principle (pp. 51, 52): The least successful teams receive the first choices in the drafting of college athletes. Through that mechanism, competition ideally increases, improving the strength of the league and the resultant profits for league members. Just as with the orchestra, this might be a perfect example of the difference principle. However, if the weaker teams are in that position because of avoidable poor decisions by players or management, the example loses some of its power.

Perhaps a better example of reciprocity within the difference principle, one with which readers of this book might sympathize, involves research: As scholars of public relations, we rely on access to current research in journals and from academic presses. In a modified original position (not knowing where in the world we might end up as public relations scholars), we surely would want to address the issue of unequal access to current scholarship due to unequal and sometimes inadequate university budgets. Knowing that such inequalities would exist in the world to which we returned, we would not wish to restrict the access of fortunate individuals with excellent access to scholarship. Rather, for the good of our discipline (and in our own self-interest), we would wish them well—but we would ask that they use their privileged status to help the less fortunate improve their degree of access to scholarship. Such assistance would enrich everyone's research.

Though Rawls does not cite the work of Thomas Henry Huxley, it is worth noting that Huxley, who generally had a less favorable view of human nature than Rawls, developed much the same idea of reciprocity—that "a man has only a partial right to the fruits of his own labor because he did not produce the mental and physical endowments which performed the labor" (Irvine, 1955, p. 336). In "Natural Rights and Political Rights," (1898), Huxley asserts:

> No gratuitous offering of Nature can be the subject of. . . private owner-ship. Therefore a man can have no exclusive possession of himself, except in so far as he is the product of the exertion of his own labour and not a gratuitous offering of Nature. But it is only a very small part of him which can in any sense be said to be the product of his own labour. The man's physical and mental tendencies and capacities, dependent to a very large extent on heredity, are certainly the "gratuitous offering of Nature;" if they belong to anybody, therefore, they must belong to the whole of mankind.
>
> (p. 366)

Huxley, the empiricist who was so strict that he would not wholly accept natural selection without proof, helps build a foundation for Rawls' difference principle.

Rawls was unaware of a second compelling area of support from evolutionary biology: Mischaracterizing game theory, an emerging area that actually strongly supports the viability of the difference principle, Rawls (2001) declares, "Political and social cooperation would quickly break down if everyone, or even many people, acted self- or group-interestedly in a purely strategic, or game-theoretic fashion" (p. 125). His equation of selfishness with game-theory behavior suggests a lack of knowledge of the persistent and unrivaled success of the cooperative and reciprocal Tit for Tat program in Axelrod's and Nowak's iterated Prisoner's Dilemma experiments. Yet Rawls realized that reciprocity and cooperation had deep origins in human nature and self-interest. In *A Theory of Justice* (1971), he asserts, "Reciprocity. . . is a deep psychological fact. Without it our nature would be very different and fruitful social cooperation fragile if not impossible" (pp. 494–495). Game theory actually supports Rawls' contention that the reciprocity embedded in the difference principle is part of human nature and not an impossibly normative ideal.

Modern game theory also affirms Rawls' assessment of the connection of indirect reciprocity and reputation. (Again, indirect reciprocity involves A helping B without the expectation of direct return; this is observed by C, who then seeks a relationship with the socially responsible A.) "When others. . .

do their part in just or fair institutions," Rawls (2001) writes, "citizens tend to develop trust and confidence in them" (p. 196); this leads to "a tendency to answer in kind" (p. 196). Again, of his own iterated Prisoner's Dilemma experiments, Nowak (Nowak & Highfield, 2011) has concluded, "Natural selection favors strategies that base their decision to cooperate (or defect) on the reputation of the recipient . . . As one would expect, Bad Samaritans with a poor reputation receive less help. . ." (p. 60). In rhetoric, Isocrates (trans. 1928/1991) makes much the same point: "Refrain when you have your fair share, so that men may think that you strive for justice, not from weakness, but from a sense of equity" (*To Demonicus*, 38).

Justice, cooperation, and society

Like both Hume and Aristotle, Rawls believes that time and custom can turn habit into virtue, or at least into human nature. For Rawls (2001), enduring social experience with the relative success of the two principles of justice as fairness will diminish "envy, spite, the will to dominate, and the temptation to deprive others of justice"—though the process will take place "gradually over generations" (pp. 202, 198). The powerful contribution of Hume and Rawls to the focus of this book is this: Evolutionary biologists from Darwin to Dawkins and beyond have shown the strategic advantages of cooperation over conflict. But Hume and Rawls, like Kropotkin, show that human cooperation is impossible without justice.

The cooperation catalyzed by justice in turn catalyzes society. As Rawls (2001) repeats throughout *Justice as Fairness*, society is "a fair system of cooperation over time" (p. 4): It is "the most fundamental idea" of his justice as fairness philosophy (p. 5). In a statement that bodes well for envisioning public relations as a form of negotiating group relationships, Rawls (2001) holds that society is "a social union of social unions" enabled by justice (p. 142). He notes that such unity can extend to international relations—a society of societies, perhaps—but realistically cautions that justice as fairness may not travel smoothly across all borders (Rawls, 2001, p. 11). Justice as fairness, after all, is best suited to property-owning democracies.

In a statement reminiscent of Peter Kropotkin's analysis of individualism and collectivism (the "double tendency" described in Chapter 5), Rawls believes that individuals gain from participating in a social union of social unions. Acknowledging that conflict will always exist, he still declares, "Society is a cooperative venture for mutual advantage" (Rawls, 1971, p. 4). For Rawls, self-interest leads to a desire for property, which leads to justice, which leads to cooperation, which leads to society, which leads to advantage—which thus strengthens property and justice, completing the cycle. And the process begins not with widespread altruism or normative ethics or unrealistic self-sacrifice. It begins with self-interest.

Political realism

That focus on self-interest, which Rawls openly attributes to Hume, is an element of the political realism that runs throughout *Justice as Fairness*. As Rawls (2001) notes in his preface to that work, though he is not rejecting the moral foundations of his earlier *Theory of Justice*, his restatement focuses on "a political conception of justice rather than. . . a comprehensive moral doctrine" (p. xvi). People unite in social cooperation, he maintains, because they seek the "rational advantage" (Rawls, 2001, p. 6) inherent in such an arrangement. Self-interest in the social peace that protects personal property leads us, he believes, to justice and fairness with its difference principle. The advantages of indirect reciprocity, including the building of a productive reputation, lead us, he believes, to justice and fairness with its difference principle. Rawls (2001) thus concludes that "justice as fairness is realistically utopian" (p. 13). In keeping with the focus of this book, the reciprocal justice that leads to cooperation and that defends stable property is not based on an appeal to hopeful idealism. It is based on self-interest.

Of Rawls' justice as fairness philosophy, Sandel (2009) concludes:

> [Rawls'] distributive justice philosophy is not about rewarding virtue or moral desert. Instead, it's about meeting the legitimate expectations that arise once the rules of the game are in place . . . Whether or not his theory of justice ultimately succeeds, it represents the most compelling case for a more equal society that American political philosophy has yet produced.
> (pp. 161, 166)

Summary

John Rawls' analysis of justice leads us to at least four important points for the understanding and practice of public relations:

1. The stable, transferable property essential to public relations relies on justice. In circular fashion, justice catalyzes cooperation, which catalyzes society, which enhances the stability and transferability of property.
2. Reciprocity in relationships is beneficial, earning trust, building reputation, and leading to mutual advantage.
3. Public relations is essential to the overlapping consensus that builds social cooperation in the midst of reasonable pluralism. A lack of overlapping consensus threatens social cooperation; that lack would undermine the legitimacy of justice, which, in turn, would undermine the stability of property and property exchange. The establishment of social legitimacy is a particular function of the reflective paradigm of public relations.
4. Rawls' difference principle, with its philosophy of the advantaged assisting the disadvantaged, already has been recommended for public relations

via Moloney's "theory of equalising PR resources." For Rawls, the difference principle does not penalize initiative: Rather, it seeks a mutually beneficial balance between equality and efficiency and between altruism and mutual advantage.

These four points address three of the Nine Tenets of public relations' social harmony frameworks outlined in Chapter 1:

IV.   Justice begins in the social defense of resources, both our own and the resources of others. Based in self-interest, a quest for justice is not normative or contrary to human nature. Justice is inseparable from the processes of sustainable resource acquisition and thus is inherent within the processes of cooperation and public relations.
V.   Biological and social tensions between individualism and collectivism are most sustainably resolved in favor of collectivism that defends individualism.
VIII. Acts of cooperation and justice are the most effective builders of a positive reputation. A positive reputation is a powerful, productive force within the processes of public relations and resource acquisition.

Rhetoric, public relations, and cooperation

Chapter 11

Introduction to Part IV

Persuasion and cooperation

Public relations scholars have, since at least the 1990s, included rhetoric in their calls for wide-ranging explorations of potential theoretical bases for the young discipline. In the seminal *Rhetorical and Critical Approaches to Public Relations*, Elizabeth Toth (1992) asserts, "Rhetorical and critical scholars must at least define what they mean by rhetoric and public relations; and, at best argue how their findings contribute to our theoretical understanding of the domain" (p. 12). In the 2009 update of that work, Heath, Toth, and Waymer call for "pluralistic studies in public relations" (p. 14), and, of course, they include rhetoric. Earlier, Heath (2008) traced public relations' origins to the rhetorics of Plato, Aristotle, and Isocrates. A continuing research project led by Lynne M. Sallot has identified 27 "theory development" categories within current public relations research, including "Rhetorical Underpinnings" (Sallot, Lyon, Acosta-Alzuru, & Ogata Jones, 2008, pp. 356, 357).

Toth's request that scholars "define what they mean by rhetoric" provides an important starting point for this section of this book, the section on rhetoric and public relations. In a moment, I will offer four standard, complementary definitions of rhetoric—but after offering those definitions, I hope to show that our vision of classical rhetoric, the beginning of the formal study of persuasion, has been blurred by an overemphasis on Aristotle's important definition and contributions. For all its brilliance, Aristotelian rhetoric is grounded in conflict and competition, and by contemporaneous as well as current accounts it was not the most successful, effective of the classical Greek rhetorics. That honor belonged to Isocratean rhetoric (Chapter 12). An overemphasis on Aristotelian rhetoric, I believe, can bolster a vision of public relations as the strategic management of conflict and as an inherent contributor to an adversarial society—not, conversely, as a historic means of cooperation and as a participant within a fully functioning society.

In keeping with this book's theme of the consilience of cooperation, this section (Chapters 11–13) will, I hope, demonstrate that the most effective rhetoric, both past and present, focuses on cooperation, justice, and moderation, as opposed to egoistic conflict and competition. In fact, the emphasis within evolutionary biology (Part II) on the role of language in developing the social instinct as well as in driving influential cultural memes makes this section a practical necessity. In the words of evolutionary biologist Martin Nowak (Nowak & Highfield, 2011):

> Language allows people to work together . . . Language is intimately linked with cooperation . . . Language propelled human evolution out of a purely genetic realm, where it still operates, into the realm of culture. Language offers a way to take the thoughts of one person, encode them, and insert them into the minds of others . . . When [among our human ancestors] there were more opportunities for deception, manipulation, cooperation, conflict—what we call politics—language became a necessity to gain support of others to make deals, to forge alliances, and to collaborate.
>
> (pp. 171, 172, 187)

Dominic Johnson (2013), the Alastair Buchan professor of international relations at Oxford, even asserts that our evolving, interactive language skills drive down the egoistic behaviors that can trigger conflict and competition:

> There was. . . a defining moment at some point in our evolutionary history where the entire cost-benefit calculus of selfishness was more or less thrown out of the window . . . After the evolution of theory of mind [understanding what others think] and complex language. . . it was now in our genes' interests to avoid selfish behavior in many contexts that might bring negative repercussions for fitness . . . The advent of theory of mind and complex language increased the likelihood of public exposure for selfish behavior and could bring high costs of retaliation . . . Natural selection should favor more efficient traits that constrain selfishness.
>
> (pp. 172, 175, 176)

Johnson (2013) holds that our use of language has created a "new currency to trade in—social information," a currency that promotes "restraint, self-control, sacrifice, sharing, patience, etc." (p. 176). As we saw in earlier chapters, Nowak's (Nowak & Highfield, 2011) game-theory experiments have shown that "natural selection favors strategies that base [a] decision to cooperate (or defect) on the reputation of the recipient . . . As one would expect, Bad Samaritans with a poor reputation receive less help" (p. 60).

Rhetoric is deeply embedded within our new social currency. According to Edward P.J. Corbett (1990a), author of *Classical Rhetoric for the Modern Student*, rhetoric is "the art or the discipline that deals with the use of discourse, either spoken or written, to inform or persuade or motivate an audience, whether that audience is made up of one person or a group of persons" (p. 3). Ott and Dickinson (2013) have expanded the definition to "any discourse, art form, performance, cultural object, or event that—by symbolic and/or material means—has the capacity to move someone" (p. 2). Perhaps more familiar to public relations scholars are the definitions (still complementary to those of Corbett and Ott and Dickinson) of Donald Bryant and Kenneth Burke. Bryant (1953) holds that rhetoric is "the function of adjusting ideas to people and people to ideas" (p. 413), and Burke (1950/1969) defines it as *the use of language as a symbolic means of inducing cooperation in beings that by nature respond to symbols. . .* the use of words by human agents to form attitudes or induce actions in other human agents. . ." (pp. 39, 41). Given the breadth and mission of rhetoric in these definitions, we no doubt are on solid ground in accepting *strategic communication* as a modern synonym for that ancient art and science.

The most famous (and complicating) definition of rhetoric, however, probably belongs to Aristotle (trans. 1954): "Rhetoric may be defined as the faculty of observing in any given case the available means of persuasion" (1355b). As Lunsford and Ede (1994) have noted, to the degree that current scholars consider classical rhetoric at all, we tend to embrace the rhetoric of Aristotle's *Rhetoric*, which contains and champions that well-known definition. In fact, Lunsford and Ede (1994) approvingly cite a colleague's "very persuasive argument. . . for all of classical rhetoric as sharing what we argue is an Aristotelian view of communication" (p. 410). This certainly seems at odds with historian Donald Clark's (1957) assessment that "in Greece of the fourth century BC there was a three-cornered quarrel among the leading teachers [Aristotle, Plato, and Isocrates] concerning what it takes to make a successful speaker" (p. 5). Ricoeur (1996) offers a more nuanced description of Aristotle's modern dominance: "Although our understanding of the art of rhetoric has its origins in Aristotle's analysis of the craft, we need to approach his account cautiously" (p. 324). Within public relations, Aristotelian rhetoric certainly seems to dominate the rival rhetorics of Plato and Isocrates. For example, a Google Scholar search, through May 2016, for the key terms *Aristotle* and *rhetoric* in the journals *Public Relations Review*, *Journal of Public Relations Research*, and *Public Relations Inquiry* locates 50 articles. A similar search for *Plato* and *rhetoric* identifies 28 articles; a similar search for *Isocrates* and *rhetoric* identifies 13. Even such cursory evidence as this suggests the current dominance of Aristotelian rhetoric among the classical variants. A goal of this chapter, however, is to show that, after much public and cross-disciplinary deliberation, the Athens of Aristotle achieved a consilience that favors a very different form of rhetoric, one closer to Isocratean rhetoric. A later chapter, Chapter 12, will focus on Isocrates; this chapter, instead, will show ancient Athens' movement away from a rhetoric based on conflict and competition—one willing to function "in any given case"—and toward one based on cooperation and justice. But we should begin with a brief analysis of that most famous of classical rhetorics, the rhetoric— and *Rhetoric*—of Aristotle.

The rhetoric of Aristotle

Aristotle (384–322 BCE) remains the best known of the classical Greek rhetoricians, owing, in large part, to the survival of his *Rhetoric*, an analysis of the art of persuasion—a so-called metarhetoric. Neither of his greatest contemporary rivals in rhetorical theory, Plato and Isocrates, left such a work. In their aforementioned analysis of "distinctions between classical and modern rhetoric," Lunsford and Ede (1994) use only the Aristotelian variety to represent classical rhetoric, bypassing the competing rhetorics of Plato and Isocrates (p. 397).

With his famous definition of rhetoric—"the faculty of observing in any given case the available means of persuasion" (1355b)—Aristotle (trans. 1954) diverges from the rhetoric of Plato, his teacher, as we shall see more fully below. For Aristotle, rhetoric need not flow from and lead others to a precise knowledge of ultimate truth, as Plato had asserted; instead, it can be applied to "any given case." In Cicero's *De Oratore* (trans. 1942/1979), in fact, Crassus wonders if gifted rhetoricians truly are able "in Aristotelian fashion to speak on both sides about every subject and by means of knowing Aristotle's rules to reel off two speeches on opposite sides on every case" (III.xxi.80). Comparing the rhetorics of Plato and Aristotle, Black (1958/1994) observes, "[Plato] did not reject the attempt to suffuse an investigation of rhetoric with a moral concern. It is on this very point that his great disciple departed from him" (p. 99). Aristotle's departure from Plato's truth-based rhetorical model does not, of course, mean that he proposes an immoral rhetoric; amoral might be a better (if somewhat controversial) description. Wardy (1996), however, compiles Aristotle's "catalogue of fishy persuasive techniques" in *Rhetoric* and *Topics* and concludes that Aristotle "subordinates truth to victory" (pp. 74, 81)—an assessment similar to an adversarial society view of public relations (Chapter 1). Garver (2004) maintains that for the Aristotelian rhetorician, "good. . . means something more than technical prowess and something less than moral goodness" (p. 200).

Kennedy (1994) believes that Aristotle's *Rhetoric* is descriptive rather than prescriptive, and he compares that work to Aristotle's objective, "dispassionate" descriptions of plants and animals in his scientific treatises (p. 56). Brockriede (1971) highlights that same empiricism in suggesting that Aristotelian rhetoric had its provenance in "the assembly, the law courts, and the ceremonies of his day" (p. 41). Given rhetoric's origins in such venues, Black (1994) maintains that Aristotle "affirmed the moral neutrality of rhetoric" (p. 99). Early in the *Rhetoric*, Aristotle (trans. 1954) does write, "We must not make people believe what is wrong" (1355a)—but he later discusses how to generate a "misleading inference" and notes that in some cases "we must assert coincidences and accidents to have been intended" (1367b). Lunsford and Ede (1994) vigorously defend what they view as the solid moral ground of Aristotle's *Rhetoric*—but at no point in their article do they cite his seminal definition of rhetoric: "the faculty of observing in *any given case* the available means of persuasion" (Aristotle, trans. 1954, 1355b, emphasis added). The notion of *any*, of course, opens the door to the "moral neutrality" that Black and others find.

We should clarify again that Aristotle, in his *Rhetoric*, is not aggressively or even tacitly immoral; instead, his analysis of rhetoric is, in the words of Corbett (1990a), "morally indifferent" (p. 544). Yoos (1984) neatly sums up this indifference and neutrality:

> In defining rhetoric as the art of finding all the available means of persuasion, Aristotle must recommend selecting, compiling, and arranging arguments to gain maximum persuasive advantage. Such strategies to gain the prize need to hide the weakness of one's own position. They need to divert an audience's attention away from the strength of an opponent's argument . . . And finally they need to put the audience in a receptive form of mind that will lull their "natural reason."
>
> (p. 96)

Aristotle's empirical, egoistic focus on what will persuade, as opposed to what is in the best interests of both the speaker and the listener, renders his rhetoric—and his *Rhetoric*—a questionable model for social harmony frameworks of modern public relations such as communitarianism, two-way symmetry, and fully functioning society theory. Critical consensus, however, is surely correct in maintaining that, today, Aristotelian rhetoric is the best known and most influential of the classical rhetorics.

Rhetoric and persuasion in ancient Athens

For Aristotle, rhetoric is an amoral, methodical discovery of means to an end—and that end is persuasion, which is a charged word and concept in modern public relations. "The role of persuasion in public relations," write Pfau and Wan (2009), "is the focus of considerable controversy" (p. 88). A generation ago, McBride (1989) asserted that public relations scholars' ambivalence toward persuasion had led to "a crippling inferiority complex" (p. 5) for the discipline. More recently, Messina (2007) has examined "whether ethical persuasion can be part of public relations practice" (p. 29), and Ihlen (2010) has reviewed enduring concerns regarding "whether persuasion can be considered a legitimate activity" within public relations (p. 64). Moloney (2006) and Porter (2010) have defended the role of persuasion in public relations; at the onset of excellence theory, Dozier and Ehling (1992) viewed persuasion as "less relevant than other processes" (p. 175) in their normative two-way symmetrical model. Both Moloney (2006) and L'Etang (2008) note its association with propaganda. Summarizing the debate, Edgett (2002) has asked "whether persuasion is a legitimate public relations function. . . [and] whether it can be performed to high ethical standards" (p. 1).

It may be reassuring to discover that our modern ambivalence regarding persuasion has deep historical roots—and, I believe, historical solutions. In the Athens of approximately 400 BCE–200 CE, persuasion actually was a powerful female deity: Peitho (Smith, 2005, 2011). The purpose of much of the rest of this chapter is twofold: To chart Peitho's diverse nature via her bewildering history and genealogy in classical Greek literature and art; and to study how the Greeks found, to borrow from Shakespeare's (1969) Theseus, "the concord of [the] discord" within Peitho's contradictory character (*A Midsummer Night's Dream*, V.i.60). Led by the dramatist Aeschylus, the rhetorician Isocrates, and, to some degree, the philosopher Plato, the Greeks determined that Peitho/Persuasion, at her best, was honest, respectful of others, and mindful of community wellbeing—hardly an Aristotelian view of neutral rhetoric. Ideally, the Greeks' resolution of the nature of persuasion might hold lessons for the tension within modern public relations between frameworks of egoism and those of social harmony.

Pfau and Wan (2009) define persuasion as "the use of communication in an attempt to shape, change, and/or reinforce perception, affect (feelings), cognition (thinking), and/or behavior" (p. 89)—a definition that Aristotle himself surely would accept. Over the past generation, scholars have identified several challenges to the ethical use and social acceptance of persuasion within public relations:

* Persuasion clashes with the objectivity promised in Ivy Lee's 1906 Declaration of Principles, which pledged to "supply news" and "prompt and accurate information" (as cited in Cutlip, 1994, p. 45) to the news media (McBride, 1989; Olasky, 1984).
* Many early public relations practitioners in the United States were, like Ivy Lee, former journalists who favored an ideal of objective communication over persuasion (McBride, 1989).
* The pervasive use of propaganda in World War I and thereafter cast suspicion on persuasion directed at groups (McBride, 1989). In his seminal *Propaganda Technique in the World War*, Harold Lasswell (1938) wrote, "We live among more people than ever, who are puzzled, uneasy, or vexed at the unknown cunning which seems to have duped and degraded them" (p. 2).
* The publication of Vance Packard's influential *The Hidden Persuaders* in 1957 cast additional suspicion on techniques of persuasion deployed by the advertising and public relations professions (Gower, 2005; McBride, 1989).
* Persuasion is not a primary function within the two-way symmetrical model of public relations, the ideal model within excellence theory (Curtin & Gaither, 2005; Pfau & Wan, 2009; Porter, 2010).

- Historically, persuasion is associated with rhetoric, a word that "in every-day parlance" often is "reserved for empty words and deception" (Ihlen, 2010, p. 59).

Such distrust seems surprisingly at odds with the modern advocacy of adversarial society theory and the definition of public relations as the "strategic management of competition and conflict for the benefit of one's own organization" (Wilcox & Cameron, 2009, p. 7).

Millennia ago, the Greek rhetorician Isocrates (trans. 1929/1992) decried his fellow Athenians' similar ambivalence regarding persuasion:

> As a symptom, not only of [the Athenians'] confusion of mind, but of their contempt for the gods, they recognize that Persuasion [Peitho] is one of the gods, and they observe that the city makes sacrifices to her every year, but when men aspire to share the power which the goddess possesses, they claim that such aspirants are being corrupted, as though their desire were for some evil thing.
>
> (*Antidosis*, 249)

A secular version of Isocrates' charge would not seem out of place in our current debates regarding persuasion.

The tangled lineage of the deity Peitho offers additional evidence of the ancient Greeks' confusion regarding persuasion. Classical sources ranging from Hesiod to Sappho and beyond cast Peitho as the daughter of Ate, the female deity of "infatuation and rashness," and the granddaughter of Eris, the female deity "of strife" (Kane, 1986, p. 101); or the daughter of Oceanus and Tethys, the generic parents of thousands of deities; or the daughter of Aphrodite, the female deity of love, revered in Athens as a source of civic harmony. Some sources have Peitho present at Aphrodite's birth. Peitho was the wife of Phoroneus, the first king of Argos and a civic unifier—or of Argos, who would be her own grandson if she, indeed, were the wife of Phoroneus. Or she was the wife of Hermes, the messenger of the gods and a trickster. She was the sister, in some accounts, of Tuche (the female deity of luck) and Metis (the female deity of cunning or, alternately, wisdom)—and, perhaps, of Eunomia (the female deity of good laws). In short, by birth and association Peitho was anything from a deceiver and manipulator to a source of concord and civic harmony. Again, the Greeks' eventual resolution of the contradictory nature of Peitho—their ancient consilience—may hold lessons for modern public relations. Before proceeding, however, I must acknowledge my indebtedness to Atsma (2014), Breitenberger (2007), Buxton (1982), Kirby (1994), and Smith (2005, 2011) for the attributions of these and following genealogies to original classical sources.

The Greek word *peitho*

In the Greek of classical Athens, *peitho* was both a proper noun (the name of a female deity) and a common noun, the name of a concept and activity. As such, the word's denotation was both sacred and secular, both a personi- fication and an abstraction. In the assessments of modern critics, the word is "multifaceted" (Smith, 2011, p. 57) and "polysemous" (Kirby, 1994, p. 3). In his study of persuasion in Greek tragedy, however, Buxton (1982) cau- tions that modern distinctions between personification and abstraction don't time-travel well: "There is no hard and fast dichotomy between *Peitho* and *peitho*: at most they may be thought of as occupying two ends of a spectrum" (p. 30). Smith (2011) cites evidence from Hesiod that the proper noun, the female deity, preceded the common noun, the activity. Studying the deity Persuasion, therefore, may tell us much about the activity she preceded and engendered.

Buxton's notion of a spectrum of meaning is a useful way of indicating the range of connotations and applications of *peitho*, particularly if we add a verti- cal axis and create a Cartesian grid. Given the range of lineages, meanings, and enactments that our research reveals, such a chart might look something like Figure 11.1.

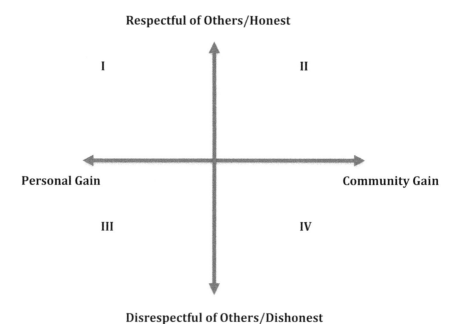

Figure 11.1 The meanings of *peitho*

One limitation of this chart would be the incorrect interpretation that an action promoting community gain invariably would have no trace of intentional personal gain.

Clarifying the range of possibilities for persuasion and how it might function in civil society mattered mightily to the Greeks, particularly to the Athenians in history's first democracy:

> In the fifth and fourth centuries [BCE], no one could avoid such questions for very long. From tragic drama to philosophical dialogue to lyric poetry, discourses and arguments about the nature of persuasion can be found just about everywhere. Praised here, condemned there, allied with subversion and rebellion in one place and with harmony and accord in another, persuasion is one of the most elusive and, yet, significant "concepts" or "activities" in classical Greek literature and philosophy.
>
> (Naas, 1995, p. 8)

Indeed, as this chapter ideally will show, three of the most significant, enduring, and complementary findings of concord within the discord of *peitho*'s guises come from a dramatist, Aeschylus; a rhetorician, Isocrates; and a philosopher, Plato.

Because much of this chapter focuses on the range of Peitho's varied nature within our Cartesian grid, it is worth noting that enactments of modern public relations easily supply examples of persuasive communication for each quadrant. The following examples are guided by Pfau and Wan's (2009) definition of persuasion as communication-based attempts to shape, change, and/or reinforce perceptions, feelings, thinking, and/or behavior:

- Quadrant I, the confluence of respect, honesty, and personal gain, is typified by Virgin Atlantic Airways Chairman Richard Branson's response to a humorous online complaint, addressed to him, about the airline's food. Branson phoned the writer with an apology and explanation, praised his wit, and invited him to help advise Virgin on meals and wines. Media responses were highly favorable toward Branson (Allen, 2009).
- Quadrant II, the confluence of respect, honesty, and community gain, is typified by Patagonia CEO Yvon Chouinard's decision to take his management team "to the windswept mountains of the real Patagonia, for a walkabout . . . We talked about the values we had in common, and the shared culture that had brought everyone to Patagonia, Inc., and not another company" (Chouinard, 2006, p. 71). Patagonia's shared culture and values include donating 1 percent of corporate profits to environmental causes (Patagonia, 2015).
- Quadrant III, the confluence of dishonesty, disrespect, and personal gain, is typified by a Washington, DC, lobbying agency's use of forged letters, purportedly sent by minority-rights groups, to urge members of Congress

to vote against the American Clean Energy and Security Act (McNeill, 2009).

- Quadrant IV, the confluence of dishonesty, disrespect, and community gain, is typified by the false communications, including bogus news conferences, issued by the activist group the Yes Men. For example, a member of the Yes Men falsely identified himself as a spokesperson for the U.S. Chamber of Commerce and hosted a fake news conference in support of climate remediation (Milbank, 2009).

As this chapter will show, the nature of ancient *peitho*/persuasion supplies antecedents for these modern instances.

Peitho in genealogy and art

In the literature of classical Greek mythology and the related pottery art, the deity Peitho appears as daughter, sister, wife, mother, and key companion. Buxton (1982) observes that the inconsistencies of Peitho's role within these relationships can result in the portrayal of "an absurdly split" personality (p. 29). Kane (1986) generously concludes that "Peitho seems to have a dual nature reflected in her ambiguous genealogy" (p. 101)—dual in the senses noted in our Cartesian grid. Despite the complexities and contradictions within the following summary, it is not comprehensive.

In Aeschylus' play *Agamemnon* (trans. 2008), Clytemnestra describes "miserable" Peitho as the "unendurable child of scheming Ruin [Ate]" (385–386). "Ate, the goddess of infatuation and rashness," writes Kane (1986), "was the daughter of Eris, goddess of strife" (p. 101). Other evidence suggests that Peitho was the daughter of Aphrodite, the female deity of love. An anonymous annotation in an early copy of Hesiod's *Works and Days*, for example, "reports that Sappho called Peitho the daughter of Aphrodite" (Kirby, 1994, p. 3). Such a relationship would be particularly significant in Athens, where Aphrodite also was known as Aphrodite Pandemos, or Aphrodite of the People. Like Peitho, Aphrodite had a multifaceted nature, focusing on both individual relationships and the social bonds that unite and sustain a community. Athenian legend holds that in gratitude for the roles played by Aphrodite Pandemos and Peitho in helping to create Athens, Theseus, Athens' first king, had a temple built in their honor in the Acropolis (Smith, 2011). Thus, as a daughter, Peitho may embody the heritage of the divisive deities of rashness and strife (quadrant III of our Cartesian grid, focusing on dishonesty, disrespect, and personal gain)—or the deity of civic harmony who helped found and sustain Athens (quadrant II of our Cartesian grid, focusing on honesty, respect, and community gain).

In *Theogony*, Hesiod (trans. 1991) asserts that Peitho is the sister of Metis, female deity of cunning and wisdom. Metis, declares Long (2007), represents a "sense of cunning, deception, and craftiness as much as that of wise counsel and political acumen" (p. 67). Conversely, the poet Alcman writes that

Peitho—via yet another mother, Promatheia, was the sister of Eunomia, female deity of good laws and social order (Smith, 2005). Under Eunomia's guidance, holds Solon (trans. 2008), the Athenian lawmaker and poet, "all things among men are fitting and rational" (p. 172). Peitho's sibling relationships, thus, indicate the same duality found in the contradictory versions of her parentage: inconsistencies regarding honesty, respect, and community wellbeing.

Buxton cites a marginal note in an early copy of Euripides' *Orestes* identifying Peitho as the wife of Phoroneus, the first king of Argos, in Greece, "who brought mankind together for the first time; for hitherto they had lived scattered and solitary" (Pausanias, trans. 1965, II.xv.v). The symbolic value of the marriage, in Buxton's (1982) words, is that "*peitho* is a central quality in a civilized polis" (p. 36). However, Nonnus, a Greek poet of the fifth century CE, casts Peitho as the wife of Hermes, the fleet-footed messenger of the gods, known for "deceitful eloquence and cunning" and for being the male deity "of thieves and rogues" (Kirkwood, 1959, p. 55). With the addition of Hermes as a reputed husband, Peitho's range of marriages includes contradictions in the qualities of persuasion represented by our Cartesian grid: Honesty/dishonesty; respect/disrespect; and personal gain/community gain.

As the wife of Phoroneus, Peitho might have been mother of the sons Aigialeus and Apis, thus helping to ensure the royal lineage of Argos. So important was that community to ancient Greece that Homer, in *The Iliad* (trans. 2011), repeatedly calls the assembled Greeks "the Argives"—people of Argos (I. 80). Alternately, the *Suda*, a tenth century CE compendium of historical data, asserts that Peitho was the mother of Iynx, whom Hera transformed into a bird for attempting to surreptitiously enchant Zeus (Atsma, 2014). The English word *jinx* traces origins to her name. Peitho's status as a mother thus suggests, again, strong contradictions in both axes of our Cartesian grid: Honesty versus dishonesty and community gain versus personal gain.

Peitho's most enduring role as a companion, or attendant, is with Aphrodite. Calling Peitho a "major figure in Aphrodite's entourage" (p. 177), Breitenberger (2007) adds that "we can infer from Sappho's extant fragments that Peitho as a personified deity is featured in the environment of Aphrodite: either as her daughter or her attendant" (p. 127). In describing the temple of Aphrodite Pandemos and Peitho in the Athenian Acropolis, the ancient Greek geographer Pausanias (trans. 1965) writes:

> The worship of . . .Aphrodite [Pandemos] and of Persuasion [Peitho] was instituted by Theseus when he gathered the Athenians from the townships into a single city. In my time the ancient images were gone, but the existing images were by no obscure artists.
>
> (I.xxii.iii)

Pausanias thus suggests that ancient architectural adornments—just as their replacements—featured an enduring association of Peitho with Aphrodite

Pandemos. This civic association with Aphrodite Pandemos is the strongest indication that a significant aspect of Peitho did indeed skew to the community-gain extreme of the horizontal axis in our Cartesian grid:

> Pausanias'. . . story connects Aphrodite Pandemos and Peitho to Theseus, the mythical and thus undatable king of Athens—to emphasise the role of these goddesses in civic cooperation and democratic spirit on which their polis was supposed to have been founded.
>
> (Smith, 2011, p. 56)

As noted below, however, Greek pottery depicts both Aphrodite and Peitho as active participants in Paris' adulterous and disastrous disrespectful/personal-gain seduction of Helen.

The rise of Peitho as a deity in the fifth century BCE was preceded by a "mighty artistic sixth-century accomplishment" in Greece: "the uniquely rich, rapid, and varied evolution of painting on pottery" (Grant, 1987, pp. 26–27). Peitho figured prominently in such art, which, taken as a whole, echoes the multifaceted personality of Peitho found in written accounts of her lineage. Her appearance in pottery that portrays peaceful, joyful marriage scenes would, traditionally, be located somewhere in quadrant I of our Cartesian grid: The intersection of personal gain and respect for others/honesty. Of such artistic scenes, Smith (2005) writes, "The erotic role of Peitho is emphasised in many . . . mythological scenes that concern courtship and marriage" (p. 15). As we might now expect, however, a contradictory image is readily available. In another pottery-vase image, Peitho appears as an influential figure in Paris' adulterous seduction of Helen, an event that occurred in the home of Menelaus, Helen's husband, and helped trigger the Trojan War. In the words of Aeschylus' Clytemnestra, who only moments earlier had condemned "miserable" Peitho, Paris "went to the house of [Menelaus] and shamed the table of hospitality by stealing away a wife" (Aeschylus, *Agamemnon*, trans. 2008, 385ff.). The image shows Aphrodite and Peitho seemingly cooperating with Paris as he takes Helen's arm to lead her away (Buxton, 1982). Such an instance of Peitho clearly would be located in the third quadrant of our grid, the intersection of personal gain and disrespect for others/dishonesty.

The image with Helen and Paris is important, for throughout classical Greek literature and art, Peitho generally is presented as an alternative to Bia, the female deity of force and compulsion (Kirby, 1994). Another extant vase, for example, shows Peitho fleeing the sexual attack by the twins Castor and Pollux on two female priests. The clear suggestion is that Peitho works through communication rather than physical violence—though, as Foley (2012), like modern critics of power disparities within public relations (Curtin & Gaither, 2005), notes, a powerful gray area can exist between Peitho and Bia. Of this particular scene, Smith (2005) writes, "Peitho's dramatic escape. . . implies that she did not condone this union in accordance with Athenian standards;

the scene thus serves as a counterexample of the ideal marriage" (p. 15). In terms of our Cartesian grid, the scene suggests that the disrespect of quadrants 3 and 4 cannot descend to the level of physical violence and remain a form of persuasion. In such instances, Bia has replaced Peitho.

Of these depictions of Peitho—at weddings and, conversely, in dishonest seductions—Buxton (1982) concludes, "In the right place—marriage—Peitho brings men and women harmonious delight; in the wrong place—illicit sexual relationships—Peitho can be an agent of discord and catastrophe" (p. 37).

Although each of these scenes focuses more on individual than civic relationships, Smith (2005) cautions against ignoring the broader social nature of such depictions: "Civic personifications could be interpreted on the private level—as personal virtues—and on the public level—as civic virtues— especially because they appeared on vases that functioned both in public and private" (p. 26). Peitho's image in Greek pottery, thus, spans our two continuums of personal/communal and respect/disrespect for others.

The Greeks' resolution: Peitho at her best

Naas (1995), as cited earlier, holds that "discourses and arguments about the nature of persuasion can be found just about everywhere" (p. 8) in the art and writings of the ancient Greeks. Significantly, three of the greatest minds in classical Athens arrived at largely the same conclusion about persuasion: Like the deity herself, persuasion is multifaceted; but—unlike the general persuasion of Aristotelian rhetoric—*peitho* is at its best when used to build respectful, honest relationships, particularly those that benefit the community. This was the message of the dramatist Aeschylus in his *Oresteia* trilogy; of the rhetorician Isocrates throughout his works; and, to a large degree, of the philosopher Plato in his *Phaedrus*.

Aeschylus and Peitho

Aeschylus' *Oresteia* trilogy tells an elaborate tale of murder, revenge, and justice: Clytemnestra murders her husband, Agamemnon, for sacrificing their daughter Iphigenia to appease the gods; their son, Orestes, then murders Clytemnestra in revenge and is pursued by the Furies, who avenge wrongs, particularly betrayals within families. In Athens, the deity Athena convenes a trial to determine Orestes' fate. In each key phase of the trilogy—murder, revenge, and the quest for justice—Peitho plays an essential role. In the first two plays of the trilogy, *Agamemnon* and *Libation-Bearers*, Peitho is seen as a self-serving, destructive, dishonest force. We already have noted Clytemnestra's condemnation of "miserable" Peitho as the descendant of the deities of ruin and strife (Aeschylus, *Agamemnon*, trans. 2008, 385ff). An individual who succumbs to Peitho, Clytemnestra warns, "inflicts unendurable harm on his community" (Aeschylus, *Agamemnon*, trans. 2008, 395), and she cites Paris and his seduction of Helen as an example. The deity Peitho fares little better in *Libation-Bearers*, in which the Chorus summons "guileful Persuasion [Peitho]" to "enter the arena" (Aeschylus, trans. 2008, 727–728) with Orestes, who has lied about his identity to gain entrance into the palace in Argos in hopes of killing Clytemnestra. In our Cartesian grid, these descriptions and actions of Peitho would fall primarily into the third quadrant: Personal-gain/disrespectful and dishonest persuasion. Clytemnestra's censure of Paris and "miserable" Peitho, however, shows that personal-gain instances of *peitho* can have profound social impacts.

As a secular noun—a distinction, again, that Buxton (1982) challenges— *peitho* appears in Clytemnestra's comment to the Chorus that "what I say is getting inside her [Cassandra's] mind and my words are persuading [*peitho*] her" (Aeschylus, *Agamemnon*, trans. 2008, 1050–1052). At this point in the first play, Clytemnestra has been urging Cassandra, Agamemnon's Trojan mistress, to enter the palace in Argos, where Clytemnestra hopes to—and does—murder her. Such usage of *peitho*, again, would fall into the personal- gain/disrespectful and dishonest quadrant.

In *Eumenides* (trans. 2008), however, the trilogy's third play, Aeschylus offers a momentous re-envisioning of Peitho. Hitherto in the trilogy, when not reviled, Peitho has been invoked by mortals for dishonest and disrespectful personal gain. In *Eumenides*, however, Athena, the female deity of wisdom, convenes a trial of Orestes, in which she invokes Peitho to help placate the Furies; Rynearson (2013) casts the trial as "the moment of truth for the entire trilogy" (p. 1). Remarkably, Athena succeeds, and she openly credits Peitho for helping her to introduce the notions of compassion and fairness into a new concept of justice. As Athena tries to persuade the Furies to release Orestes and remain in Athens as honored deities, she urges, "If you have reverence for the awesome power of Persuasion [*Peitho*], the charm and enchantment of my tongue. . . please do stay" (Aeschylus, trans. 2008, 885ff). When the Furies agree to stand down and remain peacefully in Athens, Athena declares, "I rejoice; and I am happy that the eyes of Persuasion [*Peitho*] watched over my tongue and lips when they responded to these beings [the Furies] who were savagely rebuffing me" (Aeschylus, trans. 2008, 969ff).

Significantly, Athena and Peitho cleave to respectful honesty in negotiating with the Furies: Athena promises the Furies that, in return for relinquishing their traditional roles as avengers, they may remain in Athens as revered household deities. As Athena leads them to their promised abode in sacred caverns, the reformed Furies speak against conflict, praying that "civil strife, insatiate of evil, may never rage in this city" (Aeschylus, trans. 2008, 976ff), and the grateful citizens of Athens respond, "In the age-old recesses of the earth may you receive great reverence with rituals and sacrifices" (Aeschylus, trans. 2008, 1036ff). Clearly, the Peitho of *Eumenides* falls into the community-gain/respectful and honest quadrant of our Cartesian grid. Winnington-Ingram (1951) declares that Aeschylus' new concept of *peitho* is "perhaps the most striking of all the conceptions which we find in Aeschylus, and the most original" (p. 420).

One key message of the *Oresteia* trilogy thus seems clear: Persuasion is at its best when filtered through wisdom (Athena) and directed, at least in part, toward community good. Several scholars echo Winnington-Ingram's assessment of Aeschylus' achievement. Noting "the transformation of peitho" within the trilogy, Kennedy (2009) concludes, "Where *peitho* leads to the destruction of Troy [and] Agamemnon. . . in the earlier plays of the *Oresteia*, it leads to the salvation of Orestes and of Athens in *Eumenides*" (p. 36). In "Peitho and the Polis," Kane (1986) writes, "At the end of the trilogy, Peitho has been transformed into a benign deity, the goddess of political persuasion whose awesome majesty Athena asks the Furies to revere" (p. 101). And Long (2007), observing Aeschylus' innovative fusion of wisdom, persuasion, and honesty, declares, "[Athena] opens the possibility for human flourishing in a city founded not upon violence, but upon the powers associated with. . . Peitho and Styx [deity of promises], the powers of persuasion and respect for honor" (p. 72).

Isocrates and Peitho

Born roughly two decades after Aeschylus' death in the fifth century BCE, Isocrates was praised by the Romans Cicero and Quintilian as the greatest of the Greek rhetoricians (Benoit, 1990). Isocratean rhetoric, described as "the values-driven discourse of responsible citizenship" (Marsh, 2013, p. 12), features a version of *peitho* infused with the values of moderation and justice (Poulakos, 1997). Like Aeschylus, Isocrates favored a form of persuasion that was respectful, honest, and mindful of community wellbeing (Chapter 12). Significantly, this form of rhetoric proved to be highly successful in Athens and beyond:

> There is no doubt that Isocrates has one claim to fame at least, and that is as the supreme master of oratorical culture . . . On the whole, it was Isocrates, not Plato, who educated fourth-century Greece and subsequently the Hellenistic and Roman worlds.
>
> (Marrou, trans. 1956/1982, p. 79)

In a passage modern scholars have dubbed "The Hymn to Logos" (Jaeger, 1944, pp. 89–90), Isocrates (trans. 1928/1991)—forecasting Nowak's assessment of language that appears earlier in this chapter—acknowledges the twined importance of *peitho* and logos [speech and reasoning] in building communities:

> Because there has been implanted in us the power to persuade [*peithein*] each other and to make clear to each other whatever we desire, not only

have we escaped the life of wild beasts, but we have come together and founded cities and made laws and invented arts; and, generally speaking, there is no institution devised by man which the power of speech [*logos*] has not helped us to establish . . . With this faculty we both contend against others on matters which are open to dispute and seek light for ourselves on things which are unknown; for the same arguments which we use in persuading [*peithomen*] others when we speak in public, we employ also when we deliberate in our own thoughts . . . And, if there is need to speak in brief summary of this power, we shall find that. . . in all our actions as well as in all our thoughts speech [*logon*] is our guide, and is most employed by those who have the most wisdom.

(*Nicocles*, 6–9)

Logos thus enables *peitho*, which, in turn, enables introspection, cooperation, and civilization.

For Isocrates, all such enactments of *peitho* embrace, ideally, the values of justice (*dikaiosyne*) and moderation (*sophrosyne*). Of Isocratean rhetoric, Poulakos (1997) asserts, "Dikaiosyne and sophrosyne do not merely determine the horizon of an agent's moral conduct. Because they circumscribe political identities, they also implicate the conduct of the entire polis" (p. 35). Marsh (2013) has described Isocratean rhetoric as being "concentric" (p. 23), with the values of moderation and justice first influencing internal dialogues and personal behavior and relationships and then radiating outward to community and international relationships.

Like Aeschylus, Isocrates believes that *peitho*, at its best, should be filtered through wisdom. In his essay *Panathenaicus*, he describes "wise" and "complete" rhetoricians as being, in part, individuals who

possess a judgement which is accurate in meeting occasions as they arise and rarely misses the expedient course of action. . . [and] who are decent and honourable in their intercourse with all with whom they associate, tolerating easily and good-naturedly what is unpleasant or offensive in others and being themselves as agreeable and reasonable to their associates as it is possible to be.

(Isocrates, trans. 1929/1992, 30–31)

In his essay *On the Peace*, Isocrates (trans. 1929/1992) asserts, "Arrogance and insolence have been the cause of our misfortunes while sobriety and self-control [*sophrosyne*] have been the source of our blessings" (119). Isocrates clearly favored and taught much the same form of persuasion that Aeschylus fashioned in *Eumenides*: A form of persuasion filtered through wisdom and driven by respect for others and a commitment to community wellbeing. Like the *peitho* of *Eumenides*, we locate this form of persuasion in the community-gain/respectful and honest quadrant of our Cartesian grid. Little wonder, then, that critic Henri Marrou, in his *History of Education in Antiquity* (trans. 1956/1982), concludes, "In the hands of Isocrates rhetoric is gradually transformed into ethics" (p. 89). A more detailed description of Isocratean rhetoric, particularly its success vis-à-vis Aristotelian rhetoric, is in Chapter 12.

Plato and Peitho

Born eight years after Isocrates, Plato championed a form of persuasion that differs from the ideal *peitho* described by Aeschylus and Isocrates. Plato's ideal persuasion is, indeed, directed toward the wellbeing of others—but honesty, as we shall see, is not inherent in the concept. Plato's dialogue *Phaedrus* features three speeches, ostensibly about lovers. The first, actually Phaedrus' reading of a speech by Lysias, contends that love should not be part of seeming loving relationships; the instigating lover thus would have no emotional attachment and, therefore, could not be hurt. Socrates cleverly counters with a speech maintaining that the instigating lover should, rather, avoid pain by selecting an immature lover and keeping that individual in a state of subservient inferiority. Then, fearing that he has offended Eros, the male deity of love, Socrates composes a third speech that presents the instigating lover as one concerned primarily for the spiritual and intellectual improvement of the beloved.

In his landmark essay "The *Phaedrus* and the Nature of Rhetoric," Richard Weaver (1953) labels the three lovers the nonlover, the evil lover, and the noble lover—and he compellingly demonstrates that the three speeches are metaphors for three kinds of rhetoric and that art's inherent *peitho*: "[*Phaedrus*] is consistently, and from beginning to end, about one thing, which is the nature of rhetoric" (p. 3). The three forms of love thus symbolize a sterile, uncaring rhetoric; a self-serving, potentially dishonest rhetoric; and an altruistic rhetoric that seeks to improve the lot of others. Plato, as well as Phaedrus and Socrates within the dialogue, clearly opts for the third form, the noble lover, the altruistic rhetoric. For the moment, this would seem to align Plato with Aeschylus and Isocrates.

In *Phaedrus*, however, Plato adds a requirement found elsewhere in his dialogues: Rhetoricians must know the absolute truth of a situation before they use *peitho* to bring others to that truth. Midway through *Phaedrus*, Socrates personifies logos and has her say, "Why do you talk nonsense, you strange men? I do not compel anyone to learn to speak without knowing the truth, but if my advice is of any value, he learns that first and then acquires me" (Plato, trans. 1914/1928, 260D). Paradoxically, this knowledge of absolute truth allows Plato's ideal rhetorician to lie to persuade the unenlightened. In *Republic*, for example, Socrates declares that ruling philosopher-kings—rulers because they have divined absolute truth—may deceive their subjects:

> The rulers then of the city may, if anybody, fitly lie. . . for the benefit of the state . . . It seems likely that our rulers will have to make considerable use of falsehood and deception for the benefit of their subjects.
>
> (Plato, trans. 1989, 389B, 459C)

Plato's ideal form of *peitho* thus would fall into the fourth quadrant of our Cartesian grid: The intersection of community gain with dishonesty. Philosopher-kings would use *peitho* for the benefit of their subjects, but it would not always be honest *peitho*.

Peitho at her best

This examination of the deity Peitho has shown that in classical Greece, particularly Athens, she had many natures—but, according to the dramatist Aeschylus, the rhetorician Isocrates, and, to some degree, the philosopher Plato, Peitho had a best nature: At its best, persuasion was honest, respectful of others, and mindful of community wellbeing. Peitho at her best was filtered through—if not absolute truth—at least wisdom. This is a key point: Classical Athens achieved its own form of consilience on the troubled relationship between egoism and cooperation; the Athenians' cross-disciplinary approach to this challenge yielded results that predict later conclusions within evolutionary biology, philosophy, and rhetoric. The findings of the aforementioned sections, in fact, can provide an example for each quadrant of our Cartesian grid (11.2):

*   Peitho's role in peaceful, joyful marriage scenes falls into the first quadrant, the intersection of personal gain and respect for others/honesty.
*   Peitho's role in placating the Furies in *Eumenides*—the Greeks' normative role for persuasion—falls into the second quadrant, the intersection of community gain and respect for others/honesty.
*   Peitho's role in the seduction of Helen falls into the third quadrant, the intersection of personal gain and disrespect for others/dishonesty.
*   Peitho's unpersonified role in Plato's dialogues falls into the fourth quadrant, the intersection of community gain and disrespect for others/dishonesty.

The Greeks' key distinctions among these forms of *peitho* forecast McBride's (1989) finding that acceptance of persuasion within modern public relations must distinguish between "methods and motives" (p. 12).

Ideally, this powerful consensus on *peitho*/persuasion at its best helps lessen the competition/conflict legacy of Aristotle's *Rhetoric*, as valuable as that analysis remains. As Heath (2009), Ihlen (2010), Marsh (2013), and other scholars have demonstrated, public relations owe much to the intellectual achievements of classical Greece. As modern scholars and practitioners of

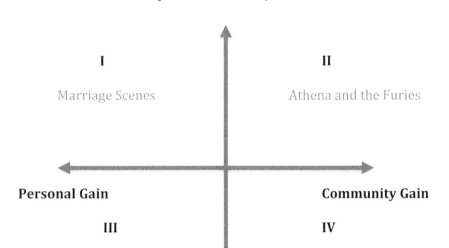

Respectful of Others/Honest

I

Marriage Scenes

II

Athena and the Furies

Personal Gain

III

Peitho and Paris

Community Gain

IV

Plato's Philosopher-King

Disrespectful of Others/Dishonest

Figure 11.2 Versions of *Peitho*

public relations wrestle the nature of persuasion within their discipline, they may wish to consider the Greeks' conclusions regarding the deity Peitho.

Modern studies do suggest the continued validity of the ancient Athenians' conclusions regarding *peitho*. For example, a 2015 study of legislative use of "prosocial" words such as "gentle, involve, educate, contribute, concerned, give, tolerate, trust, and cooperate" showed that public approval of the U.S. Congress correlated with increased use of those words. Conversely, "a text analysis of all 124 million words spoken in the House of Representatives between 1996 and 2014 found that declining levels of prosocial language strongly predicted public disapproval of Congress" (Frimer, Aquino, Gebauer, Zhub, & Oakes 2015, pp. 6, 591).

The remainder of Part IV will expand this initial account of Isocratean rhetoric (Chapter 12) and then will detail ancient and modern concurrence with Isocrates' emphases on cooperation and community wellbeing (Chapter 13).

Summary

This overview of classical rhetoric leads us to at least two important points for the understanding and practice of public relations:

1. A historical misperception of the success of Aristotelian conflict-oriented rhetoric may have impaired public relations' ability to discover and model the most effective forms of classical rhetoric.
2. After much public and cross-disciplinary deliberation, the ancient Athenians determined that persuasion/*peitho* at its best is honest, respect-ful of others, and mindful of community wellbeing.

These two points address one of the Nine Tenets of public relations' social harmony frameworks outlined in Chapter 1:

II. Cooperation is the relationship strategy best suited to resource acquisition. Evidence from evolutionary biology, philosophy, and rhetoric shows that, in general, cooperative relationships are more successful in sustained resource acquisition than relationships based on egoism, conflict, and competition.

Chapter 12

Isocrates, moderation, and justice

The Greek rhetorician Isocrates is the earliest historical figure studied in this book. In his essays and correspondence we find, arguably, Western civilization's first sustained discussion of seminal topics that now characterize public relations: The need for overlapping consensus amid reasonable pluralism (to use Rawls' language); the connection between reciprocity and reputation; the potentially destructive nature of power disparities in relationships; the importance of seeking and valuing dissent—and, most important, the role of justice and moderation in successful relationships and social stability. For Isocrates, civic rhetoric is not, ideally, an Aristotelian amoral instrument in the service of whoever chooses to wield it; it is not the "mere rhetoric" impugned by Rawls. Rather, the purpose of rhetoric is (in our own self-interest) to advance the values of justice, moderation, and dissent in the service of social harmony.

Isocrates was born in Athens in 436 BCE. His father was a financially successful flute maker, but the family fortune suffered during Athens' 30-year war with Sparta. To regroup financially, Isocrates became a logographer—a writer of judicial speeches for Athenian litigants—and then opened a school that became, in the words of Corbett (1989), "the true fountainhead of humanistic rhetoric" (p. 275). He was the contemporary of Socrates, Plato, and Aristotle, having been born 37 years before Socrates' death, eight years before the birth of Plato and 52 years before the birth of Aristotle. He died in 338 BCE at the age of 98, shortly after writing a major discourse (*Panathenaicus*) and a letter to Philip of Macedonia. Some 30 of Isocrates' discourses (actually, written essays) and letters survive.

Isocrates preferred the written essay to the public discourse because—an odd thing for a rhetorician—he was a poor public speaker. In his essay *Panathenaicus*, he concedes:

> As to my nature, however, I realized that it was not robust and vigorous enough for public affairs and that it was not adequate nor altogether suited to public discourse . . . For expounding the truth before an assemblage of many people it was, if I may say so, the least competent in all the world. For I was born more lacking in the two things which have the greatest

power in Athens—a strong voice and ready assurance—than, I dare say, any of my fellow-citizens.

(Isocrates, trans. 1929/1992, 9–10)

He confesses the same deficiencies in other essays, including *To Philip* (Isocrates, trans. 1928/1991, 81) and *To the Rulers of the Mytilenaeans* (Isocrates, trans. 1945/1986, 7). So severe was his lack of assurance, in fact, that Pseudo-Plutarch (trans. 1936/1969) alleges that "when three persons came to hear him, he retained two but let the third go, telling him to come the next day, since now the lecture-room had a full audience" (838D-E). Pondering such evidence, historian Henri Marrou (trans. 1956/1982) diagnoses "a kind of neurotic shyness which has been described as agoraphobia" (p. 85). In his preference for being a public voice emerging from a private study, Isocrates thus joins Charles Darwin, with his shyness and poor health (Irvine, 1955), and David Hume, who was embarrassed by his own ineradicable Scottish accent (Baillie, 2000).

For Isocrates, rhetoric is the discourse of responsible citizenship and is built upon the primary values of justice (*dikaiosyne*) and moderation (*sophrosyne*) (Marsh, 2013). Far from focusing on "the faculty of observing in *any given case* the available means of persuasion," as Aristotle (trans. 1954, 1355b, emphasis added) would have it, or the delivery of absolute truth—even, ironically, through deception—as Plato (trans. 1989) would have it (389B, 459C), Isocrates envisions rhetoric as a community-building discipline in an uncertain world that lacks Platonic absolutes (Plato, trans. 1989, 484B). "What raises Isocrates above the crowd of unscrupulous teachers of rhetoric," writes Erika Rummel (1994), "is his willingness to assume moral responsibility and to consider the ethics of persuasion" (p. 154).

Isocrates' success

Isocrates was not a disengaged philosopher spinning a normative rhetoric for a world that doesn't exist. For students throughout Greece, he led a for-profit school that outperformed the rival schools of Plato and Aristotle. "In Greece of the fourth century BC," writes historian Donald Clark (1957), "there was a three-cornered quarrel among the leading teachers concerning what it takes to make a successful speaker. From this quarrel Isocrates (436–338 BC) came out triumphant . . . For forty years Isocrates was the most influential teacher in Athens" (pp. 5, 58). While we lack definitive criteria for comparing the success of the competing rhetorics of Plato, Aristotle, and Isocrates, it seems logical to compare them by what they had in common: A school with, consequently, a reputation; graduates of the schools; and the evaluation of the later *Roman* rhetoricians—primarily Cicero, Dionysius of Halicarnassus, and Quintilian—who could survey the whole of classical Greek rhetoric.

Following the lead of Cicero (trans. 1939/1971), who in *Brutus* pronounces, "[Isocrates'] house stood open to all Greece as the *school of eloquence*" (8), historians have given top-school laurels to Isocrates. Freeman (1907) asserts that "Isokrates was [rhetoric's] greatest professor" (p. 161). Gwynn (1926/ 1966) says that Isocrates reigned "high above other teachers of rhetoric" (p. 48). Isocrates' reputation among students outstripped that of Plato (Hunt, 1990, p. 147) as well as that of Aristotle (Corbett, 1990b, p. 167). Venerated as Plato's Academy may be, scholars of higher education generally agree that Isocrates' school was more influential in classical Athens than the Academy. Marrou (trans. 1956/1982), who clearly feels more loyalty to Plato (p. 79), grudgingly concedes:

> There is no doubt that Isocrates has one claim to fame at least, and that is as the supreme master of oratorical culture . . . On the whole, it was Isocrates, not Plato, who educated fourth-century Greece and subsequently the Hellenistic and Roman worlds.
>
> (p. 79)

In the words of Grube (1965), "it was [Isocrates'] kind of education which triumphed over all others and dominated the Graeco-Roman world" (p. 38).

The most dramatic assessment of the three teachers' students comes, again, from Cicero (trans. 1942/1979): "Then behold Isocrates arose, from whose school, as from the Trojan horse, none but real heroes proceeded" (II.xxii). Cicero's contemporary, Dionysius of Halicarnassus (trans. 1974), concurs: "[Isocrates] became. . . the teacher of the most eminent men at Athens and in Greece at large, both the best forensic orators, and those who distinguished themselves in politics and public life" (1). And in his *Institutio Oratoria*, Quintilian writes, "The pupils of Isocrates were eminent in every branch of study" (trans. 1920/1980, III.i.14), adding that "it is to the school of Isocrates that we owe the greatest orators" (trans. 1922/1979, XII.x.22). Jebb (1876) echoes Cicero's praise of Isocrates' students and adds an anecdote about an oratorical competition of the fourth-century BCE:

> In the year 351 Mausolos, dynast of Karia, died; and his widow Artemesia proposed in honour of his memory a contest of panegyrical eloquence which brought a throng of brilliant rhetoricians to Halikarnassos. No competitor (it is said) presented himself who had not been a pupil of Isokrates; and it was certainly a pupil of Isokrates—Theopompos the historian—who gained the prize.
>
> (p. 11)

Scholars and rhetoricians past and present tend to echo Freeman (1907): "The pupils of Isokrates became the most eminent politicians and the most eminent prose-writers of the time" (p. 186). In M.I. Finley's (1987) words, they were "an entire Who's Who of Greek intellectuals and public figures" (p. 198).

We already have seen something of the preference of classical Rome's greatest rhetoricians—Cicero, Dionysius of Halicarnassus, and Quintilian—for Isocrates. Their praise of him was effusive, and their preference for his rhetoric, as opposed to that of Plato or Aristotle, was pronounced. In Cicero's (trans. 1942/1979) *De Oratore*, Isocrates is called the "father of eloquence" (II.iii). In *Brutus*, Cicero (trans. 1939/1971) writes that Isocrates "cherished and improved within the walls of an obscure academy, that glory which, in my opinion, no orator has since acquired. He. . . excelled his predecessors" (8). Dionysius of Halicarnassus (trans. 1974) praises Isocrates' "unrivalled power to persuade men and states" (9). Quintilian (trans. 1920/1980) calls Isocrates "the prince of instructors" (II.viii.11), and he accords to no one a higher rank.

Modern critics agree that Isocrates, not Plato or Aristotle, inspired the central rhetorical theorists of classical Rome. Too (1995) writes, "Scholars in Antiquity and in the Renaissance regarded Isocrates. . . as the pre-eminent rhetorician of ancient Athens" (p. 1). Katula and Murphy (1994) assert that "Isocrates' school is largely responsible for making rhetoric the accepted basis of education in Greece and later in Rome. His is the chief influence on the oratorical style and rhetorical theory of Cicero" (p. 46). Hubbell (1913) contends that "Cicero derived from Isocrates the function of the orator which he presents in *De Oratore*" (p. 16). Welch (1990) and Corbett (1989) note Isocrates' primary influence on both Cicero's and Quintilian's characterizations of the qualities and preparation of the ideal orator. As orators in the judicial and political spheres, Cicero and Quintilian could not afford ineffective rhetoric. Their clear preference for the rhetoric of Isocrates is perhaps its most compelling endorsement.

Isocratean rhetoric was not normative or utopian. It was designed for success, particularly in an Athens that Isocrates (trans. 1929/1992) describes in words that evoke Kenneth Burke's (1950/1969) later "Wrangle of the Market Place, the flurries and flare-ups of the Human Barnyard" (p. 23):

> Athens is so large and the multitude of people living here is so great, that the city does not present to the mind an image easily grasped or sharply defined, but, like a turbid flood, whatever it catches up in its course, whether men or things, in each case it sweeps them along pell-mell, and in some cases it imbues them with a reputation which is the opposite of the true.
>
> (*Antidosis*, 172)

Isocratean rhetoric, in other words, functioned in a contentious, litigious society "so like our own anguished times," according to Marrou (trans. 1956/1982, p. 87). Western civilization's most successful rhetoric advocated social unity, which was to be built—as we shall see—by the sincere advocacy of justice and moderation and the protection of dissent.

Rhetoric and social unity

In perhaps the most famous passage from the Isocratean canon, the so-called Hymn to Logos (Jaeger, 1944, pp. 89–90), Isocrates (trans. 1928/1991) describes the connection between persuasive language (*logos* and *peitho*) and social unity.

> Because there has been implanted in us the power to persuade [*peithein*] each other and to make clear to each other whatever we desire, not only have we escaped the life of wild beasts, but we have come together and founded cities and made laws and invented arts; and, generally speaking, there is no institution devised by man which the power of speech [*logos*] has not helped us to establish. For this it is which has laid down laws concerning things just and unjust, and things base and honorable; and if it were not for these ordinances we should not be able to live with one another. It is by this also that we confute the bad and extol the good. Through this we educate the ignorant and appraise the wise; for the power to speak well is taken as the surest index of a sound understanding, and discourse which is true and lawful and just is the outward image of a good and faithful soul. With this faculty we both contend against others on matters which are open to dispute and seek light for ourselves on things which are unknown; for the same arguments which we use in persuading [*peithomen*] others when we speak in public, we employ also when we deliberate in our own thoughts.
>
> (*Nicocles*, 6–8)

Modern evolutionary psychologist Michael Tomasello (2009), co-director of the Max Planck Institute for Evolutionary Anthropology, makes much the same point in *Why We Cooperate*: Because humans can teach and imitate one another, he maintains, we develop "shared intentionality," with the result that "all of humans' most impressive cognitive achievements—from complex technologies to linguistic and mathematical symbols to intricate social institutions—are the products not of individuals acting alone, but of individuals interacting" (pp. xiv–xv).

For Isocrates, the highest purpose of persuasive language was social unity in general and panhellenic unity in particular. The mission of Isocratean rhetoric was, ultimately, to unite the Greek city-states—to create, in Rawls' (2001) words, "a social union of social unions" (p. 142), a political form of Tomasello's "shared intentionality." During Isocrates' life, Greece, or Hellas, existed primarily as an idea, not a reality. It was a loose confederation of city-states, often at war with one another and continually threatened by the Persian

Empire to the east. Throughout his essays, Isocrates worked toward a pan-hellenic confederacy, designed, he hoped, to resist increasing encroachments from Persian armies. "His own political writings, read throughout Greece, gave him greater influence upon popular opinion than belonged to any other literary man of the time," declares Jebb (1876), "and he used this influence principally to enforce one idea" (p. 13). That idea was panhellenic unity. In a letter to Philip of Macedonia (father of Alexander the Great), Isocrates (trans. 1928/1991) asserts that "throughout my whole life I have constantly employed such powers as I possess" to foster panhellenic unity in the face of the threat from Persia (*To Philip*, 130). Later, in *To the Rulers of the Mytilenaeans*, he declares, "I have myself composed more discourses on behalf of the freedom and independence of the Greeks than all those together who have worn smooth the floor of our platforms" (Isocrates, trans. 1945/1986, 7). According to Too (1995), Isocrates is "the author who more than any other sets out and effects an apparently *panhellenic programme*" (p. 138). Too's use of the word *effects* is significant in gauging the effectiveness of a rhetoric built upon justice and moderation. "The new era actually did fall into the forms which Isocrates had thought out before its advent," Jaeger (1944) concludes. "Without [Isocrates' ideas]. . . the universal culture which we call Hellenistic would never have existed" (pp. 80–81).

Nor was Isocrates' successful panhellenism an extended form of what evolutionary biologists would term kin selection, a union of broad family groups among the city-states. Instead, Isocrates (trans. 1928/1991) disavows an ethnic foundation for panhellenism in favor of a wider concept: "The name 'Hellenes' suggests no longer a race but an intelligence, and . . . the title 'Hellenes' is applied rather to those who share our culture than to those who share a common blood" (*Panegyricus*, 149). In the words of Norlin (1928/1991), Isocrates "seems to conceive of Hellenism as a brotherhood of culture, transcending the bounds of race" (p. xxxiv.) Isocrates even pioneered a new medium—the written document/*syggramma*—to send his message throughout Greece (Marsh, 2013).

Unlike Aristotelian rhetoric, in which, according to Cicero (trans. 1942/1979), speakers can "reel off two speeches on opposite sides on every case" (III.xxi), Isocratean rhetoric focuses on building (in Rawlsian terms) over-lapping consensus amid the reasonable pluralism of a democracy. "[Isocrates] assigns discourse a socially constitutive, not merely instrumental, function," writes Haskins (2004)—and she further notes the current relevance of that view: "His pedagogical and political emphasis on language as a renewable source of both community and identity resonates with the postmodern search for community in the age of lost (or renounced) foundations" (pp. 11, 126). Isocrates "gave rhetoric the realistic content which it had long been accused of lacking," Jaeger declares (1944, p. 54). And he adds:

> The older type of rhetoric missed many important opportunities because it was content to serve day-to-day politics as an instrument, instead of

rising above it ... Isocrates has deliberately shifted the emphasis from style and form to the content of the "advice" which the orator imparts ... And the content, the subject of rhetoric, is the world of politics and ethics.

(pp. 67, 90)

We know that Isocratean rhetoric focused on social unity and that it succeeded; we know that rhetoricians past and present found it to be more successful than rival rhetorics. Next we turn to what values inform this singular rhetoric.

The values of Isocratean rhetoric: Justice and moderation

Throughout his essays, Isocrates worked toward a panhellenic confederacy unified by the twin virtues of justice and moderation. In his landmark *History of Education in Antiquity*, Henri Marrou (trans. 1956/1982) offers this remarkable assessment of Isocrates' strategy: "In the hands of Isocrates rhetoric is gradually transformed into ethics" (p. 89). As impressive and important as that statement may be, we might amend it—essentially reverse it: "In the hands of Isocrates, ethics is gradually transformed into rhetoric." When we examine the entire Isocratean canon, it becomes clear that Isocrates begins with and consistently champions two relationship-oriented core values: Justice (*dikaiosyne*) and moderation (*sophrosyne*). Further, he seeks to embed those relational values at several levels: Within the individual; within the family; within the city-state; and within Greece itself and beyond. Finally, Isocrates makes it clear that the process is concentric and graduated: That is, moderation and justice must first be implanted within the individual; that individual can then seek to inculcate those values into the household, then the city-state and, ultimately, into Greece itself and beyond, with each realm serving as a model for the next, more populous level—building, again, to a social union of social unions. Of Isocratean rhetoric, Dionysius of Halicarnassus (trans. 1974) declares:

> Most significant of all are the themes upon which [Isocrates] chose to concentrate, and the nobility of the subjects which he spent his time in studying. The influence of these would make anyone who applied himself to his works not only good orators, but men of sterling character, of positive service to their families, to their state and to Greece at large.
>
> (4)

Centuries later, Kropotkin (trans. 1924/1992) made a similar claim for the concentric growth of mutual aid and relationship-oriented ethics, both of which, he and Darwin first asserted, are cultivated by natural selection:

It is already possible to conceive the history of mankind as the evolution of an ethical factor, as the evolution of an inherent tendency of man to organize his life on the basis of mutual aid, first within the tribe, then in the village community, and in the republics of the free cities,—these forms of social organization becoming in turn the bases of further progress, periods of retrogression notwithstanding.

(p. 17)

In transforming ethics into rhetoric, Isocrates does not forsake the former for the latter; rather, he establishes ethics—values in action—as the indispensable core of effective, relationship-building discourse. In Isocratean rhetoric—as, perhaps, in modern public relations—the values-driven individual is the indispensable element. Neuroscientist Donald Pfaff (Pfaff & Sherman, 2015) believes that the history of biological "prosocial behavior" is similarly concentric, beginning with the individual's relationship with "the immediate family" and, eventually, expanding to larger communities:

Kindness is something that we learn, as individuals, as we begin to experience sexual intimacy and parenthood. Kindness is, as it were, reimprinted on our brains as we *choose* it for the pleasurable associations that it entails. Sex and parenthood are thus still at work in our lives in secondary capacities, reinforcing traits that we are already inclined to express.

(pp. 93, 101, 102)

Dikaiosyne and Sophrosyne

For Isocrates, the core values of the excellent individual are clear: Justice (*dikaiosyne*) and self-control/moderation/temperance (*sophrosyne*). In *Nicocles*, he writes, "If we should be minded to look into the natures, powers, and uses of human relations, we would find that those... which are attended by temperance [*sophrosynes*] and justice [*dikaiosynes*] are greatly beneficial..." (Isocrates, trans. 1928/1991, 30). Isocrates (trans. 1929/1992) articulates these twin values at the beginning of his career in *Against the Sophists*—"There does not exist an art of the kind which can implant sobriety [*sophrosynen*] and justice [*dikaiosynen*] in depraved natures" (21)—and holds fast to them at the end of his career, as we see in *Panathenaicus*: "For it was they [the ancient Athenian kings] who trained the multitude in the ways of virtue [*arete*] and justice [*dikaiosyne*] and great sobriety [*sophrosyne*]..." (138). In *Archidamus* (trans. 1928/1991), *On the Peace* (trans. 1929/1992), and *Areopagiticus* (trans. 1929/1992), Isocrates criticizes the leadership of democratic Athens for a lack of moderation and justice; he believed that any hegemonic system that ran roughshod over others' rights was ultimately self-destructive. As Jebb (1876) concludes, "Isokrates held that hegemony passes into empire, and that empire begets an insolence which at last ruins the imperial State" (pp. 28–29).

For both Plato and Aristotle, *sophrosyne* tended to address moderation in bodily pleasures (North, 1966)—control of "motley appetites and pleasures and pains" in the words of Plato (trans. 1989) in *Republic* (431B). For Aristotle (trans. 1984b), "Temperance [*sophrosyne*] must be concerned with bodily pleasures" (1118a). For Isocrates, however, *sophrosyne* meant much more; it meant self-control and moderation in all relationships, internal and external. In discussing magnanimity in victory in *On the Peace*, he declares, "Nor could we ourselves have failed to realize how much better moderation [*sophronein*] is than meddlesomeness" (Isocrates, trans. 1929/1992, 58). Later in the same written oration, in detailing Athens' turbulent political fortunes, he concludes, "Arrogance and insolence have been the cause of our misfortunes while sobriety and self-control [*sophrosynen*] have been the source of our blessings" (Isocrates, trans. 1929/1992, 119). For Isocrates, *sophrosyne* seems akin to the lack of enviousness that Axelrod (2006), in his Prisoner's Dilemma experiments, identified as a key strategy for successful relationships. In fact, Harvard psychologist Steven Pinker's (2011) studies of self-control may do much to explain why Isocratean rhetoric outperformed its Athenian rivals and dominated centuries of higher education: "Aside from intelligence, no other trait augurs as well for a healthy and successful life" (p. 598). Extensive longitudinal studies show that individuals who cultivate self-control "had higher self-esteem, had better relationships, were better at handling stress, . . . obtained higher degrees, and earned more money" (Pinker, 2011, pp.598–599). Conversely, Pinker (2011) found that contests for dominance "are like to be a net loss for everyone" (p. 542). As we shall see below, Isocrates, like Pinker, directly connects self-control/*sophrosyne* to a wide range of personal benefits.

Isocrates' concept of justice involves the related, familiar concept of treating others as we would wish to be treated—initially akin to direct reciprocity. In *To Demonicus*, Isocrates (trans. 1928/1991) writes, "Manage your temper towards those who offend against you as you would expect others to do if you offended against them. . ." (21). Isocrates even extends and diffuses the policy into what evolutionary biologists would recognize as indirect reciprocity: Urging individuals to treat others as they themselves hope to be treated by still others: "You should be such in your dealings with others as you expect me to be in my dealings with you" (Isocrates, trans. 1928/1991, *Nicocles*, 49). Evolutionary biologists (Axelrod, 2006; Nowak, 2011) and philosophers (Hume, 1739/1968; Rawls, 2001) alike acknowledge that justice enacted through indirect reciprocity is a powerful builder of productive reputation. And this is true of organizations as well as individuals: As we know, Isocrates believes that the twin virtues of moderation and justice begin within the individual and move progressively to larger groups. According to Poulakos (1997), in the works of Isocrates "attention to conduct at multiple registers (the moral, the political, the socio-economic, the oratorical) prevents us from understanding *dikaiosyne* and *sophrosyne* solely as virtues governing individual behavior" (p. 36). Isocrates' explanation of justice also reflects a particular idea found in Judaism, Hinduism, Buddhism, Confucianism, Islam, and other world religions (Küng & Kuschel, 1993), which, in Christianity, is known as the Golden Rule: "In everything, do to others as you would have them do to you" (*Gospel According to Matthew*, 8:4). For Isocrates (trans. 1945/1986), justice clearly is fluid—both more and less than following the letter of the law: In *Aegineticus*, he speaks of actions "strictly in accordance, not only with the law [*nomous*], but also with justice [*dikaios*]" (16).

For Isocrates, just and moderate behavior often was enabled by a third value, the value of dissent. In *On the Peace*, he asks, "How can men wisely pass judgement on the past or take counsel for the future unless they examine and compare the arguments of opposing speakers, themselves giving an unbiased hearing to both sides?" (Isocrates, trans. 1929/1992, 11). In *To Dionysius*, he adds, "No one could persuade me that it is possible that a man should so surpass others in both judgement and action, unless he has become a learner, a listener, and a discoverer, and has drawn to himself and collected from every possible source those means which will enable him to exercise his own intellectual ability" (Isocrates, trans. 1928/1991, 4). Millennia later, rhetorical theorist Kenneth Burke (1957) would echo Isocrates, noting that the suppression of dissent destroys the essential social dialectic that can prevent unopposed bad ideas from confronting the facts that will doom them:

> Dictatorships, in silencing the opposition, remove the intermediary between error and reality. Silence the *human* opponent, and you are brought flat against the *unanswerable* opponent, the nature of brute reality itself . . . This "unanswerable opponent" is the actual state of affairs that is of one sort while the authority would decree it another.
>
> (p. 328)

A dramatic example of Isocrates' own solicitation of dissent to ensure just and moderate behavior comes at the conclusion of *Panathenaicus* with his moving—Isocrates was in his late 90s—recollection of recently having asked a former student, an admirer of Sparta, to evaluate the fairness of earlier passages in that essay that compare Athens and Sparta. By his own account, Isocrates (trans. 1929/1992) listened, considered, rebuked, and triumphed. And yet . . .

> [The former student] went away wiser and more humble in his mind, as sensible men should . . . I, on the other hand, was left thinking that I may have argued successfully, but I felt that I was more foolish because of it and that I thought more of myself than is fitting for someone my age, so I was filled with youthful agitation.
>
> (230)

Confessing to "such a state of mind" (231), Isocrates revised the speech—and, concerned that he still had not treated Sparta with "moderation" [*metrios*] (232), he again summoned his former student, and he quotes that student's evaluation at length in the finished *Panathenaicus*. Isocrates (trans. 1929/1992) worries, perhaps ironically, that in closing *Panathenaicus* with this prolonged anecdote, he fails to follow the lead of other orators who "close their discourses with the greatest and most memorable deeds" (199). Surely, however, some readers might disagree, finding, rather, inspiration in this final example of an old man still striving for justice and moderation by inviting dissent. Within public relations, such instances are examples of the mode of reflexive behavior encouraged by McKie (2001), Pal and Dutta (2008), Aldoory (2009), Heath (2006), and others. As we shall see in Chapter 14, the welcoming of dissent is an essential ingredient of open societies that otherwise might suffer from such "groupthink" errors as believing that humans default toward conflict rather than cooperation: "One vaccine is an open society in which people and ideas move freely and no one is punished for airing dissenting views" (Pinker, 2011, pp. 557, 569).

Yet another way Isocrates sought to create just and moderate behavior was the imitation of successful cultural examples—*mimesis*, in the original Greek, which, of course, is the noun that Richard Dawkins (2006a) used to create his concept of the cultural meme. In *Antidosis*, Isocrates (trans. 1929/1992) explains how the study of rhetoric and persuasion can influence character:

> [The student] will select from all the actions of men which bear upon his subject those examples which are the most illustrious and the most edifying; and, habituating himself to contemplate and appraise such examples, he will feel their influence not only in the preparation of a given discourse but in all the actions of his life.
>
> (277)

He concludes the essay *Areopagiticus* by declaring, "If we will only imitate [*mimesometha*] our ancestors we shall both deliver ourselves from our present ills and become the saviours, not of Athens alone, but of all the Hellenes . . ." (Isocrates, trans. 1929/1992, 84). Such mimesis, however, was not meant to be rote: Words and actions of noble ancestors provided inspiration rather than rigid templates. In fact, such examples provided benchmarks for the ambitious orator to surpass. In *Panegyricus*, Isocrates (trans. 1928/1991) urges contemporary orators to be cognizant of "the deeds of the past" but also to exceed those accomplishments and "speak as no one else could" (9, 10). In advising Timotheus, ruler of Heracleia, he states that the young leader "should. . . emulate those rulers who govern their states well and should endeavour to surpass them" (Isocrates, trans. 1945/1986, *To Timotheus*, 7).

Isocrates' concentric ethics: From the citizen to the world

Isocrates stands in vivid contrast to Plato and Aristotle regarding the role of the citizen in building a virtuous society. Plato (trans. 1989) believed that the primary duty of the citizen was to know his place and function and to be willingly led by an all-knowing philosopher-king (441D-E). Aristotle (trans. 1984b) suggests separating the ethics of the public and private realms: "Perhaps it is not the same in every case to be a good man and a good citizen" (1130b). Isocrates (trans. 2000), however, could not docilely accept the infallible leadership of a divinely inspired philosopher-king because he rejects the possibility of gaining such a certain hold on absolute truth: "Since human nature cannot attain knowledge that would enable us to know what we must say or do, after this I think that the wise (*sophoi*) are those who have the ability to reach the best opinions (*doxai*) most of the time. . ." (*Antidosis*, 271). Isocrates' embrace of what we now would recognize as postmodern ambiguity and uncertainty, particularly vis-à-vis Plato's positivistic certainty, was echoed millennia later by evolutionary biologist Stephen Jay Gould (1999) in his summary of French scientist Pierre-Simon Laplace's exploration of probability: "Since we cannot obtain the requisite knowledge for prediction, the mathematics of probability provides our best practical guide for prognosis. In other words. . . human limitations inject uncertainty and apparent randomness into the best assessments we can make" (p. 15). Though Gould does challenge Laplace's exaltation of mathematics as the "best" approach, this passage does provide another example of consilience (and support for Isocrates) across disciplines and millennia.

As for Aristotle's assertion that a citizen need only be as good as the constitution requires, Isocrates believes, conversely, that it is the duty of the virtuous citizen to improve a flawed government—to speak truth to power, in the language of civil dissent. In *On the Peace*, for example, Isocrates (trans. 1929/1992) once again instructs Athens' leaders on the value of dissent:

> If you really desired to find out what is advantageous to the state, you ought to give your attention more to those who oppose your views than to those who seek to gratify you . . . You ought to commend those who admonish you for your good and to esteem them as the best of your fellow-citizens, and him most of all, even among them, who is able to point out most vividly the evils of your practices and the disasters which result from them.
>
> (10, 72–73)

For Isocrates, tolerance of dissenting voices allows leaders to receive counsel regarding justice and moderation.

Before promulgating and inculcating the virtues of *dikaiosyne* and *sophrosyne* elsewhere, however, Isocrates' (trans. 2000) virtuous citizen—the orator who transforms ethics into rhetoric—first ensures that he or she has embraced those particular values:

> Anyone who wishes to persuade others will not neglect virtue but will devote even more attention to ensuring that he achieves a most honorable reputation among his fellow citizens. Who could fail to know that speeches seem truer when spoken by those of good name than by the disreputable, and that arguments acquire more authority when they come from one's life than from mere words. The more ardently someone wants to persuade his audience, the more he will strive to be a gentleman (*kalos kagathos*) and to have a good reputation among the citizens.
>
> (*Antidosis*, 278)

For Isocrates, Morgan (2004) contends, "Consistency begins within the soul, where it monitors individual behavior" (p. 126). Again and again, Isocrates asserts that this development of individual character involves the inherency of *dikaiosyne* and *sophrosyne*:

- Consider that no adornment so becomes you as modesty, justice [*dikaiosynen*], and self-control [*sophrosynen*] (Isocrates, trans. 1928/1991, *To Demonicus*,15).
- I think you would all agree that the most sovereign of the virtues are temperance [*sophrosynen*] and justice [*dikaiosynen*] (Isocrates, trans. 1928/1991, *Nicocles*, 29).
- For it was they [the ancient Athenian kings] who trained the multitude in the ways of virtue [*arete*] and justice [*dikaiosyne*] and great sobriety [*sophrosyne*] (Isocrates, trans. 1929/1992, *Panathenaicus*, 138)

Throughout his works, Isocrates advocated, in the words of Poulakos (1997), an internal "dialectic of justice and temperance" (p. 46).

Isocrates declares that he, himself, acts with moderation (*metrios*) (Isocrates, trans. 1928/1991, *To Philip*, 22) and that when audiences have heard/read his discourses, "you will easily recognize my true character" (Isocrates, trans. 1929/1992, *Antidosis*, 54). In *Antidosis*, he adds, "All my writings tend toward virtue and justice . . . I thought my advice [in the essay *To Nicocles*] would be the best means of aiding his understanding and at the same time the readiest means of publishing my own principles" (Isocrates, trans. 1929/1992, 67, 69). Isocrates (trans. 1945/1986) expected his students to "imitate my manner of life" (*To the Rulers of the Mytilenaeans*, 10), and he seemed to have taken genuine pleasure and pride in their later ethos-driven triumphs. In *Antidosis*, he names his students who "were crowned by Athens with chaplets of gold. . . because they were honourable men. . ." (Isocrates, trans. 1929/1992, 94). Near the end of his life, he wrote, "I take more pleasure in those of my disciples who are distinguished for the character of their lives and deeds than in those who are reputed to be able speakers" (Isocrates, trans. 1929/1992, *Panathenaicus*, 87). In *The Attic Orators*, Jebb (1876) concludes his chapter on the life of Isocrates by making much the same point:

> In his school he did a service peculiarly valuable to that age by raising the tone and widening the circle of the popular education, by bringing high aims and large sympathies into the preparation for active life, and by making good citizens of many who perhaps would not have aspired to become philosophers.
>
> (p. 35)

Isocrates presumed to advise rulers as well as students. Those leaders, given their sway, constitute a particular category of individuals charged with the promulgation of moderation and justice. Leaders of Athens from the times of Solon and Cleisthenes, Isocrates (trans. 1929/1992) maintains, "believed that the rest of the people would reflect the character of those who were placed in charge of their affairs" (*Areopagiticus*, 22). His model speech for Nicocles takes that idea to heart as he has the young leader of Salamis declare, "I desired. . . to set up my conduct as a pattern to my people, knowing that the multitude are likely to spend their lives in practices in which they see their rulers occupied" (Isocrates, trans. 1928/1991, *Nicocles*, 37). In his advice to Nicocles, Isocrates (trans. 1929/1992) enjoins, "Let your own self-control [*sophrosynen*] stand as an example to the rest, realizing that the manners of the whole state are copied from its rulers" (*To Nicocles*, 31). Like other individuals who aspire to leadership, kings must embrace the philosophy of the Hymn to Logos and become proficient in the inner-dialogues that initiate self-improvement, virtue, and reliability: "No athlete is so called upon to train his body as is a king to train his soul. . ." (Isocrates, trans. 1928/1991, *To Nicocles*, 11). Although he cherished Athenian democracy (Isocrates, trans. 1928/1991, *Panegyricus*, 106), Isocrates, it seems safe to say, placed greater emphasis on the virtues of a government's leaders than he did on the form of government itself: "Isocrates offers as the criterion of political excellence the moral character of the government" (Konstan, 2004, p. 116).

From the citizen to the household

As we have seen already in the Hymn to Logos, Isocrates' ideal rhetoricians, because they first "most skillfully debate their problems in their own minds" (Isocrates, trans. 1928/1991, *Nicocles*, 8), are prepared to advise others, particularly if they have "natural ability" in oratory:

> Someone must have a mind capable of inventing, learning, working hard, and memorizing; a voice and clarity of speech that has the capacity to persuade audiences not only by what he says but also by his harmonious

diction; and furthermore, courage that does not signify shamelessness but prepares the soul with moderation (*sophrosyne*) so that it has as much confidence in addressing all the citizens as in deliberating with himself.

(Isocrates, trans. 1929/1992, *Antidosis*, 189–190)

We should recall, of course, that by his own admission Isocrates (trans. 1928/1991) lacked such assurance (*To Philip*, 81)—yet two millennia after that confession, he still serves as an inspiring adviser to those who would build honorable relationships.

Further, whereas Plato posits ultimate knowledge as the indispensable element of persuasive leadership, Isocrates (trans. 2000), as we know, posits character: "The more ardently someone wants to persuade his audience, the more he will strive to be a gentleman (*kalos kagathos*) and to have a good reputation among the citizens" (*Antidosis*, 278). And so Isocrates proposes the virtuous individual as the model for and the prime mover of the virtuous household, the first community that must embrace the values of *dikaiosyne* and *sophrosyne*:

- [Philosophy enables] us to govern wisely both our own households and the commonwealth—which should be the objects of our toil, of our study, and of our every act. (Isocrates, trans. 1929/1992, *Antidosis*, 285)
- Exhort the young to virtue not only by your precepts but by exemplifying in your conduct what good men ought to be. Teach your children. (Isocrates, trans. 1928/1991, *Nicocles*, 57)
- Progress in virtue comes. . . from everyday activities: most people turn out to conduct themselves according to the habits in which they were educated . . . Those who have been badly brought up will venture to transgress even meticulously written laws. (Isocrates, trans. 1929/1992, *Areopagiticus*, 40, 41)

Additionally, in *Aegineticus* (Isocrates, trans. 1945/1986), protection of the home as an indicator of character emerges as a key issue, with variants of the word *home—oikos*—appearing several times in that brief speech. *Oikonomia*, from which derives our modern *economics*, meant "the management of a household or family" (Liddell & Scott, 1889, p. 546). In *Antidosis*, Isocrates (trans. 1929/1992) condemns those "who have chosen to neglect what is their own and to plot against what belongs to others. . ." (24). Building virtuous households not only continues the promulgation of justice and moderation; it also qualifies citizens for leadership in more populous realms by demonstrating their ability to build virtuous communities and relationships. "It hardly stands to reason that mastery of one's own financial matters or household affairs ought to be regarded as required activity to good oratorical practices," writes Poulakos (1997). "Yet this a connection that Isocrates requires us to make" (p. 39).

Expanding to the city-state

From the household, Isocrates (trans. 1928/1991), moves to the city-state, asserting that the well-run home is the model for the well-run city: "Manage the city as you would your ancestral estate" (*To Nicocles*, 19). Because many sophists, in fact, are neither virtuous individuals nor leaders of virtuous households, Isocrates (trans. 1929/1992) maintains, they should not be considered sources of wisdom in civic debates:

> For I know that the majority even of these men have not set their own house in order, that they are insupportable in their private intercourse, that they belittle the opinions of their fellow-citizens, and that they are given over to many other grave offences. So that I do not think that even these may be said to partake of the state of culture of which I am speaking.
>
> (*Panathenaicus*, 29)

That state of culture, rather, owes its furtherance to citizens who carry their desirable, personal core values through their households and to that larger stage; Isocrates believed, in Simmons' (2002) words, that "we must educate our rulers" (p. 63). For Isocrates, "dikaiosyne and sophrosyne do not merely determine the horizon of an agent's moral conduct," writes Poulakos (1997). "Because they circumscribe political identities, they also implicate the conduct of the entire polis" (p. 35).

Isocrates (trans. 1929/1992), in fact, twice directly compares the state to an individual, maintaining that "the soul of a state is nothing else than its polity, having as much power over it as does the mind over the body. . ." (*Antidosis*, 14); in *Panathenaicus*, he writes, "Every polity is the soul of the state, having as much power over it as the mind over the body" (trans. 1929/1992, 138). Throughout his works, he repeatedly addresses the importance of the values of the city-state:

- There are several ways we can restore the state of our city and make it better. First, we should make our advisors on public issues the same sort as we would want for our private affairs. (Isocrates, trans. 1929/1992, *On the Peace*, 133)
- But no such thing [deliverance from our present ills] can come to pass until you [citizens of Athens] are persuaded that tranquillity is more advantageous and more profitable than meddlesomeness, justice than injustice, and attention to one's own affairs than covetousness of the possessions of others. (Isocrates, trans. 1929/1992, *On the Peace*, 26)

In *Archidamus*, he adds, "But no one could persuade me that we should value anything above justice . . . Cities that are governed well take it very seriously . . ." (Isocrates, trans 2004, 35).

Athens' inability to cleave to clear, enduring values that governed its actions complicated its relationships with potential allies. In detailing Isocrates' catalog of such complaints, Morgan (2004) concludes, "All these passages make the same argument: The Athenians use different standards in different situations and this means that their decisions and policies are incoherent" (p. 144). We may recall that in his Prisoner's Dilemma experiments, Axelrod (2006) found "clarity of behavior" to be an essential ingredient of success in strategic relationships (p. 20). Similarly, public relations research by Bowen (2007) has shown that organizations gain public trust when their decisions and actions are consistent and considerate of both internal and external values (p. 287). Such findings would seem to challenge one facet of contingency theory, with its 80-plus stance-shaping variables that create different standards for different situations and relationships. Despite what he saw as Athens' self-defeating inconsistency, Isocrates—until his late-in-life appeal to Philip of Macedonia to unify Greece—believed that Athens could embrace the proper values and assume moral, if unofficial, leadership of Greece: "Isocrates has an ideal of a free confederacy which experience has not taught him to be impossible," writes Jebb (1876), "and for the attainment of this ideal he believes nothing to be needful but that Athens should become and appear virtuous" (p. 193).

Expanding to Greece

From the city-state, Isocrates moves to panhellenic relationships. *Homonoia* (concord/harmony), he notes, must exist at a higher level than the city-state (Isocrates, trans. 1929/1992, *Panegyricus*, 104)—and *homonoia* can only be the result of the same paired virtues that inspire the individual and the household:

> If kings are to rule well, they must try to preserve harmony [*homonoia*], not only in the states over which over which they hold dominion, but also in their own households and in their places of abode; for all these things are the works of temperance [*sophrosynes*] and justice [*dikaiosynes*].
> (Isocrates, trans. 1928/1991, *Nicocles*, 41)

We have noted Isocrates' reminder that Athenian forebears chose leaders characterized by *dikaiosyne* and *sophrosyne* (Isocrates, trans. 1929/1992, *Panathenaicus*, 138); now he adds that those leaders also sent such values-driven individuals to other city-states as ambassadors (Isocrates, trans. 1929/ 1992, *Panathenaicus*, 143). Throughout his works, Isocrates (trans. 1929/1992) seeks not only a peaceful panhellenic confederacy but also a panhellenism characterized and inspired by the ideal virtues of Athens:

> It is a noble enterprise for us [Athens], in the midst of the injustice and madness of the rest of the world, to be the first to adopt a sane policy

and stand forth as the champions of the freedom of the Hellenes, to be acclaimed as their saviours, not their destroyers, and to become illustrious for our virtues and regain the good repute which our ancestors possessed.

(*On the Peace*, 141)

In a footnote in his translation of *On the Peace*, Norlin (Isocrates, trans. 1929/1992) writes, "Isocrates throughout this discourse proposes to make the moral code within the state the basis of her foreign policy" (p. 9). Hearkening back to the influence of individual values on the state, Jaeger (1944) observes that, for Isocrates, "the rules of private ethics are expressly declared valid for the relation of state to state" (pp. 128–129).

Advantages of concentric ethics: Reciprocity, reputation, rewards

We know, in the words of Norlin (1928/1991), that Isocrates "prides himself more upon the sound moral influence of his work and teaching than upon any other thing" (p. xxv). But Isocrates also posits a more worldly reward for concentric ethics: The idea of true advantage (*pleonektema*). For Isocrates, advantage is the reputation, power, and even material wealth gained from a life built on the reciprocity inherent in the values of moderation and justice. Advantage is the rewards bestowed by grateful communities:

> I do not mean "advantage" [*pleonexias*] in the sense given to that word by the empty-minded, but advantage in the true meaning of that term (Isocrates, trans. 1929/1992, *Antidosis*, 275) . . . Nothing in the world can contribute so powerfully to material gain, to good repute, to right action, in a word, to happiness, as virtue and the qualities of virtue. For it is by the good qualities which we have in our souls that we acquire also the other advantages of which we stand in need.
>
> (Isocrates, trans. 1929/1992, *On the Peace*, 32)

This key point—the direct association of virtue, reputation, influence, and material success—appears again in *On the Peace* and elsewhere in the Isocratean canon:

- Nothing is more important, save only to show reverence to the gods, than to have a good name among the Hellenes. For upon those who are so regarded they willingly confer both sovereign power and leadership. (Isocrates, trans. 1929/1992, *On the Peace*, 135)
- A good name may bring wealth, but wealth cannot buy a good name. (Isocrates, trans. 1928/1991, *To Nicocles*, 32)
- Do not strive to gain riches rather than a good name, knowing that both among the Hellenes and the barbarians as well those who have the highest

reputation for virtue have at their command the greatest number of good things. (Isocrates, trans. 1928/1991, *Nicocles*, 50)

In *Plataicus*, Isocrates (trans. 1945/1986) asserts that a reputation for seeking justice attracts allies in times of war: "Let no one of you, then, be afraid, if Justice is with him, to take such dangers upon himself, nor think that allies will be lacking" (42). As if directly addressing the continuing question in public relations of the relationship between ethical behavior and material benefit, Poulakos (1997) asserts that Isocrates strove "to show that being a good citizen. . . could still on many occasions lead to socio-economic success" (p. 33).

Summary

Isocrates' concept of ethics as rhetoric leads us to at least eight important points for the understanding and practice of public relations:

1. Successful relationships within homes, organizations, societies, and unions of societies are built upon the values of justice and moderation. Justice and moderation are the core values of what historians have labeled the most successful rhetoric, to date, of Western civilization: The rhetoric of Isocrates.
2. The enactment of justice and moderation is concentric, beginning with individual commitment and behavior, then moving to organizations, and building to enactment within a Rawlsian social union of social unions.
3. Studying examples of justice and moderation improves the character of the rhetorician.
4. The solicitation of dissent is essential for the maintenance of relationships characterized by justice and moderation.
5. The enactment of justice and moderation is characterized by indirect reciprocity—by treating a second party the way we wish third parties would treat us.
6. The enactment of justice and moderation builds reputation, which brings the rewards of social influence and material wealth.
7. Consistency of values and values-driven behavior, as opposed to highly variable situational stances, is conducive to clarity of reputation and productive relationships.
8. Abuse of superior power in a relationship—that is, basing relationships on force rather than the values of justice, moderation, and a respect for dissent—ultimately leads to failure.

These eight points address four of the Nine Tenets of public relations' social harmony frameworks outlined in Chapter 1:

II. Cooperation is the relationship strategy best suited to resource acquisition. Evidence from evolutionary biology, philosophy, and rhetoric shows that, in general, cooperative relationships are more successful in sustained resource acquisition than relationships based on egoism, conflict, and competition.

IV.   Justice begins in the social defense of resources, both our own and the resources of others. Based in self-interest, a quest for justice is not normative or contrary to human nature. Justice is inseparable from the processes of sustainable resource acquisition and thus is inherent within the processes of cooperation and public relations.

VIII. Acts of cooperation and justice are the most effective builders of a positive reputation. A positive reputation is a powerful, productive force within the processes of public relations and resource acquisition.

IX.   Public relations practitioners can take specific actions, drawn from evolutionary biology, philosophy, and rhetoric, to build and enhance relationships built upon cooperation and justice.

Chapter 13

Isocrates' legacy

The Roman rhetoricians and beyond

In the history of rhetoric, had Isocrates been a lone voice for moderation and justice, a lone advocate for a rhetoric based on cooperation rather than egoistic conflict and competition, his success would remain impressive—but he would have been an aberration, relegated to some kind of atypical utopian moment in the long and uneven evolution of human relationships. Such is not the case, however. We can easily argue that, apart from Aristotle (trans. 1954) and his values-neutral concept of rhetoric as "the faculty of observing in any given case the available means of persuasion" (1355b), the best-known rhetorical theorists both ancient and modern skew toward an Isocratean vision of rhetoric. In ancient times, those individuals surely would be Cicero and Quintilian; in modern times, it arguably would be Kenneth Burke, with his rich expansion of I.A. Richards' (1936/1964) notion that rhetoric is "a study of misunderstanding and its remedies" (p. 3). In fact, several scholars argue that Aristotle's conflict-oriented assessment of rhetoric, brilliant as it surely is, stumbled when it entered the "the Wrangle of the Market Place," to use Burke's (1950/1969) famous phrase (p. 23). Hunt (1925/1990) writes that Aristotle's school "seems to have been productive of little eloquence" (p. 132). Jebb (1876) adds that "the school of Aristotle—in which Rhetoric was both scientifically and assiduously taught—produced not a single orator of note except Demetrios Phalereus; the school of Isokrates produced a host" (p. 431). Cahn (1989) holds that "the limited success of Aristotle's rhetorical teaching, as well as its integration into the corpus of his political writings, proves the practical superiority of Isocrates' approach" (p. 139). The purpose of this chapter is to examine the rhetorics of Cicero, Quintilian, Burke, and, to a lesser degree, Richards. While they certainly recognize the uncooperative possibilities of the discipline, each of those theorists (like Athena in Aeschylus' *Eumenides*) views rhetoric, at its best, as a force of social cohesion—in Burke's (1950/1969) words, a "*symbolic means of inducing cooperation in beings that by nature respond to symbols*" (p. 43).

The rhetoric of Cicero

Cicero lived from 106 to 43 BCE and rose from the upper middle class to hold the office of consul, the highest governmental position in the Roman Republic. He studied and practiced rhetoric during the turmoil of Julius Caesar's rise to power and murder and the transition from the Republic to the Empire. As an eloquent leader of the opposition to the Empire, he was executed by the Triumvirate of Imperial Rome: Mark Antony, Octavian, and Marcus Aemilius Lepidus. Cicero was a prolific author, publishing everything from transcripts of his speeches to letters to several analyses of rhetoric. "Of all Roman orators," writes historian M.L. Clarke (1996) in *Rhetoric at Rome*, "none devoted so much thought and study to oratory as Cicero" (p. 62).

In addition to his political achievements, Cicero was a lawyer throughout his professional life, winning, by one count, 82 percent of his cases in the Roman courts (Pernot, trans. 2005, p. 106). His professional background provides an important lens through which we must view his rhetoric: Cicero was not an ivory tower, normative theorist. Rather, he was in the arena, "pitting his genius and talent against gifted opponents in the Roman Senate and the Roman Courts" (Ochs, 1994, p. 129). In fact, in the opinion of rhetorical scholar Donovan Ochs (1994), Cicero's first major work on rhetoric, *De Inventione*, "reads like a manual for courtroom lawyers" (p. 136). Cicero, in other words, had no use for an overly idealistic rhetoric designed to, improbably, usher in a better world. Instead, he needed a rhetoric that won. His core notions (as we shall see) that language should be a means of cooperation and that rhetoricians should seek honor and the public good are powerful endorsements of an Isocratean vision of rhetoric—a connection that, as we have seen, Cicero acknowledged (Chapter 12). Cicero's analysis of effective rhetoric strengthens the realistic, not idealistic, vision of public relations as means of social harmony, not as an egoistic force of division operating in an adversarial society. In *Rhetoric in Antiquity*, Laurent Pernot (trans. 2005), past president of the International Society for the History of Rhetoric, holds that Ciceronian rhetoric "completely dominates rhetoric in the Hellenistic and Roman era" (p. 105).

H.M. Hubbell (1913), translator of four of Cicero's primary works on rhetoric, believes that Cicero directly "adopted" (p. 27) the idea of language as a force of social unity, not division, from Isocrates (trans. 1928/1991) and his famed Hymn to Logos, in which that earlier rhetorician declares:

> Because there has been implanted in us the power to persuade each other and to make clear to each other whatever we desire, not only have we escaped the life of wild beasts, but we have come together and founded cities and made laws and invented arts; and, generally speaking, there is no institution devised by man which the power of speech has not helped us to establish.
>
> (*Nicocles*, 7)

In *De Inventione*, Cicero praises persuasive language as a force of social unity, delivering humans from savagery to social harmony and civilization. Like Hume (Chapter 9), Cicero (trans. 1949/1976) asserts that justice enables human societies—but he takes a further step back, noting that without language in the form of oratory and rhetoric, justice would be impossible:

> There was a time when men wandered at large in the fields like animals and lived on wild fare; they did nothing by the guidance of reason, but relied chiefly on physical strength; there was as yet no ordered system of religious worship nor of social duties . . . How could it have been brought to pass that men should learn to keep faith and observe justice and become accustomed to obey others voluntarily and believe not only that they must work for the common good but even sacrifice life itself, unless men had been able by eloquence to persuade their fellows. . .?
>
> (I.ii.2, 3)

With its focus on "sacrifice" and the "common good," this description even places rhetoric in the service of the cooperation—perhaps even the altruism?—inherent in the group selection and kin selection theories of evolutionary biologists since the nineteenth century (Chapters 3–7). Only "evil men," Cicero (trans. 1949/1976) adds, would use eloquence "to the detriment of good citizens and the common disaster of the community" (I.iv.5).

Twenty years after *De Inventione*, Cicero (trans. 1942/1979) makes much the same point in *De Oratore*:

> What other power could have been strong enough either to gather scattered humanity into one place, or to lead it out of its brutish existence in the wilderness up to our present condition of civilization as men and as citizens, or, after the establishment of social communities, to give shape to laws, tribunals, and civic rights? The wise control of the complete orator is that which chiefly upholds not only his own dignity, but the safety of countless individuals and of the entire State.
>
> (I.viii.33–34)

In introducing this passage, in fact, Cicero (trans. 1942/1979) says this of rhetoric:

> What function again is so kingly, so worthy of the free, so generous, as to bring help to the suppliant, to raise up those that are cast down, to bestow security, to set free from peril, to maintain men in their civil rights?
>
> (I.viii.32)

This clearly is not a vision of rhetoric as contributing to the "strategic management of competition and conflict for the benefit of one's own organization" or some other vision of egoistic, asymmetrical public relations. Rather, it echoes Isocrates' vision of inclusiveness and support of the marginalized. (The deep irony that Cicero was a slave-owner in a male-privileged society is not lost on me.) In *De Oratore*, Cicero, somewhat like John Rawls millennia later, is "setting forth. . . the conditions for the healthy functioning of the State" (Pernot, trans. 2005, p. 115). Hubbell (1913) concludes, "Cicero derived from Isocrates the idea of the function of the orator which he presents in the *De Oratore* . . . His whole attitude toward oratory as an art is drawn from Isocrates" (pp. 16, 17).

Given this vision of rhetoric as a catalyst of social harmony, it may be unnecessary to add that Cicero echoes Isocrates—and forecasts Quintilian—on the character of the ideal orator. "Moral conduct," he announces at the beginning of *De Inventione*, his first work on rhetoric, "is the highest and most honorable of pursuits" for the orator (Cicero, trans. 1949/1976, I.i.i). And he approaches Isocrates' belief that moral rhetoric leads to economic success: "From eloquence those who have acquired it obtain glory and honor and high esteem" (Cicero, trans. 1949/1976, I.iv.5). Cicero (trans. 1942/1979), like Isocrates, links reputation to "moral conduct" and a rhetoric that upholds "civic rights" (*De Oratore*, I.viii.33). Cicero's "ideal is the philosopher-statesman-orator" (Clarke, 1996, p. 55)—not the client-bound advocate of some frame-works of rhetoric and public relations.

Of Isocrates' influence on both Cicero and Quintilian, Kathleen Welch (1990), author of *The Contemporary Reception of Classical Rhetoric*, concludes:

> The psychological issues attending the idea of the speaker's or writer's integrity led Isocrates to emphasize value-laden conduct. Isocrates' emphasis on this training became an important basis for Cicero's ideal orator (*vir bonus*, or the good person) and later Quintilian's ideal orator (*vir bonus dicendi peritus*, or the good person speaking well).
>
> (p. 123)

The rhetoric of Quintilian

Quintilian lived, primarily in Rome, from 35 to 100 CE. Like Cicero, he was a lawyer, "a highly successful pleader in the courts and fully alive to the factors that made for professional success" (Clarke, 1996, p. 109). Like Cicero, Quintilian had no use for a normative rhetoric too idealistic to function in the Roman legal system. Unlike Cicero, however, Quintilian opened a school of rhetoric and ultimately distilled his practical approach into the 12 books of the *Institutio Oratoria*. He was "the preeminent teacher in Rome of the first Christian century, and second only to Cicero in his later influence on Euro-pean rhetorical education. . . right up to the present time" (Murphy & Meador, 1994, p. 177, 178). The *Institutio Oratoria*, according to Pernot (trans. 2005), "provides the best overview we have of ancient rhetoric and is the major work to read when seeking to understand this discipline in depth" (p. 159). Regarding the extensive scope of that work, many readers, consciously or otherwise, may have applied Samuel Johnson's (1779/1971) famous assessment of Milton's *Paradise Lost*: "None ever wished it longer" (p. 348). That magnum opus of classical rhetoric, however, contains three by-now familiar, Isocratean ideas:

- The indispensable ingredient of effective rhetoric is a speaker motivated by justice and moderation.
- Rhetoric, at its best, unifies society. At its best, rhetoric is not an amoral instrument ready to serve any cause.
- The study and practice of rhetoric can improve one's character.

Quintilian's rhetoric, like those of Isocrates and Cicero, clearly supports the social harmony frameworks of public relations rather than their more egoistic counterparts.

In the preface to *Institutio Oratoria*, Quintilian (trans. 1920/1980) makes this declaration:

> My aim, then, is the education of the perfect orator. The first essential for such [a] one is that he should be a good man, and consequently we demand of him not merely the possession of exceptional gifts of speech, but of all the excellences of character as well.
>
> (I.Pr.9)

Quintilian repeats this core idea throughout the 12 books of the *Institutio*; Murphy and Meador (1994) count 23 separate assertions of the point. Again, near the beginning of the work, Quintilian (trans. 1920/1980) repeats, "He who is really gifted will also above all else be good" (I.iii.2). And in the 12th and final book, devoted primarily to the orator's character, he rarely strays far from his governing idea:

> The orator then, whom I am concerned to form, shall be the orator as defined by Marcus Cato, "a good man, skilled in speaking." But above all he must possess the quality which Cato places first and which is in the very nature of things the greatest and most important, that is, he must be a good man.
>
> (Quintilian, trans. 1922/1979, XII.i.1)

This, writes Clarke (1996), is "the fundamental idea that informs the *Institutio*, the idea that the orator must be a good man" (p. 115).

Quintilian (trans. 1922/1979) even extends his core idea to hold that a bad individual cannot be a good rhetorician: "I do not merely assert that the ideal orator should be a good man, but I affirm that no man can be an orator unless he is a good man . . . The bad man and the perfect orator can never be identical" (XII.i.3, 9). Of a similar declaration in earlier in the *Institutio*, Murphy and Meador (1994) write, "This last statement indicates the association between rhetoric and virtue that existed for Quintilian" (p. 201).

But what kind of virtue? What particular qualities, for Quintilian, combine to form the character of the ideal orator? Perhaps inspired by Isocrates—who, he holds, produced "the greatest orators" of Greece (Quintilian, trans. 1922/ 1979, XII.x.22)—Quintilian focuses on justice and moderation. Generally associating the virtue of justice with honor, he writes:

> Surely every one of my readers must by now have realised that oratory is in the main concerned with the treatment of what is just and honourable . . . The orator must above all things devote his attention to the formation of moral character and must acquire a complete knowledge of all that is just and honourable. For without this knowledge no one can be either a good man or skilled in speaking . . . He must inspire his soul with justice.
> (Quintilian, trans. 1922/1979, XII.i.8; ii.1, 31)

Of moderation and self-control, he adds:

> As regards the orator himself, the qualities which will most commend him are courtesy, kindliness, moderation and benevolence . . . For the orator will assuredly have much to say on such topics as justice, fortitude, abstinence, self-control and piety . . . If the origin of our souls be divine, we must win our way towards virtue and abjure the service of the lusts of our earthly body . . .
> To conclude, then, the orator will not seek to make more money than is sufficient for his needs.
> (Quintilian, trans. 1922/1979, XI.iv.42; XII.ii.17; iii.21; vii.12)

The practice of virtue increases eloquence and persuasiveness, Quintilian (trans. 1921) believes, because it endows a speaker with a compelling ethos:

> Finally *ethos* in all its forms requires the speaker to be a man of good character and courtesy . . . The excellence of his own character will make his pleading all the more convincing and will be of the utmost service to the cases which he undertakes.
> (VI.ii.18)

A final virtue—a fastidious detail typical of Quintilian—is too entertaining to exclude: The virtuous orator, Quintilian (trans. 1922/1979) writes, will not defend pirates (XII.vii.4).

Like both Isocrates and Cicero before him, Quintilian believes that persuasive language, at its best, is a force of social unity. Nature itself, he maintains, would have betrayed humans if eloquence—"her greatest gift to man, the gift that distinguishes us from other living things"—were to become "the accomplice of crime, the foe to innocency and the enemy of truth" (Quintilian, trans. 1922/1979, XII.i.2). And though Quintilian (trans. 1922/1979) idolized Cicero—"Cicero was a perfect orator" (XII.i.19)—he extends the unifying power of eloquence beyond Cicero's assessment to embrace Isocrates' earlier point, in his Hymn to Logos, that we use eloquence to right ourselves before we address others. In Book XII, Quintilian (trans. 1922/1979) writes:

> Assuredly the man who will best inspire such feelings in others [i.e. the duty that they owe their country] is he who has first inspired them in himself. For however we strive to conceal it, insincerity will always betray itself, and there was never in any man so great eloquence as would not begin to stumble and hesitate so soon as his words ran counter to his inmost thoughts.
>
> (XII.i.29)

For Quintilian, rhetoric was not for egoistic, divisive purposes: "Quintilian emphasizes the value of rhetoric as a moral force in the community" (Murphy & Meador, 1994, p. 177).

Quintilian's rhetoric, then, is not a neutral instrument, ready to be pressed into service for any cause. His vision of rhetoric at its best is not "the faculty of observing in any given case the available means of persuasion" (Aristotle, trans. 1954, 1355b). This is a crucial distinction that, earlier, helped separate Isocratean rhetoric from its Aristotelian counterpart. For Isocrates, rhetoric was an instrument of panhellenism—"a socially constitutive, not merely instrumental, function," writes Haskins (2004, p. 11). For Quintilian (trans. 1922/1979), rhetoric itself becomes a virtue by serving to advance the virtues of the "good man skilled in speaking":

> More important is the question whether rhetoric is to be regarded as one of the indifferent arts, which in themselves deserve neither praise nor blame, but are useful or the reverse according to the character of the artist; or whether it should, as not a few even among philosophers hold, be considered as a virtue . . . The rhetoric. . . which I am endeavouring to establish and the ideal of which I have in my mind's eye, that rhetoric which befits a good man and is in a word the only true rhetoric, will be a virtue.
>
> (XII.xx.1, 4)

Kenneth Burke (1950/1969) holds that Quintilian's "notion of 'speaking well' implies the moralistically hortatory, not just pragmatic skill at the service of any cause" (p. 49).

For Quintilian, as for Isocrates, rhetoric becomes a virtue not only by lending its power to the concepts of justice and moderation but also by gradually shaping the character of the rhetorician. By studying the discourses of previous orators who were known as good individuals skilled in speaking, Quintilian's (trans. 1922/1979) student orator strengthens the virtues essential for success:

> He will consequently select as his models of eloquence all the greatest masters of oratory, and will choose the noblest precepts and the most direct road to virtue as the means for the formation of an upright character. He will. . . devote special attention to those which are of the highest and fairest nature . . . Who will teach courage, justice, loyalty, self-control, simplicity, and contempt of grief and pain better than men like Fabricius, Curius, Regulus, Decius, Mucius and countless others?
>
> (XII.ii.27, 30)

Of Isocrates' similar belief, Haskins (2004) declares, "Isocrates insists that training in eloquence is also training in moral action . . . [It] engenders, rather than merely serves, the rhetor's political identity" (pp. 7, 11).

Like Isocrates, Quintilian surely would defend the idea that, for modern practitioners, studying enactments of harmonious public relations—and engaging in such enactments—strengthens both the desire for and the ability to achieve cooperative relationships. Should that idea seem overly idealistic, we should recall Quintilian's success both as a lawyer and a teacher. In Rome, just as in Athens, rhetorics that championed cooperation and social harmony triumphed over more competitive, conflict-oriented rivals.

The rhetoric of I.A. Richards

Both Ivor Armstrong Richards (1893–1979) and Kenneth Burke (1897–1993) approached rhetoric—in fact, re-envisioned rhetoric—from a literary background, Richards as a poet and professor of literary studies at Cambridge and Harvard and Burke, among other literary functions, as editor of the literary magazine *The Dial*. As Corbett notes in his "Survey of Rhetoric" (1990), by the early twentieth century rhetorical studies became the property of university English departments, and "the term *rhetoric* fell out of fashion, being replaced by the term *composition*" (p. 571). Richards (1936/1964) himself charged that rhetorical studies survived only as "the dreariest and least profitable part of the waste . . . in Freshman English" (p. 3). In explaining the retreat of rhetorical studies into that relative backwater, Corbett (1990), Wallace (1943), and others point to the enduring influence of sixteenth-century French rhetorical theorist Peter Ramus, who "distributed the traditional parts of rhetoric between logic and rhetoric. *Inventio* and *dispositio*—that is, the discovery and arrangement of matter—he assigned to the province of logic.

Rhetoric had a franchise only on *elocutio* (style) and *pronuntiatio* (delivery)" (Corbett, 1990, p. 556). That placid summary hardly captures the tumult of Ramus' (1549/1986) *Arguments in Rhetoric Against Quintilian*, in which he calls Quintilian's definition of the ideal orator "useless and stupid" (p. 84). In an earlier attack on Cicero, Ramus simultaneously pillories Aristotle: "Wake yourself up" he imagines saying to that Roman orator, "and observe the uselessness and the absurdity of Aristotle" (Murphy, 1992, p. xxviii). By whatever routes rhetoric had retreated into English departments, however, this is where Richards and Burke encountered it.

Richards' definition of rhetoric helped awaken that formerly vast enterprise from its comparative slumber. In a 1936 lecture series at Bryn Mawr, Richards (1936/1964) defined rhetoric as "a study of misunderstanding and its remedies" (p. 3)—a definition well-suited for the social harmony frameworks of public relations and one that forecasts Bryant's (1953) later vision of rhetoric as "the function of adjusting ideas to people and people to ideas" (p. 413). Richards' elaboration of his definition evokes many of the ideas expressed in earlier chapters of this book: Misunderstandings can bar the way to the "reasonable pluralism" that Rawls seeks as the essential foundation for justice and democracy; Richards (1936/1965) even characterizes rhetoric as communal and "a branch of biology" (p. 12), in the sense that "a word is always a cooperative member of an organism, the utterance" (p. 69). In a later essay, he defines grammar as "the study of the cooperation of words with one another in their contexts" (Richards, 1938/1991, p. 95). In fact, Richards' rhetoric/ biology linkage foreshadows Nobel laureate Daniel Kahneman's (2011) goal in seeking to understand how the human brain makes decisions: "So this is my aim for watercooler conversations: improve the ability to identify and understand errors of judgment and choice, in others and eventually in ourselves, by providing a richer and more precise language to discuss them" (p. 4). The following brief summary of Richards' cooperative rhetoric will review its definition, its analogies with biology, its postmodern aspects, and its limitations—limitations fortunately addressed by Kenneth Burke.

For Richards (1936/1965), a "new Rhetoric" should relinquish "the combative impulse" that has us "take another man's words in the ways in which we can down him with least trouble" (pp. 26, 24–25). Conversely, a new rhetoric should lead us to understand and remedy the causes of misunderstanding, helping us to answer the question of "how much and in how many ways may good communication different from bad?" (Richards, 1936/1965, p. 3). We have no business, he adds, in resurrecting rhetoric unless it can "minister successfully to important needs" (Richards, 1936/1965, p. 3). Significant for public relations and for the core idea of this book, the goal of Richards' (1936/1965) new rhetoric is cooperation:

> We have instead to consider much more closely how words work in discourse . . . When our skill [in interpretation] fails, misunderstanding

of others and ourselves comes in . . . A persistent, systematic, detailed inquiry into how words work. . . will take the place of the discredited subject which goes by the name of Rhetoric . . . A revived Rhetoric, or study of verbal understanding and misunderstanding, must undertake its own inquiry into the modes of meaning . . . And with such a clarification, such a translation of our skills into comprehension, a new era of human understanding and co-operation in thinking would be at hand.

(pp. 5, 11, 23, 73)

Richards' (1936/1965) new rhetoric is based, in part, on answering the question "How does a word mean?" and in avoiding "the Proper Meaning Superstition," which limits a word to one standard, unchanging, shared definition (pp. 15, 73).

Richards' comparison of his new rhetoric to biology also forecasts modern emphases on cooperation and group selection within that related discipline. Sounding like Darwin gently backing away from the idea of unique species fashioned in isolation by an intentional creator, Richards (1936/1965) declares:

We shall do better to think of a meaning as though it were a plant that has grown—not a can that has been filled or a lump of clay that has been moulded . . . It is important. . . to realize how far back into the past all our meanings go, how they grow out of one another much as an organism grows, and how inseparable they are from one another.

(pp. 12, 30)

Defending his persistent comparisons of his new rhetoric to biology, Richards (1936/1965) quotes Spinoza as an epigraph to the fourth and final of his Bryn Mawr lectures: "The more [the mind] understands the order of nature, the more easily it will be able to liberate itself from useless things" (p. 86). Primary among useless things for Richards is the mistaken notion that a single, isolated word (similar, perhaps, to a gene?) has meaning and power apart from its participation in a larger group of words and associations. For Richards, shared meaning—a goal of his new rhetoric—is derived through an understanding of cooperation within language. "A word is always a cooperative member of an organism, the utterance," he writes in *The Philosophy of Rhetoric* (Richards, 1936/1965, p. 69)—and, as noted above, he reasserts that key point in a later essay. In this belief, Richards pushes the idea of cooperation even beyond the horizons of Isocrates and Cicero: For those earlier rhetoricians, language enables social cooperation—recall Isocrates' (trans. 1928/1991) "There is no institution devised by man which the power of speech [*logos*] has not helped us to establish" (*Nicocles*, 7) and Cicero's (trans. 1949/1976) "How could it have been brought to pass that men should learn to keep faith and observe justice . . .unless men had been able by eloquence to persuade their fellows . . .?" (I.ii.3). For Richards, however, language, with its inherent meaning, is formed by cooperation, the cooperation of words within context, within organic constructions. That initial, internal cooperation enables language to become the instrument of cooperation described by Isocrates, Cicero, Quintilian, Richards, and— as we shall see—Burke.

Richards (1936/1965) asserts that words, in large part, draw meaning from a cooperative relationship with the words that surround them:

> It is the peculiarity of meanings that they do so mind their company . . . Any part of a discourse, in the last resort, does what it does only because the other parts of the surrounding, uttered or unuttered discourse . . . Most words, as they pass from context to context, change their meanings . . . Other words. . . before and after a given word. . . determine how it is to be interpreted.
>
> (pp. 10, 11, 32)

Richards (1936/1965) titled the third of his four Bryn Mawr lectures "The Interanimation of Words," and in it he declares, "The opening words have to wait for those that follow to settle what they shall mean—if indeed that ever gets settled . . . No word can be judged. . . in isolation" (pp. 50, 51). Additionally, he holds, words draw meaning from the past definitions established by earlier acts of such linguistic cooperation as well as from the groups of individuals who use them. Of such group influence, Richards (1936/1965) writes, "This specialized form of control by usage, this social or snob control over all language, is obviously very wide and rigorous. One of the tasks of an improved Rhetoric is to question it" (p. 78).

In his belief that meaning is fluid, is derived through discourse, and is subject to hegemonic influences, Richards (1936/1965) establishes himself as an early postmodernist in language studies:

> The whole business of Rhetoric comes down to comparisons between the meaning of words . . . A controversy is normally an exploitation of a systematic set of misunderstandings for warlike purposes. This theorem [of fluid, debatable meaning] suggests that the swords of dispute might be turned into plough shares.
>
> (pp. 37, 39)

For Richards (1936/1965), ambiguity, as well as the incorrect rejection of the inevitability of ambiguity, is the enduring source of misunderstanding—and "the remedy is not to resist these shifts but to learn to follow them" (p. 73). In a later essay titled "The First Three Liberal Arts" (rhetoric, grammar, and logic), Richards (1938/1991) calls for "reflective study" of language and how meaning but acknowledges that "there can be no pretence, of course, that language works can be fully explained" (pp. 88, 89). Rather, like Kahneman (2011), he seeks "a richer and more precise language" (p. 4).

Unfortunately—and this certainly is my personal opinion—Richards does not deliver a comprehensive, applied follow-up to this promising re-envisioning of rhetoric. He devotes his final Bryn Mawr lectures to an extended analysis of metaphors, which, as deliberate examples of ambiguity, provide a good starting point for examining the sources of misunderstanding and of fluid meanings—but the pleasing depth of the analysis is, for me, offset by a lack of width: Richards seems to deliver little specific advice for embracing and deciphering ambiguity; he seems unable, or perhaps just unwilling, to escape the gravitational pull of the literary studies that had absorbed rhetoric. Fortunately—again, in my own opinion—the rhetoric of Kenneth Burke addresses this deficit. Still, for public relations theorists and practitioners, Richards (1936/1965) adds a compelling voice to the powerful idea that rhetoric, at its best, is a force for "a new era of human understanding and co-operation" (p. 73).

The rhetoric of Kenneth Burke

Within public relations research, "rhetorical studies rely heavily on the work of Kenneth Burke," wrote Elizabeth Toth (1992) in the first edition of *Rhetorical and Critical Approaches to Public Relations* (p. 6)—and, decades later, that assessment remains accurate. For Burke (1950/1969), rhetoric is "the use of words by human agents to form attitudes or induce actions in other human agents" (p. 41). In a powerful link to Richards' (1936/1965) concept of rhetoric as "a study of misunderstanding and its remedies" (p. 3), however, Burke (1950/1969) adds:

> But one can systematically extend the range of rhetoric, if one studies the persuasiveness of false or inadequate terms which may not be directly imposed upon us from without by some skillful speaker, but which we impose upon ourselves . . . Only those voices from without are effective which can speak in the language of a voice within . . . [It is] *the use of language as a symbolic means of inducing cooperation in beings that by nature respond to symbols.*
>
> (pp. 35, 39, 43)

Burke's extension of rhetoric's range leads us to his key concept of identification. The following summary of Burke's rhetoric will focus on identification, with its inherent links to consubstantiality and property; the connection of identification to social cohesion and cooperation; the transcending of Richard-sonian misunderstandings through identification; and Burke's acknowledgment of power disparities and lesser, destructive forms of rhetoric.

For Burke (1950/1969), if a sender, in the terminology of the familiar communication model, can speak "the language of a voice within" the receiver—if the sender can convincingly show common ground with the values and interests of the receiver—then identification occurs:

> A is not identical with his colleague, B. But insofar as their interests are joined, A is *identified* with B. Or he may *identify himself* with B even when their interests are not joined if he assumes they are, or is persuaded to believe so.
>
> (p. 20)

The concept of identification is at the heart of Burke's (1951) formulation of a new rhetoric: "The key term for the old rhetoric was 'persuasion' and its stress was upon deliberate design. The key term for the 'new' rhetoric would be 'identification'" (p. 203). He adds, however, that notions of persuasion and identification cannot be cleanly separated: "You persuade a man... [by] *identifying* your ways with his" (Burke, 1950/1969, p. 55). For Heath and Waymer (2009), "Identification is a vital part of communication in general... and public relations in specific" (p. 201). Burke (1950/1969) cites Aristotle in noting that shared virtues provide a traditional foundation for establishing identification, and he lists the virtues that, in *Rhetoric*, Aristotle analyzes—primary among them the familiar justice and moderation (p. 55). As such, identification certainly would be at odds with the adversarial society approach to public relations, in which "truth is not so important as the obligation of opposing counsel to create scenarios that conflict with those of their opponents" (Barney & Black, 1994, p. 244).

Individuals or publics that achieve identification have, still in Burke's (1950/1969) terminology, consubstantiality—hardly a term for characterizing adversarial or separate, competitive publics: "In being identified with B, A is 'substantially one' with a person other than himself... To identify A with B is to make A 'consubstantial' with B" (p. 21). As we know from Chapter 3, with its review of neuroscientist Donald Pfaff's altruistic brain theory, Burke is biologically, neurologically accurate with the concept of consubstantiality. Neuroscientists now believe that when we contemplate an action toward another, the image of that person—even the image of a generic representative of a group—fuses with our image of ourself within our prefrontal cortex: "A multiplicity of nerve cell mechanisms [including mirror neurons] underlies the merging of your image with mine ... As a result, instead of literally seeing the consequence of [our] act for another person, we automatically envision the consequences as pertaining to our own self" (Pfaff & Sherman, 2015, pp. 58, 60). Consubstantiality, a foundation of cooperation as opposed to conflict and competition, has a solid biological basis.

In *A Rhetoric of Motives*, Burke (1950/1969) notes several times that an individual establishes his or her identity—the source material for consubstantiality—in part via property "in the most materialistic sense of the term, economic property. . .properties that name his number or establish his identity" (pp. 23–24, 24). Thus, respect for another's "material interests," Burke (1950/1969) holds, is one means of "identifying your cause with his" (p. 24). This assertion, by way of David Hume, ties the identification inherent in public relations to a quest for justice: If Hume (Chapter 9) is correct in asserting that respect for others' property and the orderly exchange of properties inevitably leads both to justice and to reputation—and if public relations, with its foundations in resource dependency theory, is about the orderly possession and exchange of property/resources—then property-oriented identification within public relations would seem to be inseparably associated with the promotion of justice and the establishment of beneficial reputation. In fact, this leads us back to Burke's earlier point that identification and consubstantiality can be achieved by compelling agreement on the virtue of justice.

For Burke (1950/1969), identification leads to social cohesion—which, he acknowledges, sometimes can be manipulated by egoistic groups: There are "ways of identification that contribute variously to social cohesion (either for the advantage of the community as a whole, or for the advantage of special groups whose interests are a burden on the community. . .)" (p. 44). Of egoistic identification, however, he writes, "The rhetorical concept of 'identification' does not justify the excesses to which such doctrinaire tendencies can be carried" (Burke, 1950/1969, p. 31). Burke's (1950/1969) ideal rhetoric of identification, instead, becomes a social dialectic that leads to cooperation and transcendence beyond narrow egoistic interests:

> Bring several *rhetoricians* together, let their speeches contribute to the maturing of one another by the give and take of question and answer, and you have the *dialectic* of Platonic dialogue. But ideally the dialogue seeks to attain a higher order of truth, as the speakers, in competing with one another, cooperate towards an end transcending their individual positions. Here is the paradigm of the dialectical process for "reconciling opposites" in a "higher synthesis."
>
> (p. 53)

Competition thus becomes cooperation. At its best—and, for Burke (1951), this is not inevitable—identification leads us beyond narrow self-interests, just as empathy, for evolutionary biologists, can lead us to cooperation (Chapter 7): "In such identification there is a partially dreamlike, idealistic motive, somewhat compensatory to real differences or divisions, which the rhetoric of identification would transcend" (p. 203). Besides its clear link to biological empathy, this belief returns us to the functioning of Rawls' "reasonable pluralism" (Chapter 10) in pursuit of democracy and justice—"I take democracy to be a device for institutionalizing the dialectical process" (Burke, 1957, pp. 327–328)—as well as to Kropotkin's (Chapter 5) use of the same word—*synthesis*—to acknowledge the reality of balancing biologically derived individual and social interests. In fact, in the sentence immediately following his famous "Wrangle of the Market Place" passage, Burke (1950/1969) writes, "In ways of its own, [rhetoric] can move from the factional to the universal" (p. 23). Heath and Waymer (2009) thus conclude, "Cooperation and communion, sharing in common, is a theme central to Burke's approach to the most fundamental role public relations can play in society" (p. 201).

As we have seen, despite this vision of a cooperative, communal rhetoric based on identification and consubstantiality, Burke is no idealist. He persistently acknowledges the possibility of misusing, by his lights, identification, property, and power disparities among rhetoricians for egoistic purposes. In a comment that forecasts Moloney's (2006) advocacy of "a subsidy, a transfer of PR productive resources from the resource rich to the resource poor" (p. 169), Burke (1950/1969) writes, "[Rival rhetoricians'] persuasiveness varies with the resources each has at his command ... A 'good' rhetoric neglected by the press obviously cannot be so 'communicative' as a poor rhetoric backed nation-wide by headlines" (pp. 25–26). Burke (1950/1969) strongly echoes Kropotkin's (trans. 1924/1992) "double tendency" (p. 19) of individualistic and social instincts in declaring, "This wavering line between identification and division [is] forever bringing rhetoric against the possibility of malice and the lie" (p. 45). Without division, however, there would be no need for identification and consubstantiality: "Identification is affirmed with earnestness precisely because there is division. Identifica-tion is compensatory to division. If men were not apart from one another, there would be no need for the rhetorician to proclaim their unity" (Burke, 1950/1969, p. 22). Burke's optimism that we can transcend division and move from "the factional to the universal" again echoes Kropotkin's—and Darwin's—deep belief in the growing power of the social instinct, in the increasing realization, particularly for Kropotkin (Chapter 5) and Hume (Chapter 9), that we best defend individual liberties through cooperation. As Kropotkin (trans. 1924/1992) concludes, "In proportion as mutual aid becomes an established custom in a human community, and so to say instinctive, it leads to a parallel development of the sense of justice, with its necessary accompaniment of the sense of equity and equalitarian self-restraint" (p. 30). (At the risk of excessively linking this book's chapters, justice and self-restraint are the two core virtues of Isocratean rhetoric—more affirmation of our basic consilience of cooperation.)

Burke's (1950/1969) idealistic hope for a rhetorical identification grounded in virtue and transcendence, not denial, of individual interests has a strong foundation in the realistic rhetorics of Isocrates, Cicero, and Quintilian, which were tested and proven in "the Scramble, the Wrangle of the Market Place, the flurries and flare-ups of the Human Barnyard, the Give and Take, the wavering line of pressure and counterpressure, the Logomachy, the onus of ownership, the Wars of Nerves, the War" (p. 23). Identification further has a strong a basis in neuroscience: "Humans feature complexes of personality traits that have stood the test of time and allowed them to develop a basic, shared, indeed universal personality substrait" (Pfaff & Sherman, 2015, p. 49). Similarly, consubstantiality has a physical reality in the actions of mirror neurons, oxytocin, and related cooperation-inducing neurological phenomena (Chapter 3). In his introduction to *A Rhetoric of Motives*, Burke (1950/1969) writes, "The more strident our journalists, politicians, and alas! even many of our churchmen become, the more convinced we are that books should be written for tolerance and contemplation" (p. xv). In developing his new rhetoric, Burke wrote such books, and it is my hope that the book you now are reading contributes to his wish.

Summary

A review of the rhetorics of Cicero, Quintilian, Richards, and Burke leads us to at least 11 important points for the understanding and practice of public relations:

1. Though Aristotle's conflict-oriented rhetoric is the best known of the Greek and Roman classical rhetorics, it is not the rhetoric of top Western rhetoricians and rhetorical theorists past and present. That honor belongs to Isocratean rhetoric with its core values of moderation and justice.
2. Rhetoric is the foundation of social stability. The primary role of rhetoric is to encourage the common good. The use of rhetoric for egoistic, anti-social ends is counterproductive. (Cicero)
3. Rhetoric was a catalyst for the beginnings of justice. Humans originally had to persuade one another of the advantages of "social duties." (Cicero)
4. The indispensable ingredient of effective rhetoric is a speaker motivated by the values of justice and moderation. The most effective rhetorician is an ethical individual skilled in communication. (Quintilian)
5. Rhetoric at its best unifies society. Rhetoric at its best is not an amoral instrument ready to serve any cause. (Quintilian)
6. The study and practice of socially unifying rhetoric improves the rhetorician's character. (Quintilian)
7. Modern rhetoric should be a study of misunderstandings that undermine the social communication necessary for justice and democracy. To assume that role, rhetoric must surrender its combative impulses. The goal of modern rhetoric is social cooperation. (Richards)
8. Cooperation is inherent within the mechanics of rhetoric, particularly the cooperation of one word with surrounding words. Thus, not only does language enable cooperation; cooperation enables language. (Richards)
9. "The key term for the old rhetoric was 'persuasion' . . . The key term for the 'new' rhetoric would be 'identification' . . . In being identified with B, A is 'substantially one' with a person other than himself . . . To identify

A with B is to make A 'consubstantial' with B'" (Burke). Modern scholars note the centrality of identification to public relations.

10. Modern neurological research (Chapter 3) provides a scientific foundation for the reality and workings of Burke's rhetorical processes of identification and consubstantiality.

11. Respect for the property of another is a powerful means of identification and consubstantiality (Burke). As David Hume (Chapter 9) asserts, respect for property is the origin of justice and of positive reputation. Resource dependency theory holds that the exchange of resources/properties is a foundation of modern public relations. Justice, identification, consubstantiality, property, reputation, and public relations thus seem inextricably fused.

These 11 points address five of the Nine Tenets of public relations' social harmony frameworks outlined in Chapter 1:

II. Cooperation is the relationship strategy best suited to resource acquisition. Evidence from evolutionary biology, philosophy, and rhetoric shows that, in general, cooperative relationships are more successful in sustained resource acquisition than relationships based on egoism, conflict, and competition.

III. Cooperative relationships are not merely normative, idealistic, or utopian. Rather, evidence from evolutionary biology, philosophy, and rhetoric shows that cooperation is a stronger instinct within human nature than the competing instincts of egoism, conflict, and competition.

IV. Justice begins in the social defense of resources, both our own and the resources of others. Based in self-interest, a quest for justice is not normative or contrary to human nature. Justice is inseparable from the processes of sustainable resource acquisition and thus is inherent within the processes of cooperation and public relations.

VI. Ethical behavior that accommodates the needs of others has enduring foundations in the biological and social origins of cooperation. Such behavior is not normative, idealistic, or contrary to human nature.

IX. Public relations practitioners can take specific actions, drawn from evolutionary biology, philosophy, and rhetoric, to build and enhance relationships built upon cooperation and justice.

Part V

Conclusions

Chapter 14

Summaries and strategies

The social harmony frameworks of public relations are not utopian or contrary to human nature. In fact, they are the most effective frameworks for resource acquisition.

Extensive evidence from evolutionary biology, philosophy, and rhetoric coalesces into what scientist Edward O. Wilson (1998) has termed a "consilience" (p. 8), a strong multidisciplinary consensus on a key point: Quests for cooperation and justice are, originally, driven by self-interest and are deeply embedded within human nature, more so than our egoistic instincts for conflict and competition. Evidence from these three disciplines shows that, in general, consistent enactments of cooperation and justice create the best, most effective strategy for the sustained acquisition of essential resources. Because we are motivated by the desire to survive and thrive, we are and should be motivated by the values of cooperation and justice. Survival of the fittest leads us to cooperation, not to egoistic conflict.

As reviewed in Chapter 1, the social harmony frameworks of public relations include fully functioning society theory, civil society theory, communitarianism, two-way symmetry, and Isocratean rhetoric. Elements of the reflective paradigm also align with a social harmony focus, as do some established functions within public relations, such as corporate social responsibility.

This closing chapter has two goals:

1. to reassert the Nine Tenets of public relations' social harmony frameworks from Chapter 1, which are the core ideas of this book, by adding the amassed evidentiary support of the summary points that close the individual chapters on evolutionary biology, philosophy, and rhetoric.
2. to turn one last time to the scientists who have established the primacy of cooperation to see what advice they might have for developing that powerful social instinct.

The Nine Tenets revisited

The Nine Tenets of public relations' social harmony frameworks grew out of the findings of this book's individual chapters. Rather than guiding the content of the book, they arose, chronologically, only after I had completed first drafts of the chapters and could see, for the first time, the scaffolding of the con- silience of cooperation. Additional research certainly might reveal more tenets; I doubt that it would reveal fewer, though I realize there is some overlap among the nine. There is, of course, much overlap among the summary points that conclude each chapter; that overlap forms the consilience of cooperation. Once again, I believe it is important to emphasize that the tenets and their support- ing evidence rest on self-interested, empirical, materialistic foundations—as opposed to idealistic and utopian support. The passage that follows aligns the key summary points from individual chapters with the Nine Tenets of social harmony frameworks first outlined in Chapter 1. Ideally, this section con- solidates the book's multidisciplinary support for public relations' social harmony frameworks.

I   A core function of public relations is resource acquisition. Resources range from small to large, from tangible to abstract, from raw materials to employee commitment to social legitimacy.
   • Whether we envision public relations as a quest for social legitimacy, as the management of relationships with key stakeholders, as a func- tion of marketing, or as something else altogether, the securing of resources controlled by others is, in all likelihood, central to our vision of the discipline. (Chapter 1)

II   Cooperation is the relationship strategy best suited to resource acqui- sition. Evidence from evolutionary biology, philosophy, and rhetoric shows that, in general, cooperative relationships are more successful in sustained resource acquisition than relationships based on egoism, con- flict, and competition.
   • Cooperation is an evolutionary advantage. Cultures in which indi- viduals cooperate outcompete less cohesive cultures. (Darwin, Chap- ter 4)
   • Mutual aid is a more powerful instinct within social species than instincts of competition and conflict. Mutual aid has "the greatest importance for the maintenance of life, the preservation of each spe- cies, and its further evolution." (Kropotkin, Chapter 5)
   • In the words of evolutionary biologist Richard Dawkins, author of *The Selfish Gene*, "nice guys finish first"—with *nice* denoting the initial and consistent enactment of cooperation within relationships. (Chapter 6)
   • In the competition for resources, the most effective tactics, over time, are niceness (beginning a relationship with cooperation), forgiveness, and a lack of envy. Game theory experiments show that, in the social competition for resources, individuals succeed over time only if their relationship partners also succeed. (Chapter 7)

- The practical strategy of cooperation, as opposed to egoistic conflict and competition, is not aberrant. It consistently arises from the "primordial chaos" of computer programs that randomly generate cooperate/defect strategies, and it consistently grows to dominate such multi-generational experiments as, essentially, an evolutionarily stable strategy. (Chapter 7)
- A historical misperception of the success of Aristotelian conflict-oriented rhetoric may have impaired public relations' ability to discover and model the most effective forms of classical rhetoric. (Chapter 11)
- After much public and cross-disciplinary deliberation, the ancient Athenians determined that persuasion/*peitho* at its best is honest, respectful of others, and mindful of community wellbeing. (Chapter 11)
- Abuse of superior power in a relationship—that is, basing relationships on force rather than the values of justice, moderation, and a respect for dissent—ultimately leads to failure. (Isocrates, Chapter 12)
- Though Aristotle's conflict-oriented rhetoric is the best known of the Greek and Roman classical rhetorics, it is not the rhetoric of top Western rhetoricians and rhetorical theorists past and present. That honor belongs to Isocratean rhetoric with its core values of moderation and justice. (Chapter 13)
- Rhetoric is the foundation of social stability. The primary role of rhetoric is to encourage the common good. The use of rhetoric for egoistic, antisocial ends is counterproductive. (Cicero, Chapter 13)
- Rhetoric at its best unifies society. Rhetoric at its best is not an amoral instrument ready to serve any cause. (Quintilian, Chapter 13)
- Modern rhetoric should be a study of misunderstandings that undermine the social communication necessary for justice and democracy. To assume that role, rhetoric must surrender its combative impulses. The goal of modern rhetoric is social cooperation. (Richards, Chapter 13)
- Cooperation is inherent within the mechanics of rhetoric, particularly the cooperation of one word with surrounding words. Thus, not only does language enable cooperation; cooperation enables language. (Richards, Chapter 13)
- "The key term for the old rhetoric was 'persuasion' . . . The key term for the 'new' rhetoric would be 'identification' . . . In being identified with B, A is 'substantially one' with a person other than himself . . . To identify A with B is to make A 'consubstantial' with B.'" Modern scholars note the centrality of identification to public relations. (Burke, Chapter 13)

III   Cooperative relationships are not merely normative, idealistic, or utopian. Rather, evidence from evolutionary biology, philosophy, and rhetoric shows that cooperation is a stronger instinct within human nature than the competing instincts of egoism, conflict, and competition.

- Rather than being "wired" for conflict and competition, humans are neurologically wired for cooperation. Cooperation, not conflict, is our default setting. (Chapter 3)
- The social instinct in humans, which gives rise to empathy and cooperation, is not an aberration. It is a powerful product of natural selection. Denying the social instinct is painful for humans. Acting against that instinct is increasingly contrary to our nature. (Darwin, Chapter 4)
- The biological basis for cooperation is not idealistic. Rather, that basis is grounded in materialism and empiricism. (Darwin, Chapter 4)
- Mutual aid within social species is not antithetical to the processes of natural selection. Rather, cooperation is cultivated by natural selection; it is a strategic advantage for resource acquisition and survival. (Kropotkin, Chapter 5)
- There is powerful consensus among modern evolutionary biologists that humans are a cooperative species. Cooperation, not egoistic conflict and competition (which indeed exist), is our default position. (Chapter 6)
- Modern evolutionary biologists concur that cooperation is not utopian, normative, or idealistic. Developed by natural selection, its origins are biological. The basis of social harmony frameworks of public relations can be purely materialistic, with no trappings at all of idealism. (Chapter 6)
- Game theory affirms that the cooperation inherent in public relations' social harmony frameworks, far from being overly idealistic or utopian, is a powerful, inexorable fact in the ongoing survival and evolution of humans. (Chapter 7)
- We do not need philosophical idealism to defend the social harmony frameworks of public relations. Philosophical materialism, grounded in empiricism and even, sometimes, in pessimism, clearly offers firm foundations for the discipline's social harmony frameworks. (Chapter 8)
- Modern neurological research (Chapter 3) provides a scientific foundation for the reality and workings of Burke's rhetorical processes of identification and consubstantiality. (Chapter 13)

IV   Justice begins in the social defense of resources, both our own and the resources of others. Based in self-interest, a quest for justice is not normative or contrary to human nature. Justice is inseparable from the processes of sustainable resource acquisition and thus is inherent within the processes of cooperation and public relations.

- The social instinct for cooperation, derived through natural selection, engenders justice, which is an ongoing calibration of individual and collective rights. In free societies, a collectivist emphasis on justice ensures individual rights. Kropotkin's mutual aid philosophy thus addresses the seeming conflict within public relations between individual and collectivist tendencies. (Kropotkin, Chapter 5)

- Envisioning transactional justice as a core value of public relations is not idealistic or normative. Rather, it seems unavoidable. If the exchange of resources truly is indispensable to the practice of public relations, then enacting justice—which (Hume holds) was created by the self-interested need for stable and transferable property— is inevitable. Deliberately working for transactional justice ensures the continued effectiveness of public relations. (Hume, Chapter 9)
- The stable, transferable property essential to public relations relies on justice. In circular fashion, justice catalyzes cooperation, which catalyzes society, which enhances the stability and transferability of property. (Rawls, Chapter 10)
- Public relations is essential to the overlapping consensus that builds social cooperation in the midst of reasonable pluralism. A lack of overlapping consensus threatens social cooperation; that lack would undermine the legitimacy of justice, which, in turn, would undermine the stability of property and property exchange. The establishment of social legitimacy is a particular function of the reflective paradigm of public relations. (Rawls, Chapter 10)
- Successful relationships within homes, organizations, societies, and unions of societies are built upon the values of justice and moderation. Justice and moderation are the core values of what historians have labeled the most successful rhetoric, to date, of Western civilization: The rhetoric of Isocrates. (Isocrates, Chapter 12)
- Rhetoric was a catalyst for the beginnings of justice. Humans originally had to persuade one another of the advantages of "social duties." (Cicero, Chapter 13)
- Respect for the property of another is a powerful means of identification and consubstantiality. As David Hume (Chapter 9) asserts, respect for property is the origin of justice and of positive reputation. Resource dependency theory holds that the exchange of resources/ properties is a foundation of modern public relations. Justice, identification, consubstantiality, property, reputation, and public relations thus seem inextricably fused. (Chapter 13)

V   Biological and social tensions between individualism and collectivism are most sustainably resolved in favor of collectivism that defends individualism.
- Individual autonomy cannot be sustained through disregard of others' needs. Conversely, social cooperation can be sustained only through honoring individual rights. (Kropotkin, Chapter 5)

- Modern evolutionary biologists concur that cooperation does not inhibit self-interest. Rather, cooperation generally is the most successful path to long-term self-interest. (Chapter 6)
- Rawls' difference principle, with its philosophy of the advantaged assisting the disadvantaged, already has been recommended for public relations via Moloney's "theory of equalising PR resources." For Rawls, the difference principle does not penalize initiative: Rather, it seeks a mutually beneficial balance between equality and efficiency and between altruism and mutual advantage. (Rawls, Chapter 10)

VI Ethical behavior that accommodates the needs of others has enduring foundations in the biological and social origins of cooperation. Such behavior is not normative, idealistic, or contrary to human nature.
- Modern relationship-oriented ethics originates in the same social instinct, derived through natural selection, that gives rise to cooperation. (Darwin, Chapter 4)
- The foundation of modern ethics—including public relations ethics—is the biological instinct, derived through natural selection, to harmonize individualistic and collectivist tendencies. Ethical behavior that accommodates the needs of others is, thus, not normative, idealistic, or contrary to human nature; it is, rather, the satisfying of an urge no less inherent, according to Darwin and Kropotkin, than hunger. (Kropotkin, Chapter 5)
- The indispensable ingredient of effective rhetoric is a speaker motivated by the values of justice and moderation. The most effective rhetorician is an ethical individual skilled in communication. (Quintilian, Chapter 13)

VII Building relationships on the principles of cooperation and justice does not exclude the option of refusing to cooperate with hostile or destructive publics.
- Social cooperation does not mean invariable accommodation of publics with incompatible, or even hostile, values, or intentions. (Kropotkin, Chapter 5)
- Vigilance within relationships is required. A relationship strategy that never retaliates against defection cannot be an evolutionarily stable strategy. (Chapter 7)
- A quest for justice does not imply unfettered cooperation and benevolence, which would be detrimental to the overall fairness of society. The transactional justice that Hume envisions and that he expands into a broader "justice as fairness" concept both creates social cooperation and, ideally, prevents cooperative excesses that would favor particular individuals or groups. (Hume, Chapter 9)

VIII Acts of cooperation and justice are the most effective builders of a positive reputation. A positive reputation is a powerful, productive force
within the processes of public relations and resource acquisition.

- Reputation, with its inherent social capital, is built primarily by acts
  of cooperation and indirect reciprocity. (Darwin, Chapter 4)
- Consistent enactments of indirect reciprocity build reputation. A
  reputation built upon cooperation produces more benefits than one
  built upon conflict. (Chapter 7)
- Respect for transactional justice—that is, respect for the sanctity of
  others' property and the social norms of resource exchange—builds
  reputation. For Hume, nothing is more powerful in the building of a
  positive reputation than enactments of justice. (Hume, Chapter 9)
- Another powerful driver of reputation is benevolence, which Hume
  characterizes as a disinterested passion for the wellbeing of others.
  This reflects game theory findings that establish indirect reciprocity
  as a significant creator of positive reputation. (Hume, Chapter 9)
- Reciprocity in relationships is beneficial, earning trust, building
  reputation, and leading to mutual advantage. (Rawls, Chapter 10)
- The enactment of justice and moderation builds reputation, which
  brings the rewards of social influence and material wealth. (Isocrates,
  Chapter 12)
- Consistency of values and values-driven behavior, as opposed to
  highly variable situational stances, is conducive to clarity of reputation
  and productive relationships. (Isocrates, Chapter 12)

IX Public relations practitioners can take specific actions, drawn from
evolutionary biology, philosophy, and rhetoric, to build and enhance relationships built upon cooperation and justice.

- The way we begin relationships and individual encounters matters:
  Studies of mirror neurons and similar neurological phenomena show
  that the self we initially present to others influences their immediate
  reaction to us as well as their consequent behavior within the relationship. (Chapter 3)
- An early impulse toward violence or distrust, particularly in the face
  of a perceived threat, can literally short-circuit the evaluative functions of the human brain. Recognizing our snap judgments and,
  when advisable, subjecting them to slower, more considered assessments—including organizational decision-making processes—offers
  the possibility of better decisions and improved relationships. (Chapter 3)
- Simplicity, predictability, and the clarity of cooperate/defect behaviors are keys to successful resource acquisition. Complex cooperate/
  defect strategies can baffle relationship partners and do not fare well

in Prisoner's Dilemma games. An uncomplicated preference for cooperation—"avoidance of unnecessary conflict," in Axelrod's words—consistently defeats more complex, stance-calculating programs in iterated Prisoner's Dilemma tournaments. (Chapter 7)

- Traditional public relations practices such as boundary spanning, coorientation, and the reflective paradigm's inclination to move beyond organizational walls are essential for intergroup cooperation. Increasing contact and understanding among groups can increase the cooperation that generates resources. (Chapter 7)
- Habit is both essential and effective in forming the values inherent in ethical behavior. Enacting cooperation and justice within public relations can strengthen the commitment to and the prevalence of those values. (Chapter 8)
- As a creator of sustainable societies, justice is essential to social theories of public relations and particularly to the reflective paradigm, which emphasizes the maintenance of an entity's social legitimacy. Hume would argue that nothing does more to establish social legitimacy than a respect for justice, with its inherent honoring of others' property. (Hume, Chapter 9)
- The enactment of justice and moderation is concentric, beginning with individual commitment and behavior, then moving to organizations, and building to enactment within a Rawlsian social union of social unions. (Isocrates, Chapter 12)
- The solicitation of dissent is essential for the maintenance of relationships characterized by justice and moderation. (Isocrates, Chapter 12)
- The enactment of justice and moderation is characterized by indirect reciprocity—by treating a second party the way we wish third parties would treat us. (Isocrates, Chapter 12)
- Studying examples of justice and moderation improves the character of the rhetorician. (Isocrates, Chapter 12)
- The study and practice of socially unifying rhetoric improves the rhetorician's character. (Quintilian, Chapter 13)

With such extensive multidisciplinary foundations, the social harmony frameworks of public relations clearly are not idealistic or utopian. On the contrary, these frameworks are more closely aligned with human nature than rival frameworks that focus on egoistic conflict and competition.

Additional strategies of cooperation

Enduring voices within evolutionary biology, philosophy, and rhetoric concur that cooperation is not merely the best strategy for resource acquisition; it is the indispensable ingredient in the survival of our species. In *Man's Peril*, philosopher Bertrand Russell (2003) concludes:

The only thing that will redeem mankind is cooperation, and the first step towards cooperation lies in the hearts of individuals. It is common to wish well to one's self, but, in our technically unified world, wishing well to oneself is sure to be futile unless it is combined with wishing well to others.

(p. 12)

Similarly, evolutionary biologist Edward O. Wilson (2012) has written:

Beyond the ordinary instincts of altruism, there is something more, delicate and ephemeral in character but, when experienced, transformative. It is *honor*, a feeling born of innate empathy and cooperativeness. It is the final reserve of altruism that may yet save our race.

(p. 251)

Millennia before these more recent voices, the rhetorician Isocrates (trans. 1929/1992) surveyed the beginnings of Athenian democracy and the shifting alliances among Greek city-states and concluded, "Arrogance and insolence have been the cause of our misfortunes while sobriety and self-control have been the source of our blessings" (*On the Peace*, 119). If cooperation, then, presents the only sustainable path forward, how should we enact it? The last of the Nine Tenets, above, offers some specifics—but to what other sources might we turn for guidance?

The evidence within this book began with science, and to that we now return: Three important scientists within this book—psychologist Steven Pinker, neuroscientist Donald Pfaff, and evolutionary biologist Martin Nowak—each present, within their research, findings and suggestions that might enhance cooperation among individuals and groups. Writing of rhetorical research, Ihlen (2002) has observed that "too often the studies concentrate on meta-theoretical questions and are satisfied merely to indicate the *potential*" of new or evolving ideas (pp. 259–260). To avoid such generalities and to provide additional strategies for enacting cooperation and justice, this chapter turns to the advice of Pinker, Pfaff, and Nowak.

Steven Pinker and the Five Historical Forces

In *The Better Angels of Our Nature: Why Violence Has Declined*, Steven Pinker (2011), the Harvard College professor of psychology at Harvard University, outlines "Four Better Angels" of our nature and "Five Historical Forces" that have led, over eons, to an increase of cooperation and a reduction of violence within our species (p. xxv). Pinker's Four Better Angels—empathy, self-control, the moral sense, and reason—have been addressed in earlier chapters, and self-control will be touched on again below. His related Five

Historical Forces are summarized here, the idea being that public relations scholars and practitioners might examine and, possibly, further them.

1. **The leviathan.** This is philosopher Thomas Hobbes' term for a central government strong and credible enough to ensure social peace and, ideally, enforce civil rights. Within their bounds, stable central governments can enact policies "making peace more attractive than war" (Pinker, 2011, p. 680). Peaceful societies, Pinker (2011) notes, "tend to be richer, healthier, better educated, better governed, more respectful of their women, and more likely to engage in trade"—a conclusion related to the four remaining historical forces that he cites (p. xxiii).

2. **Gentle commerce.** "Voluntary exchanges" within noncoercive trade relationships generally lead to our improved understanding of those different from ourselves, which leads to additional foundations for cooperation (Pinker, 2011, p. 683). Historical trends show that stable commercial systems correlate positively with indicators of peace such as a decrease in homicides (Pinker, 2011, p. xxiv). "Countries that trade with each other," Pinker (2011) adds, "are less likely to cross swords . . . Countries that are more open to the world economy are less likely to host genocides and civil wars" (pp. xxiv, 683).

3. **Feminization.** Societies in which women have socioeconomic autonomy are less violent than those in which women suffer repression (Pinker, 2011, p. 686)—a conclusion that Pinker (2011) supports with voluminous evidence: Reproductive freedom, for example, can reduce birthrate and population, a key to defusing potentially violent competition for resources (p. 688). Reproductive freedom and equal status also reduce the prospects of gynecide, which can involve the aborting of female fetuses and the murder of female newborns in favor of male progeny; such a practice can lead to a population rife with "violent male-male competition" for women (Pinker, 2011, p. 687). Neurological research and game theory studies show that women are, in general, more suited to forming cooperative relationships than men: Women tend to fare better in resource-competition games than men (Pinker, 2011, p. 513), in part because, to a higher degree than males, they can empathize with the plight of competitors (Pinker, 2011, pp. 530–531). (Again, Chapter 7 shows that cooperative strategies outperform competitive strategies in such games.) Pinker (2011) in part attributes men's more competitive/less successful resource acquisition in such games to their relatively higher levels of testosterone and the relatively higher number of testosterone receptors within the male brain (p. 518). Goleman (2006, p. 245) notes that testosterone reduces the effectiveness of oxytocin, a hormone that encourages cooperation (Chapter 3).

   Pinker (2011) presents evidence that societies that embrace women's rights also tend to shun war as a solution to disagreements (p. 526), and he concludes by posing this question: "Would the world be more peaceful if women were in charge? . . . The answer. . . is a qualified yes" (p. 527).

4. **The expanding circle.** The more we know about potential rivals—and the more potential rivals we know—the more we increase the odds of empathy and cooperation. The act of reading, even with its fictional "others," expands our ability to empathize with the needs of currently unfamiliar individuals and groups (Pinker, 2011, p. 689). "Anything that creates a communal relationship . . .should also create sympathy," Pinker (2011) writes, and he cites experiments showing that hearing a potential rival in resource-acquisition games describe his or her circumstances "can enhance people's sympathy" (pp. 585, 690). Conversely, violence is enabled by "distancing" (Pinker, 2011, p. 568).

5. **The escalator of reason.** People of higher intelligence tend to perform better in experimental resource-acquisition games; they are more likely to cooperate (Pinker, 2011, pp. 661–662). The process of reasoning allows such individuals to engage in reflection and to "extricate ourselves from our parochial vantage points" (Pinker, 2011, p. xxv). Reasoning and reflection help individuals to envision a potentially violent situation "as a problem to be solved rather than a contest to be won" (Pinker, 2011, p. 646). Pinker (2011) asserts that as human intelligence increases (the Flynn Effect), our desire and ability to cooperate also will increase (p. 660).

Donald Pfaff and the cultivation of cooperation

In the closing chapters of *The Altruistic Brain*, award-winning neuroscientist Donald Pfaff (Pfaff & Sherman, 2015), professor at Rockefeller University, explores "how our propensity for trust and cooperation can be stimulated" (p. 155). An important element of his answer involves epigenetics, which is "the study of ways the experiences we undergo change how our genes operate —without altering our DNA sequences one iota" (Goleman, 2006, p. 150). Epigenetic studies indicate that our environments, particularly enduring environments, can affect which genes and gene sequences within our DNA turn on and turn off, so to speak (Pfaff & Sherman, 2015; Goleman, 2006; Wilson, 2012). Though he does not use the term *epigenetics*, Pinker (2011) also acknowledges the impact of sustained environment and culture upon human genetic functioning: "Genes often act in networks regulated by feedback loops, so in populations in which a particular gene is less effective, other genes may step up their activity to compensate" (p. 620). A related concept is "neural plasticity," which Pfaff (Pfaff & Sherman, 2015) defines as "the changeability and indeed the improvability of the human brain" (p. 168). With practice and habit, our considered judgments, for example, can increase their control over our snap judgments (Pfaff & Sherman, 2015; Goleman, 2006; Kahneman, 2011). In short, we can change ourselves.

Especially via epigenetics, Pfaff's recommended strategies for stimulating trust and cooperation address not only individuals: By recommending attainable tweaks to our sustained environments, he also targets the species-shaping processes of natural selection. In particular, Pfaff recommends four broad strategies to strengthen cooperation: Framing, early intervention, education, and professional conduct.

1. **Framing.** To increase cooperative behavior, Pfaff (Pfaff & Sherman, 2015) asserts, we must understand—and believe—that we truly are cooperative, that we are not, somehow, acting against human nature when we work for the wellbeing of others:

    > We are naturally inclined toward empathy . . . The way that we view ourselves and others is crucial to our social interactions. Thus if we know with certainty that we can tap into our own and others' altruistic capacities, then we can work toward transcending obstacles that prevent our giving effect to those capacities . . . We can proceed with enhanced trust in ourselves and in those with whom we interact.
    >
    > (p. 157)

    Pfaff (Pfaff & Sherman, 2015) asserts that we must overcome the "cognitive dissonance" generated by an incorrect belief that we are wired for competition (p. 159). Empirical evidence increasingly shows that cooperation "is everyone's default condition, which should be encouraged at the outset" (Pfaff & Sherman, 2015, p. 176).

2. **Early intervention.** Society should intervene to protect children from poverty, neglect, physical abuse, and other threats to their wellbeing and development. Such early intervention should also cultivate the qualities of self-esteem and empathy (Pfaff & Sherman, 2015, p. 163). Pfaff (Pfaff & Sherman, 2015) cites research showing that childhood mistreatment and low self-esteem inhibit the growth of the hippocampus, "a crucial part of the brain involved in both cognitive and emotional behavior" (p. 159). In contrast, "children with high levels of maternal support had much larger hippocampal sizes" (Pfaff & Sherman, 2015, p. 255). Like Pinker, Pfaff (Pfaff & Sherman, 2015) singles out the particular importance of early intervention for at-risk young males, noting that effects of testosterone can include a reduced tendency to trust and the reduction of friendly relationships with competitors (pp. 206, 234).

3. **Education.** Just as early intervention is, in Pfaff's (Pfaff & Sherman, 2015) view, particularly important for young males, he asserts that education is particularly important for young females. "The empowerment of women," he writes, begins with access to education and, consequently, "providing career paths to power" (Pfaff & Sherman, 2015, pp. 251, 243). Like Pinker, Pfaff (Pfaff & Sherman, 2015) cites the positive correlation

of increased socioeconomic autonomy for women with increased peace and cooperation (pp. 243–244). Educational curricula, Pfaff (Pfaff & Sherman, 2015) suggests, should include the biological origins of empathy and cooperation (a return to his emphasis on framing), activities that increase empathy, and training in conflict resolution (pp. 176, 178, 249). Such curricula could generate an "altruistic 'multiplier effect,'" he concludes (Pfaff & Sherman, 2015, p. 249).

4. **Professional conduct.** In addition to recommending specific curricular goals for educators, Pfaff (Pfaff & Sherman, 2015) directs specific attention to the legal profession, which, he suggests, should emphasize dispute-resolution processes rather than the zero-sum approach of many traditional legal procedures (p. 173). Pfaff does not mention public relations—but discipline's emphasis and reliance on positive reputation, resource acquisition, and sustained relationships surely indicates that it also should be an advocate for cooperation and justice.

Martin Nowak and the five mechanisms of cooperation

Through years of computer-generated game-theory experiments, evolutionary biologist Martin Nowak (Nowak & Highfield, 2011), director of Harvard University's Program for Evolutionary Dynamics, has identified "five mechanisms of cooperation" that account not only for the unrivaled success of cooperative strategies within resource-acquisition games, but, in a broader sense, for the rise of the human species: Direct reciprocity, indirect reciprocity, spatial relationships, group selection, and kin selection (pp. 270–271). "Using these five mechanisms of cooperation," Nowak (Nowak & Highfield, 2011) declares, "natural selection has ensured that we are able to get more from social living than from the pursuit of a solitary, selfish life" (p. 272). In even bolder language, he asserts, "Previously, there were only two basic principles of evolution—mutation and selection . . . We must now accept that cooperation is the third principle . . . Cooperation is the master architect of evolution" (Nowak & Highfield, 2011, p. xviii).

1. **Direct reciprocity.** Direct reciprocity is *quid pro quo*—or, in game theory language, tit for tat: "When I scratch your back, I expect you to scratch mine in return" (Nowak & Highfield, 2011, p. 22). Evolutionary biologist Robert Trivers has termed direct reciprocity "reciprocal altruism" (Nowak & Highfield, 2011, p. 27). Direct reciprocity drives cooperation because relationship partners recognize one another and recall the success or failure of past interactions (Nowak & Highfield, 2011, p. 24).

2. **Indirect reciprocity.** Indirect reciprocity has been cited throughout this book as a driver of positive reputation and as a strategy that leads to resource acquisition in a variety of relationships. Indirect reciprocity builds trust. Continuing the familiar backscratching analogy, Nowak describes

indirect reciprocity as A scratching B's back without thought of immediate return; social communication ensures that C, D, and others will learn of this behavior and will seek mutual backscratching relationships with the trustworthy and generous A. Nowak (Nowak & Highfield, 2011) explains:

> The point is that this little generous act secures you a reputation, which might be worth a great deal—more than the initial cost—in the long run. Thanks to the power of reputation, we help others without expecting an immediate return ... Making a reputation has been shown to engage much of the same reward circuitry in the brain as making money.
>
> (pp. 54–55)

Nowak (Nowak & Highfield, 2011) contends that the success of indirect reciprocity within social environments has, through natural selection, helped build compassion for others into a biological reality within humans (p. 55).

3. **Spatial relationships.** "All we mean by this is that some individuals interact with each other more often than with others," Nowak (Nowak & Highfield, 2011) explains (p. 270). Such interactions increase the importance of reputation and, thus, the importance of caring for others. Nowak's (Nowak & Highfield, 2011) game-theory experiments have shown that determined groups of cooperators can survive even when in a minority and surrounded by conflict-oriented defectors. The earlier game theory experiments of Axelrod (2006) forecast Nowak's findings: "Cooperation can evolve from small clusters of individuals who base their cooperation on reciprocity and have even a small proportion of interactions with each other" (p. 21).

4. **Group selection.** Again, group selection holds that a group, such as a community or species, can be a unit of selection within the processes of natural selection—just as for Charles Darwin, the individual organism is generally the unit of selection and, for Richard Dawkins, the gene plays that role. As both Darwin and Kropotkin had earlier concluded, Nowak (Nowak & Highfield, 2011) finds that "groups with meaningful social norms outcompete other groups" (p. 83). As we saw in Chapter 7, Nowak's (Nowak & Highfield, 2011) research also shows that groups that cooperate with other groups improve resource acquisition (p. 84).

5. **Kin selection.** Kin selection holds that we act to enhance not only our own survival but also the survival of relatives who share our genes (Dawkins, 2006a). Though Nowak, unlike some other evolutionary biologists, does not see kin selection as the core of group selection (Chapter 6), he does see it as a force in the evolution of cooperation. "I can envision it working whenever there is conditional behavior based on

kin recognition," he concedes. "So depending on whether I am looking at a brother or a stranger, I will behave accordingly" (Nowak & Highfield, 2011, pp. 110–111).

Self-control

The importance of self-control to cooperation is a persistent theme in the findings of the scientists within this book—an idea, actually, that dates at least to Isocrates and the concept of *sophrosyne* (Chapter 12). This important quality merits its own brief section as a strategy for building cooperation. Apart from "intelligence," no human quality correlates more with "a healthy and successful life" than self-control—and self-control correlates positively with intelligence (Pinker, 2011, pp. 598, 601). A decades-long experiment, testing subjects over their lifetimes, has shown that individuals with high levels of self-control "had higher self-esteem, had better relationships, were better at handling stress . . . and earned more money" (Pinker, 2011, pp. 598–599). Some evidence shows that women are better at exercising self-control than men (Pinker, 2011, p. 604).

Because its sources can be mapped within the human brain, Pinker (2011) contends that self-control is inheritable—and that through use and awareness of its advantages, we can strengthen our self-control (pp. 608, 609, 618). Nobel Prize-winning economist Daniel Kahneman (2011) adds that self-control can diminish when exerted over long periods, particularly within situations characterized by conflict. In such periods, a diet high in glucose actually can help an individual sustain self-control (pp. 41, 43). Self-control and empathy diminish the possibility of using force within relationships; successful exercise of self-control leads to social influence (Goleman, 2006, p. 95). Pfaff (Pfaff & Sherman, 2015) asserts that individuals who understand these aspects of self-control increase their odds of achieving it (p. 158).

Final suggestions for the enactment of cooperation and justice

Within this chapter, the ideas grouped under the final tenet of our Nine Tenets suggest 11 specific strategies for building relationships characterized by cooperation and justice:

1. Begin relationships with enactments of cooperation and justice. Such an approach can engender reciprocal behavior from relationship partners. Such a beginning has proven to be the most effective strategy in decades of game-theory experiments.
2. Forgive transgressions by relationship partners unless such actions become part of a deliberate strategy. Game theory experiments show that, over time,

the most successful resource acquisition strategies are nice (cooperative), forgiving, and, when warranted, retaliatory.

3. Avoid snap judgments regarding relationships, especially judgments that might generate conflict. Organizational decision-making processes increase the odds of self-control and cooperative measures.

4. Be simple, predictable, and clear in relationship strategies. Complex strategies with many contingencies and variables can baffle relationship partners and diminish cooperation.

5. Use traditional public relations practices such as boundary spanning, coorientation, and the reflective paradigm's inclination to move beyond organizational walls to increase contact among groups. Increased contact correlates with increased understanding and empathy, which can lead to productive cooperation.

6. Continually enact cooperation and justice within relationships to strengthen the commitment to and the prevalence of those values. Experts from all three disciplines of this book (evolutionary biology, philosophy, and rhetoric) agree that conscience enactment of values strengthens those values.

7. Study and discuss examples of justice and moderation. Doing so strengthens commitment to those values.

8. Understand that, ideally, cooperation and justice begin as personal values that spread to larger groups such as families, organizations, communities, nations, and international relationships.

9. Respect the ownership of others' property and resources. According to Hume, nothing is more effective in building a positive reputation than honoring the sanctity of others' property.

10. Solicit dissent. Acceptance of dissent is essential for cooperation and justice.

11. Enact indirect reciprocity, treating a second party as we would wish third parties would treat us. Indirect reciprocity is a powerful builder of reputation and success in relationships.

Based on the above recommendations of Pinker, Pfaff, and Nowak—and supplemented by the complementary research of Goleman and Kahneman—we may add nine additional strategies, some of which clearly operate at the societal and organizational levels:

12. Understand that, genetically, humans are cooperators. Share the evidence for this reality with colleagues and relationship partners. The multi-disciplinary evidence—the consilience—for this aspect of human nature is overwhelming. We should approach relationships by offering and expecting cooperation, not conflict. We shouldn't simply concede that we're too cynical and worldly wise to accept this reality. As Stephen Jay Gould (1996) lamented, "The most erroneous stories are those we think we know best—and therefore never scrutinize or question" (p. 57).

A reluctance to step back from egoistic frameworks of public relations may be what Kahneman (2011) labels "theory-induced blindness" (p. 279). Like Gould, he believes that "the errors of a theory. . . hide in what it ignores or tacitly assumes" (Kahneman, 2011, pp. 274–275). Compelling multidisciplinary evidence challenges the wide validity of egoistic, conflict-oriented theories of public relations.

13. Support central governments that value social peace and civil rights. These qualities are essential to the justice inherent in effective, sustainable cooperation and resource acquisition.
14. Empower women, particularly through equal rights that include equal access to education and equal paths to all levels of employment and leadership.
15. Support education. Intelligence correlates positively with self-control and cooperation. Educational curricula should include the biological origins of empathy and cooperation, activities that increase empathy, and training in conflict resolution.
16. Support early intervention programs for at-risk children and youth. Early neglect diminishes an individual's ability to cooperate.
17. Promote contact with unfamiliar others, possibly at the international level. Increased familiarity generally correlates positively with increased cooperation and increased success in resource exchange.
18. Discuss new research in cooperation and justice with other public relations professionals and with relationship partners.
19. Enact direct reciprocity, treating others as we would want them to treat us.
20. Strengthen self-control through practice and, in times of stress and conflict, through diet and awareness of that quality's heightened vulnerability.

Many of these strategies, such as early intervention for at-risk children and the empowerment of women, surely strike us as the right thing to do regardless of their impact on resource acquisition. (Darwin and Hume would argue that our feelings in this area have evolved from artificial, self-interested, instrumental virtues to natural virtues that stand on their own.) Translating these 20 strategies to specific actions could give rise to several innovative, productive tactics: Internal and external programs to ensure equal opportunity for women; social responsibility programs addressing early intervention for at-risk children; perhaps book clubs for public relations units—because reading the narratives of others increases empathy; perhaps learning a new language— because increased understanding of other cultures boosts the odds of cooperation, which, in turn, boosts the likelihood of resource acquisition. Ideally, these strategies, operating within the larger understanding of the Nine Tenets of public relations' social harmony frameworks, offer the beginnings of a plan for enacting justice and cooperation in relationships at many levels.

Conclusion

In the final chapter of *On the Origin of Species*, Charles Darwin (1859) refers to his great book as "one long argument" for evolution by means of natural selection (p. 459). This book too is an argument—not too long, I hope—for a related idea: Relationships built upon cooperation and justice are not counter to human nature—exactly the opposite, in fact—and they are more successful in resource acquisition than are relationships characterized by egoism, conflict, and competition. In the early twentieth century, rhetorical scholar I.A. Richards (1936/1964) held that the new mission of rhetoric was "a study of misunderstanding and its remedies" (p. 3). A misunderstanding that, in my opinion, haunts public relations is the belief that the discipline's social harmony frameworks, though desirable, are unrealistic—normative, idealistic, utopian fantasies designed for a better but nonexistent world. In this book, I have attempted to counter that misunderstanding with the *logos* of self-interest, empiricism, and materialism rather than the *pathos* of idealism and wishful thinking. The disciplines of evolutionary biology, philosophy, and rhetoric contribute to a consilience of cooperation, to a well-grounded assertion that humans truly can and should build successful, productive relationships by treating others as we would wish to be treated—even when those others are not in a position to help us in return. One of the clearest ideas in this book, I hope, is the repeated, multidisciplinary finding that indirect reciprocity is probably the strongest driver of positive reputation and productive relationships.

To end where we began: Why was Isocrates the most successful rhetorician of Western civilization? As a rhetorician, he understood what influential philosophers have long believed and what evolutionary biologists have now proven: The most productive relationships are built upon cooperation and justice.

References

Abbot, P., Abe, J., Alcock, J., Alizon, S., Alpedrinha, J.A.C., Andersson, M., ...
Zink, A. (2011, March 24). Inclusive fitness theory and eusociality. *Nature*, *466*,
E1-E4.

Aeschylus. (2008). *Oresteia*. (A. H. Sommerstein, Trans.). Cambridge, MA: Harvard
University Press.

Aldoory, L. (2009). Feminist criticism in public relations: How gender can impact
public relations texts and contexts. In R.L. Heath, E.L. Toth, & D. Waymer (Eds.),
Rhetorical and critical approaches to public relations II (pp. 110–123). New York:
Routledge.

Allen, N. (2009, Jan. 29). Virgin complaint letter's author revealed. *The Telegraph*.
Retrieved from www.telegraph. co.uk/travel/travelnews/4383938/Virgin-complaint-
letters-author-revealed-as-Oliver-Beale.html.

Almenberg, J., & Dreber, A. (2013). Economics and evolution: Complementary
perspectives on cooperation. In M.A. Nowak & S. Coakley (Eds.), *Evolution, games,
and God: The principle of cooperation* (pp. 132–149). Cambridge, MA: Harvard
University Press.

Angeles, P.A. (1981). *Dictionary of philosophy*. New York: Barnes & Noble.

Aristotle. (1934). *Physics*. (P. H. Wicksteed & F.M. Cornford, Trans.). Cambridge,
MA: Harvard University Press.

Aristotle. (1954). *The rhetoric and the poetics of Aristotle*. (W. R. Roberts & I.
Bywater, Trans.). New York: The Modern Library.

Aristotle. (1984a). *Generation of animals*. (A. Platt, Trans). In J. Barnes (Ed.), *The
complete works of Aristotle*, *Vol. I* (pp. 1,111–1,218). Princeton, NJ: Princeton
University Press.

Aristotle. (1984b). *Nicomachean ethics*. (W.D. Ross & J.O. Urmson, Trans). In J.
Barnes (Ed.), *The complete works of Aristotle*, *Vol. II* (pp. 1,728–1,867). Princeton,
NJ: Princeton University Press.

Aristotle. (2003). *Nicomachean ethics*. (H. Rackham, Trans.). Cambridge, MA:
Harvard University Press. (Original work published 1926)

Atsma, A.J. (2014). *Theoi Greek mythology*. Retrieved from www.theoi.com.

Axelrod, R. (2006). *The evolution of cooperation* (Rev. ed.). New York: Basic Books.

Baier, A.C. (2010). *The cautious jealous virtue*. Cambridge, MA: Harvard University
Press.

Baillie, J. (2000). *Hume on morality*. London, UK: Routledge.

Baker, G., & Morris, K.J. (2005). *Descartes' dualism*. London, UK: Routledge.

Baker, S. (1999). Five baselines for justification in persuasion. *Journal of Mass Media Ethics*, *14*, 69–81.

Barash, D.P. (2015, Oct. 27). Paradigms lost. *Aeon*. Retrieved from https://aeon.co/essays/science-needs-the-freedom-to-constantly-change-its-mind.

Barash, D.P. (2016, Feb. 13). Five blockbuster evolutionary insights and one wild life: Robert Trivers. *Los Angeles Review of Books*. Retrieved from https://lareviewof books.org/article/five-blockbuster-evolutionary-insights-and-one-wild-life-on-robert-trivers/.

Bardhan, N., & Weaver, C.K. (2011). Introduction: Public relations in global cultural contexts. In N. Bardhan & C.K. Weaver (Eds.), *Public relations in global cultural contexts: Multiparadigmatic perspectives* (pp. 1–28). New York: Routledge.

Barney, R., & Black, J. (1994). Ethics and professional persuasive communication. *Public Relations Review*, 20, 233–249.

Barrett, P.H., Gautrey, P.J., Herbert, S., Kohn, D., & Smith, S. (Eds.) (1987). *Charles Darwin's notebooks, 1836–1844*. Ithaca, NY: Cornell University Press.

Batson, C.D., & Ahmad, N. (2001). Empathy-induced altruism in a prisoner's dilemma: What if the target of empathy has defected? *European Journal of Social Psychology*, *31*, 25–36.

Benoit, W. (1990). Isocrates and Aristotle on rhetoric. *Rhetoric Society Quarterly*, *20*, 251–259.

Benoit, W. (1995). *Accounts, excuses, and apologies: A theory of image restoration strategies*. Albany, NY: State University of New York Press.

Berneri, C. (1942). *Peter Kropotkin: His federalist ideas*. London, UK: Freedom Press.

Birx, H.J. (1998). Introduction. In C. Darwin, *The descent of man* (pp. ix–xxviii). Amherst, NY: Prometheus Books.

Black, E. (1994). Plato's view of rhetoric. In E. Schiappa (Ed.), *Landmark essays on classical Greek rhetoric* (pp. 83–99). Davis, CA: Hermagoras. (Original work published 1958)

Booth, W. (1989). *The vocation of a teacher*. Chicago, IL: University of Chicago Press.

Bourke, V.J. (1968). *History of ethics, volume 2: Modern and contemporary ethics*. Mount Jackson, VA: Axios Press.

Bowen, S.A. (2007). The extent of ethics. In E.L. Toth (Ed.), *The future of excellence in public relations and communication management: Challenges for the next generation*, (pp. 275–298). Mahwah, NJ: Lawrence Erlbaum Associates.

Bowen, S.A. (2010). The nature of good in public relations. In R.L. Heath (Ed.), *The Sage handbook of public relations* (pp. 569–583). Thousand Oaks, CA: Sage.

Breitenberger, B. (2007). *Aphrodite and Eros: The development of erotic mythology in early Greek poetry and cult*. New York: Routledge.

Brockriede, W.E. (1971). Toward a contemporary Aristotelian theory of rhetoric. In R.L. Johannesen (Ed.), *Contemporary theories of rhetoric: Selected readings* (pp. 39–49). New York: Harper & Row.

Brooke, J.H. (2013). "Ready to aid one another": Darwin on nature, God, and cooperation. In M.A. Nowak & S. Coakley (Eds.), *Evolution, games, and God: The principle of cooperation* (pp. 37–59). Cambridge, MA: Harvard University Press.

Broom, G., Casey, S., & Ritchey, J. (2000). Concept and theory of organization-public relationships. In J.A. Ledingham & S.D. Bruning (Eds.), *Public relations as relationship management: A relational approach to the study and practice of public relations* (pp. 3–24). Mahwah, NJ: Lawrence Erlbaum Associates.

Brown, R.E. (2003). A matter of chance: The emergence of probability and the rise of public relations. *Public Relations Review*, *29*, 385–399.

Brown, R.E. (2006). Myth of symmetry: Public relations as cultural styles. *Public Relations Review*, *32*, 206–212.

Browne, J. (2002). *The power of place: Volume II of a biography*. New York: Alfred A. Knopf.

Browne, J. (2006). *Darwin's Origin of Species: A biography*. New York: Atlantic Monthly Press.

Bryant, D.C. (1953). Rhetoric: Its function and scope. *Quarterly Journal of Speech*, *39*, 410–424.

Burge, R. (2013). Using matching to investigate the relationship between religion and tolerance. *Politics and Religion*, *6*, 264–281.

Burke, K. (1951). Rhetoric—old and new. *The Journal of General Education*, *5*, 202–209.

Burke, K. (1957). *The philosophy of literary form* (Rev. ed.). New York: Vintage Books.

Burke, K. (1969). *A rhetoric of motives*. Berkeley, CA: University of California Press. (Original work published 1950)

Burkhardt, F., Porter, D.M., Browne, J., & Richmond, M. (1993). *The correspondence of Charles Darwin: Volume 8, 1860*. Cambridge, UK: Cambridge University Press.

Burkhardt, F., & Smith, S. (1987). *The correspondence of Charles Darwin: Volume 3, 1844–1846*. Cambridge, UK: Cambridge University Press.

Burkhardt, F., & Smith, S. (1990). *The correspondence of Charles Darwin: Volume 6, 1856–1857*. Cambridge, UK: Cambridge University Press.

Burkhardt, F., & Smith, S. (1991). *The correspondence of Charles Darwin: Volume 7, 1858–1859*. Cambridge, UK: Cambridge University Press.

Buss, D.M. (1995). Evolutionary psychology: A new paradigm for psychological science. *Psychological Inquiry*, *6*, 1–30.

Buss, D.M., Haselton, M.G., Shackelford, T.K., Bleske, A.L., & Wakefield, J.C. (1998). Adaptations, exaptations, and spandrels. *American Psychologist*, *53*, 533–548.

Buxton, R.G.A. (1982). *Persuasion in Greek tragedy: A study of Peitho*. London, UK: Cambridge University Press.

Cahn, M. (1989). Reading rhetoric rhetorically: Isocrates and the marketing of insight. *Rhetorica*, *7*, 121–44.

Cameron, G.T., Pang, A., & Jin, Y. (2008). Contingency theory. In T. L. Hansen-Horn & B. D. Neff (Eds.), *Public relations: From theory to practice* (pp. 134–157). Boston, MA: Allyn & Bacon.

Campbell, J.A. (1989). The invisible rhetorician: Charles Darwin's "third party" Strategy. *Rhetorica*, *7*, 55–85.

Campbell, J.A. (2003). Why was Darwin believed? Darwin's *Origin* and the problem of intellectual revolution. *Configurations*, *11*, 203–237.

Cancel, A.E., Cameron, G.T., Sallot, L.M., & Mitrook, M.A. (1997). It depends: A contingency theory of accommodation in public relations. *Journal of Public Relation Research*, *9*, 31–63.

Caudill, E. (1994). The bishop-eaters: The publicity campaign for Darwin and *On the Origin of Species*. *Journal of the History of Ideas*, *55*, 441–460.

Chandebois, R. (1976). Cell sociology: A way of reconsidering the current concepts of morphogenesis. *Acta Biotheoretica*, *25*, 71–102.

Choi, Y., & Cameron, G.T. (2005). Overcoming ethnocentrism: The role of identity in contingent practice of international public relations. *Journal of Public Relations Research, 17*, 171–189.

Chouinard, Y. (2006). *Let my people go surfing: The education of a reluctant businessman.* New York: Penguin Books.

Christen, C.T. (2005). The restructuring and reengineering of AT&T: Analysis of a public relations crisis using organizational theory. *Public Relations Review, 31*, 239–251.

Cicero, M.T. (1971). *Brutus.* (G.L. Hendrikson, Trans.). Cambridge, MA: Harvard University Press. (Original work published 1939)

Cicero, M.T. (1971). *Orator.* (H.M. Hubbell, Trans.). Cambridge, MA: Harvard University Press. (Original work published 1939)

Cicero, M.T. (1976). *De inventione.* (H.M. Hubbell, Trans.). Cambridge, MA: Harvard University Press. (Original work published 1949)

Cicero, M.T. (1979). *De oratore.* (E.W. Sutton & H. Rackham, Trans.). Cambridge, MA: Harvard University Press. (Original work published 1942)

Clark, D.L. (1957). *Rhetoric in Greco-Roman education.* Morningside Heights, NY: Columbia University Press.

Clark, J.W., & Hughes, T.M. (1890). *The life and letters of the reverend Adam Sedgwick, Vol. II.* Cambridge, UK: Cambridge University Press.

Clarke, M.L. (1996). *Rhetoric at Rome* (Rev. ed.). London, UK: Routledge.

Clayton, P. (2013). Evolution, altruism, and God. Why the levels of emergent complexity matter. In M.A. Nowak & S. Coakley (Eds.), *Evolution, games, and God: The principle of cooperation* (pp. 343–361). Cambridge, MA: Harvard University Press.

Coakley, S., & Nowak, M.A. (2013). Why cooperation makes a difference. In S. Coakley & M.A. Nowak (Eds.), *Evolution, games, and God: The principle of cooperation* (pp. 1–34). Cambridge, MA: Harvard University Press.

Conlin, J. (2014). *Evolution and the Victorians: Science, culture and politics in Darwin's Britain.* London, UK: Bloomsbury.

Coombs, W.T. (1993). Philosophical underpinnings: Ramifications of a pluralist paradigm. *Public Relations Review, 19*, 111–119.

Coombs, W.T., & Holladay, S.J. (2008). Comparing apology to equivalent crisis response strategies: Clarifying apology's role and value in crisis communication. *Public Relations Review, 34*, 252–257.

Coombs, W.T., & Holladay, S.J. (2012). Fringe public relations: How activism moves critical PR toward the mainstream. *Public Relations Review, 38*, 880–887.

Corbett, E.P.J. (1989). Isocrates' legacy: The humanistic strand in classical rhetoric. In R.J. Connors (Ed.), *Selected essays of Edward P.J. Corbett* (pp. 267–277). Dallas, TX: Southern Methodist University Press.

Corbett, E.P.J. (1990a). *Classical rhetoric for the modern student* (3rd ed.). New York: Oxford University Press.

Corbett, E.P.J. (1990b). Introduction to *The Rhetoric and Poetics of Aristotle.* In E.P.J. Corbett, J.L. Golden, & G.F. Berquist (Eds.), *Essays on the rhetoric of the western world* (pp. 162–167). Dubuque, IA: Kendall/Hunt. (Original work published 1984)

Culbertson, H.M., & Knott, D. (2004). Communitarianism: Part of a world view for symmetry in communication. In D. W. Stacks (Ed.), *Globalization: Challenges &*

opportunities for public relations (pp. 27–38). Gainesville, FL: Institute for Public Relations Research.

Curtin, P.A. (2011). Public relations and philosophy: Parsing paradigms. *Public Relations Inquiry, 1*, 31–47.

Curtin, P.A., & Boynton, L.A. (2001). Ethics in public relations: Theory and practice. In R.L. Heath (Ed.), *Handbook of public relations* (pp. 411–422). Thousand Oaks, CA: Sage.

Curtin, P.A., & Gaither, T.K. (2005). Privileging identity, difference, and power: The circuit of culture as a basis for public relations theory. *Journal of Public Relations Research, 17*, 91–115.

Cutlip, S. (1994). *The unseen power*. Hillsdale, NJ: Lawrence Erlbaum Associates.

Darwin, C. (1859). *On the origin of species by means of natural selection, or the preservation of favoured races in the struggle for life*. London, UK: John Murray.

Darwin, C. (1860). *On the origin of species by means of natural selection, or the preservation of favoured races in the struggle for life* (2nd ed.). London, UK: John Murray.

Darwin, C. (1872). *The origin of species by means of natural selection, or the preservation of favoured races in the struggle for life* (6th ed.). London, UK: John Murray.

Darwin, C. (1983). *Autobiography*. In G. de Beer (Ed.), *Charles Darwin and Thomas Henry Huxley: Autobiographies* (pp. 1–88). Oxford, UK: Oxford University Press. (Original work published 1887)

Darwin, C. (1998). *The descent of man*. Amherst, NY: Prometheus Books. (Original work published 1871)

Darwin, F. (1888). *The life and letters of Charles Darwin, Vol. II*. London, UK: John Murray.

Dawkins, R. (1996). *The blind watchmaker* (Rev. ed.). New York: W.W. Norton & Company.

Dawkins, R. (2006a). *The selfish gene: 30th anniversary edition*. Oxford, UK: Oxford University Press.

Dawkins, R. (2006b). Foreword to the new edition of *The evolution of cooperation*. In R. Axelrod, *The evolution of cooperation* (pp. xi–xvi). New York: Basic Books.

Dawkins, R. (2008). The evolution of altruism—what matters is gene selection. *New Scientist, 197*, 17.

Dawkins, R. (2012, May 24). The descent of Edward Wilson. *Prospect, 12*, 1–5.

Dennett, D.C. (1995). *Darwin's dangerous idea: Evolution and the meanings of life*. New York: Touchstone.

Dennett, D.C. (1997, Aug. 14). Letter to the editor. *New York Review of Books, 44* (13). Retrieved from www.nybooks.com/articles/1997/08/14/darwinian-fundamentalism-an-exchange/.

Dionysius of Halicarnassus. (1974). Isocrates. In *Dionysius of Halicarnassus: The critical essays in two volumes* (S. Usher). Cambridge, MA: Harvard University Press.

DiStaso, M.W., Vafeiadis, M., & Amaral, C. (2015). Managing a health crisis on Facebook: How the response strategies of apology, sympathy, and information influence public relations. *Public Relations Review, 41*, 222–231.

Dixon, T. (2013). Altruism: Morals from history. In M.A. Nowak & S. Coakley (Eds.), *Evolution, games, and God: The principle of cooperation* (pp. 60–81). Cambridge, MA: Harvard University Press.

Downs, R.B. (2004). *Books that changed the world.* New York: Signet Classics.

Dozier, D.M., & Ehling, W.P. (1992). Evaluation of public relations programs: What the literature tells us about their effects. In J.E. Grunig (Ed.), *Excellence in public relations and communication management* (pp. 159–184). Hillsdale, NJ: Lawrence Erlbaum Associates.

Dworkin, R. (2003). John Rawls. *The Harvard Review of Philosophy, 11,* 7–8.

Edgett, R. (2002). Toward an ethical framework for advocacy in public relations. *Journal of Public Relations Research, 14,* 1–26.

Editorial Advisory Board, Easton Press. (2006). *Books that changed the world.* Retrieved from www.listsofbests.com/list/5867-books-that-changed-the-world-easton-press.

Edmonds, D., & Eidinow, J. (2006). *Rousseau's dog: Two great thinkers at war in the age of enlightenment.* New York: HarperCollins.

Edwards, L. (2012). Defining the "object" of public relations research: A new starting point. *Public Relations Inquiry, 1,* 7–30.

Everett, J.L., & Johnston, K.A. (2012). Toward an ethnographic imperative in public relations research. *Public Relations Review, 38,* 522–528.

Ferry, G. (2010). The exception and the rule: Women and the Royal Society 1945–2010. *Notes and Records of the Royal Society, 64,* S163–S172.

Finley, M.I. (1987). *The use and abuse of history.* New York: Peregrine.

Foley, M. (2012). Peitho and bia: The force of language. *Symploke, 20,* 173–181.

Frandsen, F., & Johansen, W. (2010). Strategy, management, leadership, and public relations. In R.L. Heath (Ed.), *The Sage handbook of public relations* (pp. 293–306). Thousand Oaks, CA: Sage.

Franklin, B. (1888). *The autobiography of Benjamin Franklin.* Boston, MA: Houghton, Mifflin and Company. (Original work published 1818)

Freeman, K.J. (1907). *Schools of Hellas: An essay on the practice and theory of ancient Greek education.* London, UK: Macmillan.

Freud, S. (1961). *Civilization and its discontents.* (J. Strachey, Trans.). New York: W.W. Norton & Company. (Original work published 1930)

Fried, A., & Sanders, R. (1992). *Socialist thought.* New York: Columbia University Press.

Friedman, M. (2002). *Capitalism and freedom.* Chicago, IL: University of Chicago Press.

Frimer, J.A., Aquino, K., Gebauer, J.E., Zhub, L., & Oakes, H. (2015). A decline in prosocial language helps explain public disapproval of the U.S. Congress. *Proceedings of the National Academy of Sciences of the United States of America, 112,* 6, 591–6,594.

Frost, S.E. (1962). *Basic teachings of the great philosophers.* New York: Anchor Books.

Gandy, O.H. (1982). *Beyond agenda setting: Information subsidies and public policy.* Norwood, NJ: Ablex Publishing Company.

Garver, E. (2004). Philosophy, rhetoric, and civic education in Aristotle and Isocrates. In T. Poulakos & D. Depew (Eds.), *Isocrates and civic education* (pp. 186–213). Austin, TX: University of Texas Press.

Gauthier, D. (1998). David Hume, contractarian. In D. Boucher & P. Kelly (Eds.), *Social justice: From Hume to Walzer* (pp. 17–44). London, UK: Routledge.

Goldstein, E.B. (2010). *Encyclopedia of perception.* Los Angeles, CA: Sage.

Goleman, D. (2006). *Social intelligence: The new science of human relationships*. New York: Bantam Books.

Golob, U., & Bartlett, J.L. (2007). Communicating about corporate social responsibility: A comparative study of CSR reporting in Australia and Slovenia. *Public Relations Review, 33*, 1–9.

Gottlieb, A. (2016). Who was David Hume? *New York Review of Books, 63*(9). Retrieved from www.nybooks.com/issues/2016/05/26/.

Gould, S.J. (1977). *Ever since Darwin: Reflections in natural history*. New York: W.W. Norton & Company.

Gould, S.J. (1980). Is a new and general theory of evolution emerging? *Paleontology, 6*, 119–130.

Gould, S.J. (1990). *An urchin in the storm: Essays about books and ideas*. London, UK: Penguin Books.

Gould, S.J. (1991a). Exaptation: A crucial tool for evolutionary psychology. *Journal of Social Issues, 47*, 43–65.

Gould, S.J. (1991b). Kropotkin was no crackpot. In S.J. Gould (Ed.), *Bully for brontosaurus* (pp. 325–339). New York: W.W. Norton & Company.

Gould, S.J. (1996). *Full house: The spread of excellence from Plato to Darwin*. New York: Harmony Books.

Gould, S.J. (1997a, June 12). Darwinian fundamentalism. *New York Review of Books, 44*(10). Retrieved from www.nybooks.com/articles/1997/06/12/darwinian-fundamentalism/.

Gould, S.J. (1997b, June 26). The pleasures of pluralism. *New York Review of Books, 44*(11). Retrieved from www.nybooks.com/articles/1997/06/26/evolution-the-pleasures-of-pluralism/.

Gould, S.J. (1997c, August 14). Letter to the editor. *New York Review of Books, 44* (13). Retrieved from www.nybooks.com/articles/1997/08/14/darwinian-fundamentalism-an-exchange/.

Gould, S.J. (1999). *Questioning the millennium*. New York: Harmony Books.

Gould, S.J. (2002). *The structure of evolutionary theory*. Cambridge, MA: The Belknap Press.

Gould, S.J., & Lewontin, R.C. (1979). The spandrels of San Marco and the Panglossian paradigm: A critique of the adaptationist programme. *Proceedings of the Royal Society of London, 205*, 581–598.

Gouldner, A.W. (1960). The norm of reciprocity: A preliminary statement. *American Sociological Review, 25*, 161–178.

Gower, K.K. (2005). The fear of public relations in foreign affairs: An examination of the 1963 Fulbright Hearings into foreign agents. *Public Relations Review, 31*, 37–46.

A Grandmother's Tales. (1898, October). *Macmillan's Magazine, 78*, 425–435.

Grant, M. (1987). *The rise of the Greeks*. New York: Collier Books.

Greenwood, C.A. (2010). Evolutionary theory: The missing link for conceptualizing public relations. *Journal of Public Relations Research, 22*, 456–476.

Gross, C.G. (1993). Huxley versus Owen: The hippocampus minor and evolution. *Trends in Neurosciences, 16*, 493–498.

Grube, G.M.A. (1965). *The Greek and Roman critics*. London, UK: Methuen.

Grunig, J.E. (1989). Symmetrical presuppositions as a framework for public relations theory. In C.H. Botan & V. Hazleton (Eds.), *Public relations theory* (pp. 17–44). Hillsdale, NJ: Lawrence Erlbaum Associates.

272   References

Grunig, J.E. (1993). Image and substance: From symbolic to behavioral relationships. *Public Relations Review, 19*, 121–139.

Grunig, J.E. (2000). Collectivism, collaboration, and societal corporatism as core professional values in public relations. *Journal of Public Relations Research, 12*, 23–48.

Grunig, J.E. (2006). Furnishing the edifice: Ongoing research on public relations as a strategic management function. *Journal of Public Relations Research, 18*, 151–176.

Grunig, J.E., & White, J. (1992). The effect of worldviews on public relations theory and practice. In J.E. Grunig (Ed.), *Excellence in public relations and communication management* (pp. 31–64). Hillsdale, NJ: Lawrence Erlbaum Associates.

Grunig, L.A. (1992). Toward the philosophy of public relations. In E.L. Toth & R.L. Heath (Eds.), *Rhetorical and critical approaches to public relations* (pp. 65–91). Hillsdale, NJ: Lawrence Erlbaum Associates.

Grunig, L.A., Grunig, J.E., & Ehling, W.P. (1992). What is an effective organization? In J.E. Grunig (Ed.), *Excellence in public relations and communication management* (pp. 65–90). Hillsdale, NJ: Lawrence Erlbaum Associates.

Grunig, L.A., Toth, E.L., & Hon, L.C. (2000). Feminist values in public relations. *Journal of Public Relations Research, 12*, 49–68.

Guth, D.W., & Marsh, C. (2000). *Public relations: A values-driven approach*. Boston, MA: Allyn & Bacon.

Guth, D.W., & Marsh, C. (2017). *Public relations: A values-driven approach* (6th ed.). New York: Pearson.

Gwynn, A.O. (1966). *Roman education from Cicero to Quintilian*. New York: Teachers College Press. (Original work published 1926)

Habermas, J. (1989). *The structural transformation of the public sphere: An inquiry into a category of bourgeois society* (T. Burger & F. Lawrence, Trans.). Cambridge, UK: Polity Press.

Hallahan, K. (2001). The dynamics of issues activation and response: An issues processes model. *Journal of Public Relations Research, 13*, 27–59.

Hallahan, K. (2003). W.L. Mackenzie King: Rockefeller's "other" public relations counselor in Colorado. *Public Relations Review, 29*, 401–414.

Hallahan, K. (2010). Being public: Publicity as public relations. In R.L. Heath (Ed.), *The Sage handbook of public relations* (pp. 523–545). Thousand Oaks, CA: Sage.

Halliday, R.J. (1971). Social Darwinism: A definition. *Victorian Studies, 14*, 389–405.

Harrison, J. (1981). *Hume's theory of justice*. Oxford, UK: Clarendon Press.

Harrison, J. (2004). Conflicts of duty and the virtues of Aristotle in public relations ethics: Continuing the conversation commenced by Monica Walle. *PRism, 2*, 1–7.

Haskins, E.V. (2004). *Logos and power in Isocrates and Aristotle*. Columbia, SC: University of South Carolina Press.

Hatfield, E., Bensman, L., Thornton, P.D., & Rapson, R.L. (2014). New perspectives on emotional contagion: A review of classic and recent research on facial mimicry and contagion. *Interpersona, 8*, 159–179.

Hauert, C. (2013). Mathematical models of cooperation. In M.A. Nowak & S. Coakley (Eds.), *Evolution, games, and God: The principle of cooperation* (pp. 115–131). Cambridge, MA: Harvard University Press.

Hauser, M.D. (2013). The moral organ: A prophylaxis against the whims of culture. In M.A. Nowak & S. Coakley (Eds.), *Evolution, games, and God: The principle of cooperation* (pp. 253–272). Cambridge, MA: Harvard University Press.

Heath, R.L. (2000). A rhetorical perspective on the values of public relations: Crossroads and pathways toward concurrence. *Journal of Public Relations Research, 12*, 69–91.

Heath, R.L. (2006). Onward into more fog: Thoughts on public relations' research directions. *Journal of Public Relations Research, 18*, 93–114.

Heath, R.L. (2009). The rhetorical tradition: Wrangle in the marketplace. In R.L Heath, E.L. Toth, & D. Waymer (Eds.), *Rhetorical and critical approaches to public relations II* (pp. 17–47). New York: Routledge.

Heath, R.L., & Frandsen, F. (2008). Rhetorical perspective and public relations: Meaning matters. In A. Zerfass, B. van Ruler, & K. Sriramesh (Eds.), *Public relations research: European and international perspectives and innovations* (pp. 349–364). Weisbaden, DE: V.S. Verlag.

Heath, R.L., Toth, E.L., & Waymer, D. (2009). Section one: Rhetorical tradition and critical tradition. In R.L Heath, E.L. Toth, & D. Waymer (Eds.), *Rhetorical and critical approaches to public relations II* (pp. 13–16). New York: Routledge.

Heath, R.L., & Waymer, D. (2009). Activist public relations and the paradox of the positive. In R.L. Heath, E.L. Toth, & D. Waymer (Eds.), *Rhetorical and critical approaches to public relations II* (pp. 195–215). New York: Routledge.

Hellman, H. (1998). *Great feuds in science: Ten disputes that shaped the world.* New York: Barnes & Noble.

Herre, E.A., & Wcislo, W.T. (2011, March 24). In defence of inclusive fitness theory. *Nature, 466*, E8-E9.

Hesiod. (1991). *Theogony.* (R. Lattimore, Trans.). In R. Lattimore (Ed.), *The works and days, Theogony, the shield of Herakles* (pp. 119–186). Ann Arbor, MI: University of Michigan Press.

Hobbes, T. (1985). *Leviathan.* New York: Penguin. (Original work published 1651).

Hölldobler, B., & Wilson, E.O. (2011). *The leafcutter ants: Civilization by instinct.* New York: W.W. Norton & Company.

Holmström, S. (2004). Intermezzo: The reflective paradigm of public relations. In B. van Ruler & D. Verčič (Eds.), *Public relations and communication management in Europe* (pp. 121–133). Berlin, DE: Mouton de Gruyter.

Holmström, S. (2009). On Luhmann: Contingency, risk, trust, and reflection. In Ø. Ihlen, B. van Ruler, & M. Fredriksson, (Eds.), *Public relations and social theory: Key figures and concepts* (pp. 187–211). New York: Routledge.

Holtzhausen, D.R. (2000). Postmodern values in public relations. *Journal of Public Relations Research, 12*, 93–114.

Homer. (2011). *The Iliad.* (S. Mitchell, Trans.). New York: Atria Books.

Hooker, J.D. (1860). *Flora Tasmaniae.* London, UK: Lovell Reeve.

Hubbell, H.M. (1913). *The influence of Isocrates on Cicero, Dionysius, and Aristides.* New Haven, CT: Yale University Press.

Hume, D. (1777). *The life of David Hume.* London, UK: W. Strahan and T. Cadell.

Hume, D. (1968). *A treatise of human nature.* Oxford, UK: Clarendon Press. (Original work published 1739).

Hume, D. (1983). *An enquiry concerning the principles of morals.* Indianapolis, IN: Hackett Publishing Company. (Original work published 1751).

Hunt, E.L. (1990). Plato and Aristotle on rhetoric and rhetoricians. In E.P.J. Corbett, J.L. Golden, & G.F. Berquist (Eds.), *Essays on the rhetoric of the western world* (pp. 129–161). Dubuque, IA: Kendall/Hunt. (Original work published 1925).

Hutton, J.G., Goodman, M.B., Alexander, J.B., & Genest, C.M. (2001). Reputation management: The new face of corporate public relations? *Public Relations Review*, *27*, 247–261.

Huxley, L. (1901a). *Life and letters of Thomas Henry Huxley, Vol. I*. New York: D. Appleton and Company.

Huxley, L. (1901b). *Life and letters of Thomas Henry Huxley, Vol. II*. New York: D. Appleton and Company.

Huxley, T.H. (1860). Darwin on the origin of species. *Westminster Review*, 17, 541–570.

Huxley, T.H. (1897). *Evolution and ethics*. New York: D. Appleton and Company.

Huxley, T.H. (1898). Natural rights and political rights. In T.H. Huxley, *Collected Essays, Vol. I* (pp. 336–382). New York: D. Appleton and Company.

Huxley, T.H. (1908). *Twelve lectures and essays*. London, UK: Watts & Co.

Huxley, T.H. (1983). Speech at the Royal Society Dinner. In G. de Beer (Ed.), *Charles Darwin and Thomas Henry Huxley: Autobiographies* (pp. 110–112). Oxford, UK: Oxford University Press. (Original published 1894).

Huxley, T.H. (1983). Notebook: Thoughts and doings. In G. de Beer (Ed.), *Charles Darwin and Thomas Henry Huxley: Autobiographies* (pp. 91–99). Oxford, UK: Oxford University Press.

Huxley, T.H. (2001). *Man's place in nature*. New York: Modern Library. (Original published 1863).

Ihlen, Ø. (2002). Rhetoric and resources: Notes for a new approach to public relations and issues management. *Journal of Public Affairs*, *2*, 259–269.

Ihlen, Ø. (2009). On Bourdieu: Public relations in field struggles. In Ø. Ihlen, B. van Ruler, & M. Fredriksson, (Eds.), *Public relations and social theory: Key figures and concepts* (pp. 62–82). New York: Routledge.

Ihlen, Ø. (2010). The cursed sisters: Public relations and rhetoric. In R.L. Heath (Ed.), *Sage handbook of public relations* (pp. 59–70). Thousand Oaks, CA: Sage.

Ihlen, Ø., van Ruler, B., & Fredriksson, M. (Eds.) (2009). *Public relations and social theory: Key figures and concepts*. New York: Routledge.

Ihlen, Ø., & Verhoeven, P. (2012). A public relations identity for the 2010s. *Public Relations Inquiry*, *1*, 159–176.

Irvine, W. (1955). *Apes, angels, and Victorians: The story of Darwin, Huxley, and evolution*. New York: McGraw-Hill.

Isocrates. (1991). *Isocrates, Vol. I*. (G. Norlin, Ed. & Trans.). Cambridge, MA: Harvard University Press. (Original work published 1928).

Isocrates. (1992). *Isocrates, Vol. II*. (G. Norlin, Ed. & Trans.). Cambridge, MA: Harvard University Press. (Original work published 1929).

Isocrates. (1986). *Isocrates, Vol. III*. (L. Van Hook, Ed. & Trans.). Cambridge, MA: Harvard University Press. (Original work published 1945).

Isocrates. (2000). *Isocrates I*. (D.C. Mirhady & Y.L. Too, Trans.). Austin, TX: University of Texas Press.

Isocrates. (2004). *Isocrates II*. (T.L. Papillon, Trans.). Austin, TX: University of Texas Press.

Jaeger, W. (1944). *Paideia: The ideals of Greek culture: Vol. III. The conflict of cultural ideals in the age of Plato*. (G. Highet, Trans.). New York: Oxford University Press.

Jebb, R.C. (1876). *The Attic orators from Antiphon to Isaeos*. London, UK: Macmillan and Company.

Johnson, D.D.P. (2013). The uniqueness of human cooperation. In M.A. Nowak & S. Coakley (Eds.), *Evolution, games, and God: The principle of cooperation* (pp. 168–185). Cambridge, MA: Harvard University Press.

Johnson, S. (1971). Milton. In B.H. Bronson (Ed.), *Samuel Johnson* (3rd ed.) (pp. 331–352). New York: Holt, Rinehart, Winston. (Original work published 1779).

Kahneman, D. (2011). *Thinking, fast and slow*. New York: Farrar, Straus and Giroux.

Kane, F.I. (1986). Peitho and the polis. *Philosophy and Rhetoric, 19*, 99–124.

Kant, I. (1836). *The metaphysic of ethics*. (J. W. Semple, Trans.). Edinburgh, UK: Thomas Clark.

Kant, I. (1897). *Perpetual peace*. (B.F. Trueblood, Trans.). Washington, DC.: American Peace Society.

Kant, I. (1997). *Lectures on ethics*. (P. Heath & J.B. Schneewind, Eds; P. Heath, Trans.). Cambridge, UK: Cambridge University Press.

Katula, R., & Murphy, J. (1994). The sophists and rhetorical consciousness. In R. Katula & J. Murphy (Eds.), *A synoptic history of classical rhetoric* (pp. 17–50). Davis, CA: Hermagoras.

Kelly, E. (2001). Editor's foreword. In J. Rawls, *Justice as fairness* (pp. xi–xiii). Cambridge, MA: Harvard University Press.

Kelly, K.S. (2001). Stewardship: The fifth step in the public relations process. In R.L. Heath (Ed.), *Handbook of public relations* (pp. 279–291). Thousand Oaks, CA: Sage.

Kennedy, G.A. (1994). *A new history of classical rhetoric*. Princeton, NJ: Princeton University Press.

Kennedy, R.F. (2009). *Athena's justice*. New York: Peter Lang.

Kent, M.L., Sommerfeldt, E.J., & Saffer, A.J. (2016). Social networks, power, and public relations: *Tertius iungens* as a cocreational approach to studying relationship networks. *Public Relations Review, 42*, 91–100.

Kirby, J.T. (1994). The "great triangle" in early Greek rhetoric and politics. In E. Schiappa (Ed.), *Landmark essays on classical Greek rhetoric* (pp. 3–15). Davis, CA: Hermagoras.

Kirkwood, G.M. (1959). *A short guide to classical mythology*. New York: Holt, Rinehart and Winston.

Koller, P. (2009). International law and global justice. In L.H. Meyer (Ed.), *Legitimacy, justice, and international public law* (pp. 186–206). Cambridge, UK: Cambridge University Press.

Konstan, D. (2004). Isocrates' "Republic." In T. Poulakos & D. Depew (Eds.), *Isocrates and civic education* (pp. 107–124). Austin, TX: University of Texas Press.

Kropotkin, P. (1989). *Mutual aid: A factor of evolution*. New York: Black Rose Books. (Original work published 1902).

Kropotkin, P. (1992). *Ethics: Origin and development*. (L.S. Friedland & J.R. Piroshnikoff, Trans.). New York: Black Rose Books. (Original work published 1924).

Kropotkin, P. (1995). *Evolution and environment*. New York: Black Rose Books.

Kruckeberg, D. (1993). Universal ethics code: Both possible and feasible. *Public Relations Review, 19*, 21–32.

Küng, H., & Kuschel, K.J. (Eds). (1993). *A global ethic: The declaration of the parliament of the world's religions*. (J. Bowden, Trans.). New York: Continuum Publishing.

Lamme, M.O. (2015). "Where the quiet work is done." Biography in public relations. In T. Watson (Ed.), *Perspectives on public relations historiography and historical theorization* (pp. 48–68). Basingstoke, UK: Palgrave Macmillan.

Lasswell, H.D. (1938). *Propaganda techniques in the world war*. New York: Peter Smith.

Lauzen, M.M. (1993). When marketing involvement matters at the manager level. *Public Relations Review, 19*, 247–259.

Lawniczak, R. (2009). Re-examining the economic roots of public relations. *Public Relations Review, 35*, 346–352.

Lebacqz, K. (1986). *Six theories of justice: Perspectives from philosophical and theological ethics*. Minneapolis, MN: Augsburg.

Ledingham, J.A., & Bruning, S.D. (1998). Relationship management in public relations: Dimensions of an organization–public relationship. *Public Relations Review, 24*, 55–65.

Lee, M. (2013). Self-denial and its discontents. In M.A. Nowak and S. Coakley (Eds.), *Evolution, games, and God: The principle of cooperation* (pp. 186–197). Cambridge, MA: Harvard University Press.

Leeper, R.V. (2001). In search of a metatheory for public relations: An argument for communitarianism. In R.L. Heath (Ed.), *Handbook of public relations* (pp. 93–104). Thousand Oaks, CA: Sage.

Leeper, R.V., & Leeper, K.A. (2001). Public relations as "practice": Applying the theory of Alasdair MacIntyre. *Public Relations Review, 27*, 461–473.

Lehning, P.B. (2009). *John Rawls: An introduction*. Cambridge, UK: Cambridge University Press.

Leichty, G. (2003). The cultural tribes of public relations. *Journal of Public Relations Research, 15*, 277–304.

Lenfield, S. (2011, July/August). Ants through the ages. *Harvard Magazine, 113*, 60–63.

L'Etang, J. (1996). Corporate responsibility and public relations ethics. In J. L'Etang & M. Pieczka (Eds.), *Critical perspectives in public relations* (pp. 82–105). London, UK: International Thomson Business Press.

L'Etang, J. (2008). Public relations, persuasion, and propaganda: Truth, knowledge, spirituality and mystique. In A. Zerfass, B. van Ruler, & K. Sriramesh (Eds.), *Public relations research: European and international perspectives and innovations* (pp. 251–269). Wiesbaden, DE: VS Verlag.

Levitin, D.J. (2014). *The organized mind: Thinking straight in the age of information overload*. New York: Plume.

Liddell, H.G., & Scott, R. (1889). *An intermediate Greek–English lexicon*. Oxford, UK: Clarendon Press.

Linnean Society of London. (2016). Retrieved from www.linnean.org/the-society/medals-awards-prizes-grants/the-darwin-wallace-medal.

Long, C.P. (2007). The daughters of Metis: Patriarchal dominion and the politics of the between. *Graduate Faculty Philosophy Journal, 28*, 67–86.

Lumsden, C.J., & Wilson, E.O. (1983). *Promethean fire: Reflections on the origin of the mind*. Cambridge, MA: Harvard University Press.

Lunsford, A.A., & Ede, L.S. (1994). On distinctions between classical and modern rhetoric. In T. Enos & S.C. Brown (Eds.), *Professing the new rhetorics* (pp. 397–411). Boston, MA: Blair Press.

Luoma-aho, V. (2009). On Putnam: Bowling together. In Ø. Ihlen, B. van Ruler, & M. Fredriksson, (Eds.), *Public relations and social theory: Key figures and concepts* (pp. 231–251). New York: Routledge.

Lyon, L., & Cameron, G.T. (2004). A relational approach examining the interplay of prior reputation and immediate response to a crisis. *Journal of Public Relations Research, 16*, 213–241.

Lyotard, J.-F., & Thébaud, J.-L. (1985). *Just gaming*. (W. Godzich, Trans.). Minneapolis, MN: University of Minnesota Press.

McBride, G. (1989). Ethical thought in public relations history. *Journal of Mass Media Ethics, 4*, 5–20.

McCalman, I. (2009). *Darwin's armada: Four voyages and the battle for the theory of evolution*. New York: W.W. Norton & Company.

McKie, D. (2001). Updating public relations. In R.L. Heath (Ed.), *Handbook of public relations* (pp. 75–91). Thousand Oaks, CA: Sage.

McKie, D., & Munshi, D. (2007). *Reconfiguring public relations: Ecology, equity, and enterprise*. New York: Routledge.

McNeill, B. (2009, July 31). Forged letters to congressman anger local groups. Charlottesville (VA) *Daily Progress*. Retrieved from www.dailyprogress.com/news/forged-letters-to-congressman-anger-local-groups/article_d0472842-b253-59a1-9bb5-4d33f7956145.html.

Marrou, H.I. (1982). *A history of education in antiquity*. (G. Lamb, Trans.). Madison, WI: University of Wisconsin Press. (Original work published 1956).

Marsh, C. (2001). Public relations ethics: Contrasting models from the rhetorics of Plato, Aristotle, and Isocrates. *Journal of Mass Media Ethics, 16*(2&3), 78–98.

Marsh, C. (2003). Antecedents of two-way symmetry in classical Greek rhetoric: The rhetoric of Isocrates. *Public Relations Review, 29*, 351–367.

Marsh, C. (2012). Converging on harmony: Idealism, evolution, and the theory of mutual aid. *Public Relations Inquiry, 1*, 313–335.

Marsh, C. (2013). *Classical rhetoric and modern public relations: An Isocratean model*. New York: Routledge.

Martinson, D.L. (1994). Enlightened self-interest fails as an ethical baseline in public relations. *Journal of Mass Media Ethics, 9*, 100–108.

Mattelart, A. (1996). *The invention of communication*. Minneapolis, MN: University of Minnesota Press.

Messina, A. (2007). Public relations, the public interest and persuasion: An ethical approach. *Journal of Communication Management, 11*, 29–52.

Milbank, D. (2009, October 20). Washington sketch: When breaking news is broken. *Washington Post*. Retrieved from www.washingtonpost.com/wp-dyn/content/article/2009/10/19/AR2009101902988.html.

Mill, J.S. (1957). *Utilitarianism*. Indianapolis, IN: The Bobbs-Merrill Company. (Original work published 1863).

Miller, D. (1976). *Social justice*. Oxford, UK: Clarendon Press.

Molleda, J.-C., & Ferguson, M.A. (2004). Public relations roles in Brazil: Hierarchy eclipses gender differences. *Journal of Public Relations Research, 16*, 327–351.

Moloney, K. (2005). Trust and public relations: Center and edge. *Public Relations Review, 31*, 550–555.

Moloney, K. (2006). *Rethinking public relations: PR, propaganda and democracy* (2nd ed.). New York: Routledge.

Moore, J.R. (1979). *Post-Darwinian controversies: A study of the protestant struggle to come to terms with Darwin in Great Britain and America, 1870–1900*. New York: Cambridge University Press.

Moore, S. (2012). Ideals and realities: Renaissance state communication in Machiavelli's *The Prince* and More's *Utopia*. *Public Relations Review, 38*, 383–389.

Morgan, K. (2004). The education of Athens: Politics and rhetoric in Isocrates and Plato. In T. Poulakos & D. Depew (Eds.), *Isocrates and civic education* (pp. 125–154). Austin, TX: University of Texas Press.

Morris, B. (2004). *Kropotkin: The politics of community*. Amherst: Humanity Books.

Murphy, J.J. (Ed.). (1992). *Peter Ramus's attack on Cicero: Text and translation of Ramus's Brutinae Quaestiones*. (C. Newlands, Trans.). Davis, CA: Hermagoras.

Murphy, J.J., & Meador, P.A. (1994). Quintilian's educational and rhetorical theory. In J.J. Murphy, R.A. Katula, F.I. Hill, D.J. Ochs, & P.A. Meador (Eds.), *A synoptic history of classical rhetoric* (2nd ed.) (pp. 177–203). Davis, CA: Hermagoras.

Murphy, P. (1991). The limits of symmetry: A game theory approach to symmetric and asymmetrical public relations. *Public Relations Research Annual, 3*, 115–131.

Murphy, P. (2000). Symmetry, contingency, complexity: Accommodating uncertainty in public relations theory. *Public Relations Review, 26*, 447–462.

Naas, M. (1995). *Turning: From persuasion to philosophy*. Atlantic Highlands, NJ: Humanities Press International.

Nel, P. (2001). A justice philosophy of public relations management. *Comunicatio, 27*, 28–35.

Nietzsche, F. (2003). *The genealogy of morals*. (H.B. Samuel, Trans.). Mineola: Dover Publications. (Original published in 1913).

Noddings, N. (2010). *The maternal factor: Two paths to morality*. Berkeley, CA: University of California Press.

Norlin, G. (1991). Introduction. In G. Norlin (Trans.), *Isocrates, Vol. 1* (pp. ix–lii). Cambridge, MA: Harvard University Press. (Original work published 1928).

North, H. (1966). *Sophrosyne: Self-knowledge and self-restraint in Greek literature*. Ithaca: Cornell University Press.

Nowak, M.A. (2013). Five rules for the evolution of cooperation. In M.A. Nowak, & S. Coakley (Eds.), *Evolution, games, and God: The principle of cooperation* (pp. 99–114). Cambridge, MA: Harvard University Press.

Nowak, M.A., & Highfield, R. (2011). *SuperCooperators: Altruism, evolution, and why we need each other to succeed*. New York: Free Press.

Nowak, M.A., Tarnita, C.E., & Wilson, E.O. (2010, August 26). The evolution of eusociality. *Nature, 466*, 1057–1062.

Nowak, M.A., Tarnita, C.E., & Wilson, E.O. (2011, March 24). Nowak et al. reply. *Nature, 466*, E9-E10.

Nozick, R. (1974). *Anarchy, state, and utopia*. New York: Basic Books.

Ochs, D.J. (1994). Cicero's rhetorical theory. In J.J. Murphy, R.A. Katula, F.I. Hill, D.J. Ochs, & P.A. Meador (Eds.), *A synoptic history of classical rhetoric* (2nd ed.) (pp. 129–176). Davis, CA: Hermagoras.

Olasky, M.N. (1984). Retrospective: Bernays' doctrine of public opinion. *Public Relations Review, 10*, 3–12.

Ostrom, E. (1990). *Governing the commons: The evolution of institutions for collective action*. Cambridge, UK: Cambridge University Press.

Ott, B.L., & Dickinson, G. (2013). Entering the unending conversation: An introduction to rhetorical criticism. In B.L. Ott & G. Dickinson (Eds), *The Routledge reader in rhetorical criticism* (pp. 1–13). New York: Routledge.

Owen, R. (1860, April). Review of *On the Origin of Species*. *The Edinburgh Review, 111*, 487–532.

Packard, V. (1957). *The hidden persuaders*. New York: D. McKay.

Pal, M., & Dutta, M.J. (2008). Public relations in a global context: The relevance of critical modernism as a theoretical lens. *Journal of Public Relations Research, 20*, 159–179.

Paley, W. (1837). *Natural theology or evidences of the existence and attributes of the deity, collected from the appearances of nature*. Boston, MA: Good, Kendall and Lincoln.

Pang, A., Cropp, F., & Cameron, G.T. (2006). Corporate crisis planning: tensions, issues, and contradictions. *Journal of Communication Management, 10*, 371–389.

Patagonia. (2015). Becoming a responsible company. Retrieved from www.patagonia.com/us/patagonia.go?assetid=2329.

Pausanias. (1965). *Pausanias's description of Greece*. (J.G. Frazer, Trans.). New York: Biblo and Tannen.

Pearson, R. (1989). Beyond ethical relativism in public relations: Coorientation, rules, and the idea of communication symmetry. *Public Relations Research Annual, 1*, 67–86.

Pernot, L. (2005). *Rhetoric in antiquity*. (W.E. Higgins, Trans.). Washington, D.C.: The Catholic University of America Press.

Pfaff, D.W., & Sherman, S. (2015). *The altruistic brain*. New York: Oxford University Press.

Pfau, M., & Wan, H.-H. (2009). Persuasion: An intrinsic function of public relations. In C. H. Botan & V. Hazleton (Eds.), *Public relations theory II* (pp. 88–119). Mahwah, NJ: Lawrence Erlbaum Associates.

Pfeffer, J., & Salancik, G.R. (1978). *The external control of organizations: A resource dependence perspective*. New York: Harper & Row.

Pieczka, M. (1996). Public opinion and public relations. In J. L'Etang & M. Pieczka (Eds.), *Critical perspectives in public relations* (pp. 54–64). London, UK: International Thomson Business Press.

Pinker, S. (2011). *The better angels of our nature: Why violence has declined*. New York: Penguin.

Pinker, S. (2012, June 18). The false allure of group selection. *Edge*. Retrieved from http://edge.org/conversation/the-false-allure-of-group-selection.

Plato. (1928). *Phaedrus*. In H.N. Fowler (Trans.), *Euthyphro, Apology, Crito, Phaedo, Phaedrus*. Cambridge, MA: Harvard University Press. (Original work published in 1914).

Plato (1989). *Republic*. (P. Shorey, Trans.). In E. Hamilton & H. Cairns (Eds.), *Plato: Collected dialogues* (pp. 575–844). Princeton, NJ: Princeton University Press. (Original work published 1930).

Popper, K. (1966). *The open society and its enemies* (5th ed.). London, UK: Routledge.

Porter, L. (2010). Communicating for the good of the state: A post-symmetrical polemic on persuasion in ethical public relations. *Public Relations Review, 36*, 127–133.

Poulakos, T. (1997). *Speaking for the polis: Isocrates' rhetorical education.* Columbia, SC: University of South Carolina Press.

Pruss, A. (2013). *Altruism, normalcy, and God.* In M.A. Nowak & S. Coakley (Eds.), *Evolution, games, and God: The principle of cooperation* (pp. 329–342). Cambridge, MA: Harvard University Press.

Pseudo-Plutarch. (1969). *Plutarch's Moralia in sixteen volumes: Volume X.* (H.N. Fowler, Ed. & Trans). Cambridge, MA: Harvard University Press. (Original work published 1936).

Quintilian, M.F. (1980). *Institutio oratoria, Vol. I.* (H.E. Butler, Trans.). Cambridge, MA: Harvard University Press. (Original work published 1920).

Quintilian, M.F. (1921). *Institutio oratoria, Vol. II.* (H.E. Butler, Trans.). Cambridge, MA: Harvard University Press.

Quintilian, M.F. (1979). *Institutio oratoria, Vol. IV.* (H.E. Butler, Trans.). Cambridge, MA: Harvard University Press. (Original work published 1922).

Ramus, P. (1986). *Arguments in rhetoric against Quintilian.* (C. Newlands, Trans.). DeKalb, IL: Northern Illinois University Press. (Original work published 1549).

Rawls, J. (1971). *A theory of justice.* Cambridge, MA: Harvard University Press.

Rawls, J. (1995). Political liberalism: Reply to Habermas. *The Journal of Philosophy, 92*(3), 132–180.

Rawls, J. (1999). *The law of peoples.* Cambridge, MA: Harvard University Press.

Rawls, J. (2001). *Justice as fairness: A restatement.* Cambridge, MA: Harvard University Press.

Richards, I.A. (1964). *The philosophy of rhetoric.* London, UK: Oxford University Press. (Original work published 1936).

Richards, I.A. (1991). The first three liberal arts. In A.E. Berthoff (Ed.), *Richards on rhetoric: Selected essays, 1929–1974* (pp. 86–97). New York: Oxford University Press. (Original work published 1938).

Ricoeur, P. (1996). Between rhetoric and poetics. In A.O. Rorty (Ed.), *Essays on Aristotle's* Rhetoric (pp. 324–384). Berkeley, CA: University of California Press.

Roberts, C. (2012). Public relations and Rawls: An ill-fitting veil to wear. *Journal of Mass Media Ethics, 27,* 163–176.

Robins, R.W. (2005). The nature of personality: Genes, culture, and national character. *Science, 310,* 62–63.

Roszak, T. (2009). *The making of an elder culture: Reflections on the future of America's most audacious generation.* Gabriola Island, BC: New Society Publishers.

Ross, D. (2011). Naturalism: The place of society in nature. In I.C. Jarvie & J. Zamora-Bonilia (Eds.), *The Sage handbook of the philosophy of social sciences* (pp. 121–136). Los Angeles, CA: Sage.

Rummel, E. (1994). Isocrates' ideal of rhetoric: Criteria of evaluation. In E. Schiappa (Ed.), *Landmark essays on classical Greek rhetoric* (pp. 143–154). Davis, CA: Hermagoras. (Original work published 1979).

Ruse, M., & Wilson, E.O. (1986). Moral philosophy as applied science. *Philosophy, 61,* 173–192.

Russell, B. (1945). *The history of western philosophy.* New York: Touchstone.

Russell, B. (2003). *Man's peril, 1954–55.* London, UK: Routledge.

Rynearson, N. (2013). Courting the Erinyes: Persuasion, sacrifice, and seduction in Aeschylus's *Eumenides. Transactions of the American Philological Association, 143,* 1–22.

Sallot, L.M., Lyon, L.J., Acosta-Alzuru, C., & Ogata Jones, K. (2008). From aardvark to zebra redux: An analysis of theory development in public relations academic journals into the 21st century. In T.L. Hansen-Horn & B.D. Neff (Eds.), *Public relations: From theory to practice* (pp. 364–410). Boston, MA: Allyn & Bacon.

Sandel, M.J. (2009). *Justice: What's the right thing to do?* New York: Farrar, Straus and Giroux.

Schloss, J.P. (2013). Unpredicted outcomes in the games of life. In M.A. Nowak & S. Coakley (Eds.), *Evolution, games, and God: The principle of cooperation* (pp. 201–219). Cambridge, MA: Harvard University Press.

Secord, J.A. (1981). Nature's fancy: Charles Darwin and the breeding of pigeons. *Isis, 72,* 162–186.

Shakespeare, W. (1969). *A midsummer night's dream.* In A. Harbage (Ed.), *William Shakespeare: The complete works* (pp. 146–174). New York: Viking Press.

Shakespeare, W. (1969). *Julius Caesar.* In A. Harbage (Ed.), *William Shakespeare: The complete works* (pp. 895–929). New York: Viking Press.

Simmons, P., & Walsh, B. (2012). Public relations and organizational justice: More fairness or just more cooperation? *Public Relations Inquiry, 1,* 141–157.

Simmons, T.L. (2002). *Climbing Parnassus.* Wilmington, DE: ISI Books.

Sims, R.R. (2003). *Ethics and corporate social responsibility: Why giants fall.* Westport, CT: Praeger.

Smith, A. C. (2005). The politics of weddings at Athens: an iconographic assessment. *Leeds International Classical Studies, 4,* 1–32.

Smith, A.C. (2011). *Polis and personification in classical Athenian art.* Leiden, NL: Koninlijke Brill NV.

Smith, J.M., & Szathmáry, E. (1997). *The major transitions in evolution.* Oxford, UK: Oxford University Press.

Smudde, P.M., & Courtright, J.L. (2011). A holistic approach to stakeholder management: A rhetorical foundation. *Public Relations Review, 37,* 137–144.

Snow, C.P. (1961). *The two cultures and the scientific revolution.* New York: Cambridge University Press.

Solon. (2008). *Solon 4 (Eunomia): Appendix II.* (C.A. Faraone, Trans.). In C.A. Faraone (Ed.), *The stanzaic architecture of early Greek elegy* (pp. 168–174). Oxford, UK: Oxford University Press.

Sommerfeldt, E. (2011). Activist online resource mobilization: Relationship building features that fulfill resource dependencies. *Public Relations Review, 37,* 429–431.

Sproul, B.C. (1991). *Primal myths: Creation myths around the world.* New York: HarperCollins.

Starck, K., & Kruckeberg, D. (2001). Public relations and community: A reconstructed theory revisited. In R.L. Heath (Ed.), *Handbook of public relations* (pp. 51–60). Thousand Oaks, CA: Sage.

Sterelny, K. (2007). *Dawkins vs. Gould: Survival of the fittest.* Cambridge, UK: Icon Books.

Stuart, J.T. (2008). The question of human progress in Britain after the Great War. *British Scholar, 1,* 53–78.

Taylor, M. (2010). Public relations in the enactment of civil society. In R.L. Heath (Ed.), *The Sage handbook of public relations* (pp. 5–15). Thousand Oaks, CA: Sage.

Tennyson, A. (1851). *In memoriam* (5th ed.). London, UK: Edward Moxon.

Thaler, R.H. (2015). *Misbehaving: The making of behavioral economics*. New York: W.W. Norton & Company.

Tomasello, M. (2009). *Why we cooperate*. Cambridge, MA: The MIT Press.

Too, Y.L. (1995). *The rhetoric of identity in Isocrates*. Cambridge, UK: Cambridge University Press.

Toth, E.L. (1992). The case for pluralistic studies of public relations: Rhetorical, critical, and systems perspectives. In E.L. Toth & R.L. Heath (Eds.), *Rhetorical and critical approaches to public relations* (pp. 3–15). Hillsdale, NJ: Lawrence Erlbaum Associates.

Toth, E.L. (2002). Postmodernism for modernist public relations: The cash value and application of critical research in public relations. *Public Relations Review, 28*, 243–250.

Trivers, R. (1971). The evolution of reciprocal altruism. *Quarterly Review of Biology, 46*, 35–57.

van Ruler, B., & Verčič, D. (2005). Reflective communication management, future ways for public relations research. In P.J. Kalbfleisch (Ed.), *Communication yearbook 29* (pp. 238–273). Mahwah, NJ: Lawrence Erlbaum Associates.

Vasquez, G.M., & Taylor, M. (1999). What cultural values influence American public relations practitioners? *Public Relations Review, 25*, 433–449.

Vlastos, G. (1991). *Socrates: Ironist and moral philosopher*. Ithaca: Cornell University Press.

Waeraas, A., & Ihlen, Ø. (2009). Green legitimation: The construction of an environmental ethos. *International Journal of Organizational Analysis, 17*, 84–102.

Wallace, K.R. (1943). *Francis Bacon on communication and rhetoric*. Chapel Hill, NC: University of North Carolina Press.

Wardy, R. (1996). Mighty is the truth and it shall prevail? In A.O. Rorty (Ed.), *Essays on Aristotle's* Rhetoric (pp. 56–87). Berkeley, CA: University of California Press.

Waymer, D., & Ni, L. (2009). Connecting organizations and their employee publics: The rhetorical analysis of employee–organization relationships (EOR). In R.L. Heath, E.L. Toth, & D. Waymer (Eds.), *Rhetorical and critical approaches to public relations II* (pp. 216–232). New York: Routledge.

Weaver, R.M. (1953). *The ethics of rhetoric*. Chicago, IL: Henry Regnery.

Weber, M. (2002). Engaging globalization: Critical theory and global political change. *Alternatives, 27*, 301–325.

Welch, K.E. (1990). *The contemporary reception of classical rhetoric: Appropriations of ancient discourse*. Hillsdale, NJ: Lawrence Erlbaum Associates.

Wilberforce, S. (July–October, 1860). Review of *On the Origin of Species. The London Quarterly Review, 108*, 118–138.

Wilcox, D.L., & Cameron, G.T. (2009). *Public relations: Strategies and tactics* (9th edition). Boston, MA: Pearson Education.

Willis, P. (2012). Engaging communities: Ostrom's economic commons, social capital and public relations. *Public Relations Review, 38*, 116–122.

Wilson, D.S., & Wilson, E.O. (2007). Rethinking the theoretical foundation of sociobiology. *The Quarterly Review of Biology, 82*, 327–348.

Wilson, E.O. (1975). *Sociobiology: The new synthesis*. Cambridge, MA: The Belknap Press.

Wilson, E.O. (1998). *Consilience: The unity of knowledge*. New York: Alfred A. Knopf.

Wilson, E.O. (2004). *On human nature*. Cambridge, MA: Harvard University Press.

Wilson, E.O. (2012). *The social conquest of Earth*. New York: Liveright.

Winnington-Ingram, R.P. (1951). Review of Hesiod and Aeschylus by Friedrich Solmsen. *Gnomon, 23*, 414–421.

Wispé, L. (1991). *The psychology of sympathy*. New York: Plenum Press.

Wolfe, T. (2016). *The kingdom of speech*. New York: Little, Brown and Company.

Woodcock, G. (1989). An introduction. In P. Kropotkin, *Mutual aid: A factor of evolution* (pp. vii–xxi). New York: Black Rose Books.

Wright, R. (1997, August 14). Letter to the editor. *New York Review of Books, 44*(13). Retrieved from www.nybooks.com/articles/1997/08/14/darwinian-fundamentalism-an-exchange/.

Xifra, J., & Ordeix, E. (2009). Managing reputational risk in an economic downturn: The case of Banco Santander. *Public Relations Review, 35*, 353–360.

Yang, A., & Taylor, M. (2010). Relationship-building by Chinese ENGOs' websites: Education, not activation. *Public Relations Review, 36*, 342–351.

Yoos, G.E. (1984). Rational appeal and the ethics of advocacy. In R.J. Connors, L.S. Ede, & A.A. Lunsford (Eds.), *Essays on classical rhetoric and modern discourse* (pp. 82–97). Carbondale, IL: Southern Illinois University Press.

Yunis, H. (2003). *Written texts and the rise of literate culture in ancient Greece*. Cambridge, UK: Cambridge University Press.

Index

For Product Safety Concerns and Information please contact our EU
representative GPSR@taylorandfrancis.com
Taylor & Francis Verlag GmbH, Kaufingerstraße 24, 80331 München, Germany